**ANMOL PUBLICATIONS PVT. LTD.**
4374/4B, Ansari Road, Daryaganj
New Delhi-110 002

*Human Resource in Public Enterprises*

ISBN 81-7488-923-X



**PRINTED IN INDIA**

Published by J. L. Kumar for Anmol Publications Pvt. Ltd., New Delhi-110 002 and Printed at **Tarun** Offset Press, Delhi.

*To the Memory*
*of*
*my Father*

# CONTENTS

# FOREWORD

The pace of economic development is determined by the rate of expansion in productive resources employed in the economy and the rate of improvement in the overall efficiency in the use of resources, i.e. the total factor productivity. To most economists and planners, development is growth in national income or GNP. But the human resource approach emphasizes at the effective development and utilization of the manpower. Accordingly, the strategy of development should centre on human rather than material agents.

The public sector has been at the centre of India's planned development and massive investments have been made in a wide range of activities including manufacturing, infrastructure and services. The public enterprises, in the early stages of the country's industrialization process, proved to be the main agency for achieving the goals of our economy.

Some of the public enterprises have done exceedingly well both in terms of resource generation as well as social responsibilities. But the public sector as a whole has fallen short of the expectations of people. The large investment has not yielded the desired returns. A number of public enterprises have been making losses. There are many reasons for that but managerial inadequacies and labour troubles are mainly held responsible for this state of affairs.

The role the public sector is undergoing a change throughout the world and it has been completely redefined in the changed economic climate. The government of India has embarked upon a bold programme of public sector reforms since 1991. Unfortunately, there is not much evidence of a major change in the environment in which the public sector is now operating. However, ideological postures are no longer relevant. What is actually relevant is the need for efficiency and productivity.

In this study Dr. Suresh Aggarwal has examined productivity and its relationship with wages for Indian public enterprises. Trends in partial productivities, total factor productivity and capital intensity are analysed for different levels for the period 1974-75 to 1995-96. Dr. Aggarwal finds at the aggregate level a significantly rising trend in labour productivity and capital intensity, and a falling trend in capital productivity and in total factor productivity (Translog index). Inter-industry and inter-firm variations in productivity of selected sixteen firms in eight industrial groups have also been analysed. A number of interesting hypotheses have been tested. The statistical regression analysis indicates a strong positive relationship between productivity growth and value added growth. Capital intensity has been found to have a positive relationship with labour productivity and negative association with total factor productivity. The study finds no visible improvement in the total factor productivity of these public enterprises since 1990-91.

Wage trends along with employment, value added and wage share, have been analysed for all the levels, i.e. aggregate, industry and firm level to obtain a better understanding of the relationship of productivity with wages. A major finding of the analysis, by Dr. Aggarwal, is that employment increased only upto 1990-91 and since then there is a consistent fall in it. The study also finds that the real wages per worker increased only at a rate equal to that of national real per capita income, thus refuting the popular perception of wages to be increasing at a very fast rate in Indian public enterprises.

Dr. Aggarwal has tested a number of models indicating the relationship of wages with labour productivity and other important variables. A noteworthy finding of the econometric analysis is that real wages have a significant positive relationship with labour productivity in all the industries and the firms and real wage rates have increased faster in those industries and firms where TFP growth rates have been positive. This finding is of much significance since it points out, together with earlier findings, that employees are generally not over paid in the public enterprises and the blame on them for every malaise seems to be misplaced.

This study deals with very important aspects of India's public sector enterprises. I am sure it will be of considerable interest to policy makers, managers and workers in public enterprises and scholars engaged in research in this area.

**Professor Abad Ahmad**
Pro. Vice-Chancellor
University of Delhi

# ACKNOWLEDGEMENTS

This book is substantially based on the findings of my doctoral research at the University of Delhi. I am deeply indebted to Professor Lallan Prasad, my supervisor, for his invaluable help and guidance. I am also grateful to Professor V.N. Pandit and Professor K.L. Krishna, who have been my teachers and a sources of inspiration. I wish to extend my gratitude to Dr V.K. Seth, Prof V.K. Bhalla, Dr J.K. Goyal, Dr Ashok Seth and Dr Ravinder Gargesh, for giving me many valuable suggestions and help in my work. My thanks are due to many of my friends and colleagues both in Satyawati College (M) and the Department of Business Economics, who have helped me in different ways at various stages of this work. I am also thankful to the staff of the Delhi University Computer Centre, and Ratan Tata Library for their help. Finally, I must acknowledge the help and inspiration that I received from my family.

**Suresh C. Aggarwal**

# LIST OF TABLES

**Appendices**

# 1

# INTRODUCTION

## The Context

*Most Nations* Today are development-minded. The less developed countries which have been poor and stagnant for centuries are in a state of revolt against poverty, unemployment population growth, disease, ignorance and sustainable economic growth. Problems of poverty and low productivity continue to be real in all developing regions of the world, not least of all Asia and the Pacific. The advanced countries likewise are committed to growth, and the more rapid and spectacular the better. This almost universal quest for forward movement is in essence a revolution which has no precedent in history. The slogan of this world-wide revolution is development. Economists, generally, tend to equate modernization and development with economic growth.

Orthodox economic doctrine holds that growth is primarily a process of accumulating material wealth. Economic progress is measured by the production of goods and services, expressed for the most part in monetary terms. From this perspective unemployment and other manifestations of underutilization of human resources are mainly the consequences of an insufficient rate of economic growth. The logic holds that these problems can best be resolved by accelerating the accumulation of material wealth. Adherents to the GNP approach do not deny the existence of serious human resource problems as development proceeds—problems of transfer of rural labour to urban areas, the underutilization of human resources, the distribution of income between the rich and the poor. The importance of human capital in economic development gradually dawned, in early 1970's, on the thoughts of development 'pundits'. In advanced countries, there has been an intensive search for the missing 'residual' growth and technical progress that might account for the unexplained residual in modern growth. The 'residual' covers a wide variety of factors affecting growth, including structural changes, quality of management, and changes in the age and sex composition of the labour force, advances in science and technology and their dissemination through education, training and other means.

The welfare dimension was, thus, accorded greater attention in the early 1970s when the development debate shifted to income inequality and poverty in the wake of the dissatisfaction with the preoccupation about economic growth. It was realized that the wealth of a country is based upon its power to develop and to effectively utilize the innate capacities of its people and is not foreordained by space, energy, and cropland. Human resource not material wealth as such, are the ultimate basis of wealth. In the 'human resource' approach the goals of development are the maximum possible utilization of human beings, especially in countries like India which are rich in human resources, in more productive activity and the fullest possible development of skills, knowledge, etc. It is human capacities which transform the passive natural resources into active agents of production. The economic development of nations, therefore, is ultimately the result of human effort. It takes skilled human agents to discover and exploit natural resources, to mobilize capital, to develop technology, to produce goods and to carry on trade.

The importance of "the human factor" in economic development, which was also highlighted by Adam Smith, Alfred Marshall and a number of todays economists like T.W. Schultz, Frederick H. Harbison, forced the governments and international organizations involved in development work to focus their attention to these basic needs of education, health, nutrition, etc. Besides being an approach to enhancing productivity and earning power (wages and salaries) in the long run, meeting these needs became an integral component of short run poverty alleviation strategies. These strategies were also viewed as complementary to increasing employment in labour-intensive technologies and reducing inequalities in income and wealth.

Because of the series of economic crises spawned by the oil shocks and other unfavourable external developments which required structural adjustments and stabilization measures in developing countries, human resource issues receded to the background in the latter part of the 1970s. The 1980s brought to the fore the mounting external debt problem and various changes in the international economic environment. These not only served to accentuate the need for macroeconomic reforms, including the public sector reforms which dominated these economies, but actually also led to the reduction in public spending for basic services and programmes directly related to human resource in many developing countries. Recently, there has been a renewed interest in human resource utilization in line with the concern about issues of poverty, unemployment and growth. It is increasingly recognized that social human resource policies can make a significant contribution both to long run economic growth and poverty alleviation.

It is quite unlikely, of course, that any country will ever adopt the human resources approach completely in planning its development strategy. Indeed, few have ever followed logically and consistently the GNP approach. In practice, development strategies are the outcome of combination of different perspectives and compromises on conflicting goals. However, labour is the major beneficiary of as well as the chief contributor to prosperity and growth. The bulk of the national product is distributed in wages and salaries to individual workers, and expansion of the total product has improved the welfare of these workers. Given the pivotal role of human resources in economic development, a thorough understanding of the relationship of its productivity improvement and the reward it obtains from its contribution to output, is exceedingly important.

Labour as a distinct factor of production, as it is defined in the text books of economics, did not exist prior to advent of industrialization. There was absence of labour market, therefore, the reward of work was not mediated through the market forces. In the absence of labour market, supply of work effort was based upon customary principles and its reward also depended on non-economic considerations. The industrial revolution gave rise to labour market by destroying subsistence economies and creating an 'economic man'; who primarily gets his stimulus through market led rationality. Therefore, both worker as well as employer started responding to market forces in making their decisions regarding supply of work effort and demand for work.

The breakdown of the system of reward of workers based on customary payments necessitated the evolving of new principles on which the reward of work will be based. Since then, several attempts have been made to identify the criteria which can be used for rewarding workers. One can say, for the sake of brevity, that the entire science of economics is a grand attempt to evolve a suitable criteria for rewarding labour. In the process of evolution of a suitable criterion, the attitude of both worker and employer has undergone a change. It is due to the change in the attitude, in contrast to the workers of early industrialization, the workers today are offered astronomical amounts as compensation for their labour. The worker has come a long way-from mere subsistence to 'Winner-take-all position'.[1]

Owing to the unique position of labour as a factor of production; determining its share has always been a source of continuous, still unresolved, debate. The earliest explanation advocates that the worker should be paid not more than what is required for his subsistence. In due course of time this negative attitude towards the worker was superseded by physiocratic view; which advocated that the employer must keep a fund to be exclusively given to the workers; which meant that the wage rate depended upon the number of workers alone. In this the blame of low wages rested not with the employer but with the worker.

Adam Smith, the first pioneer of laissez-faire capitalism, believed that reward to a person is maximized in laissez-faire capitalism; including employer, and it is determined by his contribution to the creation of wealth. The classical rules state that for maximum profit (including minimum cost) the quantity of each resource input used in a process must be adjusted until the value of the product resulting from the last increment of the resource (the marginal product) is equal to the cost of the last increment of the resource (marginal cost). Hicks and Marshall had declared that the wages of labour tend to be equal to the net product of a man's labour. This 'law of marginal productivity' is regarded, even today, by most modern economists as the most fundamental principle of the theory of wages. This implies that any increase in real wages can take place only through improvements in productivity.

However, this doctrine of laissez-faire subsequently lost its trust with the gradual development of socialist ideas and collectivist doctrines. Marx (1818-1883) and Engels (1820-1895), with a stress on class struggle, gave an entirely different interpretation to the reward of labour. The exploitative element was highlighted; saying that the capitalist class owns all the means of production; whereas, labour owns only his labour power; which is perishable. In order to ensure his and his family's survival the worker must sell his labour power. The capitalist ensures that the 'use value'of labour power is in excess of its `exchange value'. This excess was called the **surplus value**.

In the process of production, whereas other factors merely transform themselves, it is labour alone which transforms more than what it receives. The capital, thus, accumulated was nothing but 'dead' labour; Marx concluded. The excessive use of capital would cause a falling rate of profit; because of over-production, which would ultimately lead to the breakdown of capitalism and usher in a classless society; where means of production would be collectively owned and used with no exploitation of labour. He finally exhorted'"Workers of the World Unite; you have nothing to lose but your chains." In the classless society the maxim of distribution would be 'from each according to his ability, to each according to his needs'. Nearly half of the Globe found the reasoning convincing and adopted this model in the early 20th century.

Occurrence of financial depression of 1930's brought into focus the importance of the increasing role of state in economies using methods of mass production. Emergence of trade unions and increasing state intervention now played a special role in wage - determination in many countries of the world, mainly to protect the labour from excessively low and oppressive wages and to generate mass consumption to maintain the system of mass production. The increasing state intervention, until the end of the 1970's, also led to a considerable increase in the number and size of the state enterprises in both the developing and developed nations. But the resulting quasi-fixity of wages, because of internalized labour markets; collective bargaining and trade unionism; and X-inefficiency were cited as the possible reasons for the explanation of the simultaneous co-existence of unemployment and high wage rates, which was a common feature of many of these countries.

The laissez-faire world which advocated that wage rate depends upon productivity and believed that 'invisible hand' will ensure this, failed to explain or was baffled at this phenomenon. However, efficiency wage models, believing that the quality of labour depends on the wage received, are also helpful in explaining this phenomenon. Indeed, the efficiency wage theory argues that real wages do not decrease, when there is unemployment; because any drop in wages causes a drop in the quality of labour; owing to the hiring of less competent individuals, or to the reduced willingness of these individuals to provide effort. The efficiency wage argument, thus, reversed what the marginalist's said earlier. Earlier the 'cause' was productivity and the 'effect' was wage rate. Here, the 'cause' is wage rate and the 'effect' is productivity. The basic idea underlying efficiency wage theory is that high wage rate leads to more efficiency which in turn increases the productivity. Thus, the link between wages and productivity is restored back by the efficiency wage theory.

Though in conventional labour markets, reward depends on absolute performance but in growing number of markets with 'winner-take-all' characteristics; Frank and Cook (1995) argue that it is relative performance, not absolute, that is rewarded.

The relative contribution of each unit of labour differs from the other to the extent the human capital is embodied in the labour. This idea has developed the concept of human capital. It is capital because it is a source of future earning, it is human because it is embodied in men. Therefore, each unit of labour, along with wages, get a return on human capital embodied in him. In this sense, each worker is a capitalist to the extent human capital is embodied in him.

This idea accepts the heterogeneity in the work force and also accepts the inequalities in rewards. This idea basically is not different from Neo-classical approach which links reward with productivity because a worker with more capital embodiment will be paid higher because of his higher productivity and contribution.

In all this debate, one thing is common; and that is the wage- productivity nexus but the area of agreement does not go beyond this. Is it a one-way nexus; (if so; which way?) or a two way nexus? Does this nexus change with change in ownership? This is a subject matter of endless debate. The present study is a humble effort which aims at addressing the above mentioned issues.

**Objectives**

The main objective of the present study is to explore the nexus between wages and productivity in the selected public sector enterprises in India. The study is confined to the public sector because of its domination in Indian economy. However, the growing criticism about its disappointing profitability and efficiency has made the study all the more necessary and relevant. In India, the major part of investment in public sector, at over 80%, went into enterprises producing goods, mostly basic and capital goods, and the remaining into services. The study has, therefore, limited itself only to the selected public sector manufacturing enterprises belonging to the Central Government.

Nehru saw the public sector and its rapid, progressive and relentless expansion as not only the path to socialism but also the mechanism to bring about India's industrialization and modernization. As a result, the public sector was assigned a place of commanding height in the Indian economic scene. It was expected to perform many economic and social objectives. It was expected to create the basic infrastructure for development, be a pace-setter in taking risk and nurturing entrepreneurship, take care of social needs, help the poor and the weak, generate employment and generate resources for future industrialization. The dream of Nehru was sought to be translated into reality through the Industrial Policy resolution of 1956 which remained the broad framework,till 1991, for demarcating the roles of public and private sectors.

In spite of the phenomenal growth and achievements, the public sector has also come in for severe criticism for its failures; especially to generate resources. Even the framers of economic policy are so much disappointed with the public sector that the Eighth Plan document in a critique states, "the public sector, as envisaged by Jawaharlal Nehru, was to contribute to growth and development of the nation by providing surplus re-investible resources. This has not happened as should have. Many PSUs make substantial losses and have become a continuing drain on the exchequer, absorbing resources which are withdrawn from sectors where these are desperately needed to achieve other developmental goals. Apart from the fact that the present fiscal situation does not permit any more accumulation of unsustainable losses, there is also the fact that many loss making PSUs do not serve the goal for which they were set up".[2] The statement highlights the progress, or otherwise, of the PSUs (public sector undertakings) in last 40 years.

Thus, the continuous resource crunch and the unprofitability of the public sector gradually led to a shift from reliance on the public sector to the private sector as an engine of growth in the future. The present economic reforms, since 1991, justifiably bring the public sector into close scrutiny and to ask searching questions about the productivity and efficiency of the factors of production especially the human resources employed in the public sector.

However, the shift in reliance, from public sector to the private sector is not confined to India alone but the entire globe is paying attention to the merits of this change. The thrust towards privatization as a policy tool was initiated in the U.K. in mid-1970s. It gradually picked up momentum in developing countries in the second half of the eighties when a number of countries in Latin America and Africa adopted privatization as a means of solving the resource problems of debt-ridden and loss making enterprises. World Bank and I.M.F. have also supported and advocated the policy of privatization as part of their structural adjustment programmes in developing countries. The gradual failure, and the consequent disappearance; of the erstwhile Soviet model,which was adopted in different degrees by almost half of the Globe as the planning strategy for their economic development, also gave a boost to the proponents of privatization.

While the ideological and efficiency arguments for privatization have been advanced vigorously by the proponents of privatization, there however, seems to be no unanimity in the literature on the relationship between ownership **perse** and industrial performance.[3] It is being argued that there were efficient and inefficient public enterprises, and efficient and inefficient private enterprises. However, existence of efficient public enterprises seems to be more of an exception rather than the rule. Public sector, everywhere, is now being criticized and condemned for its major shortfalls. The whole blame of slow economic growth in many countries of the world, including India, is being put on the dominance of inefficient public sector in these countries.

The government's role as an investor in and manager of public enterprises, because of the severe criticism, has probably become the most crucial issue for the future. It is also the most difficult and controversial. In India, not even the most ardent defenders of public enterprises can ignore the substantial inefficiencies that afflict the commercial public enterprises; nearly half of which are incurring losses. One of the major shortcomings attributed to these public enterprises is over-manning and labour inefficiency. Major blame of the inefficiency of public enterprises is put on the labour and labour is being accused of getting high wages, under various pressures, which has no link to their contribution to output i.e. productivity.

It is in this context that the study is undertaken so as to find the link between wages and productivity in selected public enterprises in India.

## Methodology

The methodology used in the present study is such that it can effectively account for the estimation of productivity, measurement of output, inputs and wages, the choice of industries and their representative firms, within a specified time frame.

Productivity, both single factor and total factor are measured by different methods. Single factor productivity refers to the ratio of an output to an input, which could be labour,capital or even raw-material. Since gross value added has been selected as a measure of output because of its superiority over others, therefore, the study has concentrated on the calculation of labour and capital productivity alone.

Since single factor productivities suffer from certain limitations, total factor productivities, defined as the ratio of output to weighted inputs, have also been calculated for all the three levels. The different productivity indices will be calculated and presented in chapter IV. It will also include the trends of capital-intensity in each industry and firm. Total factor productivities are estimated by all the three methods, i.e. Kendrick, Solow and Translog method.

As total factor productivities are based on certain restrictive assumptions, therefore, the alternative approach to production function will also be used, where mainly Cobb-Douglas production function and CES production functions are fitted to each industry/firm and estimates of productivities will be obtained.

Once the productivity estimates are obtained, the study will try to analyse the variations in productivities within an industry/firm and at the aggregate level. Inter-industry and inter-firm variations in productivities will also be analysed with the help of regression analysis, which would include gross value added as the scale parameter, the real wage rate, capital intensity and trend variable '**t**' representing institutional factors including embodiments in labour and capital.

The study, during the discussion of methodology will also highlight the issues relating to (a) measurement of output, i.e., why gross value added is preferred (b) measurement of inputs-labour and capital, and, (c) other recent developments in the measurement of productivity, i.e., problem of duality, general specification of functional forms, embodied technical progress, and labour embodiment. Capital has been measured with the help of the perpetual inventory method. Wages in the study include all wages, salaries and other benefits. The real wage rate is obtained by dividing the deflated wages and salaries by the number of employees.

The present study has been conducted only for selected public sector enterprises in India. As mentioned earlier, over 80% of the investment in public sector went into enterprises producing goods. Out of the eleven groups of manufacturing industries in India's public sector (as classified by Public Enterprises Survey, Department of Public Enterprises, Government of India, New Delhi) the study has limited itself to the following eight groups, i.e.,

1. Steel Industry;
2. Power Industry;
3. Petroleum Industry;
4. Fertilizers, Chemicals and Pharmaceuticals Industry;
5. Heavy Engineering Industry;
6. Medium and Light Engineering Goods Industry;
7. Transportation Equipment Industry;
8. Consumer Goods Industry.

The study, besides the eight industrial groups, has also been conducted for (a) aggregate of the selected eight groups of manufacturing industries, and (b) firms. Within each group of an industry, two firms each have been selected which are generally the oldest and the largest in terms of the amount of capital employed.

The period selected for the present study is 1974-75 to 1995-96. However, the period of study differs for the Power industry and for a few firms depending on the availability of data.

**Sources of Data**

The basic data source for the study is the Public Enterprises Survey, Department of Public Enterprises, Government of India, New Delhi. Data relating to value added, number of employees, Wages, salaries and other benefits, and value of gross fixed capital are taken from various issues of this survey. The data on prices, for deflating different variables, has been taken from Chandok (1990), R.B.I. Bulletin, National Income Accounts and the Index of Wholesale Prices in India by making suitable and necessary adjustments.

**Organisation of the Study**

Chapter II discusses the wage-productivity nexus at length and contains the experience of the earlier studies relating to the nexus in the context of Indian industry. Chapter III deals with the methodology related to the study. Different methods, both parametric and non-parametric, of estimating productivity have been presented in detail. The chapter also highlights some recent developments in the estimation of productivity. Measurement of output, inputs and wages have also been described in this chapter. The chapter also includes the methodology used for explaining the variations in productivity and its nexus with wages. Chapter IV constitutes sources of data and measurement of variables in the study. It provides the experience of some significant studies on productivity in public enterprises in India. Analysis of productivity trends by both parametric and non-parametric methods of the selected public sector enterprises also form part of chapter IV. The chapter also examines the regression equations fitted to different productivity indices to explain the changes in them. Chapter V investigates the wage trends in selected public sector enterprises. The wage-productivity nexus in selected public sector enterprises is empirically analysed in chapter VI with the help of the regression analysis. A summary of our findings and concluding remarks are presented in Chapter VII.

## NOTES

1. Frank (1995) has mentioned how Berry Bonds was offered a contract of $43.7 million in 1992 by the San Francisco Giants Club, p 6.
2. Eighth Plan, p 16.
3. Diverse conclusions of the studies by Kay and Thomson (1986); Vickers and Yarrow (1988); Bhaya (1990) and others on the one hand and Boardman and Vining (1989), Majumdar (1995) and others on the other hand is a testimony to this.

# 2

# WAGE-PRODUCTIVITY NEXUS— A THEORETICAL PERSPECTIVE

## General

It is generally believed that the compensation of workers employed in the organised sector in general and public sector in particular is not necessarily linked to their economic contribution in the productive process. It is now an accepted fact that most of the enterprises belonging to organised sector follow efficiency wage criterion to achieve their organisational goals.[1] It is also true that a very large part of the compensation package of employees working in these enterprises consists of non-wage components.[2] The enterprises belonging to this set generally follow the policy of internalized labour market which results in insulation of compensation packages from secular trends in productivity and market forces.[3] Moreover, these firms are generally operating under monopolistic or oligopolistic markets where the prices of their products are not necessarily determined by costs. Therefore, abnormal profit which they normally earn are also partly shared with their employees. The contention of real earnings of workers in the organised sector being higher is also supported by Lucas (1988) and Ahluwalia (1991). However, Tulpule and Datta (1988) and Jose (1994) concludes that improvements in real earnings of employees have been made possible due to productivity changes.[4]

Apart from these factors which facilitate in enhancing the wages of organised sector workers, these workers are also well organised into trade unions which helps in increasing their bargaining power, especially in a situation where the trade unions are promoted and patronised by political parties. The collective interest of these workers is also protected through many labour market regulations which are mostly targeted at these enterprises.

In the case of public enterprises, it is widely believed that this relationship between compensation of workers and their productivity gets further eroded; as the workers are better placed and enjoy a higher proportion of non-wage component in their compensation packages. The advantage is derived because of their capacity to earn rent as a consequence of lobbying for better compensation packages. It is now believed that the public sector unions are quite distinct from private sector unions as they are capable of shifting labour demand as well as wages through political process rather than be satisfied with their share determined by the production function.[5] Thus, in organised sector, wage rate (W) is higher than what it would have been in neo-classical market-clearing model and the causes are; (a) internalised labour market; (b) oligopolistic markets; (c) trade unionism; and (d) increased productivity. Here, an attempt has been made to study indepth the relationship between wages and productivity to explore whether wages are determined by productivity or not.

This chapter is divided into three sections. Section 2.2 describes the distinct phases of the pendulum that has swung from laissez-faire to state intervention and back to laissez-faire. The section 2.2 is divided into three sub-sections. Section 2.2.1 describes the wage-productivity nexus. Whereas section 2.2.2 deals with the 'rise of State intervention', section 2.2.3 elaborates on the drift towards market economy. Section 2.3, Public Sector in India, is further sub-divided into five parts. First part, 2.3.1, gives the rationale of the public sector. Section 2.3.2 highlights the growth and performance of India's public sector. Section 2.3.3 analyses the maladies of public sector in India. While section 2.3.5 describes the wage policy in public sector, section 2.3.4 elucidates the shifts in the objectives of public sector in India. Finally, section 2.4 contains a brief survey of some important studies linked to the wage - productivity relationship.

## Wage-Productivity Nexus: A Theoretical Perspective

In this section we will discuss the different phases of the Wage-productivity relationship. The first phase basically gives us an insight into the relationship till the emergence of the socialist doctrines. The second phase covers the phase of rise in state intervention. The third phase coincides with the emergence of laissez-faire back on the scene. The three phases are described in the following three sub-sections.

### *Wage-Productivity Nexus*

Wages constitute the only source of income to the worker. Today, the worker, especially in the public sector, is not satisfied with the wages he receives, and expects to be protected against the galloping inflation. He wants to improve his standard of living by sharing the gains of economic progress in the country. He is politically awakened and is ready to protest in order to secure his rights. In this endeavour, he has strong political allies. However, an indiscriminate upward movement of wages, or payment of monetary 'wage-supplements', may largely be reflected in the cost of production and consequently in the price of the product. Such gains may not be of any avail to the worker since inflationary pressures following such an increase would largely neutralize the increase in money wages and adversely affect the volume of employment. An increase in real wages can take place only through improvements in productivity and the linking of wages to such gains in productivity. It is in this context that nexus between wages and productivity is to be examined.

The wage in economic analysis is the price paid for labour as a factor of production. The labour is a distinct factor of production as it is the producer and also the consumer of national wealth/income. There emerges several problems when we start treating labour simply as a commodity and ignore its peculiar process of 'reproduction'. It is said by Picchio (1992) that "...other commodities do not subsist, they exist, they do not die, they are either consumed or destroyed, they are not born, they are produced, last but not the least they do not acquire habits and are not politically active".[6] Therefore, the price of labour is a unique parameter which is highly complex to determine and depends upon many factors.

Various answers have been given by various generations of economists about the problem of distribution of national Wealth produced by labour and other factors. The earliest explanation advocates that wages are historically determined and have no relationship with the market forces. At best workers should be paid not more than what is required for their subsistence. In due course of time this attitude was changed by physiocratic school. The *physiocratic school* held the notion that it was the agricultural sector which was the source of all surpluses and accumulation. Their objective was to maximize this surplus. The 'Wage Fund' doctrine advocated by them is among the most fundamental of classical economics. According to this doctrine, variations in the wage rates were explained by the principle that the level of wages is the function of labour supply and the size of wage fund available. Thus, the blame for low wages rested with the worker and not with the employer. This theory served the role of a *Theory of Wages*. In the works of Ricardo we find a theory of distribution of national product in terms of wages, rent and profit. In Ricardo's formulation, rent was determined by *marginal land*, wages were the function of wage fund, and profit was a residual element. Ricardo's concept of surplus was further developed by Karl Marx to develop the *Theory of Surplus Value* and the concept of marginal productivity was adopted by the neo-classical economists and J.B. Clark[7] extended the notion of marginal productivity to all the factors of production.

Hicks (1964) viewed wages, as the price of labour, being straight forwardly determined by the intersection of labour demand and supply curves in the market for labour. This view is clearly illustrated in the opening sentence of Hick's (1964) *Theory of Wages*. According to Hicks[8], "The theory of the determination of wages in a free market is simply a special case of the general theory of value. Wages are the price of labour, and thus, in the absence of control, they are determined, like all prices, by supply and demand." However, in the same paragraph Hicks did point out towards "certain peculiar properties" of labour. Hicks later on also emphasized that "The only wage at which equilibrium in the labour market is possible is a wage which equals the value of the marginal product of the labourers".[9] It was pointed out that the number of labourers which an employer will prefer to employ is that number which makes his profit a maximum, and that number is given by the equality of wages to the marginal product of the labour employed. Marshall[10] declared that "the wages of labour tend to equal `the net product' of a man's labour... the value of the produce which he takes part in producing after deducting all the other expenses of producing it". Theoretically[11], under competitive factor and product market situation, the wage rate (w) is determined by marginal physical product of labour (MPP), together with the ruling product prices: i.e.

W = MPP x Price of product

The marginal productivity analysis assumes that the position of the labour's marginal physical product schedule is independent of the wage level. The potential implausibility of this assumption has a long track record in the labour economics literature. Since neo-classical theory failed to explain the co-existence of high wages and unemployment, it had to incorporate 'efficiency wage theory' as a plausible reason for such phenomenon. The efficiency wage theory argues that high wage rate leads to more efficiency which in turn increases the productivity. This theory again linked wages to productivity but in the reverse direction.[12]

There are basically two routes through which a relationship between productivity and the wage rate may arise. First, there is the case where a wage increase raises the efficiency of workers, and second, there is the case where a wage increase improves the efficiency of management. The first of these mechanisms is generally referred to as the *economy of high wages*[13] while the second is termed *shock theory*[14]. According to the economy of *high wages* argument, improved wages lead to higher levels of marginal productivity at given levels of employment through improvements in worker's nutrition and health. This effect has frequently been found to be of importance in the context of less developed countries.[15] However, the same sort of mechanism is sometimes seen to be operating in developed economies, via the positive psychological effects thought to be associated with a higher wage. The basic argument lying behind the slack hypothesis is that the productivity of management is shocked into improving as the wage rate payable to the workforce increases. Underlying this hypothesis is the assumption that the employer firm, as an organisation, is operating with a degree of slack or inefficiency, which has the potential to be reduced when the organisation becomes threatened in some way. The classic example here is that of a non-union plant which becomes unionized. If, under such circumstances, there is a sudden increase in wages from the non-union to the union level, it is often argued that special managerial emphasis will be placed upon eliminating inefficiencies in the usage of labour as the factor of production whose price has increased. As a consequence of this efficiency drive the marginal productivity of labour, at given levels of employment, is seen to increase. Whether wages and labour productivity are linked via either economy of high wages or shock effects, the analysis suggests that labour's marginal physical product schedule shifts upwards as the wage rate is increased. Thus, the theory once again established the link between wages and productivity.

*Rise of State Intervention*

However, with the gradual development of socialist ideas and collectivist doctrines, the grip of the doctrine of laissez-faire, which is based upon the assumption of market clearing, with the wage rate being determined at the intersection of demand and supply curves, got weakened. The socialist ideas of Ferdinand Lassle (1815-1864), Karl Marx (1818-1883) and Friedrich Engel (1820-1895) had the most potent influence in the direction of increased state intervention in the economic field. Coker[16] has summarized the view points expressed by Marx and other earlier writers as, "these men set forth fully the doctrine that wage workers, in fields, factories and mines, are the real producers of wealth, most of which is unjustly taken away from them by employers, traders and other non-producers, and they proposed collective schemes . . .". It was this belief of Marx, that workers are exploited by the owning class that he propagated the idea of a society free from exploitation where each one is *rewarded* as per his need; underlying principle being `*From each according* to *his* ability, *to each* according to his need'. Thus, the direct link between wages and productivity of a worker was almost forgotten. However, the socialist ideas also accepted the differences in the productive contribution of different categories of workers and emphasized on the removal of differences based on ownership of property.

Some other developments and circumstances also contributed towards the movement for greater state intervention in the economic field. The notable development, besides attacks by later economists upon the doctrine of Laissez-faire, being the occurrence of frequent financial depressions; especially of 1930's which led Keynes to emphasize the importance of the increasing role of State. It became in fact increasingly evident that if the mass of the people were to rise above the level of mere wage slaves, they would have to be protected against the evils of free and unrestricted competition, by a greater measure of interference with and regulation of industry on the part of society than had been customary in the past. The earliest measures of wage regulation aimed mainly at removing sweatshop conditions (a system where payment is less than or equal to a very low living wage) and to protect the weaker sections of workmen, specially women and minors, against excessively low and oppressive wages.

Once introduced, state intervention continued. Sooner or later, it became a special feature of wage determination in many countries of the world, at least for certain categories of workmen and under special circumstances. The political and economic developments of the present century till 80's had all the more necessitated the assumption of wider state activities in this direction. In particular, the gradual change in the concept of state functions, wider application of democratic ideals and principles, establishment of socialist states, increase in the size of permanent class of wage-earners, increase in the number of industrial strifes to the detriment of the interests of the community at large, and occasional disruptions in the harmonious functioning of the economic system, have led the state to adopt more positive measures in order to regulate wage rates.

The objectives of state regulation of wages have been many, depending upon local conditions-economic and political power and the main philosophy of the role of the state in the life of a particular society. In keeping with the changing social philosophy concerning economic justice and fair play, the state intervened in the realm of wages with a view to protecting workers in the sweated industries (i.e. low wage industry). Occasionally, the purpose behind intervention has been maintenance of industrial peace in the sphere of wages - the main bone of contention between employers and workmen. Sometimes, especially during periods of economic depressions, state regulation of wages has been designed to speed up the pace of economic recovery. Similarly, preventing an inflationary spiral and maintaining economic stability during war time has been another objective of regulation of wages by the state. Finally, the most comprehensive object of state regulation of wages, which has found expression in a large number of countries, even in the capitalist societies, not to speak of the socialist ones, has been the pursuit of a national income distribution policy and fitting the wage-structure *therein* and using the wage policy as an instrument of planned economic development. Thus, wage contracts became an integral part of the government's wage policy.

Both Marxian and Neo classical theories were basically based on the assumption of homogeneity of labour. However, the theory of Human capital recognized the fact that workers can be put into different categories on the basis of amount of capital embodied in each worker in the form of experience i.e. learning by doing, education and training. These inter-personal differences also explain the dissimilar payments made to different categories of workers. Implicit in this statement, however, is the assumption that workers are rewarded in accordance to their relative contribution to the output.

*Drift towards Market Economy*

From a historical perspective, until the end of the 70's there was a considerable increase in the number and size of the state enterprises in both the developing and developed nations. In the early 1950's and 1960's there was a broad consensus that governments must intervene directly and play an activist role in development. Early development economics showed unquestioning faith in the ability of the state to correct market failures and imperfections, and to effectively direct the process of economic development. In fact even the World Bank, a capitalist institution with a development mission, was reluctant to lend to countries that did not have a government sponsored 'Development Plan'.[17] By the beginning of the 1980's there was a sharp swing away from this opinion, particularly in industrial countries and international financial institutions.

Recent writings in most of the academic journals and other forms of print media suggest that the pendulum of opinion has swung towards market not because of sudden emergence of some new philosophical insight, but due to disillusionment with the role of state. It is now an accepted fact that in most of the economies, strategies based on state intervention did not work. The State instead of promoting growth with equity created inefficiencies and distribution of resources in favour of power elites at the cost of working class and disadvantaged sections of society.

In an era of a contemporary disillusionment with state, it seems, we have forgotten our disappointment with the efficacy of market forces. It was the reliance on the market forces which led to the great depression of 1930's. It was the pursuit of the policy of free trade and free market by the imperialist forces which led to the process of deindustrialization in the colonies. We, therefore, must remind ourselves that the gains from planning and state intervention were quite remarkable in developing countries. For a century before 1950, the bulk of the population in developing countries was engaged in low productivity agricultural occupations, as a result economic growth barely kept pace with population growth. The growth rate was 2 percent per annum in UK between 1790 and 1820; 2.7 percent in Germany between 1850 and 1880; and some 4 percent in Japan between 1876 and 1900.[18] On the other hand, today's highly indebted developing countries registered an even higher growth rate of 6.6 percent per annum during this period. Therefore, one cannot ignore the acceleration of growth rates in the post 1950 period which was made possible by state intervention in these developing countries.[19]

The success of interventionist strategies in breaking away from past stagnation led to an exaggerated belief in the role of the state. The solution to every problem was found in the expansion of government activity in that area, irrespective of cost. Soon the scale of government became so large that the quality of intervention, as well as the quality of services provided by the state, deteriorated. Hirschman (1980 and 1982) has pointed out that a similar process took place in several industrialized countries. The wide expansion in government services resulted in a drop in the average quality of these services causing disenchantment with the welfare state. The disenchantment became so grave that it led to the breakdown and disintegration of U.S.S.R and its allies, who had advocated the unfettered expansion of state.

Therefore, taking a longer view, it seems that the pendulum of opinion has been swinging between two extreme positions - call for strong state (after emphasis on market failure) and call for unfettered market forces (after the emphasis on government failure). With the pendulum swinging back towards market forces; wages in the conventional labour markets are once again being determined by traditional wage theories.

Despite a swing towards market forces there, however, seems to be no unanimity in the literature about the relationship between ownership *perse* and industrial performance. Caves and Christiansen (1980); Kay and Thomson (1986); Vickers and Yarrow (1988); Bhaya (1990); Jha and Sahni (1992); Ramaswamy and Renforth (1994) all broadly concluded that there are either no substantial differences in the performance of the public sector and private sector or they cannot be just explained on the basis of ownership. It was found that a competitive environment, rather than ownership, substantially promoted allocative efficiency. Further, the policy environment within which public enterprises operate as well as their management structure, had more to do with their performance, in contrast to private enterprises, rather than the ownership of their assets (Levy, 1987). Fishlow (1990) argued that change of ownership alone will not make a crucial difference to the management of loss-making public enterprises. However, in a comprehensive study Boardman and Vining (1989) find that joint and state-owned enterprises perform worse than similar private enterprises. With respect to India, Vashist and Kundu (1990); Swamy (1994) and Majumdar (1995) conclude that public enterprises are less efficient as compared to their private counterparts and ownership does strongly matter in influencing industrial performance in the Indian context.[20]

Though, there are diverse opinions, but the existence of efficient public enterprises seems to be more of an exception rather than the rule; as the public sector, everywhere, is now being criticized and condemned for its major shortfalls. It is, therefore, necessary for the present study to describe and examine in detail the different aspects of India's public sector.

## Public Sector in India

The public sector was assigned a place of commanding height in the Indian economic scene. It was expected to create the basic infrastructure for development, be a pace setter in taking risk and nurturing entrepreneurship, take care of the social needs, help the poor and the weak and create an environment of equal opportunities and social justice. This was the role of the public sector as envisaged by Jawaharlal Nehru.

### *Rationale of the Public Sector*

The declared social objective of the Indian development strategy since Independence has been growth with equitable distribution. The problem of reconciling growth with equity in a democratic framework had provided the justification for the mixed economy as an institutional form in India. Mixed economy allows the *state* to actively intervene, through different instruments, to control the pace as well as the composition of private economic activity in the interest of equity. Since this control happens to be direct in the case of public sector, it provides the basic justification for the public sector as the most effective instrument with which the state in a mixed economy operating under the democratic framework would be able to pursue the social objectives of growth with equitable distribution.

However, whilst this ideological concern is an important justification for the existence of public enterprises in many countries, it is not necessarily the exclusive or even the most persuasive justification. In many mixed economies of developing countries there are pragmatic justifications that are free of any ideological considerations.

Many governments hold the view that certain key sectors of their economies should not be left in the hands of private citizens. These sectors are usually concerned with *infrastructure* activities, for example, the generation and distribution of energy, transportation and communications. These are usually activities that require *large initial capital* investments which are not forthcoming from the private sector. The services of such public enterprises may need to be extended to localities that cannot support them in purely economic terms. Often such infrastructure is created as a basis for regional or local development.

The government may also take initiative to produce other basic products in order not only to accelerate economic development but also to reduce its country's dependence on industrialized countries. Hence public enterprises are commonly found producing and marketing goods such as chemicals, steel, cement, textile and pharmaceuticals. These enterprises exist not necessarily as a result of political ideology, but because of government initiatives to speed up economic development.

Employment generation is another important justification for government intervention, particularly in underdeveloped regions which are unlikely to attract private sector initiatives. Economies of scale, cost of research and development and the introduction of new technologies are all frequently given as justifications for government interventions when these are beyond the capability of private investors.

For certain enterprises that provide monopolistic products or services, it may be considered in the national interest for these enterprises to be part of the public sector - either to give the benefit of monopoly profit to the state, or to ensure a pricing policy that is fair to the consumers. Other legitimate justifications are state security and defence considerations, which may require that strategically important enterprises be controlled by the state.

However, in some developing countries there have been public enterprises without any rational justification. Some enterprises are in the public sector because they have been abandoned by their private owners and no local businessman has been found who would be willing or be able to take over. One government may bring about a wholesale nationalisation which leads to the acquisition of private enterprises, with or without compensation to their owners, only to be replaced by another government with different policies, but which still retains the many enterprises nationalised under the previous regime.[21]

For these and similar reasons, many governments find that they are responsible for managing a large number of enterprises that do not contribute significantly to either employment or to wealth generation. Many of these businesses soon become ailing, unprofitable and are an administrative as well as financial burden on the state. Many of them may be small, commercial businesses which are unsuited by reason of their size and type of product or operations, to justify inclusion in a public sector portfolio.

Mehdi (1990) has divided these reasons for the growth of public enterprises into two main categories, namely, economic and socio-political. He has emphasized on the importance of socio-political reasons along with the economic ones. He says that "the specific nature of political purposes or objectives for which SOEs (*state owned enterprises*)[22] are created or used may vary from country to country and from time to time within the same country, depending upon their internal and external politico economic circumstances and the stage of their socioeconomic development. It has been pointed out by many economists e.g., Sheahan, that the establishment and expansion of SOEs is based on *political* [emphasis mine] rather than economic objectives, especially in developing countries. Experience from around the world shows that, more often than not, political objectives conflict with economic ones, and where this is the case, governments have shown partiality towards political objectives at the expense of economic objectives. The long run consequences of such preferences have often resulted in a loss of economic efficiency and dwindling operating surpluses."[23]

In India, the rationale for the public sector has been explicit or implicit in almost all the plan documents as well as in policy statements. The public sector came into being with the adoption of the Industrial Policy Resolution in 1948, which was subsequently followed by the Industries (Development and Regulations) Act of 1951. However, the Industrial Policy Resolution of 1956 formed till 1991, the broad framework for demarcating the roles of public and private sectors. In fact, the Resolution envisaged the expansion of public enterprises to serve as a powerful instrument in the armoury of the Government to gain control of the commanding heights of the economy and thereby achieve the basic national objectives mentioned in the Country's constitution. The Industrial Policy Resolution makes it explicitly clear: ". . . the state must progressively assume a predominant and direct responsibility for setting up new industrial undertakings and for developing transport facilities . . . . The adoption of the socialist pattern of society as the national objective as well as the need for planned and rapid development require that all industries of basic and strategic importance, or in the nature of public utility services, should be in the Public Sector. Other industries which are essential and require investment on a scale which only the State, in present circumstances, could provide, have also to be in the Public Sector. The State has, therefore, to assume direct responsibility for the future development of industries over a wider area".[24]

It is, therefore, hardly surprising that over the last forty years, the public sector has grown at a phenomenal rate and emerged as a crucial factor in India's economic development. The relative rapid rates of expansion and the consequent increase in the importance of public sector in the Indian economy are reflected by its share in important macro-economic aggregates.

*Growth and Performance of India's Public Sector*

During the last fortyfive years the public sector has

expanded considerably. In its process of expansion, it has made the people take the public sector for granted, oblivious of certain crucial factors like efficiency, productivity and competitive ability. Many of the public enterprises have turned into slow moving, inefficient giants. While there are several social and infrastructural sectors where only the public sector can deliver the goods, it has to be made efficient and surplus generating.

**(a) Growth of Public Sector** : At the time of Independence, activities of the public sector were restricted to a limited field. After Independence, public sector undertakings have grown rapidly in many fields of economic activity involving massive investment. Over the last four decades, the growth of public sector, especially public enterprises[25], in India has been phenomenal.

As on March 31, 1996, there were 243 central government undertakings (**Table** 2.3.2 (A)), excluding banks, financial institutions and departmental undertakings like the railways, ports, etc. The growth of investment in Central government undertakings is shown in **Table** 2.3.2. (A). It is clear from the **Table** that since 1950-51, the number of industrial and commercial undertakings of the central government has increased from 5 to 243 units in 1995-96, and the capital investment has increased from Rs 29 crores to Rs 1,78,628 crores. The major portion of the total investment is in enterprises producing goods (Capital in 164 manufacturing units is Rs 1,21,598 crores). In the goods producing public enterprises bulk of the investment is in the basic and heavy industries. **Table** 2.3.2 (B) gives us the growth in employment in Public enterprises. The total employment which was only 7 lakhs in 1971-72 increased to a level of 20.41 lakhs, a three fold increase however, there is a small decline since 1990-91. Along with increase in employment, per capita emoluments also increased during the same period. The increase was almost thirteen times while the consumer price index increased by approximately eight times making the real per capita emoluments to increase substantially, from Rs 5735 in 1971-1972 to Rs 12746 in 1995-96.

Since public sector includes not only the enterprises owned and run by central government but also the enterprises run by state governments and local bodies, therefore, all of them have been taken together in **Tables** 2.3.2 (C), 2.3.2 (D), 2.3.2 (E) and 2.3.2 (F) for a more comprehensive view of the entire public sector.

**Table** 2.3.2 (C) reveals that in 1961, the total number of workers employed in the public sector were 71 lakh out of a total employment of 121 lakhs for the economy. The number of employed grew to 194.6 lakhs in 1995 in the public sector out of a total of 275 lakhs. Thus, public sector was providing employment to 71 percent of the total labour force employed in the organised sector. This, perhaps, speaks for the importance of the employment generation objective of the public sector.

**Table** 2.3.2 (D) and 2.3.2 (E) gives us the share in gross domestic capital formation (GDCF) and gross domestic saving (GDS). During 1950-51 to 1995-96, gross domestic capital formation increased from 10.2 percent to 27.4 percent of GDP at current prices. However, the share of the public sector in GDCF improved from 2.8 percent during 1950-1951 to 8.2 percent during 1995-96 (**Table** 2.3.2 (E)). The comparative shares of the public and private sectors in gross capital formation underwent a change from 27:73 to 31:69 (**Table** 2.3.2 (D)). Thus, the share of the public sector which accounted for slightly more than one-fourth (approximately) of capital formation during the early fifties gradually increased to slightly less than one-third during the mid nineties.

However, the share of savings by the public sector has not undergone a similar change. The share of the public sector in gross domestic saving rose from 1.8 percent in 1950-51 to 3.4 percent in 1980-81 but declined sharply thereafter to only 0.6 percent in 1993-94 but rose again to 1.9 percent in 1995-96. In relative terms, the share of the public sector remained almost stagnant till 1980-81 but again dropped sharply to only 2.38 percent in 1993-1994 and was 7.51 percent in 1995-96. The basic cause of this failure seems to be the failure of the public enterprises to generate internal surplus commensurate with the increase in their capital stock. There is, however, an improvement in the saving performance of the public sector since 1990-91.

Despite the constraints, however, the public sector has been a very important factor in expanding the industrial sector of the economy. **Table** 2.3.2 (F) outlines the share of the public sector in total investment during the plans. Except in the first plan when its share in the total was low, in all the other plans the share in the total is large. In fact from the First plan to the Second plan, it was a big jump of over 30 percentage points. This took place because it was in the Second plan that the country, for the first time, embarked upon the course of a rapid industrialization of the country. Since then there has been no looking back and the share of public sector is now projected to be 45.2 percent in the Eighth Plan.

**(b) Performance of Public Sector :** Performance evaluation, a difficult task even in private enterprises, is a much more complicated exercise in PSUs. This was echoed way back in 1967 by the ARC report on Public Sector undertakings, thus :

"The task of measuring the performance of the management in the public sector is much more difficult than is the case in the private sector. The test of profitability provides a ready index for private enterprise. But in the public sector other tests such as the fulfilment of non-financial, social and national objectives prescribed by the government have to be met by the management in addition to the criterion of profitability. It is, therefore, necessary to work out a proper set of criteria for evaluating managerial performance in the public sector. These criteria have to be consistent with the objectives and obligations of the public enterprises".

The vast literature on public sector is full of this dilemma as to the choice of a suitable criterion to judge the performance of the public sector. Despite the realisation of the difficulties involved, a set of financial criteria, especially the profit ratios have been chosen to evaluate their performance. However, it may be noted that given the diversity of commercial objectives and non-commercial objectives of the public sector, the use of pure economic criteria to evaluate the public sector is wholly inadequate. Many objections have been raised against the use of an economic criterion solely. Mehdi (1990), on the basis of his cross-sectional study of 46 countries concludes that the specific characteristics of the public sector squeeze their revenue, and these contribute to the overall deficit of these enterprises, but this deficit makes a relatively small contribution to the overall deficits of government, and, hence should not be considered as a sole explanation of central government deficits. It has been suggested that if the expenditure by public enterprises on social objectives like housing, education, health, etc. is excluded, their efficiency will show better performance and is comparable to the private sector (Sen Gupta, 1988). Having agreed with the fact that the so-called social overhead is a burden on PSEs (The total expenditure on township, alone, was Rs 6613.31 crores upto 31st March 1996) which since inception are entrusted with such non-commercial responsibilities, PSEs which are making losses, tend to point to their social obligations as an alibi for poor performance. So the structure of performance evaluation system should be so designed as to prevent excuses and alibis for poor performance.

Though, there is no unanimity on the choice of the profitability criteria, the choice seems to be limited. However, some alternative criteria have been suggested by Fazal (1969), Dholakia (1978), Trivedi (1986), Sarna and Rao (1988) and Rao and Latha (1990). Fazal has included capital investment, rate of return, capacity utilization, manpower planning and development, pricing and marketing policies and morale and discipline in his evaluation criteria. On the other hand, Dholakia, Sarna and Rao, and Rao and Latha have used total factor productivity approach to find out the efficiency of the public sector enterprises in India. Roa and Latha have simultaneously used different financial ratios to evaluate the performance of public sector enterprises. Trivedi (1986) has suggested to adopt the 'public profitability at constant prices' to be an alternative. He defined public profitability as :

(Output—intermediate Inputs—Wages—Rent—Opportunity Cost of Working Capital/Fixed Capital;

where cost and benefit were taken as social cost and social benefit.

Therefore, a rational evaluation criteria may include the following objectives while evaluating its success:

(a) furthering the non-commercial objectives of the enterprise as specified by the government;

(b) furthering of the commercial objectives of the enterprise and maximization of profits, so as to generate internal resources for its expansion, subject to the constraints of government directives;

(c) improvement in the quality of products and services; and

(d) economy and efficiency in the use of resources.

**Table** 2.3.2 (G) gives a brief profitability profile of the public enterprises in India. It shows that the number of enterprises has grown from 93 to 243. During the period, 1971-72 to 1980-81, gross profit as a percentage of capital employed increased from 4 to 7.8. During the next decade it again increased from 7.8 to 10.88 and remained around 11.5 from 1990-91 to 1993-94 but increased to 16.1 in 1995-96. This distinct improvement, despite some fluctuations is a welcome development and need to be sustained. In absolute terms, the amount of gross profit increased from Rs 169 crores only to Rs 27988 crores despite the increase in the number of loss making units, which are now almost 45 percent of the total units. Net profits after tax also showed a distinct improvement over the same period. The net profits which were negative, Rs 19 crores, in 1971-72 increased to Rs 9878 crores in 1995-96. However, net profit as a percentage of capital employed was meagre 5.68, though it increased from 2.03 in 1981-82. The low net profit as a percentage of capital employed reflects on the poor financial performance of the public sector in India and has been the main basis of its criticism and condemnation. Joshi and Little (1994) have demonstrated that PSEs have performed quite poorly as compared to private sector firms in terms of real returns to investments over the period 1976-77 to 1986-87.

All these tables, show that there have been some improvements in the overall financial performance of the public sector, especially since 1990-91 when the new industrial policy was announced. Not only the percentage of gross profit and net profit to capital employed has increased over these years but the capacity utilization, the exports and the internal resources generated by them also increased. Whereas exports by the public sector increased from Rs 8980 crores in 1990-91 to Rs 15211 crores in 1995-96, the resources generated by them increased from Rs 11,296 crores to Rs 24371 crores during the same period. However, this improvement may not have come through efficiency but because of substantial market power of many PSEs.

Table 2.3.2 (A)

**Growth of Investment in Central Government Enterprises**

| *Year* | *No. of Units* | *Total Investment (Rs Crores)* |
|---|---|---|
| 1950-51 | 5 | 29 |
| 1960-61 | 48 | 953 |
| 1970-71 | 93 | 4089 |
| 1980-81 | 168 | 18231 |
| 1990-91 | 236 | 102083 |
| 1993-94 | 240 | 159307 |
| 1994-95 | 245 | 173292 |
| 1995-96 | 243 | 178628 |

*Source:* Economic Survey (1996-97)

Table 2.3.2 (B)

**Employment in the Public Enterprises**

| *Year* | *Employment (lakh)* | *Per Capita Emoluments (Rs)* | | *Consumer Price Index (1960-100)* | |
|---|---|---|---|---|---|
| 1971-72 | 7.01 | 5920 | | 192 | (-) |
| 1980-81 | 18.39 | 14239 | (140) | 401 | (109) |
| 1990-91 | 22.19 | 49179 | (730) | 951 | (395) |
| 1991-92 | 21.79 | 56508 | (854) | 1079 | (462) |
| 1992-93 | 21.52 | 64983 | (998) | 1185 | (517) |
| 1993-94 | 20.69 | 72151 | (1119) | 1272 | (562) |
| 1994-95 | 20.62 | 84429 | (1326) | 1402 | (630.21) |
| 1995-96 | 20.51 | 105879 | (1688) | 1545 | (704.7) |

*Source:* Economic Survey (1996-97)

Table 2.3.2 (C)

**Total Employment in the organised sector**

| *Year* | *Public Sector (lakh persons)* | *Total Employment (lakh persons)* | *% in Public Sector* |
|---|---|---|---|
| 1961 | 71 | 121 | 59 |
| 1971 | 107 | 175 | 61 |
| 1981 | 157 | 231 | 68 |
| 1991 | 191 | 271 | 70 |
| 1993 | 193.3 | 272 | 71 |
| 1994 | 194.4 | 273.75 | 71.01 |
| 1995 | 194.66 | 275.25 | 70.7 |

*Source* : Ministry of Labour

Table 2.3.2 (D)

**Gross Domestic Saving and Gross Domestic Capital Formation**

—Share of Public Sector

| | (at Current Prices) | | (Rs Crores) | |
|---|---|---|---|---|
| *Year GDCF* | *Aggregate GDS* | *Public Sector Sector* | *Aggregate* | *Public* |
| 1950-51 | 975 | 168 (17.23) | 954 | 259 (27.15) |
| 1960-61 | 2063 | 425 (20.6) | 2544 | 1142 (44.9) |
| 1970-71 | 6783 | 1253 (18.47) | 7177 | 2808 (39.12) |
| 1980-81 | 28786 | 4654 (16.17) | 30880 | 11767 (38.10) |
| 1990-91 | 129999 | 5436 (4.18) | 135156 | 52150 (38.6) |
| 1991-92 | 140736 | 11888 (8.44) | 140668 | 56537 (40.4) |
| 1992-93 | 155733 | 10765 (6.91) | 169656 | 62763 (37.0) |
| 1993-94 | 188707 | 4498 (2.38) | 175473 | 69426 (39.6) |
| 1994-95 | 237840 | 17240 (7.25) | 228852 | 83709 (36.6) |
| 1995-96 | 281014 | 21107 (7.51) | 288181 | 89589 (31.1) |

*Source:* Economic Survey (1996-97)

Table 2.3.2 (E)

**Gross Domestic Saving and Gross Domestic Capital Formation**

—Share of Public Sector
(as percent of GDP at Current Prices)

| *Year* | *Aggregate GDS GDCF* | *Public Sector Sector* | *Aggregate* | *Public* |
|---|---|---|---|---|
| 1950-51 | 10.4 | 1.8 | 10.2 | 2.8 |
| 1960-61 | 12.7 | 2.6 | 15.7 | 7.0 |
| 1970-71 | 15.7 | 2.9 | 16.6 | 6.5 |
| 1980-81 | 21.2 | 3.4 | 22.7 | 8.7 |
| 1990-91 | 24.3 | 1.0 | 27.7 | 9.7 |
| 1991-92 | 22.8 | 1.9 | 23.4 | 9.2 |
| 1992-93 | 22.1 | 1.5 | 24.0 | 8.9 |
| 1993-94 | 23.1 | 0.6 | 23.6 | 8.6 |
| 1994-95 | 24.9 | 1.8 | 26.0 | 8.8 |
| 1995-96 | 25.6 | 1.9 | 27.4 | 8.2 |

*Source:* Economic Survey (1996-97)

Table 2.3.2 (F)

**Share of Public Sector in Total Investment**
**(as percent of total Investment)**

| | |
|---|---|
| First Plan | 16.0 |
| Second Plan | 47.0 |
| Third Plan | 51.0 |
| Fourth Plan | 58.0 |
| Fifth Plan | 43.3 |
| Sixth Plan | 47.8 |
| Seventh Plan | 45.7 |
| Eighth Plan* | 45.2 |

*Source:* Plan Documents

* Projected

Table 2.3.2 (G)

**Profitability Profile of Public Enterprises in India**

| | 1971-72 | 1980-81 | 1990-91 | 1991-92 | 1992-93 | 1993-94 | 1994-95 | 1995-96 |
|---|---|---|---|---|---|---|---|---|
| No. of units | 93 | 168 | 236 | 237 | 239 | 240 | 245 | 243 |
| Capital Employed (Rs Crores) | 4098 | 18231 | 102083 | 117991 | 140110 | 159307 | 162450 | 173874 |
| Gross Profit/Capital Employed (%) | 4.06 | 7.8 | 10.88 | 11.59 | 11.39 | 11.59 | 13.9 | 16.10 |
| Gross Profit before Tax (Rs Crores) | 169 | 1418 | 11102 | 13675 | 15957 | 18560 | 22630 | 27988 |
| Net Profit after tax (Rs Crores) | –19 | –203 | 2272 | 2351 | 3271 | 4435 | 7187 | 9878 |
| No. of Profit making units | 56 | 93 | 123 | 133 | 131 | 120 | 130 | 134 |

*Source:* 1. Economic Survey (1996-97)
2. Public Enterprises Survey (1996-97)

### *Maladies of the Public Sector*

Regardless of the contribution made by public sector in India, it had become discredited by the early 1980's and was condemned both by academia and politicians alike. An idea about the concern for its financial failure can be gauged by a large number of Parliamentary committees like L.K. Jha Commission, Arjun Sengupta Committee, etc. appointed for evaluating Public undertakings. Public sector was seen as a drain on the Indian economy. Repeatedly the government had depended, in plan after plan, on the public sector for generation of economic surpluses, only to be rudely disappointed. The disappointment has been so grave that even socialist politicians and planners like L.K. Jha, Abid Hussain, Vasant Sathe and others advocated reforms including privatization, at one time or the other as the measure to combat the problem. By now the pride and idealism, associated with the existence and expansion of public sector, has almost totally disappeared.

There have been a variety of factors affecting the working of public sector enterprises; some of these have been economic, while others derive from social and political factors outside the enterprise or industry. It is therefore, not possible to single out any one or two elements as being the sole- or even the principal-causes of under performance by public sector enterprises. Several reasons have, therefore, been pointed out by different Parliamentary Committees (numbering more than 100) and others. Inadequate corporate planning, inaccurate designing, lack of managerial and financial autonomy, bureaucratization and politicization of management with consequent constraints on decision-making, location of plants on political consideration and over-employment under pressure from labour unions are a familiar story of public sector enterprises.

An important reason for the high costs is the cost over-runs of public sector projects. Many of the projects have taken longer to complete than was initially envisaged and in consequence (a) they have cost more than was originally estimated; (b) the benefits from them were realised later than expected; (c) the returns on the investments made have not, as a result, reached the level anticipated when the projects were sanctioned.

Another important reason cited for the poor performance of the public sector enterprises is that precise targets of production to be achieved in a prescribed period based on proper assessment of capacities are not laid down. The order book not being full, the established capacities are not fully utilised. In the absence of norms for consumption of scarce raw materials there is considerable wastage and spoilage. Inventories are heavy and unbalanced. No attempt is made to explore indigenous sources.

Manpower in excess of actual requirements; low productivity of labour as well as capital; lack of cost, budgetary or inventory controls; inadequate attention to Research and Development and development of Human Resources, and inadequate availability of skilled manpower are some other problems plaguing the public sector enterprises. There is also an extravagance in overhead expenditures, particularly, on provisions of townships and social amenities.

However, important from the financial angle is the question of pricing policies, which are generally not rational. For most of the public sector enterprises selling prices are administered rather than adopting market oriented pricing. The approach to pricing of public sector products has been influenced by conflicting considerations. The prices were generally kept low resulting in many cases in a situation of no-profit no-loss. However, in some cases like petrol, steel, etc. prices were fixed so as to yield an adequate return on capital. The conflict between the two approaches, i.e. the *public utility approach* and the *rate* of *return* approach has meant in practice the adoption of a minimal acceptable rate of return on capital and the subsidization of consumers and the private sector in many ways. The deficiencies in the system of pricing of public sector products had the effect of enlarging the burden on the budgets of the government.

Trade union activity in public enterprises is another important problem. Trade unions are resisting the moves of the government towards restructuring the public enterprises and no rational wage structure has been allowed to be implemented. The recent attempts to reduce over-staffing through proper employment policies, including the creation of a national renewal fund, have also been resisted by the trade unions in many industries. There is no unanimity in the literature about the possible effects of trade unions on productivity and wages. The common held view about the impact of unions on productivity and wages is, that unions on one hand increase wages of the worker and on the other decrease productivity through their restrictive work rules. However, recently Freeman and Medoff (1984) and other Harvard scholars have challenged the conventional view and found the net results of unions on productivity to be positive in many of their studies.

Though, no particular study has analysed the effect of trade unions on wages and productivity in India's public sector enterprises, yet a recent study conducted for selected Indian industries; has observed that there is no statistical evidence of a direct link either between unionization and wages or between unionization and productivity.[26]

There are, therefore, a whole range of circumstances such as cost overruns; delays in projects implementation, faulty pricing policy, over-employment and political interference, that ail the public sector in India. Similar problems, however, also plague the public enterprises in few other countries like France,

UK, and Philippines but the experience of Korea, Singapore and Germany indicates that public enterprises have performed better.[27]

*Shifts in the Objectives of Public Sector in India*

Despite the criticism and condemnation, public sector in India still occupies an important place in the Indian economy; because of its sheer size. Public sector in India is one of the many instruments of State intervention and as such its definition and scope can be determined only with reference to the social objectives and the development strategy to attain these objectives. The Indian development strategy has gone though distinct phases. While Tendulkar (1979) has identified the first two of these distinct phases the third phase is identified by Mehdi (1990). The first phase covering the period 1950-51 to 1964-65 was effectively dominated by the social objective of economic growth although other objectives like equity; reduction in inequalities; and generation of employment opportunities have indeed been mentioned. The second phase from 1965-66 to 1979-80 was characterized by the predominant concern for the reduction of poverty through redistribution. The third phase starting from early eighties has been characterised by the primary concern for commercial objectives of the public sector so as to contribute to the growth of the economy.

The emphasis on the role of the public sector has changed in degrees depending upon the constraints faced and the emerging major issues of the time. The Industrial Policy Resolution of 1948 declared that "a dynamic national policy must . . . be directed to a continuous increase in production by all possible means, side by side with measures to secure its equitable distribution". However, upto the Third Plan period, the growth orientation received considerably more emphasis in actual implementation than the redistributive functions of the public sector.

The mid-sixties were characterized by the suspension of the planning process and the inability of the public sector to generate internal surpluses combined with the governments inability to divert private resources for public investment. This resulted in the drying up of resources for the public sector investment which was reflected in an absolute reduction in the magnitude of public sector investment in real-terms during the mid-sixties. The overall industrial growth rate during this period also showed a decline; perhaps, because of deceleration in the rate of growth of investment in the public sector. The rate of growth of industrial production was 7.4 per cent per annum between 1950-1960, 6.3 percent between 1960-1970 and 4.2 per cent between 1970-1980.[28] Simultaneously, there was also a growing realization that the growth process during the first fifteen years of planning had not managed to make any significant dent on abject poverty in the country. The social objective of reduction/removal of poverty through redistribution came naturally into the picture in these circumstances. This also became the catchy political slogan of all political parties. This shift in emphasis changed the focus of the debate on the public sector. While in the earlier period, the much debated issue related to the relative position of the public sector in direct productive activities the focus now was on the public sector's capability to meet the redistributive objective of poverty alleviation. The strategic role played by the universal intermediate, heavy and machine building industries receded into the background. As opposed to the prominent role given to the discussion of Public Sector in the Industrial Policy Resolution of 1956, one finds it conspicuous by its almost total absence in the new Industrial Policy Statement of 1977. The discussion here concentrated on employment generation, fiscal instruments and the state intervention in the distribution of essential commodities and essential inputs to the disadvantaged sections of the society. Thus, the role by the public sector underwent a change in this period.

Because of a slowdown in the industrial growth rate (only 1.4 percent in 1979-80)[29], there appeared a new debate on the role of the public sector. This debate was further intensified because of many other internal and international factors - (a) increase in internal and external debt of the government; (b) reduction in foreign remittances to India after the second oil crises; (c) the resource crunch being faced by the Public sector whereby public investment declined; (d) existence of surplus manpower in many public enterprises; (e) continuous poor financial performance by many of the public enterprises. Thus the Industrial Policy statements of 1980 suggested an emphasis on optimum utilisation of installed capacity, raising both productivity and employment, reducing regional imbalances through preferential treatment of industrially backward areas, fostering rapid growth of export oriented industries alongside with import saving ones, expanding and consolidating agrobased industries and providing for protection of consumer interests against higher prices and poor quality of products.

Public concern for the relatively poor performance of the public sector enterprises has been growing since the early 1980's. For there is not only a micro-economic aspect of their failure in terms of economic and financial inefficiency, there is also a macro-economic dimension to the problem of low profitability. The failure to give adequate return on the huge public sector investment has been a major contributing factor towards the recent fiscal and foreign exchange crisis which has put severe strains on the Indian Economy. The urge for better performance has also grown due to tight budgetary constraints, and due to a growing and powerful cadre of professional enterprise managers and a gradual liberalisation of the economic policies with more emphasis on market forces and less on centrally directed economic planning.

A number of official committees like L.K. Jha Commission and Arjun Sen Gupta Committee, have examined various aspects of public sector performance emphasizing the need for better incentives and greater autonomy and accountability for the management of the public sector enterprises. The committee to Review Policy for Public Enterprises, known as the Arjun Sengupta Committee (1984), in particular recommended the "holding company" structure and the performance contract or Memorandum of Understanding (MOU) system with a view to ensuring an `arm's - length' relationship between the government and central government's public sector enterprises (*CPSEs*). Its other recommendations included decontrol of the prices of products of the public sector, abolition of price preferences, closure of chronically sick units and giving primacy to financial and technological upgradation.

In July 1991, the government through the new Industrial Policy, initiated programmes of economic stabilization and structural reform which aimed at creating a competitive and market-driven economic environment in India. Public sector reform is an important element of the structural reform programme. The New Industrial Policy of July 1991 stipulates that the government 'ensure that the public sector is run on business lines'. It also provides for strengthening the MOU system in order to provide the PSE's with a 'much greater degree of management autonomy', divesting of a part of the government shareholding in Public sector enterprises, reference of the chronically sick CPSEs to the Board of Industrial Financial Reconstruction (BIFR) for the reformulation of revival/ rehabilation schemes and the creation of a National Renewal Fund (NRF) as a social security mechanism to protect the interest of the workers likely to be affected by the rehabilitation packages. The Eighth Five year Plan (1992-97) also reflects this approach and lays down that the public sector investments be confined to the infrastructural areas where private participation would not be forthcoming. It stipulates that the public sector may withdraw from some areas and that the principle of market economy should be the main operative principle in the public sector operations. As a result the new Industrial Policy of July 1991 has brought down the number of areas reserved for public sector from 29 to six and the private sector is expected to play an increasing role in industrial activities. The liberalised industrial trade and foreign investment policies as also the fiscal, monetary, exchange rate and financial sector reforms which are a part of the on going structural reform programme have also radically altered the economic environment in which PSEs hitherto operated, necessitating basic reforms in their structure and framework. Thus the key elements of the Industrial Policy statement of July 1991, in the context of the reforms of the public sector, have been the strengthening of the MOU system, the disinvestment of PSU shares and creation of a National Renewal Fund.

**MOU**: MOU clearly defines the relationship of the PSU with the government and clarifies the respective roles of the PSU as well as the Government in order to achieve better performance. The MOU is also an attempt to bring a proper balance between accountability and autonomy. The emphasis is on achieving the negotiated and agreed objectives rather than interfering in the day to day affairs. It also includes the setting up of the objective performance evaluation system and introduce a performance incentive system. However, without autonomy accountability is a mirage. The government entered into MOUs with 4 PSEs in 1987-88 but the number increased to 114 in 1996-97. Out of 104 PSEs with MOUs in 1995-96, 52 PSEs were rated as excellent and 31 rated as very good. Thus, MOUs have increased the operational autonomy and fiscal discipline of the PSEs as no PSE can be rated excellent unless it has exceeded its targets (budgeted) for financial performance which is assigned 60 percent weight in the MOUs. MOUs have also enabled the PSEs to face competition and led to greater coordination among the Ministries as well as between PSEs and ministries. During 1996-97, all the sick and loss making PSEs which have not been referred to BIFR have been brought under the purview of the MOU system in order to improve their performance.

**Disinvestment**: In order to provide further market discipline to the performance of PSEs, it was envisaged to disinvest a part of government holdings in equity share capital in the case of selected PSEs. Since then the purpose of disinvestment has been to raise resources, encourage wide public participation and promote greater accountability. The total amount raised through disinvestment has, however, been short of targets. It was Rs 3038 crores in 1991-92 (budget = Rs 2500 crores), Rs 1912.42 crores in 1992-93 (target = Rs 3500 crores), Rs 2291.85 in 1993-94 (target 2500 crores), Rs 2619.62 crores in 1994-95 (target Rs 4000 crores) and Rs 168.48 crores in 1995-96 (target Rs 7000 crores).

So as to democratise the system of disinvestment the government constituted a Disinvestment Commission under the full-time chairmanship of Mr G.V. Ramakrishna, former member of Planning Commission, in August 1996 with four other numbers. Apart from drawing out a detailed disinvestment strategy the broad terms of reference set for the Commission include: (i) to draw up a comprehensive overall long term disinvestment programme within five to ten years for the PSUs referred to it; (ii) to determine the extent of disinvestment in each of the PSUs, (iii) to prioritise the PSUs referred to it by the core group on terms of overall disinvestment programme, (iv) to recommend the preferred mode or modes of disinvestment for each of the identified PSUs, (v) to recommend a mix between primary and secondary disinvestment taking into account Government objectives, the relevant PSU funding requirement, etc., (vi) to superise the overall sale process and take decision on instrument, pricing, time, etc. as appropriate, (vii) to select the financial advisors for the specified PSUs to facilitate the disinvestment process, (viii) to protect the interest of the affected employees etc. The actual disinvestment would be done by the concerned undertaking under the overall guidance of the Disinvestment Commission.

The Disinvestment Commission submitted the panel report on 20th Feb., 1997. The main recommendations of the Commission were:

——Establishment of Disinvestment Fund to be administered by the Ministry of Finance used for restructuring, Voluntary Retirement Scheme, strengthening PSEs by utilising the fund for turning around the loss making PSEs and restructuring the marginally profit making undertakings, for developing social infrastructure, etc.

——Corporate Governance and Autonomy

— create autonomy to Board of PSEs alongwith proper delineation of accountability,

— all decisions by Boards,

— Government should exercise their right only through their representatives on the board,

— practice of audit by CAG and examination by COPU needs to be reviewed in view of changing commercial environment - Government may initiate necessary dialogue.

——Delegation of Powers to PSEs:

— graded autonomy to strong/moderate and other

performers. For strong performers it is recommended that delegation of powers be maximum.

— strong performers empowered to form joint ventures upto equal stakes; with foreign parties subject to approval by FIPB.

— complete investment decisions autonomy for strong performers.

—Professionalising the Board

— select experts and professionals from outside the government for appointment as non-executive directors on the board of PSEs.

— PESB (Public Enterprises Selection Board) can prepare a comprehensive list of professionals.

— restrict the number of elected directorship held by each person in PSEs.

—Provision for Elected Directors

— Election of directors representing minority shareholders in proportion to the extent of non-government shareholding.

—Selection of Top Management:

— PESB's recommendations should be accepted by concerned ministry without having to go to the ACC

— Broad base PESB

— Five year contractual terms for CEOs and removal on non-performance.

—Salary of CEOs (Chief Executive Officers) is far lower than counterparts in Private Sector. So raise the salary of chairman and managing directors in profit making undertakings to at least Rs 50,000 per month plus incentives, performance linked Bonus, allowances etc. be paid. Salaries of Schedule 'B' and 'c' be suitably raised. The commission stated that the appointment should be on contractual basis and should be liable for termination within the contract period for proven non-performance.

——PSEs fully empowered for autonomy in price fixation.

——For accountability revamp MOU system; performance assessment on routine intervals by a joint team of secretaries of ministries, CEOs and outside senior professionals.

——Formation of Pre-investigation Board to evaluate all questionable Commercial decisions at the board of directors level to determine whether the decisions were taken with modified or corrupt intent; it could refer malfeasance only to CBI/CVC.

— Pre investigation Board could include retired financial sector top executives, former CEOs and professionals.

——Formation of Standing Empowered Group to provide continuity to the whole process of disinvestment in PSEs; selection of financial advisors, sale process supervision, pricing, timing, etc. publicity and to draw funds from disinvestment fund. SEG to comprise the Cabinet Secretary, Secretaries of the Ministry of Finance, DPE, Administrative Ministry and CEO of the concerned PSE.

——Retailing of PSE shares to small Investors and Employers:

— sizable quantity of shares to small investors and PSE employees at 10 percent below the issue price,

— a ceiling of 200 shares for such allotment,

— ceiling of 500 shares for preferential allotment to employees; payment in two instalments; lock in period of three years.

Regarding the PSUs referred to it for disinvestment, the commission identified 20 PSUs as core sector undertakings and 15 as non-core sector units. The classification of 5 was left to be decided at a later date. Disinvestment suggested for the strategic sector, which included arms and ammunition, defence equipment, aircrafts, atomic energy, etc., was nil whereas for core sector it could be upto 49% and for non-core sector upto 74% or more. The disinvestment commission also made specific recommendations relating to three of the 40 PSUs. While for

Modern Food the outright sale was recommended, it suggested 49 percent disinvestment in Gas Authority of India with immediate disinvestment of 25 percent and 74 percent or more disinvestment in ITDC.

The Disinvestment Commission, which was referred 40 PSEs at the first instance in September, 1996, had a further list of 10 PSEs added on to the list in March, 1997. Subsequently, the second, third and fourth reports were submitted in April, May, and August, 1997. In these the Commission had made various recommendations about 19 PSEs, out of the 50 referred to it, for disinvestment of varying degrees. The fifth report in November, 1997 recommended 7 more divestments but no sale of equity in NTPC.

To give shape to the changed policies relating to PSEs, the Approach paper to the Ninth Plan, presented to the National Development Council in early 1997 highlighted that the policies relating to PSEs will be fine tuned to ensure greater autonomy, their more efficient functioning and increased resource generation. Potentially viable units will be assisted through restructuring, offering a more attractive VRS package and conversion to joint ventures etc. Following up with the NDC meeting, the finance minister in his 1997-98 budget speech, announced that to begin with, nine well performing public sector enterprises had been identified for being turned into Global giants. The enterprises, whom he described as "**Navratnas**", are IOC, ONGC, HPCL, BPCL, IPCL, VSNL, BHEL, SAIL and NTPC". In a subsequent statement, the Industry Minister on July 4th, 1997 announced various measures that would help them achieve the objectives. He stated that the decision to delegate decision-making to boards of the navratnas would lead to the uncaging of the nine tigers. "We have redefined the commanding heights of the PSUs in India", he remarked. To make these navratnas truly world class entities, the strategy was to turn them into autonomous board-managed companies and extend, gradually, the model package to all profit making PSUs.

The navratna board of directors have been allowed to enter into technology joint ventures, to affect organisational restructuring including establishment of profit centres, opening of offices in India and abroad. They have been permitted to structure and implement schemes relating to personnel and human resource management, training, voluntary or compulsory retirement schemes, etc. The navratnas shall not depend upon budgetary support or Government guarantees. The resources for implementing their programmes shall have to come from their internal resources or through other resources, including capital markets. The Government also decided to induct four professional non-official directors in these PSUs. These steps were construed to be first wave of reforms and not as freedom.

In continuation of its policy on Navratnas, the government in October, 1997 announced graded financial and operational powers to the boards of 97 "mini-ratnas" and broad based their boards by inducting at least three non-official part time directors. Category I PSEs were to be given more financial and operational autonomy than category II enterprises, after the boards of these enterprises are restructured.

The government has, however, come under severe criticism for the tardy progress made in restructuring of PSUs equity structure. The Chairman of the disinvestment commission stressed the need for total acceptance of the proposals rather than selective implementation. On 22nd October, 1997, he urged that the Disinvestment Fund be created with its proceeds to be used for reviving sick PSUs and improving the general health of the PSEs and not make disinvestment as a short-term budget balancing measure. The government also failed to appoint non-executive directors on the boards of Navratnas, making autonomy meaningless. The chairman lamented that India was very slow even after the 1991 reforms to implement the world wide practice to privatise inefficient government owned enterprises.[30] The government in December, 1997 however, abolished 696 very old guidelines out of the total 892, in order to free the PSUs from the grip of the bureaucrats.

**The National Renewal Fund**: Government announced the setting up of a social safety net viz NRF on 3rd February, 1992 to protect the interest of workers affected by industrial restructuring. The NRF, *inter alia,* provides payment of compensation to rationalised workers and their retraining, counselling and redeployment. Assistance from NRF has been provided for implementing VRS of PSEs. A total of Rs 1429.76 crores has been released to 86,804 employees from April 1992 to February, 1996.

Though, a special emphasis has been given to the retraining and redeployment of workers who have either been retrenched or have availed of VRS, the NRF have come a cropper. There is thus, an urgent need for a clear-cut labour policy laying out a framework for retrenchment of redundant workers with adequate compensation packages.

The Indian Industrial policies thus, make it clear that despite the various reforms suggested for the public sector enterprises, they are to be managed within the framework of public ownership. The umbilical chord that the Government has with PSUs can not be wished away. Complete disinvestment is, therefore, no panacea for the ills of the public sector, it is rather the starting point, seems to be the thinking of the policy makers.

*Wage Policy in Public Sector*

The shift in thinking about the public sector is also evident by the wage policy as outlined in the Eighth Plan; despite the lack of consistency in approach. The question of fixation of a minimum wage has assumed considerable importance in India since the last few decades. The demand for minimum wage gathered momentum due to the awakening among workers and the active intervention of the State in labour disputes. Many considerations, like the size and composition of the family and the earners, requirements of a worker, cost of living, etc. were taken into account while fixing the minimum wages.

A majority of the public enterprises set up by the central government had in the early stages adopted wage patterns applicable to corresponding central government employees. In the case of the workers in various enterprises, the practice has been to enter into wage settlements with unions representing the employees. Prior to 1968, public enterprises were required to obtain 'Government's' approval for any general revision in the terms and conditions of service of their employees. Generally, the level of emoluments in public enterprises used to be fixed by the managements on region-cum-industry basis taking also into account the level of emoluments prevailing for central government servants of comparable categories. In view of the recommendation of the Administration Reforms Commission (1967) public enterprises were made free to make appointments irrespective of pay, for all posts below the Board level without reference to the government. It was, however, recognised that though uniformity is not possible in the matter of pay and allowances but wherever possible, rationalisation be effected. The freedom, depending upon the relative strengths and weaknesses at the bargaining **table**, led to wide differences between different enterprises *interse* and between the levels obtaining in the central government and the enterprise. The trend of distortions was arrested towards the end of 1971 when the Third Pay Commission highlighted that the public enterprises were raising their emoluments considerably despite losses suffered by them. The Government then decided that there be no general revision of wages or increase in fringe benefits in the public enterprises without prior consultations with the central government. Within the government, the then Bureau of Public Enterprises in the Ministry of Finance acted as the central coordinating point for the scrutiny of such proposals. It was felt that there is no uniformity either in the periodicity of review or the extent of neutralisation. The lack of uniformity was all prevalent between the public sector and the Central Government employees and between the central government and state government employees. Even within the same sector the practice varied from institution to institution leading to wide disparities, even within the public sector in emoluments between employees of the same status.

The Government, through the Bureau, had been trying to rationalise the wage structure and eliminate the distortions in it. The department of Public Enterprises, Ministry of Industry continues to function as a nodel agency for evolution of policy relating to wage settlements of unionised staff, etc. The subsequent wage settlements were aimed at bringing uniformity in the wage structure and it included the total package of monetary rewards from employment. The workers in public enterprises had been deriving benefits in addition to wages and perquisites, minimum bonus at the rate of 8.33 per cent of wages. Moreover, they had also been getting other opportunities of supplementing the income by overtime allowances, rapid promotion policies and favourable fringe benefits and scale revision through periodic wage settlements at a greater scale than those available to their counterparts in Central Government. The upward movement of emoluments of unionised workers had exercised pressure and led to periodical pay revision of supervisory personnel but the gap between the two had gradually narrowed down. The upward movement of emoluments of workers eroded the capacity to pay in many public enterprises.

All this led to a change in the thinking of the Government, in 1980's, which considered it necessary that the increases in wages of the workers be linked to productivity so that on the one hand, the enterprises would have the capacity to pay and, on the other hand, the increase would then appear to be sharing of the fruits of prosperity. However, pending evolution of clear guidelines on the subject, a number of wage settlements were entered into, according to earlier guidelines. But since July 1995, all public sector enterprises have been brought under the same DA pattern i.e. IDA, and the earlier distinction between industrial DA and central DA has been abolished. This step will further rationalise the wage structure.

The Eighth Plan also clearly outlines the Government's national wage policy. It says "Wide differences in wages prevail between the organised and the unorganised sectors even in similar activities and occupations and even in different regions. Even minimum wages fixed statutorily vary widely among states and regions. Further, changes in wage rates and wage levels over time vary significantly, mostly in the direction of increasing wage disparities. The levels of and changes in wages and salaries often have no relation with productivity, and, wages thus do not function as instruments that induce efficiency. It is, therefore, necessary that a national wage policy be evolved to guide steps in the direction of removing irrational and iniquitous disparities in wage and salary levels and include efficiency; and also to streamline institutional mechanisms for wage fixation . . . ."[31] The new wage policy announced in November 93 and January, 1994 emphasized that PSEs should generate their own resources for meeting enhanced liability on account of wage revision and no budgetary support to them by the government will be provided. Also no automatic increase in administered prices of their goods and services will be made.

Thus, though the need to have a rational and equitable wage policy was always felt but there has always been a lack of clarity and consistency in the Government's approach to the wage policy. Wages and salaries in public enterprises continue to be determined and revised through 'settlements' and 'understandings' between the employees and the enterprises and has no relation 'whatsoever' with market forces.

**Earlier Studies on Wage-Productivity Relationship**

Several studies have been conducted, both abroad and in India, to find out the relationship between wages and productivity. No attempt is made here to list all of them as the number is so large that it will make the task very difficult. Most of the studies confirm that there does exist a relationship between the two. However, two recent studies; Gordon (1987) and Holzer (1990), needs special mention. Gordon (1987) has studied the relationship in the U.S., Japan, and Europe for the years (1964-84) and found that nexus exists both ways; except in U.S. manufacturing where wage rigidity was higher. Holzer (1990) confirms the positive effect of both level and changes of productivity on wages in U.S. firms on the basis of information provided by them in 1980 and 1982.

In this section an attempt is being made to briefly describe a few significant studies conducted in India on the link between wages and productivity.

Johri and Aggarwal (1966), in a study on the inter-industry wage structure in India has found the correlation, both simple and partial, between wages and labour productivity for the period 1950 to 1961 for 29 industries. They calculated the simple correlation coefficients for four sub-periods, 1950-52, 1953-55, 1956-58 and 1959-1961. Though the association between wages and productivity seems to be decreasing over the period (from +0.61 to +.279) but the high values of both simple and partial correlation coefficients provide sufficient statistical evidence in support of their hypothesis of close association between wages and productivity. They conclude that the evidence strongly suggests that higher the labour productivity, the higher will be the wages and vice versa.

Sawhney (1969), in another study of 29 industries for the period 1953 and 1963 tested different hypothesis on wage differentials. In the explanation of inter-industry wage differentials, he tested the influence of labour productivity on wage levels. From the values of simple and partial correlation coefficients for the two periods (+.75 and +.71 of simple and +.68 and +.81 of partial) he arrived at the conclusion that wage rates in different industries are significantly influenced by corresponding levels of labour productivity. The regression model also corroborated the same result. The inter-temporal analysis was also conducted and again a strong relationship between labour productivity and wage rates was confirmed.

Verma (1971) also conducted an analysis of factors contributing to wage differences between manufacturing industries. He conducted a cross-section analysis of 209 industries for 1964 based upon data drawn from *Annual Survey of Industries*, 1964. He included five explanatory variables, value added per worker being one of them. Verma fitted a regression equation and found that the average annual wage differed between industries primarily due to the fact that in some industries the level of productivity (value added per worker) was higher than in other industries. This result too is in agreement with the studies by Johri and Aggarwal and Sawhney.

Dholakia (1976) has taken a cross-section data on the two-digit level manufacturing industries for two years 1960 and 1964 and applied the regression technique to test alternative models based on the 'expected ability to pay' and the 'technology' hypothesis. He included five explanatory variables in his postulated relationship. The five variables were (a) proportion of skilled workers in the total working force in the industry(s); (b) capital intensity as indicated by the value of fixed capital stock per worker employed in the industry (K); (c) average productivity of labour in the industry (P); (d) average rate of surplus originating in the industry as indicated by the ratio of non-wage income to total capital stock (R), and (e) the average size of firms in the industry as indicated by the average number of workers employed per factory (F). He formulated five alternative regression models to test the explanatory power of each of the variables. He concluded that skill-mix (reflecting technological level) and productivity were the two major determinants of inter-industry wage structure in India.

In another significant study Tulpule and Datta (1988) analysed the trend of real wages in manufacturing in India for the period 1960 to 1983. They concluded that real wages rose faster than the national per capita real income but only marginally faster. They refuted the claim that workers are appropriating a disproportionately large share of wealth and contended that labour productivity increased faster than real wages. They also found a very high (+.81) correlation between the real wages per worker and labour productivity.

Jose (1994) had undertaken a study of 19 manufacturing industries, employing about 7.6 million workers in the factory sector, for the period 1970-71 to 1987-88. The main aim was to analyse the trend of rising real wages. The main source of data was ASI i.e. *Annual Survey* of *Industries*. He noted "that 1970s was a period of relative stagnancy in real earnings amongst most industries and that any perceptible rise in real earnings came about only by the early 1980s"[32]. He also observed that it was productivity change which made it possible to bring any improvement in real earnings of employees and noted a high degree of association between the index number of real earnings and productivity in most industries.

Most of these studies, both in India and abroad, pertain to either the market economies as a whole or to the organised manufacturing sectors of the economy. These studies have made very valuable contributions but our aim is to see whether the conclusions arrived at by these studies are also valid for India's public sector enterprises. As many significant studies are not available for the erstwhile U.S.S.R or East European countries, which might have thrown more light on the relationship in the public sector; it therefore, becomes more pertinent to undertake the present study and fill the gap. Most of the studies in India have used aggregate data for manufacturing industries and did not consider either the aggregate or the disaggregate level of public enterprise. These studies also analyses only one aspect of the relationship; i.e. the effect of productivity on wages and the other side is ignored. The present study will concentrate on finding the two way nexus between wages and productivity in public enterprises especially in the firms; industries and the aggregate of industries. In order to understand this relationship, efforts have been made to first find out the behaviour of productivity trends and wage trends in these units. The detailed methodology involved in the exercise and the results thus obtained are discussed in the subsequent chapters.

## NOTES

1. Yellen (1984) defines efficiency wages as higher than market equilibrium wages.
2. Hart (1984).
3. Lindback and Snower (1988).
4. Jose (1994), p 31.
5. Freeman (1986), p 69.
6. Picchio (1992) c.f. Seth (1994).
7. Clark (1899).
8. Hicks (1964), p 1.
9. Hicks (1964), p 8.
10. Marshall, p 548 (First Edition) c.f. Hicks (1964).
11. For detailed discussion, see King (1972); Spasford and Tzannatos (1993).
12. For more details, see Yellen (1984); Akerlof and Yellen (1986).
13. Perlman (1969), pp 50-56.
14. King (1972), p 37.
15. See for example Todaro (1989), pp 35-37 and Herrick and Kindleberger (1983), p 195.
16. Coker, Francis W., 'Recent Political Thought'. c.f. Sinha (1971), p 7.

17. Even today, the Bank, which is otherwise a strong champion of free enterprise and market forces, does not lend without a government guarantee.

18. Person Commission. (1969) *Partners in Development*. New York: Praeger. p 27. c.f. Jalan (1991), p 63.

19. Jalan (1991), p 64.

20. Majumdar (1995), p 31.

21. Examples are India, Pakistan, Bangladesh, Sri Lanka, Thailand, Uganda, Kenya.

22. Brackets are mine.

23. Mehdi (1990), p 130.

24. Government of India (1956). *Industrial Policy Resolution*. April 30, 1956.

25. Public sector includes (a) administrative departments; (b) departmental enterprises; and (c) non-departmental enterprises. Public enterprises include all departmental and non-departmental enterprises. The term public enterprises has been used interchangeably with public sector.

26. For details about the literature on the effect of trade unions on wages and productivity, see Ramjash (1992).

27. For details see Seetharaman (1984-85). Vol 28 (4); 28(5); 28(6); Manason (1988), Sikorsi (1989) and Song (1988).

28. Hajela (1987), p 330.

29. Hajela (1987), p 333.

30. In 1996 alone, 88 billion US dollars were raised globally through disinvestment.

31. Government of India. (1992-97) Eighth Five Year Plan. p 126.

32. Jose (1994), p 31.

# 3

# METHODOLOGY: MEASUREMENT OF PRODUCTIVITY AND WAGES

## General

Productivity growth is important because it is the key determinant of a nation's future standard of living. The inhabitants of a country whose productivity is growing rapidly can expect to have a better quality of life by enjoying better and more food, clothes, education, environment, medical care, etc. Productivity advancement has contributed to the economic growth of many industrialized countries. Therefore, the realisation of productivity improvement is an important aspect of industrial development for the developing economies. Economic literature of the last four decades is full of issues relating to the theory and measurement of productivity. Solow (1957), Fabricant (1959) Kendrick (1961) had tried to explain the growth of output through productivity growth. Since then lot of research and debate about the measurement, determinants and consequences of factor productivity has emerged. Some of the issues and methods of measurement of productivity are covered in this chapter.

This chapter is divided into five sections. The second section (3.2) relates to the question of methodology and consists of sub-sections on measuring productivity by both parametric and non-parametric methods. It also includes few important issues relating to the measurement of productivity. Sections 3.3 and 3.4 deal with the measurement of output and inputs respectively. Section 3.5, gives an account of the measurement of wages. The last section i.e. 3.6 outlines a brief account of the methodology used in the study to explain the variations in productivity and the nexus of productivity with wages.

The section 3.2 has been sub-divided into four parts. While section 3.2.1 describes the partial productivity indices; labour and capital (also known as single factor productivities), section 3.2.2. deals with total factor productivity measures. It gives an account of Kendrick; Solow and Translog Index of total factor productivity. Section 3.2.3 talks of production function estimation which includes the discussion about Cobb-Douglas production function; CES production function and Transcendental Logarithmic Specification (Translog production function). The last part; section 3.2.4 elucidates some recent developments in the theory of productivity estimation and includes a brief review of some of these developments.

**Measures of Factor Productivity**

Productivity often refers to output-input ratios that are commonly used in economic theory and economic policy. Productivity can, hence be defined in terms of the efficiency with which inputs are transformed into useful output within the production process. It follows, that there are as many indices of productivity as there are factors of production. In each of its forms, it is basically a comparison of an output with the services of one or more of the resources used in producing the output. Since the output-input ratios of a particular time and place have limited significance, the ratios are, therefore, compared with the corresponding ratios of another time or place. The productivity ratios are usually normalized to some base year, resulting in a productivity index over time.

Productivity in a given period can be measured either by average productivity or marginal productivity. Most of the studies, including Kendrick (1961), have taken average productivity index as a measure. While each index has its own merits, the ones most often used are *partial or single factor* productivity indices of labour and capital and the *total or multifactor* productivity index. Partial productivity indices are simply the average product of labour or capital. Total factor productivity is a more comprehensive approach and has been extensively used.

*Partial Productivity Indices*

Labour productivity, i.e. output per unit of labour, is the most widely used measure of productivity. Kendrick (1961) while calculating productivity trends in the USA, defined average productivity of labour as the real gross output of the private domestic economy divided by total man-hours of labour input. Different measures of labour productivity have been adopted by different studies, depending upon the meaning given to the input labour. Because of computational simplicity and data availability, the average number of persons engaged in production is generally taken as labour input. The productivity ratio could then be called as 'output per man'. Change in output per man, then, combines the effect of changes in (1) efficiency, (2) total resources per man hour, and (3) average hours worked per man. Thus, productivity revealed by this ratio may be influenced by the substitution of capital for labour, the realization of economics of scale, the introduction of more efficient vintages of capital and the employment of better trained manpower and changes in raw material. In order to eliminate the impact of changes in raw materials, labour productivity is also defined as the ratio of value added to labour employed. Symbolically,

$$AP_L=V/L \qquad \ldots (1)$$

where $AP_L$, V and L are, respectively, the labour productivity, value added and labour input.

Other *partial* productivities like capital productivity and material productivity can be similarly defined. Capital productivity, symbolically is written as;

$$AP_K = V/K \qquad \ldots (2)$$

however, it can also be defined as

$$AP_K = V\text{-}W/K \qquad \ldots (3)$$

implying that we exclude wages from total value added so that we have mainly the contribution of capital to output, but generally the first definition given by equation (2) is preferred and used.

*Total Factor Productivity Measures*

However, because of the limitations of the partial productivity indices, it is useful to devise a composite measure of productivity which relates output to all the inputs simultaneously. Total factor productivity growth identifies the contribution to an increase in output made by factors other than increases in factor inputs. It contains the effects of technical progress and of better utilization of capacities, learning by doing, improved skills of labour, better maintenance procedures, better organizational skills, better labour-management relations, etc. It is, hence, a composite measure of technological change and changes in the efficiency with which technology is applied to production. Tinbergen (1942) and Solow (1957) were the first to develop this concept of total factor productivity. Stigler (1947) suggested that inputs be weighted by their marginal products to obtain an index of real total factor input. Griliches (1960), Denison (1962) and Griliches and Jorgenson (1966, 1967) applied almost a similar weighting scheme separately to labour and capital input. So various total factor productivity (TFP) indices differ from one another only with regard to the weighting scheme involved. The two indices most often used in empirical research have been the Kendrick's arithmetic measure and Solow's geometric index. However, in some of the recent studies, approximation to the Divisia Index has been used.

*(a) Kendrick Index*

Let there be one homogeneous output netted of material, denoted by V and two factors of production : capital denoted by K and labour denoted by L. Also, let $W_o$ and or denote the factor rewards or prices of labour and capital, respectively, in the base year of the study. Then the Kendrick index for year t may be expressed as

$$A_t = V_t/w_oL_t+r_oK_t \qquad \ldots (4)$$

Suitable adjustments can be made into the formula if there are more than two inputs. Since the index is based on the assumption of linear production function, therefore, it does not allow for the possible diminishing-marginal productivity of factors. The index is equal to unity in the base year, i.e. Ao is equal to one, because of the assumption of constant returns to scale, perfect competition and payment of factors according to their marginal product.

*(b) Solow Index*

Solow's measure is based on the Cobb-Douglas production function with constant returns to scale and autonomous and Hicks-neutral technological change. Assuming that factors are paid the value of their marginal products, we obtain the following equation in discrete form

$$\Delta A_t/A_t = \Delta V_t/V_t - [\alpha_t \Delta L_t/L_t + \beta_t \Delta Kt/K_t] \quad \ldots (5)$$

where V denotes value added, L labour, K capital, $\alpha$ the share of labour in value added and $\beta$ the share of capital in the value added.

Once computation of $\Delta A_t/A_t$ is done (for different years) with the help of equation (5), the Solow index is calculated from the following identity (taking A (O) as unity);

$$A_{(t+1)} = A(t)\,[1 + \Delta A_t/A_t] \quad \ldots (6)$$

Under the assumption of competitive equilibrium the Solow index and the Kendrick index are equivalent for *small* changes in the quantities of inputs and outputs.[1] The Solow's assumption of unitary elasticity of substitution is not very restrictive because Nelson (1965) has shown that non-unitary elasticity of substitution does not make any significant difference to the estimates of total factor productivity.

The Solow concept of total factor productivity growth is unambiguous for infinitesimally small shifts in technology in continuous time. However, empirical estimates of total factor productivity change are based on a discrete set of price and quantity data. In order to solve this problem a 'flexible' function form of production function which is a second order approximation to any arbitrary production function which is twice differentiable can be used. One such 'flexible' functional form for which the Tornquist discrete approximation is exact is the Translog (transcendental logarithmic) production function.

*(c) Translog Index*

Solow (1957) and Jorgenson and Griliches (1967) recognized the need to use the Divisia Index. In studies by Christensen and Jorgenson (1969, 1970), Jorgenson and Griliches (1972), Christensen, Cummings and Jorgenson (1980) and few others, Translog index, an approximation to the Divisia Index, has been used.

Christensen and Jorgenson (1970), Jorgenson and Griliches (1972) and others have discussed the properties of the Divisia index which makes its application highly preferable. Divisia indexes not only satisfies 'factor reversal test' and 'time reversal test' but also have the reproductive property that a "Divisia index of Divisia indexes is a Divisia index of the Components". To apply Divisia index to data at discrete points of time, an approximation of the Divisia index, the Translog index is used. Translog index numbers satisfy the time reversal test and approximately the factor reversal test but they do not have the reproductive property.

A general model of the Divisia index can be described by using an aggregate production function with two factors of production.[2] Let

$$V = F(K,L,T) \qquad \ldots (7)$$

where V denotes aggregate value added, K aggregate capital, L aggregate labour and T time. The function is continuous, twice differentiable and assumes constant returns to scale. The aggregates are functions of their components; i.e.

$$V = V(V_1,V_2,V_3 \ldots V_m) \qquad \ldots (8)$$

$$K = K(K_1,K_2 \ldots K_n) \qquad \ldots (9)$$

$$L = L(L_1, L_2 \ldots L_q) \qquad \ldots (10)$$

Correspondingly we have m output prices, n capital prices, and q labour prices, denoted respectively by $p_1, p_2 \cdots p_m$; $r_1, r_2 \ldots r_n$; $w_1, w_2 \ldots w_q$ and the respective aggregate prices are represented by p, r and w. Under the profit maximization and perfect competition assumptions, the producer's equilibrium demands that the shares of the factors be equal to their respective elasticities, so that

$$S_k = r.K/p.V = \partial \log V/\partial \log K \quad \ldots (11)$$

$$S_L = w.L/p.V = \partial \log V/\partial \log L \quad \ldots (12)$$

$$S_k + S_L = 1 \text{ ( constant returns to scale)} \quad \ldots (13)$$

Differentiating equation (7) totally with respect to time and re-arranging terms, we get

$$d \log V/dT = S_K \text{ dlog}K/dT + S_L \text{ dlog } L/dT + A_T \quad \ldots (14)$$

The expression for $A_T$ is called the Divisia quantity index of technological change.

Similarly, Divisia price index of technological change can be obtained under the same set of assumptions, i.e., constant returns to scale, perfect competition and profit maximization. Under the assumptions,

$$pV = rK + wL$$

and price function p can be stated as a function of r, w and T

$$p = p\ (r, w, T) \quad \ldots (15)$$

Since technological change is defined as

$$A_T = -\ \partial \log p/\partial T \quad \ldots (16)$$

therefore, we can express the Divisia price index as;

$$\text{dlog } p/dT = S_K \text{ dlog } r/dT + S_L \text{ dlog } w/dT - A_T \quad \ldots (17)$$

Translog index based on Translog production function is used as an approximation to the continuous Divisia index. The Translog production function[3] is expressed as :

$$\log V = \alpha_o + \alpha_K \log K + \alpha_L \log L + \alpha_T T + 1/2\ \beta_{KK} (\log K)^2$$

$$+ \beta_{KL} (\log K) (\log L) + 1/2\ \beta_{LL} (\log L)^2 + \beta_{KT} (\log K)\ T$$

$$+ \beta_{LT}\ (\log L)T + 1/2\ \beta_{TT}\ T^2 \quad \ldots (18)$$

Constant returns require

$$\alpha_K + \alpha_L = 1;$$

$\beta_{KK} + \beta_{KL} = 0; \beta_{KL} + \beta_{LL} = 0$

So corresponding to equation (14), we obtain

$$\Delta \log V = \bar{S}_K (\Delta \log K) + \bar{S}_L (\Delta \log L) + \bar{A}_T \quad \ldots (19)$$

where

$$\Delta \log V = \log V(T) - \log V(T-1) \quad \ldots (20)$$

$$\Delta \log K = \log K(T) - \log K(T-1) \quad \ldots (21)$$

$$\Delta \log L = \log L(T) - \log L(T-1) \quad \ldots (22)$$

and

$$\bar{S}_K = 1/2\ [S_K(T) + S_K(T-1)] \quad \ldots (23)$$

$$\bar{S}_L = 1/2\ [S_L(T) + S_L(T-1)] \quad \ldots (24)$$

$\bar{A}_T = \Delta \log TFP$ is the Translog quantity index of technological change.

The Translog price index of technological change can be obtained in a similar way.

Hence a number of alternative measures of total factor productivity can be obtained from alternative assumptions with respect to the underlying production function. The major differences between the alternative indices of total factor productivity such as Kendrick index, Solow index and Translog index are the different assumptions about the elasticity of substitution implicit in the underlying production function.

Though, total factor productivity measures are a clear improvement over single factor measures; however, the difficulties of disentangling technical change from the effects of scale economies and input substitution remain. Limitations of the methodology for deriving the estimates of total factor productivity have also been pointed out by Griliches and Jorgenson (1967), Nelson (1973) and Nelson (1981).

*Production Function Estimation*

An alternative approach to measuring productivity involves the explicit specification of a production function and the direct linkage of productivity growth to key parameters of this function. An additional benefit of this approach is that in the process of measuring productivity growth, the parametric estimates of the production technology are also obtained. Solow (1957), thus, demonstrated that the rate of productivity growth could be identified with the rate of Hicks-neutral technical change, assuming constant returns to scale and competitive markets. This result clearly demonstrated the correspondence between the characteristics of a neo-classical technology and improvements in total factor productivity under the given assumptions. An important aspect of production function estimate of total factor productivity growth is that while it includes the effect of technical progress, varying capacity utilization, and learning by doing, it does not include the effect of scale economies unless the assumption of constant returns to scale is imposed.

The section now briefly discusses the three commonly used production functions, namely: (a) Cobb-Douglas production function; (b) CES production function; and (c) Translog production function.

*(a) Cobb-Douglas Production Function*

One of the most popular form of the production function for statistical testing is the Cobb-Douglas production function written as

$$V = A_o e^{\lambda t} L^{\alpha} K^{\beta} \quad \ldots (25)$$

where V, L, K and T refer to value added, labour, capital and time respectively. Also

$$A > O, V \geq O, L \geq O, K \geq O$$

The function is a *linear one in the logarithms* of the inputs, output, and time. Thus, we have

$$\log V = a + \alpha \log L + \beta \log K + \lambda t \quad \ldots (26)$$

The OLS estimation of this equation yields estimates of $\alpha$, $\beta$ and $\lambda$. $\lambda$ provides a measure of the total factor productivity growth and is the rate of exponential technological progress. The constant $\alpha$ measures the *elasticity of response* of output to labour input.[4] Similarly, $\beta$ gives us the *elasticity of response* of output to capital input. So, if labour and capital are increased by one per cent, then output will increase by ($\alpha + \beta$) percent The sum of the coefficients indicates the extent of economies or diseconomies of scale. If the two coefficients just sum to unity, then it is the case of constant returns. It is, however, important to note that the same degree of economies of scale is experienced for all output levels. If the firm enjoys increasing returns over one section of the output scale it enjoys them over *all* other sections. There is no way in which we can use a *single* Cobb-Douglas function to describe the firm that enjoys increasing returns upto a certain level of output then experiences either constant returns or decreasing returns beyond that level of output.

If we differentiate equation (25) with respect to labour and capital respectively, we obtain marginal product of labour and capital; i.e.

$$MP_L = \partial V / \partial L = \alpha V/L \qquad \ldots (27)$$

$$MP_K = \partial V / \partial K = \beta V/K \qquad \ldots (28)$$

Since profit maximization entails that marginal productivity of labour is equal to the real wage and that the marginal productivity of capital is equal to the price per unit of capital, it would imply

$$w/p = \partial V/\partial L = \alpha V/L$$

$$\text{or } w.L/p.V = \alpha \qquad \ldots (29)$$

Similarly

$$r/p = \partial V/\partial K = \beta V/K$$

$$\text{or } r.K/p.V = \beta \qquad \ldots (30)$$

Equation (29) and (30) makes it clear that in the case of a Cobb-Douglas production function the factor shares are constant. Thus, in equilibrium the coefficients $\alpha$ and $\alpha$ will measure the fractions of total value added shared by labour and capital respectively. From equations (29) and (30) we may obtain the capital-labour ratio, and the capital-output ratio

$$L/K = \alpha r/\beta w\ ,\ K/V = \beta\ p/r \qquad \ldots (31)$$

$$K/L = \beta w/\alpha r$$

Thus, we observe the obvious economic fact that the ratio of labour to capital depends on the ratio of the factor prices, not their absolute levels. Similarly the capital output ratio depends only on the ratio of the price of output to the price of capital.

So far the Cobb-Douglas production function does not make the assumption of returns to scale to be constant but if one were to test it directly then the equation (26) can be transformed so as to have log (V/L) as the dependent variable.

$$\text{Log}\,(V/L) = a+\beta \log (K/L) + (\alpha+\beta-1)\log L + \lambda t \quad \ldots (32)$$

A restrictive Cobb-Douglas production function which explicitly assumes $\alpha+\beta=1$ can be written as

$$\log (V/L) = a+\beta \log (K/L) + \lambda t \quad \ldots (33)$$

The Cobb-Douglas function can be extended to cover the cases of many inputs and outputs.

*(b) The Constant Elasticity of the Substitution (CES) Production Function*

The Cobb-Douglas production function has done very valuable service as a production function both in theoretical explorations and in empirical studies. However, the critical feature of the C-D production function is that it has elasticity of substitution to be unity; one can always substitute capital for labour (or labour for capital) at this fixed elasticity of unity. But the data may have low elasticities of substitution and may not fit into the Cobb-Douglas mould. At the other extreme, it is perhaps possible to have processes where the degree of substitution is very high indeed and the iso-quants are nearly flat. Again the data will not be appropriate to fit into the Cobb-Douglas mould. Therefore, we require a production function that provides for elasticities of substitution other than unity.

A production function often used for statistical testing is the constant elasticity of substitution (CES) form written as

$$V=\gamma_o e^{\lambda t} (\delta L^{-\rho}+(1-\delta)K^{-\rho} ]^{-v/\rho} \quad \ldots (34)$$

where $\lambda$ is the efficiency parameter, $\delta$ is the distribution parameter, $\rho$ is the substitution parameter, and $v$ is the scale parameter. Also $v$, $\gamma$, $\rho$ and $\delta$ are non-negative constants and $\delta$

must not exceed unity, i.e. $0 \leq \delta \leq 1$. The elasticity of substitution, $\sigma$, is $1/(1+\rho)$ and the permissible range of $\sigma$ is between O and $\infty$.

$$\sigma = \frac{d\log(K/L)}{d\log\left[(\partial V/\partial L)/(\frac{\partial V}{\partial K})\right]} = \frac{1}{1+\rho}$$

When the elasticity of substitution approaches unity (i.e., when $\rho$ approaches zero), the CES function simplifies to the Cobb-Douglas form. When the elasticity approaches zero (i.e., when $\rho$ approaches infinity), the CES function becomes a Leontief-type input-output function. The CES function, like the Cobb-Douglas production function is Hicks-neutral and disembodied.

The empirical evidence indicates that the parameters of the CES production function are highly sensitive to slight changes in the data, measurement of variables, and methods of estimation. Nadiri[5] has pointed out several problems like the (a) differences in time series and cross-section estimates, (b) the identification problems, and (c) the estimation problems which are responsible for the instability and inconsistency of the estimated parameters of the function. For estimating the CES production function any of the approaches given by Kmenta (1967), Bodkin and Klein (1967), Bayesian estimation technique[6] or Ferguson (1965) can be adopted. The Ferguson (1965) approach uses the side relation between labour productivity and wage rate that may be derived from the CES production function under the assumptions of perfect competition and profit maximization (so that the real wage rate equals the marginal product of labour). Then a linear relationship can be expressed between labour productivity, on the one hand, and the real wage rate and the level of employment, on the other.

$$\log[V/L]=a+b\log(w)+c\log L+dt \qquad \ldots (35)$$

where

$$b = \frac{v}{(v+\rho)}\ ;\ c = \rho\left(\frac{v-1}{(v+\rho)}\right) \text{ and } d = \frac{\lambda\rho}{(v+\rho)}$$

Equation (35) is a somewhat generalized form of the well known SMAC equation and is not based upon the assumption of constant returns. The equation can be estimated by ordinary least square technique and three important parameters, i.e. $\lambda$, $v$ and $\rho$ of the CES production function can be obtained indirectly.

In estimating the parameters of a production function it is possible to fit either the function directly or through the marginal productivity conditions. Since these two sets of relations are interdependent, therefore, if the ordinary least squares technique is used, then, it has been contended[7] that, it will give biased and inconsistent estimates for a firm maximizing profits in a competitive market. However, Zellner et al (1966) have proved that under reasonable assumptions the ordinary least squares will give consistent and unbiased estimates. The same result was obtained for the CES production function by Hodges (1969).

*(c) Transcendental Logarithmic Specification*

Christensen, Jorgenson and Lau (1971, 1973) developed the transcendental logarithmic (Translog) production function as a more general specification of a production function. The Translog production function does not assume a Hicks-neutral or a constant rate of technological change and permits the elasticity of substitution between inputs to change. The production function is a flexible functional form based on a few apriori restrictions on the properties of the underlying technology. The function is expressed as

$$\log V = \alpha o + \alpha_L (\log L) + \alpha_K(\log K) + \alpha_t\, t + \tfrac{1}{2}\beta_{LL} (\log L)^2 + \tfrac{1}{2}\beta_{KK} (\log K)^2 + \beta_{LK} (\log L)(\log K) + \beta_{LT} (\log L)t + \beta_{Kt} (\log K)t + \tfrac{1}{2}\beta_{tt}\, t^2 \quad \ldots (36)$$

where the $\alpha$ and $\beta$'s are the parameters of the production function.

In equation (36), the first four terms relate to the Cobb-Douglas production function and the last three are associated to the assumptions about technical progress, and the other quadratic and interaction terms give information on the curvature of the production function.

If we differentiate log V in equation (36) with respect to log L and log K, respectively,

$$\partial \log V / \partial \log L = \alpha_L + \beta_{LL} (\log L) + \beta_{LK}(\log K) + \beta_{Lt} t \quad \ldots (37)$$

$$\partial \log V / \partial \log K = \alpha_K + \beta_{KK}(\log K) + \beta_{LK}(\log L) + \beta_{Kt} t \quad \ldots (38)$$

these two equation (37) and (38) show that the elasticities of value added with respect to labour and capital are not constant, as is the case with Cobb-Douglas production function, but depend on the input levels (log L and log K) and time (t). The β's are interpreted with the help of equations (37) and (38) and the equilibrium conditions.

Ahluwalia (1991) points out that if log V is plotted against log L assuming log K to be constant, then the Cobb-Douglas production function will be a straight line but the Translog production function will be a curve which shows that the Translog production function has a variable elasticity of value added with respect to an input (labour). The elasticity is initially higher than that of a Cobb-Douglas production function but declines as the input level increases.

Under competitive equilibrium, the marginal productivity conditions require that the elasticity of value added with respect to each input be equal to the respective factor share in value added. In Translog production function, since elasticities of value added as well as factor shares change with input levels; therefore, the elasticity of substitution is also a function of the input levels and is not a constant.

The total factor productivity growth (TFPG) in a Translog production function is given by

$$\partial \log V / \partial T = \alpha_t + \beta_{tt} t + \beta_{Lt}(\log L) + \beta_{Kt}(\log K) \quad \ldots (39)$$

where $\alpha_t$ is the rate of autonomous total factor productivity growth, $\beta_{tt}$ is the rate of change of TFPG, and $\beta_{Lt}$ and $\beta_{Kt}$ define the bias in TFPG. Therefore, in equation (39) if both $\beta_{Lt}$ and $\beta_{Kt}$ are zero, then the total factor productivity growth is Hicks-neutral type. However, if $\beta_{Lt}$ is positive, then the share of labour increases with time.

*Recent Developments—a Few Necessary Digressions*

The accurate specification of the form and estimation of the parameters of the production function, such as $\alpha$'s and $\beta$'s are crucial to the measurement of these indices. Nadiri (1970) has shown that any error due to misspecification of the form of the function, or due to erroneously measuring the inputs will spill over into the measure of total factor productivity growth. Some advancements in the field of production function estimation have been made during the last few years by Shephard (1970), Uzawa (1964), and McFadden (1978). Some significant major developments are briefly mentioned here. The section is, therefore, further divided into four parts. Section 3.2.4 (a) deals with the problem of duality. The problem of `General specification of functional forms is described in section 3.2.4 (b). Section 3.2.4 (c) explains the developments relating to the `embodied technical progress'. `Labour embodiment' is being discussed in the last sub-section 3.2.4 (d).

*(a) Duality*

One major area of development is the use of cost function model based upon duality theory[8] for the measurement of productivity. The cost function represents a unique relationship between minimal cost and given output and input prices, that is, it gives us the relationship between total cost and output for a cost minimizing firm facing competitive input markets. The most important result which duality theory gives is, that production and cost functions are dual to each other in that the cost function is an equivalent and equally fundamental specification of the underlying production technology to that of the production function, under the assumption of cost minimization. In addition the cost function can be used to relate such technological characteristics as scale economies, input substitution and technical change to observed changes in total factor productivity. So the cost function model is a powerful and flexible econometric tool for measuring total factor productivity, especially at the firm level where the required assumptions are satisfied.

*(b) Specification of Functional Forms*

Another area of development in the field of production function estimation is more general and flexible specifications of a neo-classical technology. The Cobb-Douglas and CES production functions are vary restrictive in their formulations as they assume that elasticity of substitution is either unity or constant respectively for all combinations of inputs. However, lately a number of highly general functional forms have been proposed using the duality relation between the cost and production functions. Some of these are Generalised Leontief (GL), Generalised Cobb-Douglas (GCD) and Translog (TLOG). While Diewert (1971 and 1973) introduced the GL and GCD, the TLOG was introduced by Christensen, Jorgenson and Lau (1973). On the other hand Berndt and Khaled (1979) estimated the Generalized Box-Cox form which takes on the GL, TLOG as special or limiting cases.

*(c) Embodied Technical Progress*

So far in our discussion of methodology, we have assumed technological progress as 'disembodied'. It goes on at the same rate, whatever the level of capital accumulation, or decumulation and does not need capital equipment to realise the gains in productivity. They can be implemented on old machines just as well as on new equipment and the technical progress is *neutral* in both the Hicks and Harrod sense.

The disembodied form is an extreme model of technological progress. Progress is *embodied* in the new machines and the new process. 'Embodiment' means that because of technological advance the new inputs are more efficient than the old inputs. If we rewrite the production function as

$$V = F(\lambda_1 L, \lambda_2 K)$$

where $\lambda_1$ and $\lambda_2$ are the coefficients of factor augmentation, then it can be proved that the direction of technical change depends upon the ratio $\lambda_1/\lambda_2$. The technical change is Hicks neutral if the ratio is constant, Harrod neutral (Labour augmenting) if $\lambda_2$ is constant, and Solow neutral (capital augmenting) if $\lambda_1$ is constant. Such an embodiment model puts greater importance to capital accumulation in growth process compared to the earlier model of disembodied technological change as it recognized the heterogeneity of capital goods belonging to different vintages.[9] In principle this means that one has a production function for each vintage of capital. Then the production function for capital of vintage $v$ in year $t$, with associated labour and output is expressed as

$$V(t, v)=Ae^{\lambda v}\ L(t, v)^{\alpha}.\ K(t, v)^{\beta} \qquad \ldots (40)$$

where L(t, $v$) and K(t, $v$) are the amount of labour and capital in period t with vintage v and the term $e^{\lambda v}$, denoting technical progress, has the *vintage* of capital as its exponent and *not* time. Solow (1959) has contended that higher the vintage number, or the more recent the vintage, the larger will be the value added from given amounts of labour and capital.

It is, however, necessary that for empirical analysis all these capital with different vintages be aggregated. But even labour can be heterogeneous with divergent characteristics; they differ in their longevity, productive qualities, mobility, etc. Moreover, the issue of aggregation of heterogeneous units as applicable to both capital and labour is also relevant for output. So the problem is one of the general aggregation. Fisher (1969) has shown that labour, capital, and output aggregation over all the production units is possible under certain strict assumptions. "He demonstrated that with constant returns to scale and only two factors of production, the necessary condition for aggregation is that all capital is perfectly substitutable and all technical changes are *capital-augmenting*".[10]

In empirical analysis, the problem of 'embodiment' versus 'disembodiment' has been discussed. While Jorgenson (1966) has proved that it is a matter of indifference whether embodied or disembodied model is used, in quite a few other significant studies evidence has favoured disembodied model over the embodied model. These studies are by Massell (1962), Denison (1964), Berglas (1965), Lydall (1968), Wicksen (1970) and You (1976).

*(d) Labour Embodiment*

Wright (1936) was one of the first who observed the learning process. Arrow (1962) describes a vintage model incorporating the learning aspect. Learning means the labour used in the production process becomes more efficient over time. Since the acquired knowledge is irreversible and a function of all past levels of accumulation, therefore, when the factors of production receive their private marginal products there is an increasing return due to the accumulation of knowledge. The social rate of return, thus, will be more than the private rate of return. Arrow (1962) contended that if learning activity is "...measured by cumulative output, then experience is acquired by *doing more* regardless of the length of time it takes; when it is measured by time, experience is acquired by *doing it longer* regardless of the accumulation of output".[11] While the first version suggests that labour productivity rises with a larger volume of output; the second says that labour productivity increases proportionately with time.

While the studies by Rapping (1965), Sheshinsky (1967) and David (1975) basically supports the learning hypothesis, but Chen (1976) does not find support for the hypothesis of learning by doing.

Another recent development in productivity analysis relates to the number of amendments to the early Solow model, based upon the assumption of a competitive equilibrium. While the competitive equilibrium condition of constant returns to scale, assumed in Solow's model, may be acceptable at more aggregate levels of productivity analysis, it is not likely to be generally appropriate in the case of industries or firms where economies of scale may exist.

**Measurement of Output**

Nadiri (1970) has clearly emphasized the need and importance of the proper measurement of output and inputs. Any error in measurement will have an impact on the productivity measurement. The differences in the methods of measuring them, output and inputs, may be a significant reason for differences in various productivity estimates.

Different meanings can be assigned to the output of an industry. The choice, in measurement, may be either in 'real value added' by the industry or in 'real value of product'; which gives us gross output. While real value added excludes the consumption of purchased materials, fuels and energy, the gross output includes them. If we choose value added then the specification of the production function will include only labour and capital but if gross output is opted for then it is necessary that 'material' is also included in the specification.

In the existing literature on productivity measurement both value added and gross output are used to measure output. However, Griliches and Ringstad (1971) have advanced arguments in favour of using value added. The arguments are (a) value added facilitates comparison of results for different firms each with different material consumption; (b) it facilitates aggregation of output across industries; (c) inclusion of material as an input may lead to the problem of dominant variable. All variation in productivity may be captured by material's consumption, thus neglecting the role of physical and human capital utilization.

Bruno (1978) and Diewert (1978) have noted that value added captures hybrid aspects of firm's activities. First, it captures a production relationship between primary factors and output. This relationship is based on management's capabilities. Second, it also captures a profit-generating relationship between firm-specific capital and firms output[12]. Bruno (1978, 1984) and Stoneman and Francis (1992) points out that the use of single deflated value added, deflating nominal value added by an index of manufacturing prices, leads to biased estimates. Such a single-deflation method is valid only if the price of material relative to the price of output is more or less constant for the period of study. When this relative price is changing, Bruno (1978, 1984) and Stoneman and Francis (1992) have noted that estimated productivity would, *cetris peribus*, vary inversely. Bruno (1978 and 1984) has given a formal expression of the relationship between changes in the relative price of materials and value added by single deflation[13]. It clearly shows that the problem is serious only if the relative price of materials fluctuate. This problem of biased estimate can be overcome if a Divisia index (i.e. shifting weights) of intermediate inputs can be used to obtain double-deflated value added. Double deflation basically means deflating the value of output by an output price index and the value of input by an input price index. To seek empirical evidence on this requires the construction of price index of raw-materials and other inputs.

Another choice arises between the use of either gross or net value added as the output measure. Denison (1974) advocates for the use of net value added on theoretical grounds. He argues that gross value added includes a measure of capital consumption, therefore, there is no rationale as to why capital consumption ought to be maximized - the quantity of capital used up on production-rather than minimised. However, most empirical studies have preferred to use gross value added because there is no unanimity in the literature about the definition and the rate at which depreciation is to be calculated. The diverse nature of data availability for depreciation also restricts the use of net value added as a measure of output.

## Measuring Inputs

So far we have discussed the measurement of output. But proper measurement of inputs; both labour and capital is equally important. Thus, in the subsequent sections 3.4.1 and 3.4.2 measurement of labour input and capital input is briefly described.

### *Measurement of Labour Input*

The size of labour input can be measured by different alternative measures. The choice can be between the number of 'man-hours' worked, the number of 'man-days' worked, the number of 'workers' or the average number of 'employees'.

Denison (1961) has pointed out that a reduction in man-hour per week leads to an increase in labour input per hour, therefore, he disapproves the use of 'man-hour' as a measure of labour input. The use of 'man-days' as a measure of labour input will bring in the same problem i.e. a reduction in 'man-days' worked may lead to an increase in 'man-hours' worked per day. So number of persons seems to be more satisfactory, as it will adjust this change in quality of one hour's work and change in 'man-hours' per day, measure of labour input.

If only 'number of workers' is taken as the measure of

labour input, then we are excluding from it 'persons other than workers'. 'Person other than workers' is a category of employees which includes supervisors, technicians, managers, clerks and other similar type of employees. Such employees are at least as much important, if not more, for getting the work done as the workers who operate on the machines. Thus their services should be included in the measurement of labour inputs.[14] However, when 'total number of employees' is taken as a measure of labour input then the assumption of perfect substitution between 'workers' and 'persons other than workers' is implicitly involved. A problem that arises while measuring labour input is how to make "...adjustments of labour input for health and nutritional conditions of the labour force, disequilibrium due to underemployment, age-sex composition and hours worked; ... the role of educational attainment of the labour force...."[15] Griliches (1967) suggested the use of rates of remuneration, as they reflect the differences in efficiency of different classes of labourers, for making the adjustments. Nadiri (1972) has concluded that despite the disagreement on the method to assess and measure the contribution of education to growth of output, there is general unanimity that improvement in educational attainment of workers does contribute positively to growth of output.

*Measurement of Capital Input*

In the estimation of total factor productivity and production functions capital plays a crucial role. Capital is a major factor input which consists of a multiplicity of physical objects already produced by the economy and, in turn used for the current production of other commodities. Capital has been defined differently by different people but four main definitions of real capital are : instantaneous productive capacity, long run productive capacity, cumulated consumption forgone, and real wealth.

Instantaneous productive capacity definition of capital implies that one lot of capital goods constitutes more capital than another lot of capital goods if more output can be produced this year with the first lot than with the second lot when the production function and the labour force are the same in each case. This definition of capital only considers the capital's capacity to produce *today* but does not take into account their durability. It makes, then, no difference whether the existing stock of capital $K_1$, for instance, will wear out next year, in two years, or in a hundred years. Only its effectiveness today is considered.

A measure of capital as an indicator of long run productive capacity incorporates both durability and productivity of capital goods. Such a concept will include a generalised production function which takes account of the flow of consumption goods in every future year. Thus, a mix of capital goods $K_1$ and $K_2$ would constitute more real capital than a mix $K'_1$ and $K'_2$ if people are better off with the first mix than they are with the second. 'Better off' includes potential output tomorrow as well as potential output today.

Capital can also be measured as per its opportunity cost. Capital in this sense is measured as the amount of capital goods in existence. This definition of capital is that employed by Kendrick (1964) in his measure of human capital; the forgone earnings of students and the alternative cost of research and development can be assessed in no other way.

Real wealth is the present value, at some given time series of interest rates, of the stream of consumption goods earned by the existing stock of capital goods. This definition is different from other measures of real capital in that any technical change that increases the productivity of capital goods increases the quantity of real wealth as well. Thus a given mix of capital goods $K_1$ and $K_2$ would count as the same amount of instantaneous productive capacity or long run productive capacity at all times, but it shall represent more real wealth at a time when the current technology has endowed it with a high present and future marginal product than it does at a time when it is less favoured by the existing technique. The statistical implication of this concept of real wealth is that the measure of capital should include capital gains in addition to the original cost of equipment.

Real wealth and accumulated consumption forgone are called the "forward-looking" and "backward-looking" measures of capital, while instantaneous productive capacity and long run productive capacity are measures of capital "in their own units". The choice among these concepts of real capital is, generally, governed by the purpose of the study.

The "backward looking" concept of capital, defined and measured on the basis of cost, is useful in the measurement of productivity. Measured by its cost, capital provides a basis for determining if the use of factors of production is becoming more or less efficient over time. Cost based measures of capital, however, are not suitable for determining industrial capacity, or for analysing the determinants of investment or production, because identical amounts of real capital will represent different capacities to produce goods and services. For such a purpose, the capital should be measured in terms of its ability to contribute to production.

The concept of capital measured by its cost was favoured by Denison (1957). He stated, "The value, in base period prices, of the stock of durable capital goods (before allowance for capital consumption) measures the amount it would have cost in the base period to produce the *actual* stock of capital goods existing in the given year (not its equivalent in ability to contribute to production). Similarly, gross additions to the capital stock and capital consumption are valued in terms of base year costs for the *particular* types of capital goods added or consumed. This must be modified immediately, in the case of durable capital goods not actually produced in the base year, to substitute the amount it would have cost to produce them if they had been known and actually produced. But a similar modification is required in all deflation or index number problems."[16] Therefore, by this method only cost associated quality change of capital goods is counted as quantity change. Quality change (e.g. a larger machine) that results in a change in cost is counted as a change in quantity and quality change that results in no change in cost (e.g. a more efficient machine that cost the same as an older machine) is not counted as a change in quantity. According to Prof. Joan Robinson (1960) it is this concept which "...is congenial to the production function point of view, for it corresponds to the essential nature of capital regarded as a factor of production", because "the main purpose of the production function is to show how wages and the rate of interest are determined by technical conditions and the factor ratio."[17]

The measurement of capital by cost method involves, however, some conceptual and practical problems. When prices do not change, gross addition to capital stock will be equal to the value of gross capital formation; if cost method is used. But in a situation when prices are changing, a price index for capital goods is required for deflation purposes. Deflation is particularly difficult when new products are introduced, since there is no obvious way to value these products at base period prices if they did not exist in the base period. The method generally used considers the new product equivalent to one unit of the old product multiplied by the ratio of the cost of the new product to that of the old product in an overlap period. If an overlap does not exist, a hypothetical comparison is undertaken by estimating what it would have cost to produce the new product in a period when the old one still existed.

Since capital goods prices commonly change over time, it raises several difficulties in the measurement of depreciation and income. There is, however, no agreement on a single definition of depreciation. Different procedures for estimating depreciation can lead to substantially different estimates of depreciation. Kendrick has stated on this issue, that "as non-permanent assets age, their contribution to net output declines. This is the result of declining gross output capacity, increasing maintenance and repair costs, and creeping obsolescence. Obsolescence results in the reduction in the rate of return on old equipment, not only when the installation of new equipment leads to reduced product prices or higher factor prices, but also when the old equipment is utilized less intensively or in less productive activities. Empirical and theoretical considerations suggest that these effects may be assumed to occur gradually over the life time of a group of capital equipment."[18]

Thus, Kendrick (1956) contends that while making an estimate of capital, it must be taken into account that the capital embodied in a specific asset goes on declining over time due to depreciation and obsolescence. Denison does not agree with Kendrick on the issue of obsolescence and said that obsolescence should be charged at the time the capital goods is retired and that it should be handled as a deduction from gross capital formation rather than as an addition to capital consumption. The reason for this treatment is that obsolescence has little if any effect on the time pattern of services provided by the asset before retirement, even though it is a determinant of the timing of the retirement. The Denison's method of calculating depreciation is also known as straight line depreciation procedure.

Another method used for calculating depreciation is *discounted value definition;* which can be stated as : depreciation is the decline in the value of the sum of the remaining anticipated services discounted to the present. The anticipated services taken are net of maintenance and repair expenses and net of the reduction in value occasioned by obsolescence. The effect of obsolescence is viewed as occurring at a constant rate. The total of the depreciation charges under the discounted value definition, as with the straight line definition, equals the cost of the asset. The time path of the charges, however, can vary from that based on the straight line definition.

Depreciation based on the discounted value definition can be either more or less than straight line depreciation in the early years of an asset's service life, with the reverse occurring in later years. A decline over time in the services provided by an asset because of either deterioration or constant rate obsolescence contributes to a more rapid write-off than straight line depreciation. The effect of discounting works in the opposite direction. Christensen and Jorgenson (1973) and Mendelowitz (1971) considers the use of discounted value definition as the only appropriate measure. Richard and Nancy Ruggles (1961), however, argue that when efficiency improvements have been excluded from the measurement of capital stock, it is not proper that decrease in efficiency through aging should be carefully taken into account. They feel that, for deriving a consistent estimate of capital, no allowance should be made for depreciation during the life of a machine, despite the fact that producers may for financial reasons and in order to derive a more meaningful profit figure, amortize the cost of a machine over its life.

The debate between Denison (1972) and Jorgenson and Griliches (1967) focused attention on different set of issues relating to measurement of capital input. Among these, two sets of issues are :

(i) Utilization of capacity, and (ii) relation between asset price and service price. The stock of capital would be measured in number of machines while the service flow could be measured in machine hours. The quality of capital services corresponding to each stock could, thus, be measured, directly, at least in principle. The assumptions of a constant ratio of capital service to capital stock and that asset prices are proportional to service prices, lead to errors in measurement of capital input. While the stock of equipment (capital) may be calculated by cumulating the net flow of investment goods, the relative utilization of this capital has to be estimated in order to convert stocks into flows of equipment services. For this an adjustment of relative utilization of equipment is essential. Most of the available capacity utilization measures are based on the relationship between actual output to output at full utilization of both labour and capital, so that these measures also attempt to adjust both labour and capital simultaneously. However, Jorgenson and Griliches (1970) has approached the problem by adjusting labour and capital separately. Capital was corrected by multiplying the stock of capital by the relative utilization of capital. Jorgenson-Griliches (1970) have shown that total factor productivity is quite sensitive to the index of utilization. However, this problem is basically due to disequilibrium phenomenon and does not arise in the long run. Kendrick (1973) and Denison (1974) have, however, argued strongly against making such corrections in productivity studies.

The method which is generally followed in measuring the capital input is known as Perpetual Inventory Method and was pioneered by Goldsmith in 1951. In this method the time series of the stock of capital is build up step by step from time series of values of investment and prices of capital goods.

To compute a time series of real capital according to the perpetual inventory method, we need time series of gross investment in current prices, $I_t$, where t refers to the year, time series of capital goods prices, $P_t$, and a rule, a rate of discarding, connecting values of new and old capital goods from which we can calculate time series of depreciation $D_t$. Then the increase in real capital in the year t is

$$\Delta K_t = \frac{I_t - D_t}{P_t}$$

In practice, however, a slightly modified variant of this method is often used especially in the case where a sufficiently long time series is not available. The modified variant of the perpetual inventory method requires; (a) an independently derived estate of the capital stock relating to a bench-mark year valued at constant base period prices; (b) the estimate of the gross capital formation at constant base period prices for each year in the period under study; and (c) the estimates of the actual capital consumption.

Given these estimates, the required time series of real capital stock can be obtained as

$$K_T = K_o + \sum_{t=1}^{T} I_{t*}$$

and

$$I_{t*} = I_t - D_t$$

where $K_T$ is capital stock in period T;

$I_{t*}$ denotes net investment in year t;

$I_t$ is gross investment in year t;

$K_o$ is the capital stock in bench mark year at constant prices;

and $D_t$ denotes capital consumption or depreciation in period t.

The differences in estimates may arise because of differences in the values of $K_o$ or $D_t$.

However, Usher (1980) has hinted at the possibility of using several possible alternatives to the perpetual inventory method. Book values of companies, etc.; direct surveys of capital goods in existence and statistics of fire insurance are some of the important alternatives that can be used for constructing time series of real capital.[19]

## Measurement of Wages

Wages, in economic theory, are defined as the price of labour. But wages are a unique price; as it is the cost to the employer and is one of the determinants of price of product. It is also the source of income to the workers as it determines their standard of living. The workers, therefore, would always be demanding higher wages whereas the employers would like to pay the minimum. There is, thus, a clash in the objectives of the workers and of the employers about the level of wages. 'Persons other than workers' get salaries instead of wages for the services rendered by them. In practice, however, both 'workers' and 'persons other than workers' not only get wages and salaries but also receive certain other financial benefits in the form of fringe benefits and incentive payments. Therefore, any exercise aimed at measuring wages must include salaries as well as other benefits as they are also costs to the employer. So wages, which can be more appropriately defined as *'earnings'*, include all direct wages and salaries consisting of basic wages, allowances, other compensatory and ex-gratia payments as well as the imputed value of benefits if any, received by the employees.

## Methodology : Variation in Productivity and its Nexus with Wages

This section 3.6 briefly outlines the approach adopted in the study in the later chapters. Not only the productivity estimates, through parametric and non-parametric methods, are obtained and presented subsequently in chapter IV, but an attempt has also been made to find out why productivity varies between different time periods and between different firms and industries. For this different regression functions are estimated for productivity. The explanatory variables which are expected to affect productivity have been included in the study. These are the scale parameter; represented by gross value added at constant prices, the real wage rate, the capital-labour ratio and the institutional factor's parameter; represented by the 'time' variable. Several studies including Goldar (1986); Ahluwalia

(1991) and Anita Kumari (1993) have included some of these variables in the methodology used by them. However, explaining productivity changes is only a means rather than an end of the study. Therefore, a detailed analysis of the wage trends has been undertaken in chapter V. Different models have been built in chapter VI with real wage rate as the dependent variable and a host of other explanatory variables, so as to find out the link of wages with productivity.

Generally, it is expected that the growth in real wage rate is associated with increase in productivity. However, in public enterprises wages are also influenced by other factors. Therefore, variables like value added which is an indicator of the firms capacity to pay; its proxy variable like total factor productivity indices; the capital-intensity of the unit of production, capturing the 'machine per worker' effect; the consumer price index and the time variables have been included in different models, as it is generally believed that real wage rate has a relationship with these variables.[20] Thus the endeavour is to probe and determine a link between real wages and other factors; especially productivity.

## NOTES

1. Levhari, Kleiman and Halevi (1986).
2. Goldar (1986).
3. Christensen, L.R., Jorgenson, D.W. and Lau, L.J. (1973).
4. One percent increase in labour, with the amount of capital held constant, will add $\alpha$ percent to output.
5. See Nadiri (1970), for details.
6. Zellner (1966).
7. Nadiri (1970).
8. For detailed mathematical exposition, see Goldar (1986).
9. A vintage refers to time period. A machine built in 1995, that is of vintage 1995, will be the best that can be produced with the knowledge of 1995.
10. Nadiri (1970), p 1145.
11. Nadiri (1970), p 1162.

12. Majumdar (1995).
13. The expression is also briefly discussed by Balakrishna and Pushpangadan (1994).
14. Sinha and Sawhney (1970), pp 26-27.
15. Nadiri (1972), p 132.
16. Denison (1957), pp 222-223.
17. Joan Robinson (1960), p 115.
18. Kendrick (1956), p 150.
19. Usher (1980), p 8.
20. Several earlier studies i.e. Sawheny (1969), Verma (1971), Suri (1976), Gordon (1987) and Holzer (1990), have attempted to find out the relationship between these variables.

# 4

# PRODUCTIVITY TRENDS IN SELECTED PUBLIC SECTOR ENTERPRISES

## General

In this chapter we analyse the productivity trends of selected public sector enterprises. Though public sector includes (a) administrative departments, (b) departmental enterprises and non-departmental enterprises, the present study covers only selected public enterprises engaged in manufacturing activities, wherein it is more meaningful to measure productivity trends. The period covered by this study is 1974-75 to 1995-96, i.e., a period of twenty two years. The study has been conducted for (a) eight major groups of manufacturing industries in public sector covering 80 percent of manufacturing industries, (b) the aggregate of these eight industrial groups; and (c) sixteen firms, two from each industrial groups. In 1992-93 the share of eight industrial groups, as an aggregate, in the total manufacturing industries of the public sector, was 93 percent on the basis of value added, 57.27 percent in wages and salaries, 80.85 percent in gross fixed capital formation and 50.24 percent in number of employees. It is thus, representative of the population.

The chapter has been divided into five sections. Section 4.2 highlights the sources of data used and the measurement of variables which have been used during this study. A brief review of some significant studies relating to estimation of productivity in public sector enterprises is presented in section 4.3. Section 4.4 provides a detailed discussion about the estimates of productivities in firms, industries and the aggregate of industries, both by parametric and non-parametric methods. Inter-group variations will also be discussed in this section. Finally, section 4.5 will provide the summary of the results drawn from discussions of the previous section 4.4.

**Sources of Data and Measurement of Variables**

The basic source for time series data on value added, capital stock, employment and wages and salaries are the Public Enterprises Survey published by the Bureau of Public Enterprises. Data on prices used for deflating value added, capital stock and wages and salaries has been compiled and computed from the various issues of National Income Statistics, Reserve Bank of India Bulletins, Index number of wholesale prices, and Chandok (1990).[1]

The period choosen for the study, from 1974-75 to 1995-96, almost coincides with the beginning of the V plan in India. By this time the public enterprises in India had almost matured as the foundation of most of these was laid during the Second Plan period.[2] There is also a series of evidence[3] to show that deceleration had stopped and acceleration in the industrial growth had started since the mid-seventies. Ahluwalia (1991) has also emphasized the change which period after mid-70's experienced. She showed how public investment, which had declined from 9.2 percent during 1960-61 to 1965-66 to 4.7 percent in 1965-66 to 1975-76, started rising and was 5.1 percent during 1975-76 to 1979-80 and subsequently increased to 7.5 percent during 1975-76 to 1979-85. The period after mid-70's was also characterised by 'official-reflection', as different committees were set up to review different aspects of policy[4]. Mid-70's also witnessed a reorientation of policies-especially in respect of investment in infrastructure and liberalisation of domestic industrial licensing policies. Tendulkar (1979) also highlighted the shift in the objectives of the public sector that took place around this time. Thus, we find that the year 1974-75 was a turning point in India's industrial policy and its growth.

*Measurement of Variables: Estimates of Value Added*

In most of the earlier significant studies for both Indian manufacturing and public enterprises, 'value added' has been preferred to be the best measure of output as it facilitates aggregation of output across industries. Though on theoretical grounds net value added is considered to be superior but gross value added has been accepted in the present study because of the controversy surrounding the depreciation as a measure of true capital consumption. The Public Enterprises Survey provides the size of gross value added at current prices. Value added at current prices have been deflated by indices of wholesale prices (Base 1970-1971=100) compiled and computed from different available sources such as Chandok (1990) and Index number of wholesale prices in India, etc. Chandok (1990) provides data only till 1988-1989, therefore other sources have also been relied upon though the base year in these sources, i.e., RBI Bulletins and Index Number of wholesale Prices in India is 1981-82=100. This base year 1981-82 has been changed to the comparable base (1970-71=100).

Product groups given in Chandok (1990) differ not only from what is being given by the Public Enterprise Survey for the firms and the industries but also from those of the Index Number of wholesale Prices in India. Therefore, due care and caution has been taken while making a time series of wholesale prices for a product for each firm and industry.

For making the product groups comparable for different sources regrouping has been done. For steel group and the two firms- *Steel Authority of India Ltd and Misra Dhatu Nigam Ltd* the index number of wholesale prices for the group-iron, steel and ferro alloys- has been applied. For power group and the two firms, i.e., *National Hydro-Electric Power Corporation Ltd* and *National Thermal Power Corporation,* index number of Electricity has been used. A weighted average price index of petroleum crude and mineral oil has been used for both Petroleum industry group as well as for *Indian Oil Corporation Ltd.* and *Oil and Natural Gas Commission.* The group of Chemicals, Fertilizers and Pharmaceuticals was a combined group till 1986-1987 when it was bifurcated into two separate groups of Fertilizers as one and Chemical and Pharmaceuticals as another. However, we have again combined the two for the later years, i.e. 1987-88 to 1995-96, so that a uniformity and comparability is maintained. A weighted average of price index for fertilizers, chemicals and drugs and medicine was calculated and used as a deflator for the group. However, the price index used for its firms were different - it was the Price Index of fertilizers for *National Fertilizers Ltd.* and of industrial chemicals for *Indian Petro-Chemicals Corporation Ltd.* The index number of machinery and machine tools has been used as a deflator for both Heavy engineering and Medium and Light engineering groups and their firms *Bharat Heavy Electricals Ltd, Bharat Heavy Plate and Vessels Ltd* and *Indian Telephone Industries Ltd.* However, for *Hindustan Machine Tools;* a medium and light engineering firm, we have used the weighted average price index of machine tools, watches and clocks and tractors till the year 1988-89, and that of machine tools and watches and clocks only for the year 1989-90 to 1995-96. While the price index of transport equipment has been used as a deflator for Transport equipment industry group and *Hindustan Aeronautics Ltd.,* the price index of machines and machine tools is used for *Bharat Earth Movers Ltd.* To get the deflator for the consumer goods group a weighted price index of bakery products, paper and paper products, leather and leather products, rubber and rubber products, jute manufactures and photo films has been calculated and used. Also for *Cement Corporation of India,* the price index of cement and, for *Hindustan Photo Films Manufacturing Company Ltd* the price index of photo films have been used respectively.

*Estimates of Capital Input*

We take the value of gross fixed capital stock at constant prices as the measure of capital input. We have preferred to use gross stock over net stock on the following grounds: (a) since value added is also gross and not net, therefore there will be uniformity in the analysis if capital is also gross, (b) Richard and Nancy Ruggles (1961) argue that while efficiency improvements have been excluded, then why exclude efficiency declines, (c) Barna (1961) has also favoured the use of gross stock as massive investments are generally made for maintenance of capital, so as to keep it in the same efficient from, (d) it has been reported by Banerji (1975) and others that the data of depreciation reported in different sources are not very representative of true capital consumption. Thus, the value of gross fixed capital stock has been used and taken directly from the balance sheets of the firms and industries as contained in different issues of Public Enterprises Survey. However, from 1986-87 onwards the gross fixed Capital (GFC) stock has been calculated by adding the gross block, unallocated expenditure during construction, capital work in progress, and others. We have used the perpetual inventory method which is used almost universally for the purpose. This requires a bench-mark year (1974-75 in our case) estimates of GFC stock at 1970-1971 prices and real gross investments at 1970-1971 prices over successive years for the period under consideration.

Let $\mathbf{K_o}$ denote the bench year real capital stock and $\mathbf{I_t}$, the real gross investment in fixed capital in the year **t**. Then $\mathbf{K_t}$, real gross fixed capital stock for the year **T** is obtained as :

$$K_T = K_o + \sum_{t=1}^{T} I_t$$

$I_t$ is calculated as

$$I_t = (GFC_t - GFC_{t-1})/P_t$$

where $\mathbf{GFC_t}$ is the value of gross fixed capital at the end of the year **t** and $\mathbf{P_t}$ is the capital goods price deflator. $\mathbf{K_o}$ is also at 1970-1971 prices.

Once the estimates of real gross fixed capital for the bench-year are obtained, the real gross investment of the next year is added to this to obtain real GFC for that year. In order to get the time series of real GFC for the entire period the same procedure has been followed throughout. Deflator for GFC, at 1970-1971 prices, is obtained as weighted average of wholesale price index of machinery, machine tools and building materials.

*Estimates of Factor Shares*

Labour share is calculated as the percentage share of salaries and wages including benefits in gross value added at current prices. The capital share is then obtained as the residual, i.e. if $\alpha$ is the share of labour in gross value added then share of capital is $(1 - \alpha)$.

### *Estimates of Wage Rate*

The estimates of wage rate are obtained by dividing the salaries and wages and other benefits including bonus (as given by Public Enterprises Survey) by the total number of employees. Wage rates for all the groups of public enterprises consisting of industries and firms are deflated by the corresponding consumer price indices at 1970-1971 prices. The consumer price index has been obtained from Chandok (1990) till 1988-89 and from R.B.I. Bulletins for the years 1989-90 to 1995-96. Since the price index for 1989-90 to 1995-96 was on the base year 1980-81=100, the same has been converted into the base year 1970-71=100 by the conversion formula. For 1974-75 to 1977-78, data for number of employees and their salaries, wages and other benefits is not directly available for firms from Public Enterprises Survey. To obtain the required data, we have calculated the proportion of each firm in the respective industry's employment and total salaries, wages and other benefits for the next three years, i.e. 1978-79 to 1980-81. The average proportion of these three years has been used to obtain the respective values for the firms for years 1974-75 to 1977-78.

### *Estimates of Variables for Aggregate of Industries*

Estimates of value added, wages and salaries, employment and gross fixed capital stock has been calculated by taking the summation of all eight industrial groups. The data of deflators for consumer price index and capital stock is the same but for output we compiled the deflator from wholesale price index of non-agricultrual commodities as given by Chandok (1990) and by the Index Number of wholesale prices in India.

The reason for excluding the three remaining industrial groups of public enterprises is the difference in the nature of their production activities. While Minerals and Metals and Coal groups have different manufacturing process as compared to, say, Power or Steel or any other group included in the study, the textile group has been excluded because it mainly contains those loss making units which were taken over by the government because of altogether different reasons which do not match with the ideology associated with other industrial groups. Since the three industrial groups were not included in the study, therefore, they are also excluded from the aggregate of industrial groups so that the two analyses are uniform in character and are not unduly influenced by those industrial groups which have been excluded otherwise.

**Studies on Productivity in Public Enterprises**

This section gives a brief review of some significant studies on productivity in public enterprises. Most of the studies are confined either to the industry group level or to the aggregate of industries, i.e., manufacturing as a whole.

Dholakia (1978) has used the total factor productivity (TFP) approach to measure the performance of public enterprises in India for the period 1960-61 to 1975-76. He compared the performance of public enterprises with the private sector. He advocated the use of total factor productivity as a criterion for efficiency evaluation rather than net profitability. He showed that while the index (Kendrick) of TFP for the public enterprises rose to 188.79 in 1975-76 from 100 in 1960-61, it was only 102.73 for the private sector during the same period. While calculating TFP he has used the net output instead of value added. Thus, he concluded that public enterprises performed better than the private sector.

Meena Gupta (1982) has compared the productivity of Fertilizer industry, both for the public sector and the private sector. She contended that TFP, labour and capital productivity are low in the public sector as compared to the private sector - the main reasons being excessive employment and higher capital investment in the public sector. She has, however, shown that the performance of the public sector improved more than the private sector, especially after excluding very old and obsolete units over the period of time.

Sarna and Rao (1988) have used a different method for estimating productivity for the public sector as a whole. The productivity analysis was based upon the rates of growth of GDP, i.e., gross domestic product and GDCF, i.e., gross domestic capital formation generated by both the public enterprises and the whole economy during the period 1971-72 to 1983-84. The study has compared the performance of the public and the private sector for all the sectors of economy. They have noted that the productivity of the public sector, as reflected by labour and capital productivities in the manufacturing sector has shown a declining trend. The conclusion does not conform with the conclusion reached by Dholakia (1978) for the manufacturing sector because Dholakia's estimates may have a possible upward bias for public sector productivity and downward bias for private sector productivity due to nationalization in public sector and under-reporting of output by the private sector.

Rao and Latha (1990) have analysed the performance of public enterprises during the period 1975-76 to 1985-1986. They have used different financial ratios alongwith TFP and partial productivity indices. They have concluded that in public sector manufacturing industries capital-output ratios have been very high and capital productivity has been declining over the years. Further, while labour productivity has been fluctuating over the period, the TFP indices show a very high growth rate. TFP Solow and TFP Divisia show a sharp upswing since 1979-80. The study has used value added as the output variable and has calculated the TFP for the public enterprises by all the three versions, i.e., Kendrick, Solow and Divisia. The main source of data for the study are the various issues of Public Enterprises Survey.

Vashist and Kundu (1990) have also measured the productivity of public enterprises with a view to make comparisons with the private sector. They have conducted the study for the registered manufacturing sector for the period 1960-61 to 1984-85 and have calculated TFP and productivities of labour and capital. The study concludes that the productivity in public enterprises is lower than in private enterprises at every point of time under study. Over time it finds that the performance of public enterprises has worsened since 1974-75, while that of private enterprises has improved. This conclusion contrasts with the findings of Dholakia's study. Vashist and Kundu (1990) have used net output as the variable and have used National Income Accounts Statistics as the source of data. The overall result for the 24 year period showed no average shift in productivity for public enterprises. The study also compared the labour and capital productivities in the two sectors. It found that the performance of the private sector, on this count, is also better. Labour productivity in public enterprises increased by 1.13 percent but capital productivity declined by -1.83 percent over the time period.

Anita Kumari (1993) gives us the productivity estimates at the group level of public sector enterprises for the period 1971-72 to 1987-88. She has used not only the productivity methods but has also fitted the Cobb-Douglas and CES production functions for the groups. She has used value added as the variable, and the source of data for her study are the various issues of Public Enterprises Survey. The study has also tried to explain the inter-temporal and cross-section variations in productivity with the help of regression analysis. Anita Kumari (1993) has given the productivity estimates for each industry group. She has concluded that for some industrial groups like Steel and Consumer goods TFP as well as partial productivities have been declining over the period, but, for all other industries like Minerals and Metals, Power, Petroleum, Chemicals, Heavy engineering, Medium and Light engineering and Transportation equipment, estimates of TFP and partial productivities have generally shown a rising trend.

Swamy (1994) has conducted a comparative study of public and private sector industries for the period 1980-88 by using the ASI (Annual Survey of Industries) data. Both partial productivities of Labour and Capital, as well as, Kendrick index of TFP, have been calculated along with capital intensity for each year of the study. The study concludes that the private sector industries have exhibited higher value of labour productivity, capital productivity and TFP on an average compared to public sector industries, though the public sector industries have improved their productive efficiency over the reference period. Majumdar (1995) has also obtained a similar result for the period, 1973-74 to 1988-89 while comparing the public sector, which includes the enterprises owned by both the Central Government and the State Governments, with the joint Sector and the private sector.

All the above mentioned studies, except that of Rao and Latha (1990) and Anita Kumari (1993), have concentrated on the comparison of the public sector with the private sector. Except Dholakia's study all have concluded that public sector is less efficient than the private sector. While Meena Gupta's (1982) study is very restrictive, confined only to the fertilizer industry, all other studies, except that of Anita Kumari (1993) have one major limitation; that is, they have estimated TFP and partial productivity indices for only the aggregate level of the public enterprises and no study has attempted the estimatiion at the disaggregate level. The time period and the data source being different in different studies makes it difficult to make a proper comparative analysis of the results. However, an attempt has been made at a subsequent place.

The analysis conducted in this work is close to that of Rao and Latha (1990) and Anita Kumari (1993). However, while using the same source of data, i.e., various issues of Public Enterprises Survey, the present study is completely different. While Rao and Latha (1990) have estimated the productivities only for a short period of eleven years and that too at the aggregate level, their study neither attempts to use the production function approach to estimate productivities, nor does it explain the factors contributing to the variation in productivity over time. Anita Kumari (1993) on the other hand while filling these gaps in Rao and Latha's study suffers from other limitations. Her study limits itself to the industry group level and neglects both the aggregate of industry groups as well as the disaggregation at firm's level. The regression analysis used by the study to explain time series and cross section variations in productivities is also very restrictive and includes only value added as the major variable.

The present study has tried to fill all these gaps and claims to be an improvement over the existing studies. We have not only estimated productivities at all the three levels, i.e., the firm level, the industry level and the aggregate of industries level, but have also used separate deflators for value added and wage rates. While Index number of wholesales prices has been used as a deflator for value added, consumer price index for Industrial Workers have been used for deflating the wage rate.

The present study also covers the recent years, thus updating the literature.

**Estimates of Productivities**

In this section we will discuss the estimates of single factor productivities: labour and capital, and total factor productivities for the eight industrial groups along with the sixteen firms, two each belonging to a particular industrial group. We will also analyse the estimates of productivities obtained for the aggregate of eight industrial groups. The discussion will cover both the parametric and non parametric estimates. The first section (4.4.1) examines the productivity estimates, both parametric and non parametric, and the regression functions for the aggregate of industrial groups. The study will also examine the regression functions explaining the variations in productivities over time for each industry and firm in section 4.4.2. The next section (4.4.3) will deal with the explanation of inter-firm and inter-industry variations in productivity estimates. For both production functions and regressions explaining productivity changes the study has applied first the ordinary least square method and then the Cochrane - Orcutt adjustment method of autocorrelation to eliminate autocorrelation from these estimations. The purpose is to obtain estimates free from any auto-correlation. Wherever the regression obtained from Cochrane-Orcutt method has shown a significant value of 'RHO', there the new regression has been adopted, and the coefficients obtained from ordinary least square are not reported. So the tables containing regressions show the coefficients obtained from either of the two methods. The values of 'F' for OLS and `RHO'for Cochrane-Orcutt regressions are indicated. In production functions analysis the Translog production function was applied but it did not give any meaningful results for individual firms and industry for lack of a long time-series data. The pooling of cross-section data is not desirable because of heterogeneous nature of firms and industry. Therefore, the results obtained from Translog production function have not been reported.

*Productivity in Aggregate of Industries*

In this section we present the results obtained for the

aggregate of the eight industrial groups of the public enterprises selected for the study. Thus, the aggregate is not the same as the total manufacturing industries in the public enterprises. It thus, to some extent puts a limit on the comparability of the results of this section of the study with the results obtained elsewhere. However, on comparison to the results obtained by Rao and Latha (1990) for the entire manufacturing sector of public enterprises, we find almost the same trend, i.e., that capital productivity is falling till 1985-86 (the period of study by Rao and Latha) while other productivities like labour and TFP's are increasing. However, in the present study the increase is almost negligible.

Sarna and Rao (1988) however, have concluded that both labour as well as capital productivity declined for the period 1971-72 to 1983-84. A comparison of the estimates obtained for the aggregate industries in the present study with the two recent studies is given below:

| *Sector* | *Study* | *Period* | *Labour Productivity* | *Capital Productivity* | *TFPT* |
|---|---|---|---|---|---|
| Registered Public Enterprises (Manufacturing) | Ahluwalia | 1960-86 | 2.2% | –2.5% | –0.4% |
| | Vashist & Kundu | 1960-85 | 1.13% | –1.83% | 0.0% |
| Public Enterprises (Aggregate of 8 industrial groups) | Current | 1974-96 | 7.49% | –1.56% | -0.40% |

While our estimates are relatively higher for labour productivity, they are in agreement for capital productivity and total factor productivity. The possible reason for higher labour productivity could be the exclusion of three labour-intensive industrial groups from the current study. But broadly the results of the current study are in agreement with the results obtained by the two studies. On comparison at the disaggregate level of industries, our results are broadly in agreement, especially in direction, with Ahluwalia (1991) for the corresponding nearest industrial groups. But the agreement with the results of Kumari (1993) is limited only to labour productivity and the results for capital productivity and TFP could not be reconciled for want of all necessary details about her results. The agreement of results of the present study, especially TFPT, with those of Ahluwalia (1991) clearly demonstrates the similar behaviour of the public enterprises with that of organised manufacturing enterprises.

*(a) Estimates of Factor Productivities*

The detailed time trends of single factor productivities (labour and capital productivity) and total factor productivities along with capital intensity are presented in **Table 4 (1)**. It also provides the exponential annual growth rates for the same. The **Table** indicates that labour productivity index has been almost continuously increasing during the period and reaches an index of 412 over the period, the annual growth rate being 7.49 percent. But we find fluctuations in capital productivity and TFP indices over the same period. Capital productivity index declined to 62, the decline being more noticeable since 1988-89 with the rate of growth being - 1.56 percent. The trends of TFPK, TFPS and TFPT also show a similar fluctuation in the indices. However, while Kendrick index show a marginal positive growth rate of 0.68 percent, both the TFPS and TFPT show a negative growth rate of -0.40 percent. Thus, total factor productivity over the period has remained almost stagnant. On the other hand capital intensity in the aggregate of these eight industrial groups increased from 6.202 thousand per employee to 40.90 thousand at an annual growth rate of 9.06 percent. Thus, capital deepening in the public enterprises has taken place. But increase in capital deepening along with decline in capital productivity reveals that capital output ratio in the manufacturing industries has increased. This fact along with almost stagnant, though a little negative, growth in TFP indicates the inefficiency in the use of the scarce factors in the public enterprises. The increase in labour productivity, it seems, has been made possible due to 'more machines per employee' effect.

*(b) Production Function Estimates*

The estimates of the production function of the aggregate industries are summarized in **Table 4 (2)**. Though originally ordinary least square (OLS) method was applied but it provided results which had high degree of autocorrelation.

Therefore, Cochrane-Orcutt adjustment method has also been applied in order to get rid of auto-correlation, as will be evident later for all the production functions. The new auto-regressive method not only eliminates the auto-correlation which is present in OLS estimates but also increases the explanatory power, i.e., $\bar{R}^2$ of the functions. The C-D function illustrates that the coefficients of both log (K/L) and log (L) are significant. It, thus, implies that the manufacturing sector has experienced increasing returns to scale, and the assumption of constant returns to scale of TFP measures is not satisfied. The function provides a growth rate of technological progress (TP) to be -13.8 percent, which is higher than that given by TFP indices. The CES production function, however, confirms the results obtained from C-D function. The CES function has both the coefficients of log (L) and Log (W) to be significant for the value zero, but log (W)'s coefficient is insignificant for unity. It, therefore, implies that there is no evidence of constant returns to scale and the elasticity of substitution is unity, as is assumed by C-D function. The growth rate of TP as computed from CES function is -1.58 percent, which is again an overestimation but not to the same extent as the C-D function. The Translog production function is limited by low value of $\bar{R}^2$ (.285 only) but shows that coefficient of log(L) is significant, thus confirming the results obtained from C-D and CES production functions. The results, thus, show that though there is a confirmity between the results obtained separately from production functions and TFP but between them such confirmity and consistency is missing; mainly because of the differences in the set of assumptions underlying the two procedures.

*(c) Estimates of Functions Explaining Productivity Changes—Aggregate of Industries*

Different studies for India and other countries for manufacturing industries have tried to explain productivity changes through regression analysis (Kendrick; 1973, Gordon; 1987, Goldar; 1986, Ahluwalia; 1991 and others). Some of the commonly used explanatory variables are value added, capital intensity, labour input, capital input, capacity utilization, unionization ratio, etc. However, each study has used different set of explanatory variables. For the present study the

Table 4 (1)

**Estimates of Productivity and Capital Intensity : Aggregate of Industries**

| *Variable* | *Indices of Single Factor Productivity* | | *Indices of Total Factor Productivity* | | | *Capital Intensity (Rs' 000)* |
|---|---|---|---|---|---|---|
| *Year* | *Labour* | *Capital* | *Kendrick* | *Solow* | *Translog* | |
| 1974-75 | 100.00 | 100.00 | 100.00 | 100.00 | 100.00 | 6.20 |
| 1975-76 | 105.50 | 97.74 | 100.89 | 100.80 | 100.79 | 6.69 |
| 1976-77 | 117.29 | 101.09 | 107.39 | 105.81 | 105.99 | 7.19 |
| 1977-78 | 129.31 | 100.79 | 111.20 | 109.02 | 109.16 | 7.95 |
| 1978-79 | 130.99 | 90.50 | 104.17 | 102.80 | 102.78 | 8.97 |
| 1979-80 | 120.27 | 77.88 | 91.59 | 90.07 | 90.10 | 9.57 |
| 1980-81 | 103.35 | 62.50 | 75.10 | 72.12 | 72.10 | 10.25 |
| 1981-82 | 139.48 | 81.04 | 98.58 | 87.12 | 87.22 | 10.67 |
| 1982-83 | 175.00 | 90.26 | 113.62 | 96.91 | 97.20 | 12.02 |
| 1983-84 | 196.94 | 92.13 | 119.03 | 100.74 | 101.08 | 13.25 |
| 1984-85 | 215.96 | 92.13 | 121.79 | 102.64 | 103.06 | 14.53 |
| 1985-86 | 229.08 | 89.23 | 120.46 | 101.53 | 101.98 | 15.92 |
| 1986-87 | 241.60 | 87.22 | 119.70 | 100.97 | 101.41 | 17.18 |
| 1987-88 | 287.14 | 91.10 | 128.30 | 107.00 | 107.62 | 19.34 |
| 1988-89 | 324.95 | 93.40 | 133.93 | 111.33 | 111.96 | 21.37 |

| | | | | | | |
|---|---|---|---|---|---|---|
| 1989-90 | 315.64 | 84.03 | 122.07 | 101.56 | 102.12 | 23.29 |
| 1990-91 | 335.90 | 79.08 | 117.10 | 98.20 | 98.77 | 26.34 |
| 1991-92 | 328.16 | 70.18 | 105.35 | 88.60 | 89.09 | 29.00 |
| 1992-93 | 327.96 | 65.66 | 99.43 | 83.93 | 84.39 | 30.98 |
| 1993-94 | 338.20 | 61.38 | 94.08 | 80.06 | 80.50 | 34.17 |
| 1994-95 | 365.77 | 59.69 | 92.60 | 79.65 | 80.05 | 37.98 |
| 1995-96 | 412.02 | 62.45 | 97.64 | 84.21 | 84.60 | 40.90 |
| Growth rate % | 7.49 | –1.56 | 0.68 | –0.44 | –0.40 | 9.06 |

*Notes* : 1. Data computed and compiled from various issues of Public Enterprises Survey, Deptt. of Public Enterprises, GOI, New Delhi.

2. Growth rates are annual exponential growth rates over time.

Table 4 (2)

**Production Function Estimates : Aggregate of Industries**

| *Explanatory variable* / *Dependent Variable Productivity* | Coefficients of *Constant* | *Log (K/L)* | *Log L* | *T* | *Low (W)* | *Log (K)* | $\bar{R}^2$ | *DW* | *F/RHO* |
|---|---|---|---|---|---|---|---|---|---|
| 1. **Cobb-Douglas** | –26.720 | 2.305** | 3.338* | –0.138 | | | .975 | 1.948 | RHO=.871* |
| Log (V/L) | (-4.723) | (2.773) | (4.684) | (-1.691) | | | | | (8.139) |
| 2. **CES** | –19.783 | | 2.888* | 0.007 | 1.441* | | .972 | 1.848 | RHO=.763* |
| Log (V/L) | (-4.081) | | (4.115) | (0.337) | (2.149) | | | | (5.526) |
| 3. Translog | 1.663 | | 2.441** | 0.177 | | –2.115 | .285 | 1.893 | F=3.39 |
| Log (V) | (0.326) | | (2.306) | (1.347) | | (-1.581) | | | (3,15) |

*Note* : 1. The significance of coefficient of W is tested for both zero and unity while that of the other coefficients are tested against zero.

2. Figures in brackets give the T-values.
3. * denotes significance at 1% level.

   ** denotes significance at 5% level.

   *** denotes significance at 10% level.
4. Figures in brackets in the last column i.e. F/RHO, give either the degree of freedom of F-values or t-values of RHO.

Table 4 (3)

**Regression Functions for Productivity Changes—Aggregate of Industries**

| *Explanatory variable* / *Dependent Variable Productivity* | *Constant* | *Log (V)* | *T* | *Low (WR)* | *Log (K/L)* | $\bar{R}^2$ | *DW* | *F/RHO* |
|---|---|---|---|---|---|---|---|---|
| Labour Productivity | -7.219 | 0.842* | -0.011 | 0.213** | 0.425* | .999 | 1.50 | RHO=.924* |
| log (LP) | (-24.538) | (36.711) | (-0.838) | (2.314) | (3.335) | | | (12.317) |
| Kendrick (TFP) | -0.528 | 0.830* | -0.048** | 0.261** | -0.322** | .992 | 1.396 | RHO=.754* |
| log (TFPK) | (-1.908) | (34.570) | (-3.694) | (2.571) | (-2.238) | | | (4.764) |
| Solow (TFP) | -1.932 | 0.729* | -0.042 | 0.404* | -0.012 | .979 | 1.466 | RHO=.955* |
| log (TFPS) | (-2.987) | (22.394) | (-1.731) | (3.116) | (0.071) | | | (5.906) |
| Translog (TFP) | -2.074 | 0.734* | -0.040 | 0.395* | 0.012 | .979 | 1.450 | RHO=.957* |
| log (TFPT) | (-3.094) | (22.730) | (-1.619) | (3.072) | (0.007) | | | (6.038) |

*Note* : 1. Figures in brackets give T values

2. * denotes significance at 1% level.

** denotes significance at 5% level.

*** denotes significance at 10% level.

Table 4 (A)

**Gross Value added and Gross Capital Formation (at Current prices) in 1995-96: Eight industrial groups and their aggregate**

| *Industries* | *Value Added (Rs lakhs)* | | *Gross Fixed Capital (Rs lakhs)* | |
|---|---|---|---|---|
| AGGREGATE (of 8 groups) | 4404860 | | 17126731 | |
| I Steel | 772422 | (17.53%) | 3407532 | (19.90%) |
| II Power | 529312 | (12.02%) | 4160714 | (24.29%) |
| III Petroleum | 2021707 | (45.90%) | 6985951 | (40.79%) |
| IV Fertilizers, chemicals & Pharmaceuticals | 406330 | (9.22%) | 1419941 | (8.29%) |
| V Heavy Engineering | 248028 | (5.63%) | 257832 | (1.51%) |
| VI Medium & Light Engineering | 170633 | (3.87%) | 375640 | (2.19%) |
| VII Transport Equipment | 188535 | (4.28%) | 234789 | (1.37%) |
| VIII Consumer Goods | 68293 | (1.55%) | 284332 | (1.66%) |

*Notes* : 1. Figures in the brackets are share of the industry out of the aggregate total of the eight industrial groups.

2. Source of data used is various issues of Public Enterprises Survey, Deptt. of Public Enterprises, Govt. of India, New Delhi.

Table 4 (B)

**Gross Value added and Gross Capital Formation (at Current prices) in 1995-96 : 16 Firms from 8 industrial groups**

| *Firms* | | *Value Added (Rs lakhs)* | | *Gross Fixed Capital (Rs lakhs)* | |
|---|---|---|---|---|---|
| I | SAIL | 606620 | (78.53) | 2389198 | (70.11) |
| II | MDNL | 3669 | (0.47) | 11547 | (0.34) |
| III | NHPCL | 50781 | (9.59%) | 817222 | (19.64%) |
| IV | NTPC | 418367 | (79.03%) | 2435535 | (58.54%) |
| V | IOCL | 401371 | (19.85%) | 1142211 | (16.35%) |
| VI | ONGC | 850442 | (42.06%) | 4065261 | (58.19%) |
| VII | NFL | 51909 | (12.77%) | 205090 | (14.44%) |
| VIII | IPCL | 191713 | (47.18%) | 479212 | (33.75%) |
| IX | BHEL | 212463 | (85.66%) | 193105 | (74.90%) |
| X | BHPUL | 11842 | (4.77%) | 7076 | (2.74%) |
| XI | HMTL | 32035 | (18.77%) | 49748 | (13.24%) |
| XII | ITIL | 25955 | (17.06%) | 75978 | (20.22%) |
| XIII | BEML | 34837 | (18.48%) | 45290 | (19.29%) |
| XIV | HAL | 98911 | (52.46%) | 106651 | (45.42%) |
| XV | CCIL | 16417 | (24.04%) | 72513 | (25.50%) |
| XVI | HPFMCL | 726 | (1.06%) | 62777 | (22.08%) |

*Notes* : 1. Figures in the brackets are share of the firm out of the aggregate total of the industrial group.

2. Source of data used is various issues of Public Enterprises Survey, Deptt. of Public Enterprises, Govt. of India, New Delhi.

Table 4 (C)

**Estimates of Productivity and Capital Intensity : Inter-Industry Growth Rates (Percentages)**

| *Industry* | *Single Factor Productivity* | | *Total Factor Productivity* | | | *Capital Intensity* |
|---|---|---|---|---|---|---|
| | *Labour* | *Capital* | *Kendrick* | *Solow* | *Translog* | |
| Steel | 6.20 | 0.02 | 2.20 | -0.30 | -0.35 | 6.10 |
| Power | 17.70 | 8.28 | 8.70 | 3.50 | 3.50 | 9.40 |
| Petroleum | 10.69 | 0.46 | 2.25 | -2.02 | -1.99 | 10.23 |
| Fertilizers, Chemicals and Pharmaceuticals | 8.26 | 2.95 | 4.00 | 3.21 | 3.24 | 5.31 |
| Heavy Engineering | 2.70 | -1.40 | -0.30 | -0.90 | -0.90 | 4.19 |
| Medium and Light Engineering | 4.99 | -2.12 | 0.69 | -0.66 | -0.66 | 7.11 |
| Transport Equipment | 5.17 | -1.55 | 0.94 | 0.20 | 0.24 | 6.72 |
| Consumer Goods | 2.31 | -6.54 | -3.98 | 0.05 | 0.10 | 8.85 |

*Notes* : 1. Data computed and compiled from various issues of Public Enterprises Survey, Deptt. of Public Enterprises, GOI, New Delhi.

2. Growth rates are annual exponential growth rates overtime.

Table 4 (D)

**Estimates of Productivity and Capital Intensity : Inter-Firm Variations in Growth rates (%)**

| Firms | Single Factor Productivity | | Total Factor Productivity | | | Capital Intensity |
|---|---|---|---|---|---|---|
| | *Labour* | *Capital* | *Kendrick* | *Solow* | *Translog* | |
| 1. SAIL | 11.51 | 5.88 | 9.17 | 4.55 | 4.60 | 5.63 |
| 2. MDNL | 21.26 | 22.89 | 17.01 | 10.31 | 9.10 | -1.63 |
| 3. NHPCL | -0.46 | -8.53 | -8.29 | -10.48 | -10.37 | 8.06 |
| 4. NTPC | 22.99 | 9.99 | 11.16 | 4.89 | 4.92 | 12.99 |
| 5. IOCL | 4.76 | -0.42 | 0.11 | -3.86 | -3.83 | 5.18 |
| 6. ONGC | 13.99 | 2.71 | 2.84 | -3.45 | -3.45 | 11.28 |
| 7. NFL | 9.23 | 5.42 | 5.66 | 1.76 | 1.74 | 3.80 |
| 8. IPCL | 5.63 | -0.38 | 0.45 | -1.99 | -2.03 | 6.02 |
| 9. BHEL | 1.85 | -2.90 | -2.10 | -3.20 | -3.20 | 4.83 |
| 10. BHPVL | 5.20 | 2.60 | 3.50 | -0.40 | -0.47 | 2.6 |
| 11. HMTL | 1.79 | -3.41 | 1.41 | -2.20 | -2.22 | 5.21 |
| 12. ITIL | 7.58 | -3.88 | -1.72 | -1.04 | -1.00 | 11.46 |
| 13. BEML | 4.99 | -3.34 | -1.50 | -7.56 | -7.52 | 8.33 |
| 14. HAL | 5.89 | -0.63 | 1.51 | 0.82 | 0.91 | 6.53 |
| 15. CCIL | 13.54 | 2.91 | 4.70 | -0.90 | -0.70 | 10.63 |
| 16. HPFMCL | -1.82 | -13.35 | -11.36 | 4.43 | 3.83 | 12.07 |
| | (2.72*) | (-7.89*) | (-5.9*) | (-6.73)* | (-6.79)* | (10.61)* |

*Notes* : 1. Data computed and compiled from various issues of Public Enterprises Survey, Deptt. of Public Enterprises, GOI, New Delhi.

2. Growth rates are annual exponential growth rates over time

* The growth rates in the brackets are obtained for HPFMCL after excluding the last four (abnormal) years.

explanatory variables for all the regressions which have been included are real gross value added at constant prices which is also indicative of the scale of production besides capacity to pay, the real wage rate is indicative of the price of labour and its contribution to productivity, the capital-labour ratio is indicative of capital deepening, and the time period is indicative of all other changes like change in labour-management relations, labour or capital embodiment. Thus, the regression function used in the analysis is,

$$\text{Productivity} = A.e^{\lambda t}\,(V)^{\alpha}.\,(Wr)^{\beta}.\,(K/L)^{\gamma}$$

The function is log-linear, where $\lambda$, $\alpha$, $\beta$ and $\gamma$ are parameters and A is a constant. V is value added, Wr, the wage rate and K/L is capital intensity. Thus, for labour productivity, we have

$$\log (LP) = \log A + \lambda t + \alpha \log (V) + \beta \log (Wr) + \gamma \log (K/L)$$

Similar expressions have been used for TFPK, TFPS and TFPT.

For the aggregate of industrial groups the estimates are presented in **Table 4 (3)**. The result of labour productivity supports the Verdoon's law. However, not only labour productivity but all the TFP measures have been positively and significantly associated with increase in value added and wage rates. Increase in value added might have increased productivity over the period because of (a) technological progress; and (b) economies of scale. Over the period more investment may bring qualitative improvement in machines etc. and add to productivity. Productivity may also increase because of the presence of economies of scale, both internal and external, which may also arise due to specialization of both labour and machines. The positive association of productivity indices with value added is in confirmity with the findings of many earlier studies for India and other countries for the manufacturing industries (e.g. Goldar (1986), Kendrick (1973), Gordon (1987)). The positive association of increase in productivity rate with increase in wage rate supports the views of the efficiency wage hypothesis which contends that higher wages may lead to higher productivity of labour because of the improvement in the efficiency of either labour or management. Capital intensity, as usual, has 'more machines to work' with effect on labour productivity and thus has a positive and significant association. However, the association is weak in the case of TFP's as it is significantly associated with only TFPK and not with TFPS and TFPT. Though, the time variable has been associated with many individual industries but at an aggregate level the influence is not so evident.

*Group Level Factor Productivities*

*I Steel-Group*

The Steel industrial group is one of the largest industrial groups in the public sector enterprises. In terms of its contribution to value added, it was Rs 772422 lakhs in 1995-96 (**Table 4 (A)**) a share of 17.53% of the aggregate of the eight industrial groups under study. Its share in gross fixed capital formation (GFC) at current prices was 19.90%. Within the steel group the two firms selected on the basis of availability of data and size are Steel Authority of India Limited (SAIL) and Misra Dhatu Nigam Limited (MDNL). While SAIL's contribution to the total value added of steel group was 78.53%, its share in GFC was only 70.11% (**Table 4 (B)**). on the other hand, the share of MDNL in both value added and GFC was 0.47% and 0.34% respectively.

*(a) Estimates of Factor Productivity*

The estimates of single factor productivities, i.e., labour and capital (LP and CP) and total factor productivities (TFP) along with capital intensity for the steel industry have been shown in **Table 4.I.1** (Appendix). Average annual growth rates have been shown at the bottom of the tables. These growth rates have been computed as the exponential growth rates for the entire period. While the growth rates of all the industries have been summarized in **Table 4(C)** those of the firms are presented in **Table 4 (D)**.

In Steel industry both labour productivity and capital productivity growth rates have been fluctuating over the entire period. Labour productivity, however, increased over the period with a growth rate of 6.19 percent, but capital productivity's growth rate remained stagnant (0.02 percent) with its index declining during the same period. The TFPK increased at a rate of 2.24 percent and its pattern of change coinciding with that of labour productivity. On the other hand TFPS and TFPT show marked fluctuations and the two indices reduce over the period at the rates of -0.3 percent and -0.35 percent respectively (**Table 4. (C)**). Time series of all the three TFP indices indicates in **Table 4.I.1** (app.) that TFP has been gradually declining till 1982-83 and thereafter it started improving. The main reason for the improvement being the increase in capacity utilization of the industry in general and of the dominant firm SAIL in particular. While capacity utilisation increased from 66 percent in 1983-84 to almost 100 percent in 1993-94 in SAIL, it increased from 40 percent to 66 percent in MDNL during the same period.[5] During 1974-1984 the Steel group's capital intensity, defined as the ratio of gross fixed capital at constant prices to number of employees, increased at a rate of 6.1 percent per year. This reveals that there has been capital deepening in the steel industry.

**Tables 4.I.2** and **4.I.3** in the Appendix give us the detailed trends for SAIL and MDNL respectively. While the productivities for both the firms have increased faster than the Industry, MDNL registers even faster growth than SAIL. **Table 4 (D)** shows that labour productivity of SAIL rose by 11.5 percent and capital productivity by 5.8 percent. The corresponding increase being 21.2 percent and 22.9 percent respectively for MDNL. Growth of Kendrick (17.1 percent), Solow (10.3 percent) and Translog (9.1 percent) TFP indices for MDNL were also higher than those of SAIL (Kendrick = 9.1 percent, TFPS = 4.5 percent and TFPT = 4.6 percent). Whereas for SAIL the capital-labour ratio increased at a growth rate of 5.63 percent, the ratio decreased at a rate of -1.6 percent in the case of MDNL. The differences in the behaviour of the two firms can best be explained due to the differences in their size especially in terms of GFC and their capacity utilization.

Thus, over the entire period there has been fluctuations in factor productivities, both single factor and total factor, though the indices increased substantially faster for the two firms as compared to the industry.

### *(b) Production Function Estimates*

Estimates of the Cobb-Douglas (C-D) and CES production function for the steel group are given in **Table 4.I.4**. The estimates of Translog production function in all cases under study are limited by the non-availability of a long time series of data and the heterogeneity in the firms.

In C-D function for the steel industry the coefficient of log (L) is insignificant implying thereby that returns to scale is constant, supporting, thus, the assumption of TFP measure. The coefficient of log (K/L) is, however, negative but insignificant. The coefficient of **t**, which gives us TFP growth, is positive and significant showing the growth rate of TFP to be 22.1 percent which is an overestimation. The introduction of a separate trend variable may have led to an under estimation of the capital coefficient and over estimation of the coefficient of time, thus, making the coefficient of **t** to be not only significant but also very high. In CES production function for the industry, coefficient of log (L) is insignificant. Hence, it shows that returns to scale is constant, a result same as given by the C-D function. Coefficient of log (W) is statistically insignificant for both zero and unity, thus, showing the elasticity of substitution to be low. The coefficients of **t** and log (W) give us a TFP growth rate of -6.30 percent which is higher than the productivity estimates but take the same direction.

The estimates of C-D function for SAIL, as given in **Table 4.I.4**, give us a similar trend, as is obtained for the steel industry, because of its size. Coefficient of log (L) is not significant in either C-D function or in CES function, thus, supporting the result of constant returns to scale in the industry. The TFP growth presented by **t** coefficient is 9.7 percent which is close to the growth of the TFPK index. The coefficient of log (W) is again not significant, as was the case for industry. Thus, elasticity of substitution for the firm SAIL is also low. The TFP growth rate indicated by the CES function is -14.15 percent which is higher than the productivity estimates.

MDNL's C-D function indicates in **Table 4.I.4** that coefficient of log (L) is not only significant but negative for the firm. Thus the firm does not experience constant returns to scale.

Table 4.I.4

**Production Function Estimates : Steel Group**

| | Coefficients of | | | | | | | |
|---|---|---|---|---|---|---|---|---|
| *Explanatory variable* | *Constant* | *Log (K/L)* | *Log L* | *T* | *Log (W)* | $\bar{R}^2$ | *DW* | *F/RHO* |
| *Dependent Variable Productivity* | | | | | | | | |
| **Steel Industry** | | | | | | | | |
| 1. **Cobb-Douglas** | -2.950 | -0.914 | 0.453 | .221** | | .886 | 1.807 | RHO=.859* |
| Log (V/L) | (-0.457) | (-1.216) | (0.456) | (2.851) | | | | (8.212) |
| 2. **CES** | -12.719 | | 1.846 | 0.066 | 2.046 | .896 | 1.810 | RHO=.806* |
| Log (V/L) | (-1.968) | | (1.705) | (1.364) | (1.749) | | | (7.657) |
| **SAIL** | | | | | | | | |
| 1. **Cobb-Douglas** | 5.433 | +0.680 | -1.570 | 0.097 | | .917 | 1.703 | RHO=.488*** |
| Log (V/L) | (0.371) | (0.552) | (-0.581) | (1.349) | | | | (1.774) |
| 2. **CES** | 1.551 | | -0.672 | 0.075 | 1.530 | .921 | 1.643 | RHO=.426 |
| Log (V/L) | (0.112) | | (-0.265) | (1.213) | (0.968) | | | (1.363) |

Contd. . . .

| | | | | | | | | |
|---|---|---|---|---|---|---|---|---|
| **MDNL** | | | | | | | | |
| 1. **Cobb-Douglas** | 7.823 | -1.319 | -3.442*** | -0.074 | | .922 | 2.063 | RHO=.745* |
| Log (V/L) | (2.229) | (-1.413) | (-1.993) | (-0.864) | | | | (5.455) |
| 2. **CES** | 4.988 | | -2.918 | -0.110 | -0.712 | .905 | 1.773 | RHO=.771* |
| Log (V/L) | (1.963) | | (-1.606) | (-1.022) | (-0.686) | | | (5.638) |

*Note* :
1. The significance of coefficient of W is tested for both zero and unity while that of the other coefficients are tested against zero.
2. Figures in brackets give the T-values.
3. * denotes significance at 1% level.

   ** denotes significance at 5% level.

   *** denotes significance at 10% level.
4. Figures in brackets in the last column i.e. F/RHO, give either the degree of freedom of F-values or t-values of RHO.

Table 4.I.5

**Regression Functions for Productivity Changes—Steel Group**

| *Explanatory variable*<br>*Dependent Variable Productivity* | *Constant* | *Log (V)* | *T* | *Log (WR)* | *Log (K/L)* | $\overline{R}^2$ | *DW* | *F/RHO* |
|---|---|---|---|---|---|---|---|---|
| **Steel Industry** | | | | | | | | |
| Labour Productivity | -5.993 | 0.927* | -0.034** | 0.730* | 0.253*** | .996 | 1.640 | RHO=.698* |
| log (LP) | (-15.618) | (21.606) | (-2.568) | (3.944) | (1.894) | | | (4.98) |
| Kendrick (TFP) | 0.095 | 0.910* | -0.033** | 0.775* | -0.439** | .990 | 1.612 | RHO=.669* |
| log (TFPK) | (0.223) | (18.868) | (-2.313) | (3.674) | (-2.924) | | | (4.018) |
| Solow (TFP) | 0.272 | 0.833* | -0.044*** | 0.650** | -0.378 | .974 | 1.638 | RHO=.741* |
| log (TFPS) | (0.432) | (11.921) | (-1.937) | (2.197) | (-1.734) | | | (4.781) |
| Translog (TFP) | 0.187 | 0.844* | -0.044*** | 0.646*** | -0.376 | .973 | 1.628 | RHO=.743* |
| log (TFPT) | (0.285) | (11.582) | (-1.865) | (2.099) | (-1.653) | | | (4.83) |
| **SAIL** | | | | | | | | |
| Labour Productivity | -5.710 | 1.019* | 0.017 | 0.039 | -0.012 | .995 | 2.491 | RHO=.809* |
| log (LP) | (-24.216) | (42.198) | (1.669) | (0.301) | (-0.114) | | | (8.291) |
| Kendrick (TFP) | 0.088 | 1.019* | 0.014 | 0.052 | -0.498* | .999 | 2.449 | RHO=.775* |

Contd. . . .

| | | | | | | | | |
|---|---|---|---|---|---|---|---|---|
| log (TFPK) | (0.328) | (36.543) | (1.224) | (0.345) | (-4.105) | | | (5.961) |
| Solow (TFP) | 1.565 | 0.722* | -0.015 | 0.288 | -0.464*** | .988 | 1.908 | RHO=.280 |
| log (TFPS) | (2.889) | (11.915) | (-0.795) | (0.967) | (-1.857) | | | (1.628) |
| Translog (TFP) | 1.564 | 0.733* | -0.013 | 0.263 | -0.484*** | .989 | 1.907 | RHO=.287 |
| log (TFPT) | (2.868) | (12.012) | (-0.710) | (0.875) | (-1.925) | | | (1.689) |
| **MDNL** | | | | | | | | |
| Labour Productivity | -1.103 | 1.056* | -0.001 | 0.054 | 0.190 | .997 | 2.151 | RHO=.529** |
| log (LP) | (-1.848) | (21.583) | (-0.112) | (0.317) | (0.995) | | | (2.582) |
| Kendrick (TFP) | -1.40 | +1.034* | -0.006 | 0.055 | 2.169* | .999 | 2.137 | RHO=.284* |
| log (TFPK) | (-4.676) | (57.541) | (-1.599) | (0.729) | (22.496) | | | (4.449) |
| Solow (TFP) | 3.825 | 0.652* | -0.049* | 0.393 | 0.611 | .979 | 2.249 | 141.83(4,8) |
| log (TFPS) | (2.823) | (9.397) | (-3.063) | (1.264) | (1.382) | | | |
| Translog (TFP) | 2.523 | 0.623* | -0.049 | 0.386 | 0.956 | .959 | 2.005 | 72.83(4,8) |
| log (TFPT) | (1.512) | (7.301) | (-2.475) | (1.007) | (1.755) | | | |

*Note* : 1. Figures in brackets give T values.

2. * denotes significance at 1% level.

** denotes significance at 5% level.

*** denotes significance at 10% level.

3. Figures in brackets in the last column; i.e. F/RHO, give either the degree of freedom of F-values or t-values of RHO.

The firm shows that the TFP growth rate is -7.4 percent which is contrary to those given by the productivity indices. In CES production function the coefficients of log (W) as well as log (L) are insignificant. This implies that returns to scale is constant in the firm contrary to C-D function estimate. The elasticity of substitution is positive but less than one. The TFP growth rate for MDNL by CES production function is -38.1 percent which is a highly overestimated value. In all the production functions we have used the Cochrane-Orcutt method of estimation, for ordinary least square method gave a high degree of auto-correlation. The last column of the **Table** shows the significance of the auto-correlation coefficient. The present exercise has improved the explanatory power (i.e. $\bar{R}^2$) of the new functions.

*(c) Estimates of Functions Explaining Productivity Changes—Steel Group*

**Table 4.I.5** details the different regression function estimates explaining the changes in labour productivity and TFP indices over time. It is noticed from **Table 4.I.5** that in the function of labour productivity for Steel industry as an aggregate, the coefficients of log (V), log (Wr) and log (K/L) are positive and significant. Thus, as scale, wage rate and capital per unit of labour expands the productivity of labour increases. The significance of log (W), not only for labour productivity but also for other TFP measures, supports the efficiency wage hypothesis, i.e., higher wage rate tends to push up the level of productivity.

The coefficient of time is significant but negative implying thereby that the deterioration in labour-management relations and other institutional factors have been depressing labour productivity over time. The analysis of all three TFP measures indicate that while the coefficient of log (V) and **t**, which is negative, have been significant in all the three cases, the coefficient of log (K/L) is also significant (though at 5 percent level of significance) for the Kendrick index. Thus, while the increase in scale of output and wage rate have helped increase in TFP, the negative impact of other factors, captured by the coefficient **t** have been pushing down the productivity.

As expected, the role of the scale parameter, i.e., the value added as observed from **Table 4.I.5** is same for the firms SAIL and MDNL in relation to explaining labour productivity and TFP variations. Capital intensity is an important and significant coefficient in explaining TFP in SAIL but not in MDNL. Here the time coefficient and the wage rate coefficient are not significant in explaining the productivity variations.

*II Power-Group*

The Power group in public sector manufacturing enterprises is a late entrant. It started only in 1982-83 but is an important sector. It employs 24.29% of the total GFC at current prices of the eight industrial groups and contributes 12.02% to the value added (**Table 4 (A)**). It is a highly capital intensive industry with capital-labour ratio, not only increasing at a rate of 9.4 percent but also it is the highest in the manufacturing sector, the ratio being 154.08 thousand per employee. The firms selected here are (a) National Hydro-Electric Power Corporation Ltd (NHPCL), and (b) National Thermal Power Corporation Ltd. (NTPC Ltd.). While NHPCL contributed 9.59% to the total value added of the Power group, the share of NTPC is 79.03%. Their shares in GFC are 19.64% and 58.54% respectively (**Table 4 (B)**).

*(a) Estimates of Factor Productivities*

**Table 4. II.1** (Appendix) contains the year-to-year partial factor and total factor productivity indices for the Power industry. The **Table 4 (C)** illustrates that while the index of labour productivity increased at an annual growth rate of 17.7 percent, the index of capital productivity increased at a growth rate of 8.28 percent during the period 1982-83 to 1995-96. While the labour productivity index increased almost continuously, there has been some fluctuations in capital productivity index; especially it has declined during the three years from 1992-93 to 1994-95. The three TFP measures have been following the fluctuating path of capital productivity as the share of capital in total value added is close to 94 percent. While the Kendrick index of TFP increased at an annual growth rate of 8.7 percent, the Solow and Translog indices rose with an identical growth rates of 3.5 percent. The difference in growth rates, as shown in **Table 4 (C)**, of TFP by Kendrick, Solow and Translog, is explained in the changing share of labour and capital in value added. During the same period the capital-labour ratio in the

Table 4.II.4

**Production Function Estimates : Power Group**

Coefficients of

| *Explanatory variable* / *Dependent Variable Productivity* | *Constant* | *Log (K/L)* | *Log L* | *T* | *Log (W)* | $\bar{R}^2$ | *DW* | *F/RHO* |
|---|---|---|---|---|---|---|---|---|
| **Power Industry** | | | | | | | | |
| 1. **Cobb-Douglas** | -10.609 | 3.038** | -0.041 | -0.104 | | .934 | 2.052 | 52.94 |
| Log (V/L) | (-3.559) | (3.001) | (-0.106) | (-1.183) | | | | (3,8) |
| 2. **CES** | -1.356 | | 0.494 | 0.037 | 1.503 | .870 | 2.107 | 25.64 |
| Log (V/L) | (-1.455) | | (0.997) | (0.321) | (0.810) | | | (3,8) |
| **NHPCL** | | | | | | | | |
| 1. **Cobb-Douglas** | -2.571 | 1.275* | 0.086 | -0.122 | | .759 | 1.044 | 12.59 |
| Log (V/L) | (-3.943) | | (4.976) | (0.221) | (-1.490) | | | (3,8) |
| 2. **CES** | 0.340 | | -0.397 | 0.053 | 2.113* | .537 | 1.201 | 5.25 |
| Log (V/L) | (0.722) | | (-0.812) | (0.610) | (3.001) | | | (3,8) |

Contd. . . .

| NTPC | | | | | | | | |
|---|---|---|---|---|---|---|---|---|
| 1. **Cobb-Douglas** | -5.173 | 0.822 | 0.599 | 0.091 | | .898 | 2.035 | 27.45 |
| Log (V/L) | (-1.55) | (.641) | (0.715) | (0.587) | | | | (3,6) |
| 2. **CES** | -2.733 | | 0.228 | 0.291 | -0.866 | .894 | 2.336 | 26.32 |
| Log (V/L) | (-1.234) | | (0.138) | (1.111) | (-0.406) | | | (3,6) |

*Note* :
1. The significance of coefficient of W is tested for both zero and unity while that of the other coefficients are tested against zero.
2. Figures in brackets give the T-values.
3. * denotes significance at 1% level.
   ** denotes significance at 5% level.
   *** denotes significance at 10% level.
4. Figures in brackets in the last column i.e. F/RHO, give either the degree of freedom of F-values or t-values of RHO.

Table 4.II.5

**Regression Functions for Productivity Changes - Power Group**

| *Explanatory variable* / *Dependent Variable Productivity* | *Constant* | *Log (V)* | *T* | *Log (WR)* | *Log (K/L)* | $\bar{R}^2$ | *DW* | *F/RHO* |
|---|---|---|---|---|---|---|---|---|
| **Power Industry** | | | | | | | | |
| Labour Productivity | -18.078 | 0.934* | 0.244 | 0.116 | 0.811 | .961 | 2.335 | RHO=.946** |
| log (LP) | (-2.209) | (5.144) | (1.033) | (0.153) | (1.161) | | | (3.22) |
| Kendrick (TFP) | -9.585 | 0.936* | 0.298 | 0.109 | -0.147 | .847 | 2.334 | RHO=.945* |
| log (TFPK) | (-1.170) | (5.134) | (1.006) | (0.143) | (-0.210) | | | (3.27)* |
| Solow (TFP) | 1.242 | 0.616* | -0.012 | 0.309 | -0.078 | .848 | 2.331 | RHO=.873* |
| log (TFPS) | (0.765) | (5.989) | (-0.226) | (0.716) | (-0.196) | | | (5.076) |
| Translog (TFP) | 1.108 | 0.617* | -0.009 | 0.290 | -0.064 | .849 | 2.333 | RHO=.875* |
| log (TFPT) | (0.675) | (6.004) | (-0.174) | (0.674) | (-0.162) | | | (5.089) |
| **NHPCL** | | | | | | | | |
| Labour Productivity | -4.507 | 0.426** | -0.041 | 0.530 | 0.946* | .933 | 1.747 | RHO=.891 |
| log (LP) | (-2.249) | (3.257) | (-0.476) | (1.732) | (6.552) | | | (2.073) |
| Kendrick (TFP) | 2.677 | 0.427** | -0.044 | 0.527 | -0.033 | .913 | 1.775 | RHO=.888 |

Contd. . . .

| | | | | | | | | |
|---|---|---|---|---|---|---|---|---|
| log (TFPK) | (1.381) | (3.276) | (-0.525) | (1.726) | (-0.232) | | | (2.051) |
| Solow (TFP) | 5.915 | 0.412** | -0.158* | 0.357 | -0.194 | .935 | 1.788 | RHO=41.11 |
| log (TFPS) | (10.247) | (2.608) | (-6.489) | (0.807) | (-0.894) | | | (4.7) |
| Translog (TFP) | 5.934 | 0.414** | -0.157* | 0.355 | -0.205 | .934 | 1.790 | RHO=39.91 |
| log (TFPT) | (10.241) | (2.610) | (-6.394) | (-0.801) | (-0.941) | | | (4.7) |
| **NTPC** | | | | | | | | |
| Labour Productivity | -16.651 | 1.000* | 0.320 | 0.273 | 0.148 | .995 | 1.873 | RHO=.948 |
| log (LP) | (-2.690) | (18.831) | (1.817) | (1.042) | (0.893) | | | (3.990) |
| Kendrick (TFP) | -8.977 | 1.004* | 0.316 | 0.262 | -0.722** | .982 | 1.604 | RHO=.951 |
| log (TFPK) | (-1.365) | (19.052) | (1.725) | (1.010) | (-4.677) | | | (3.706) |
| Solow (TFP) | 4.119 | 0.586* | -0.010 | 0.179 | -0.462** | .966 | 3.280 | RHO=.702 |
| log (TFPS) | (5.427) | (12.515) | (-0.338) | (0.882) | (-3.162) | | | (4.38) |
| Translog (TFP) | 4.040 | 0.589* | -0.007 | 0.173 | -0.461 | .966 | 3.287 | RHO=.715 |
| log (TFPT) | (5.154) | (12.542) | (-0.228) | (0.845) | (-3.146) | | | (4.428) |

*Note :* 1. Figures in brackets give T values.

2. * denotes significance at 1% level.
   ** denotes significance at 5% level.
   *** denotes significance at 10% level.

3. Figures in brackets in the last column; i.e. F/RHO, give either the degree of freedom of F-values or t-values of RHO.

industry increased from 51.619 thousand to 154.08 thousand per employee with an annual growth rate of 9.4 percent. Since the growth rate in capital productivity is lower than the capital intensity growth rate, therefore, part of the increase in capital intensity must have helped in increasing the labour productivity.

**Tables 4. II.2** and **4.II.3** (Appendix) provide the estimates for the two firms NHPCL and NTPC. The trend of productivity estimates for NHPCL is completely at variance with that of NTPC. **Table 4 (D)** shows that while all the five productivity growth rates for NHPCL are negative over the period, those of NTPC are positive showing a rising trend. The differences in growth rates of the two firms can be partly due to high manpower and material cost in NHPCL and partly due to high capital-labour ratio in NTPC giving rise to 'more machine per labour' effect. The growth rates of the power sector were, thus, more influenced by the growth rates of NTPC, the dominant firm.

*(b) Production Function Estimates*

**Table 4.II.4** provides the estimates of C-D and CES or SMAC production function for the Power group and the two firms. The coefficient of log (L) in C-D production function for the Power industry is insignificant, thus supporting the constant returns to scale assumption of TFP. The coefficient of **t** gives us the TFP growth rate of -10.40 percent, however, the coefficient is statistically insignificant. In CES production function the coefficient of log (L) is insignificant, thus supporting the results of C-D function about returns to scale being constant. The coefficient of log (W) is insignificant for both zero and unity, thus, proving that elasticity of substitution is low. TFP growth by CES function is -7.4 percent which is near to the C-D estimate.

The estimates of C-D function for NHPCL from **Table 4.II.4** give us a similar picture as is obtained for the industry. The coefficient of log (L) is insignificant, thus supporting the constant returns to scale hypothesis. Log (K/L) is significant, as earlier, and the coefficient of **t** gives us a negative TFP growth rate of -12.2 percent. The value is high but takes the same direction as given by productivity estimates. The CES production function indicates that coefficient of log (L) is insignificant i.e., returns to scale is constant. Coefficient of log (W) which is significant for zero value but insignificant for unity, leads to the conclusion that elasticity of substitution is unity. The TFP growth rate is -4.77 percent, which is low but supports the direction pointed out by productivity estimates.

The production function estimates for NTPC are given in **Table 4.II.4**. The coefficients of C-D function are all statistically insignificant. It supports the assumption of TFP that returns to scale is constant. The TFP growth rate of 9.10 percent, as shown by coefficient of **t**, is close to the estimate of Kendrick TFP. The CES production function has insignificant values of both log (L) and log (W), thus supporting the results of the industry that returns to scale is constant and elasticity of substitution is low but negative. Low elasticity of substitution may be possibly due to highly capital intensive nature of the firm and the industry. The TFP growth rate by CES function is 15.59 percent, which is a slight overestimation.

*Estimates of Function Explaining Productivity Changes - Power Group*

**Table 4.II.5** accounts for the different regression functions for the Power industry and to the two firms NHPCL and NTPC. As expected, value added is an important and significant variable in explaining productivity differences for the industry and the firms in all the regressions.

No other variable is found to be significant to explain productivity variations for the Power industry. However, out of the two firms, log (K/L)'s coefficient is also significant for TFPK, TFPT and TFPS in NTPC, though it has a negative sign indicating that capital deepening does not go hand in hand with TFP because of under-utilization of capital. However, the results support the contention that as scale expands the TFP increases, either because of technological progress, or specialisation, or both.

*III. Petroleum-Group*

It is a core industrial group of the manufacturing sector in India's public sector. The total value added by this group is highest of all industrial groups. It is also the most profitable group of the public enterprises. It contributed a gross value added at current prices of Rs 2021307 lakhs in 1995-96, a share of 45.90 percent of the eight industrial groups. The share in GFC at current prices was 40.79 percent (**Table 4 (A)**). The amount of value added for the Petroleum industry and for Indian Oil Corporation, a firm selected for the study, for the base year 1974-75 was very high it being an abnormal year for the Petroleum industry because of international oil crises in 1973-1974. Since an abnormal base year for the study has an adverse impact, therefore, intrapolation for the year was done for the value added. Like Power, the Petroleum group is also a highly capital intensive industry. The capital-labour ratio increased at the rate of 10.23 percent during 1974-1975 to 1995-96. The two firms selected from this group are (a) Indian Oil Corporation Limited (IOC), contributing 19.85% to total value added of the group and 16.35% to the total GFC; and (b) Oil and Natural Gas Commission Ltd (ONGC) with a contribution of 42.06% in value added and 58.19% to the GFC (**Table 4 (B)**).

*(a) Estimates of Factor Productivities*

**Table 4.III.I** (Appendix) illustrates the estimates of single factor and multi-factor productivity estimates of the Petroleum industry along with capital intensity. The labour and capital productivity reached their peak in 1990-91 but thereafter declined gradually. While the index of labour productivity increased at an annual growth rate of 10.69 percent, capital productivity index not only declined but fluctuated throughout this period. It registered a meagre growth rate of .46 percent. Similar to capital productivity index, there have been wide fluctuations in TFP indices. While the TFPK increased at a growth rate of 2.25 percent, the TFPS and TFPT declined over the period with growth rates of -2.02 percent and -1.99 percent respectively (**Table 4 (C)**). However, there has been a gradual increase in capital intensity ratio at the rate of 10.23 percent. The increase in capital-labour ratio along with a declining capital productivity has meant that capital-output ratio in the industry has increased. This does not auger well for the industry as well as for the economy. The sharp decline in all the indices of productivity since 1991-92 has been partly due to the Gulf war in 1990 resulting in an international oil crisis immediately thereafter.

The productivity trends for IOC and ONGC as revealed by **Tables 4.III.2** and **4.III.3** (app.) are almost similar in nature. While in the case of IOC labour productivity increased at a rate of 4.76 percent and capital productivity declined at a moderate rate of -0.42 percent, for ONGC both increased at the rates of 13.99 percent and 2.71 percent respectively. TFPS and TFPT have declined nearly at the same rates in both the firms but TFPK increased at the rate of 2.84 percent for ONGC while remaining almost stagnant for IOC. However, the index reduced though fluctuating, from 100 in base year to only 63.36 in 1995-96. Capital deepening has taken place faster in ONGC (where it grew at the rate of 11.28 percent) than in IOC (where the rate is 5.18 percent). The growth rates of Petroleum group, i.e., industry and the two firms specify that higher growth in productivities have been possible due to capital deepening only.

*(b) Production Function Estimates*

The production function estimates of the Petroleum group are presented in **Table 4.III.4.** The coefficient of log (L) in C-D function for the industry, being significant reveals the absence of constant returns to scale. The coefficient of **t** gives us a TFP growth rate of -2.05 percent, a growth rate close to that of TFPS. In CES production function the coefficient of log (L) is significant at a 10 percent level of significance, thus implying that returns to scale is not constant and confirming the results of C-D function. Since coefficient of log (W) is insignificant the elasticity of substitution is low, almost zero. The TFP growth by this function is -1.25 percent which is close to that of TFPT.

In the estimates of C-D function for IOC all the three parameters are significant showing that constant returns to scale does not exist and the firm has decreasing returns. A very high value of **t** i.e., 36.6 percent, is reflective of over-estimation of this

Table 4.III.4

**Production Function Estimates : Petroleum Group**

Coefficients of

| *Explanatory variable* <br> *Dependent Variable Productivity* | *Constant* | *Log (K/L)* | *Log L* | *T* | *Log (W)* | $\bar{R}^2$ | *DW* | *F/RHO* |
|---|---|---|---|---|---|---|---|---|
| **Petroleum Industry** | | | | | | | | |
| 1. **Cobb-Douglas** | -20.223 | 3.425*** | 2.311*** | -0.205 | | .922 | 1.583 | RHO=.891* |
| Log (V/L) | (-2.229) | (1.960) | (2.108) | (-1.419) | | | | (6.58) |
| 2. **CES** | -7.018 | | 1.781*** | .001 | 1.080 | .930 | 1.409 | 85.72 |
| Log (V/L) | (-1.712) | | (1.900) | (.026) | (1.58) | | | (3,16) |
| **IOC Ltd.** | | | | | | | | |
| 1. **Cobb-Douglas** | 19.586 | -2.538** | -4.173* | 0.366* | | .890 | 1.737 | RHO=.493 |
| Log (V/L) | (3.838) | (-2.456) | (-4.467) | (4.335) | | | | (1.752) |
| 2. **CES** | 4.702 | | -1.690 | 0.129* | 0.746* | .870 | 1.704 | RHO=.739* |
| Log (V/L) | (1.409) | | (-1.703) | (2.483) | (0.915) | | | (3.156) |

| | | | | | | | | |
|---|---|---|---|---|---|---|---|---|
| **ONGC** | | | | | | | | |
| 1. **Cobb-Douglas** | -7.461* | 1.217*** | 1.495 | -0.064 | | .911 | 1.61 | 56.13 |
| Log (V/L) | (-3.346) | (1.731) | (1.401) | (-1.196) | | | | (3,13) |
| 2. **CES** | -4.857 | | 1.692 | 0.123 | -4.500 | .905 | 1.678 | 51.88 |
| Log (V/L) | (-1.398) | | (1.485) | (1.367) | (-1.368) | | | (3,13) |

*Note* : 1. The significance of coefficient of W is tested for both zero and unity while that of the other coefficients are tested against zero.

2. Figures in brackets give the T-values.

3. * denotes significance at 1% level.

** denotes significance at 5% level.

*** denotes significance at 10% level.

4. Figures in brackets in the last column i.e. F/RHO, give either the degree of freedom of F-values or t-values of RHO.

Table 4.III.5

**Regression Functions for Productivity Changes—Petroleum Group**

| *Explanatory variable* / *Dependent Variable Productivity* | *Constant* | *Log (V)* | *T* | *Log (WR)* | *Log (K/L)* | $\bar{R}^2$ | *DW* | *F/RHO* |
|---|---|---|---|---|---|---|---|---|
| **Petroleum Industry** | | | | | | | | |
| Labour Productivity | -10.172 | 0.939* | 0.045*** | 0.296* | 0.441*** | .998 | 1.614 | RHO=.964** |
| log (LP) | (-5.875) | (34.70191) | (1.79684) | (3.916) | (2.029) | | | (13.682) |
| Kendrick (TFP) | -3.558 | 0.942* | 0.016 | 0.323* | -0.413*** | .989 | 1.535 | RHO=.969* |
| log (TFPK) | (-1.509) | (32.285) | (0.496) | (3.945) | (-1.764) | | | (8.664) |
| Solow (TFP) | 3.457 | 0.907* | -0.017 | 0.863* | -1.502* | .985 | 1.96 | 334.76 |
| log (TFPS) | (12.017) | (27.364) | (-1.660) | (14.740) | (-15.321) | | | (4,15) |
| Translog (TFP) | 3.410 | 0.908* | -0.018*** | 0.863* | -1.485* | .985 | 1.97 | 334.59 |
| log (TFPT) | (11.915) | (27.540) | (-1.832) | (14.825) | (-15.221) | | | (4,15) |
| **IOC Ltd.** | | | | | | | | |
| Labour Productivity | -5.588 | 1.031* | -0.054* | 0.121 | 0.712* | .998 | 1.908 | RHO=.869 |
| log (LP) | (18.514) | (36.026) | (-6.095) | (1.452) | (7.362) | | | (13.820) |
| Kendrick (TFP) | -0.199 | 1.034* | -0.059* | 0.123 | -0.181*** | .997 | 1.902 | RHO=.865 |
| log (TFPK) | (-0.667) | (36.223) | (-6.792) | (1.476) | (-1.877) | | | (12.911) |

| | | | | | | | | |
|---|---|---|---|---|---|---|---|---|
| Solow (TFP) | -1.982 | 0.962* | -0.095* | 0.316 | 0.320 | .989 | 1.685 | RHO=.897* |
| log (TFPS) | (-2.692) | (14.962) | (-4.039) | (1.691) | (1.470) | | | (7.766) |
| Translog (TFP) | -1.973 | 0.962* | -0.093* | 0.310 | 0.304 | .989 | 1.681 | RHO=.900 |
| log (TFPT) | (-2.684) | (15.126) | (-3.916) | (1.681) | (1.412) | | | (7.830) |
| **ONGC** | | | | | | | | |
| Labour Productivity | -2.620 | 0.889* | -0.035 | 0.995 | -0.021 | .995 | 1.305 | 936.43 |
| log (LP) | (-3.953) | (17.117) | (-0.839) | (0.891) | (-0.080) | | | (4,12) |
| Kendrick (TFP) | 4.000 | 0.887* | -0.036 | 0.981 | -0.995* | .969 | 1.306 | 129.06 |
| log (TFPK) | (6.006) | (16.990) | (-0.856) | (0.874) | (-3.737) | | | (4,12) |
| Solow (TFP) | -2.868 | 0.737* | 0.056 | -0.110 | -0.132 | .798 | 1.201 | RHO=.919* |
| log (TFPS) | (-0.584) | (6.180) | (0.439) | (-0.0144) | (-0.188) | | | (6.381) |
| Translog (TFP) | -2.872 | 0.738* | 0.057 | -0.112 | -0.133 | .798 | 1.201 | RHO=.919* |
| log (TFPT) | (-0.584) | (6.181) | (0.439) | (-0.045) | (-0.189) | | | (6.376) |

*Note :* 1. Figures in brackets give T values.

2. * denotes significance at 1% level.

** denotes significance at 5% level.

*** denotes significance at 10% level.

3. Figures in brackets in the last column; i.e. F/RHO, give either the degree of freedom of F-values or t-values of RHO.

variable. In CES for IOC the coefficient of log (L) and log (W) is insignificant, portraying that scale is constant but elasticity of substitution is close to zero. The function provides a TFP growth rate of 50.78 percent, which is an overestimation. *ONGC's* Cobb-Douglas production function in **Table 4.III.4** narrates that coefficient of log (L) is insignificant, showing thereby constant returns to scale, and the TFP growth rate is -6.4 percent, a value which takes the same direction as TFPS and TFPT estimates. The CES function confirms the results of C-D function that there are constant returns to scale and elasticity of substitution is zero; as the coefficients of both log (W) and log (L) are insignificant for value to be zero. Since the estimation has high value of $\bar{R}^2$ and low **t**-statistics, it might suffer from multcollinearity.

*(c) Estimates of function explaining productivity changes - Petroleum Group*

The estimates are reported in **Table 4.III.5** for both the industry and the two firms. The significance of log (V) is not lost in all the productivity estimates for the Petroleum industry as well as the firms.

However, in industry's labour productivity estimates one finds that all the coefficients are positive and significant. Thus, labour productivity of the petroleum industry has been pushed up by the increase in scale, increase in wages, increase in capital per employee and better labour-management relations. Coefficients of log (W) and log (K/L) are significant for TFPK, TFPS and TFPT, thus supporting the efficiency wage hypothesis. Capital deepening has, however, reduced the TFP growth in the industry. In the case of IOC Ltd besides value added, we find only the significant effect of **t** thus concluding that adverse labour-management relations are responsible for reducing labour productivity as well as TFP growth. However, 'more machines per employee' effect of K/L ratio is also visible for labour productivity in IOC. On the other hand, labour productivity in ONGC has improved only with an increase in scale of production. But TFPK, out of all the three TFP indices, has also been affected by capital deepening.

*IV. Fertilizers, Chemicals and Pharmaceuticals-Group*

The industrial group uses 8.29% of total GFC at current prices and contributes 9.22% to the value added (**Table 4 (A)**). The two firms selected from this group are (a) National Fertilizers Ltd (NFL) with a share of 12.77% in value added of the industry and using 14.44% of the capital and (b) Indian Petro-chemical Corporation Ltd (IPCL) with its contribution of 47.18% to value added while utilizing 33.75% of the aggregate capital of the industry (**Table 4 (B)**).

*(a) Estimates of Factor Productivities*

The estimates for the industry, as described by **Table 4.IV.1** (Appendix) show a rising trend, with some fluctuations over the period. While labour productivity for the industry grew at a rate of 8.26 percent, the capital productivity increased by 2.95 percent. The corresponding rates as summarized in **Table 4 (C)** for TFPK, TFPS and TFPT are 4.00 percent, 3.21 percent and 3.24 percent. The capital intensity increased continuously at a rate of 5.31 percent. National fertilizers Ltd (NFL) also shows a positive growth rate for all the indices over the period 1979-80 (for details see **Table 4 (D)**). However, in IPCL (**Table 4 (D)**) the growth rates are positive for labour productivity, capital intensity and TFPK but they are negative for capital productivity, TFPS and TFPT. TFP indices along with capital productivity index (**Tables 4.IV.2 and 4.IV.3 (App.)**) have been almost continuously declining since 1974-75, partly due to high capital intensity over the period.

*(b) Production Function Estimates*

The estimates for the group are expressed in **Table 4.IV.4.** The C-D function for the industry explains that the coefficient of log (L) is significant thus violating the assumption of constant returns to scale (CRS). Coefficient of **t** gives the TFP growth to be 2 percent, which is an underestimate. The CES function describes the coefficient of log (W) to be negative but insignificant, while the coefficient of log (L) is significant. Thus returns to scale is not constant and elasticity of substitution is low. The TFP growth as traced from CES function is 4.61 percent close to TFPK estimate. NFL also supports the results of the industry, that constant returns to scale does not hold valid

Table 4.IV. 4

**Production Function Estimates : Fertilizers, Chemicals and Pharmaceuticals Group**

| *Explanatory variable* | Coefficients of *Constant* | *Log (K/L)* | *Log L* | *T* | *Log (W)* | $\bar{R}^2$ | *DW* | *F/RHO* |
|---|---|---|---|---|---|---|---|---|
| *Dependent Variable Productivity* | | | | | | | | |
| Fertilizers Industry | | | | | | | | |
| 1. **Cobb-Douglas** Log (V/L) | -6.847 | 0.558* | 1.402* | 0.020*** | | .977 | 1.775 | 278.15 |
| | (-6.480) | (3.015) | (5.659) | (1.828) | | | | (3,16) |
| 2. **CES** Log (V/L) | -5.73 | | 1.509* | 0.048** | -0.039 | .964 | 1.420 | 175.46 |
| | (-3.753) | (4.423) | | (2.116) | (-0.069) | | | (3,16) |
| **NF Ltd.** | | | | | | | | |
| 1 **Cobb-Douglas** Log (V/L) | -7.523 | -1.040 | 7466*** | 0.0149 | | .771 | 1.063 | 16.76 |
| | (-1.421) | (-0.937) | (1.761) | (0.288) | | | | (3,11) |
| 2. **CES** Log (V/L) | -7.388 | | 5.215 | 0.019 | -0.149 | .754 | 1.078 | 15.36 |
| | (-1.260) | | (1.452) | (0.358) | (-1.259) | | | (3,11) |

| | | | | | | | | |
|---|---|---|---|---|---|---|---|---|
| **IPCL** | | | | | | | | |
| 1. **Cobb-Douglas** | 6.645 | -0.731 | -2.332** | 0.211* | | .782 | 1.589 | RHO=.478** |
| Log (V/L) | (3.283) | (-1.717) | (-2.293) | (3.028) | | | | (2.302) |
| 2. **CES** | 3.369 | | -1.786 | 0.133 | 0.267 | .746 | 1.629 | RHO=.617** |
| Log (V/L) | (2.329) | | (-1.676) | (1.740) | (0.444) | | | (2.282) |

*Note* : 1. The significance of coefficient of W is tested for both zero and unity while that of the other coefficients are tested against zero.

2. Figures in brackets give the T-values.

3. * denotes significance at 1% level.

** denotes significance at 5% level.

*** denotes significance at 10% level.

4. Figures in brackets in the last column i.e. F/RHO, give either the degree of freedom of F-values or t-values of RHO.

Table 4.IV.5

**Regression Functions for Productivity Changes - Fertilisers, Chemicals and Pharmaceutical**

| *Explanatory variable* / *Dependent Variable Productivity* | *Constant* | *Log (V)* | *T* | *Log (WR)* | *Log (K/L)* | $\bar{R}^2$ | *DW* | *F/RHO* |
|---|---|---|---|---|---|---|---|---|
| **Fertilizers, Chemicals & Pharmaceutical Industry** | | | | | | | | |
| Labour Productivity | -5.943 | 0.926* | 0.006 | -0.211** | 0.532* | .999 | 2.768 | RHO=.881* |
| log (LP) | (-17.431) | (29.985) | (1.316) | (-2.199) | (8.590) | | | (15.210) |
| Kendrick (TFP) | 0.331 | 0.915* | 0.003 | -0.169 | -0.246* | .997 | 2.749 | RHO=.893* |
| log (TFPK) | (0.911) | (29.009) | (0.658) | (-1.745) | (-3.974) | | | (13.329) |
| Solow (TFP) | 0.648 | 0.825* | -0.022* | 0.014 | -0.108 | .996 | 2.781 | RHO=.844* |
| log (TFPS) | (2.040) | (26.882) | (-4.748) | (0.143) | (-1.654) | | | (11.777) |
| Translog (TFP) | 0.565 | 0.835* | -0.023* | 0.002 | -0.090 | .996 | 2.736 | RHO=.840* |
| log (TFPT) | (1.877) | (28.532) | (-5.238) | (0.022) | (-1.441) | | | (12.561) |
| **NFL** | | | | | | | | |
| Labour Productivity | -1.037 | 0.970* | -0.004 | -0.041 | -0.149* | .999 | 1.759 | 4452.10 |
| log (LP) | (-6.034) | (63.740) | (-1.464) | (-1.368) | (-3.003) | | | (4,10) |
| Kendrick (TFP) | 5.171 | 0.970* | -0.004 | -0.043 | -1.085* | .998 | 1.769 | 2288.43* |
| log (TFPK) | (29.633) | (62.780) | (-1.447) | (-1.392) | (-21.407) | | | (4,10) |

| | | | | | | | | |
|---|---|---|---|---|---|---|---|---|
| Solow (TFP) | 4.699 | 0.738* | -0.041* | 0.110 | -0.731* | .903 | 1.217 | 33.70 |
| log (TFPS) | (5.805) | (10.297) | (-3.049) | (0.771) | (-3.111) | | | (4,10) |
| Translog (TFP) | 4.722 | 0.738* | -0.041** | 0.110 | -0.737 | .902 | 1.218 | 33.43 |
| log (TFPT) | (5.821) | (10.272) | (-3.042) | (0.771) | (-3.129) | | | (4,10) |
| **IPCL** | | | | | | | | |
| Labour Productivity | -1.935 | 1.099* | -0.084* | 0.186*** | 0.100*** | .992 | 2.044 | 669.17 |
| log (LP) | (-12.956) | (27.906) | (-16.499) | (1.984) | (2.460) | | | (4,15) |
| Kendrick (TFP) | 4.016 | 1.116* | -0.093 | 0.275* | -0.698* | .986 | 2.019 | 337.86 |
| log (TFPK) | (27.439) | (28.936) | (-18.621) | (3.000) | (-17.510) | | | (4,15) |
| Solow (TFP) | 4.675 | 0.801* | -0.076* | 0.059 | -0.649* | .952 | 1.699 | 95.33 |
| log (TFPS) | (20.175) | (1[illegible]12) | (-9.611) | (0.405) | (-10.269) | | | (4,15) |
| Translog (TFP) | 4.702 | 0.797* | -0.075* | 0.048 | -0.652* | .945 | 1.686 | 83.09 |
| log (TFPT) | (18.914) | (12.169) | (-8.883) | (0.309) | (-9.623) | | | (4,15) |

*Note* :

1. Figures in brackets give T values.
2. * denotes significance at 1% level.

   ** denotes significance at 5% level.

   *** denotes significance at 10% level.
3. Figures in brackets in the last column; i.e. F/RHO, give either the degree of freedom of F-values or t-values of RHO.

because coefficient of log (L) in C-D function is significant. However, in CES function none of the variables is significant. CES function, therefore, outlines that returns to scale is constant and elasticity of substitution is low. Indian Petro-chemical Corporation Ltd narrates a similar trend as witnessed for NFL, i.e., returns to scale is not constant by C-D estimates but is constant by CES estimates and elasticity of substitution is low. The growth rates derived from the two functions are 21.9 percent and 18.14 percent respectively, both are overestimates.

*(c) Estimates of functions explaining productivity changes - Fertilzer's Group*

The estimates are expressed in **Table 4.IV.5.** In the industry, as expected, value added and capital-labour coefficients are positive and significant; pointing out that as scale and capital per employee increases, the labour productivity, also increases. However, in Fertilizer industry wage rate coefficient is negatively associated with labour productivity; contrary to the experience so far. But, in TFPK regression, the capital intensity has a negative relationship. In TFPS and TFPT, the time coefficient is negative and significant. Thus, as in other industries, deteriorating institutional factors pushed down the productivity growth. In NFL, as depicted by **Table 4.IV.5**, labour productivity also has a negative relationship with capital-labour ratio. However, for TFPK, TFPS and TFPT, the results are same as are obtained for the industry. In IPCL, results are similar for TFPS and TFPT but for TFPK and labour productivity we find even the coefficient of log (W) to be significant thus reporting that higher wages did help in increasing productivity in this firm. The time coefficient is more consistently significant for this firm as compared to NFL and the industry where it was significant only for TFPS and TFPT variations. Thus we find more variations in the productivity changes in this industry which possibly may have been due to frequent changes in the Government's policy in regard to Fertilizers industry and Drug industry.

*V. Heavy Engineering-Group*

The group consists of 16 core firms of the economy. Together, as **Table 4 (A)** reveals, they account for 1.51% of the aggregate GFC of the eight industrial groups and contribute 5.63% to the value added. The two firms choosen from the industry are (a) Bharat Heavy Electricals Ltd (BHEL) which contributes 85.66% to the value added while employs 74.90% of the GFC of the industry, and (b) Bharat Heavy Plate and Vessels Limited (BHPVL); a comparative small unit with its share to value added being only 4.77% and using 2.74% of the capital (GFC) (**Table 4 (B)**).

*(a) Estimates of factor productivities*

**Table 4.V.1** (Appendix) depicts the estimates for the industry. While the labour productivity index rose at an annual rate of 2.7 percent, the indices of all other four productivities declined. The decline is more noticeable after 1988-89 mainly because of a steep fall in capacity utilization by BHEL, a dominant firm, from a peak of almost 95 percent in 1988-89 to around 47 percent in 1993-94[6]. The decline in capital productivity, TFPK, TFPS and TFPT are -1.4 percent, -0.3 percent, -0.9 percent and -0.9 respectively (**Table 4 (C)**). However, the capital intensity increased at a moderate rate of 4.19 percent. The growth rates contained in **Tables 4 (D) and 4.V.2 (App.)** for BHEL narrates the same trend as was reported for the industry, simply because of its dominance in all the important economic parameters. Thus, except for labour productivity, other productivity indices declined over the period. However, BHPVL shows, in **Table 4 (D) and 4.V.3 (App.)** a positive growth in labour productivity, capital productivity and TFPK. The rates being 5.2 percent; 2.6 percent and 3.5 percent respectively which are higher than those of BHEL. Though TFPK (-0.4 percent) and TFPT (-0.47 percent) show a decline, the decline is slower than that of BHEL and of the industry. The capital-labour ratio for BHEL increased at a rate of 4.83 percent, a rate higher than BHPVL (2.6 percent).

*(b) Production-Function Estimates*

The production function estimates for Heavy-engineering, as outlined in **Table 4.V.4**, illustrates that all of the explanatory

Table 4. V.4

**Production Function Estimates : Heavy Engineering Group**

Coefficients of

| *Explanatory variable* <br> *Dependent Variable Productivity* | *Constant* | *Log (K/L)* | *Log L* | *T* | *Log (W)* | $\bar{R}^2$ | *DW* | *F/RHO* |
|---|---|---|---|---|---|---|---|---|
| **Heavy Engineering Industry** | | | | | | | | |
| 1. **Cobb-Douglas** | -32.364 | 6.474** | 5.112** | -0.188** | | .793 | 2.379 | RHO=.794* |
| Log (V/L) | (-2.403) | (2.628) | (2.367) | (-2.195) | | | | (10.418) |
| 2. **CES** | 0.6175 | | -0.106 | 0.018 | 0.441 | .722 | 1.666 | RHO=.596 |
| Log (V/L) | (0.163) | | (-0.141) | (0.939) | (.822) | | | (2.659)** |
| **BHEL** | | | | | | | | |
| 1. **Cobb-Douglas** | 4.535 | 0.931 | -1.164 | -0.013 | | .566 | 1.617 | RHO=.474*** |
| Log (V/L) | (1.240) | (1.250) | (-1.434) | (-0.335) | | | | (1.933) |
| 2. **CES** | 6.566 | | -1.479 | 0.013 | 0.602 | .581 | 1.895 | RHO=.504 |
| Log (V/L) | (1.970) | | (-1.845) | (0.731) | (1.420) | | | (2.240) |

Contd. . . .

| | | | | | | | | |
|---|---|---|---|---|---|---|---|---|
| **BHPVL** | | | | | | | | |
| 1. **Cobb-Douglas** | -4.881 | 1.750 | 2.548*** | -0.027 | | .764 | 1.790 | 21.52 |
| Log (V/L) | (-1.391) | (1.138) | (1.746) | (-0.571) | | | | (3,16) |
| 2. **CES** | -1.088 | | 1.094 | 0.033 | 0.109 | .745 | 1.615 | 19.55 |
| Log (V/L) | (-1.035) | | (1.500) | (1.007) | (0.153) | | | (3,16) |

*Note :* 1. The significance of coefficient of W is tested for both zero and unity while that of the other coefficients are tested against zero.

2. Figures in brackets give the T-values.

3. * denotes significance at 1% level.

** denotes significance at 5% level.

*** denotes significance at 10% level.

4. Figures in brackets in the last column i.e. F/RHO, give either the degree of freedom of F-values or t-values of RHO.

Table 4.V. 5

**Regression Functions for Productivity Changes—Heavy Engineering Group**

| *Explanatory variable* / *Dependent Variable Productivity* | *Constant* | *Log (V)* | *T* | *Log (WR)* | *Log (K/L)* | $\bar{R}^2$ | *DW* | *F/RHO* |
|---|---|---|---|---|---|---|---|---|
| **Heavy Engineering Industry** | | | | | | | | |
| Labour Productivity | -5.987 | 0.943* | -0.028* | -0.003 | 1.069* | .997 | 2.250 | RHO=.833* |
| log (LP) | (-42.227) | (43.614) | (-5.366) | (-0.077) | (13.450) | | | (18.56) |
| Kendrick (TFP) | -0.968 | 0.944* | -0.037* | 0.002 | 0.391* | .994 | 2.427 | RHO=.783* |
| log (TFPK) | (-7.220) | (45.592) | (-8.107) | (0.050) | (5.087) | | | (16.544) |
| Solow (TFP) | -6.292 | 1.016** | 0.066* | 0.653 | 0.575 | .991 | 2.043 | RHO=.962* |
| log (TFPS) | (-9.877) | (34.606) | (3.467) | (0.938) | (5.425) | | | (23.265) |
| Translog (TFP) | -6.289 | 1.020* | 0.066* | 0.046 | 0.874* | .991 | 2.077 | RHO=.961* |
| log (TFPT) | (-9.994) | (34.871) | (3.501) | (0.811) | (5.435) | | | (-23.412) |
| **BHEL** | | | | | | | | |
| Labour Productivity | -6.177 | 0.982* | 0.010* | 0.021 | 0.746* | .998 | 2.210 | 0.906* |
| log (LP) | (-61.665) | (71.118) | (3.197) | (0.978) | (19.631) | | | (51.198) |

Contd. . . .

| | | | | | | | | |
|---|---|---|---|---|---|---|---|---|
| Kendrick (TFP) | -1.481 | 0.979* | 0.004 | 0.024 | -0.008 | .998 | 2.261 | .905* |
| log (TFPK) | (14.022) | (66.75) | (1.196) | (1.038) | (-0.199) | | | (46.123) |
| Solow (TFP) | -8.562 | 1.182* | 0.139* | 0.059 | -0.002 | .984 | 1.720 | .957* |
| log (TFPS) | (-6.973) | (17.588) | (4.180) | (0.530) | (-0.012) | | | (18.237) |
| Translog (TFP) | -8.690 | 1.188* | 0.140* | 0.054 | -0.000 | '.984 | 1.719 | .958* |
| log (TFPT) | (-7.003) | (17.707) | (4.205) | (0.503) | (-0.003) | | | (18.286) |
| **BHPVL** | | | | | | | | |
| Labour Productivity | -4.545 | 1.014* | 0.013 | 0.020 | 0.865* | .998 | .873 | .971* |
| log (LP) | (-4.111) | (59.029) | (0.530) | (0.346) | (9.472) | | | (6.492) |
| Kendrick (TFP) | 1.351 | 1.014* | 0.001 | 0.015 | 0.247** | .996 | .894 | .967* |
| log (TFPK) | (1.477) | (57.526) | (0.067) | (0.257) | (2.632) | | | (6.039) |
| Solow (TFP) | 0.316 | 0.805* | 0.044 | -0.267 | 0.059 | .819 | 1.374 | .962* |
| log (TFPS) | (0.123) | (12.613) | (0.576) | (-1.219) | (0.173) | | | (6.561) |
| Translog (TFP) | 0.273 | 0.808* | 0.044 | -0.272 | 0.069 | .821 | 1.381 | .963* |
| log (TFPT) | (0.105) | (12.645) | (0.575) | (-1.239) | (0.203) | | | (6.560) |

*Note* : 1. Figures in brackets give T values.

2. * denotes significance at 1% level.

** denotes significance at 5% level.

*** denotes significance at 10% level.

3. Figures in brackets in the last column; i.e. F/RHO, give either the degree of freedom of F-values or t-values of RHO.

variables are significant in C-D function. It implies that industry does not experience constant returns to scale and the industry has significant association with capital-labour ratio. The function portrays a TFP growth rate of 18.8 percent. On the other hand, the CES function has no significant explanatory variable. It depicts that the industry has constant returns to scale, a result contrary to C-D function result. The elasticity of substitution is very low and less than unity as coefficient of log (W) is insignificant for both unity and zero. The TFP growth rate as calculated from CES function is 3.2 percent, an overestimate. The C-D function for the firm, BHEL, indicates in **Table 4.V.4** that the coefficient of log (L) is negative but insignificant; thus concluding that the firm has constant returns to scale. It reports a TFP growth rate of -1.3 percent, nearest to TFPK estimate. The CES function conveys that coefficients of log (L) and log (W) are insignificant thus revealing that the firm has constant returns to scale and elasticity of substitution is low. The growth of TFP as estimated is 3.26 percent. In BHPVL, we find the coefficient of log (L) to be significant and positive indicating an increasing returns to scale. The growth rate given by this function is -2.7 percent, an overestimation of TFPS and TFPT. CES function depicts constant returns to scale and elasticity of substitution to be near zero; as both the coefficients of log (L) and low (W) are insignificant for zero values. The TFP growth rate reported by CES is 3.70 percent, which is close to that of TFPK.

*(c) Estimates of function explaining productivity changes : Heavy Engineering Group*

The estimates are outlined in **Table 4.V.5.** In heavy engineering industry, the labour productivity has log (V), **t** and log (K/L) as the significant coefficients. Thus, while an increase in scale and capital intensity increased the labour productivity, as was also the case in fertilizer group, the deteriorating impact of **t** kept labour productivity at a depressed level. The same result is obtained on the scrutiny of TFPK, TFPS and TFPT. In BHEL, we have the same factors influencing labour productivity. The three TFP indices have a positive scale effect but no impact of capital deepening. **Table 4.V.5** depicts that in BHPVL, labour productivity has the same behaviour as the industry, i.e., positive influence of increase in scale and capital intensity. The three TFP indices, like BHEL, were mainly related to positive scale effect. Thus, one may infer that it is mainly the scale parameter and time parameter which has the impact on total factor productivity in the firms but capital deepening also has its influence in the industry.

*VI. Medium and Light Engineering-Group*

The medium and light engineering industrial group has 23 units in it during the year 1995-96 and the share of the group as stated in **Table 4 (A)** in the aggregate value added and GFC is 3.87% and 2.19% respectively. Hindustan Machine Tools Limited (HMT) and Indian Telephone Industries Limited (ITI) are the two firms selected from this group. They contribute 18.77% and 13.24%, and 17.06% and 20.22% to value added and GFC of the industry respectively (**Table 4 (B)**). Thus, together the two firms have a share of almost 35% in value added and 33% in GFC during 1995-96.

*(a) Estimates of factor productivity*

The detailed time trends of estimates of productivities for the group are given in **Tables 4.VI.1**, **4.VI.2** and **4.VI.3** given in the Appendix. However **Tables 4 (C)** and **4 (D)** give us a summary of the growth rates. It is clear from the **Table 4 (C)** that while labour productivity increased continuously at an annual growth rate of almost 5 percent, capital productivity declined gradually by 2 percent. On the other hand the three TFP indices changed at the same rate (of .66 percent approximately) with TFPK increasing modestly while TFPS and TFPT showing a downward trend. However, the capital-labour ratio increased consistently at an annual rate of 7.11 percent. The growth behaviour of the two firms, as explained by **Table 4 (D)**, is nearly the same. While HMT Ltd has positive rates for labour productivity and TFPK, it is negative for other productivity measures. The sharp fall in capacity utilization rate from 92.00 percent in 1991-92 to 41 percent in 1993-94 and competition from other producers are probably partly responsible for slow growth in productivity. In case of ITI Ltd labour productivity is the only estimate to take a positive value though there is a sharp fall in its value in the last two years. Capital deepening in ITI has been at more than double the rate than in HMT Ltd. The growth figures are reported in **Table 4 (B)**.

Table 4. VI. 4

**Production Function Estimates : Medium and Light Engineering Group**

| Explanatory variable / Dependent Variable | Coefficients of Constant | Log (K/L) | Log L | T | Log (W) | $\bar{R}^2$ | DW | F/RHO |
|---|---|---|---|---|---|---|---|---|
| **Medium & Light Engineering Industry** | | | | | | | | |
| 1. **Cobb-Douglas** | -2.288 | 2.044** | 0.343 | -0.106 | | .895 | 1.99 | 55.72 |
| Log (V/L) | (-1.246) | (2.135) | (0.931) | (-1.428) | | | | (3,16) |
| 2. **CES** | -0.492 | | 0.034 | 0.032 | 0.684 | .877 | 1.70 | 46.18 |
| Log (V/L) | (-0.300) | | (0.097) | (1.690) | (1.220) | | | (3,16) |
| **HMT Ltd.** | | | | | | | | |
| 1. **Cobb-Douglas** | -1.664 | -0.504 | 0.758* | 0.029 | | .598 | 1.784 | 10.43 |
| Log (V/L) | (-1.887) | (-0.668) | (3.241) | (0.757) | | | | (3,16) |
| 2. **CES** | 2.621 | | 0.857* | -0.013 | 0.498 | .611 | 1.735 | 10.98 |
| Log (V/L) | (-2.833) | | (3.394) | (-0.739) | (1.010) | | | (3,16) |

Contd. . . .

| **ITI Ltd.** | | | | | | | | |
|---|---|---|---|---|---|---|---|---|
| 1. **Cobb-Douglas** | 8.200 | 2.551*** | -2.427*** | -0.155 | | .933 | 2.427 | RHO=.551*** |
| Log (V/L) | (1.708) | (1.883) | (-1.756) | (-1.153) | | | | (2.199) |
| 2. **CES** | -0.001 | | -0.220 | 0.064* | 0.796 | .936 | 2.461 | RHO=.527** |
| Log (V/L) | (-0.000) | | (-0.279) | (3.112) | (2.129) | | | (2.532) |

*Note* : 1. The significance of coefficient of W is tested for both zero and unity while that of the other coefficients are tested against zero.

2. Figures in brackets give the T-values.

3. * denotes significance at 1% level.

** denotes significance at 5% level.

*** denotes significance at 10% level.

4. Figures in brackets in the last column i.e. F/RHO, give either the degree of freedom of F-values or t-values of RHO.

Table 4.VI. 5

Regression Functions for Productivity Changes - Medium and Light Engineering Group

| *Explanatory variable*<br>*Dependent Variable* | *Constant* | *Log (V)* | *T* | *Log (WR)* | *Log (K/L)* | $\bar{R}^2$ | *DW* | *F/RHO* |
|---|---|---|---|---|---|---|---|---|
| **Medium & Light Engineering Industry** | | | | | | | | |
| Labour Productivity | -7.111 | 0.933* | 0.019 | 0.111 | 0.588** | .991 | 0.875 | RHO=.950* |
| log (LP) | (-8.723) | (19.927) | (0.633) | (0.897) | (2.395) | | | (7.281) |
| Kendrick (TFP) | -0.447 | 0.937* | -0.030 | 0.099 | -0.013 | .942 | 0.813 | RHO=.919* |
| log (TFPK) | (-1.043) | (20.168) | (-1.331) | (0.803) | (-0.055) | | | (5.526) |
| Solow (TFP) | -6.392 | 0.973* | 0.087*** | 0.032 | 0.141 | .923 | 2.094 | RHO=.961* |
| log (TFPS) | (-4.295) | (16.239) | (1.917) | (0.202) | (0.449) | | | (11.237) |
| Translog (TFP) | -6.908 | 0.992* | 0.092*** | 0.010 | 0.164 | .923 | 2.095 | RHO=.962* |
| log (TFPT) | (-4.343) | (16.315) | (1.952) | (0.067) | (0.517) | | | (11.201) |
| **HMT Ltd.** | | | | | | | | |
| Labour Productivity | -7.924 | 0.986* | 0.127* | 0.026 | 0.079 | .990 | 1.989 | RHO=.954* |
| log (LP) | (-13.046) | (32.759) | (7.071) | (0.298) | (0.793) | | | (19.110) |
| Kendrick (TFP) | -2.056 | 0.989* | 0.095* | 0.052 | -0.462* | .991 | 2.068 | RHO=.950* |

Contd. . . .

| | | | | | | | | |
|---|---|---|---|---|---|---|---|---|
| log (TFPK) | (-4.024) | (34.671) | (5.991) | (0.607) | (-4.887) | | | (18.150) |
| Solow (TFP) | -0.200 | 1.029* | 0.056* | -0.060 | -0.645* | .987 | 1.354 | RHO=.926* |
| log (TFPS) | (-0.451) | (24.956) | (3.387) | (-0.482) | (-4.652) | | | (17.861) |
| Translog (TFP) | -0.146 | 1.051* | 0.051** | -0.074 | -0.628* | .985 | 1.288 | RHO=.924* |
| log (TFPT) | (-0.312) | (23.454) | (2.865) | (-0.544) | (-4.161) | | | (16.628) |
| **ITI Ltd.** | | | | | | | | |
| Labour Productivity | -3.683 | 1.077* | 0.057** | -0.012 | -0.520** | .997 | 1.816 | RHO=.829* |
| log (LP) | (-22.144) | (19.024) | (2.769) | (-0.177) | (-2.150) | | | (6.726)*** |
| Kendrick (TFP) | 0.587 | 11.029* | 0.062* | -0.009 | -1.548* | .984 | 1.702 | RHO=.545 |
| log (TFPK) | (3.410) | (18.760) | (3.647) | (-0.118) | (-9.177) | | | (2.053) |
| Solow (TFP) | -8.499 | 0.980* | 0.161** | 0.093 | -0.349 | .963 | 1.898 | RHO=.968* |
| log(TFPS) | (-2.524) | (11.369) | (2.728) | (0.797) | (-0.780) | | | (8.937) |
| Translog (TFP) | -8.862 | 1.005* | 0.167* | 0.065 | -0.363 | .964 | 1.941 | RHO=.969* |
| log (TFPT) | (-2.600) | (11.734) | (2.807) | (0.567) | (-0.816) | | | (9.144) |

*Note* :
1. Figures in brackets give T values.
2. * denotes significance at 1% level.
   ** denotes significance at 5% level.
   *** denotes significance at 10% level.
3. Figures in brackets in the last column; i.e. F/RHO, give either the degree of freedom of F-values or t-values of RHO.

*(b) Production Function Estimates*

The production function estimates of the group are placed in **Table 4.VI.4.** The C-D function for medium and light engineering industry shows that the coefficient of log (L) is not significant, thus the industry experiences constant returns to scale. The growth rate given is -10.6 percent, an over estimation. Since in CES function both log (L) and log (W) coefficients are insignificant, it supports the result of CD function that there are constant returns to scale. The elasticity of substitution is also very low, i.e., near zero. The growth rate attained from the function is 10.12 percent which is close to that of C-D function in value but is opposite in direction. This is because while C-D function assumes unitary elasticity of substitution, the CES function conveys the value to be close to zero. The coefficient of log (L) is significant in both C-D function and CES function for HMT Ltd. It, therefore, infers that returns to scale is not constant but increasing and elasticity of substitution is low, because coefficient of log (W) is insignificant for value zero. The growth rates acquired from two functions are 2.9 percent (close to TFPK) and -2.6 percent (close to TFPS and TFPT). ITI Ltd's C-D function has both log (K/L) and Log (L) coefficients to be significant. Since coefficient of log (L) is negative it thus implies that the the firm has decreasing returns to scale and the elasticity of substitution is negative. Coefficient of log (W) is significant for value zero but insignificant for unity in CES function. Thus, CES function conveys that returns to scale is constant and elasticity of substitution is one, as the coefficient of log (L) is insignificant. The growth rates noticed for ITI Ltd from the two production functions are -15.5 percent and 31.37 percent respectively, both are overestimates but while the former takes the direction of TFPS and TFPT the latter takes the direction of TFPK.

*(c) Estimates of functions explaining productivity changes : Medium and Light Engineering Group*

For the industry, as **Table 4.VI.5** depicts, the labour productivity has log (V) and log (K/L) as significant explanatory variables as has been the case generally for other industries too. It confirms that not only increase in scale but capital deepening also improves labour productivity. However, for TFP's time variable **t** is significant for TFPS and TFPT only but concludes that in medium and light engineering group improved labour-management relations has helped in increasing TFP. In HMT, we find the role of time coefficient **t** and capital intensity coefficient log (K/L) to be more widespread as **t** is significant in all the productivity regressions and log (K/L) in all the TFP regression. Thus, in HMT both these variables have helped in improving the productivity. The behaviour of productivity variations is the same as far as the impact of log (V) and **t** is concerned for ITI Ltd. Capital intensity did influence only the labour productivity and TFPK. It is to be noted that in ITI Ltd the impact of capital-deepening on labour productivity is at variance with the experience so far.

*VII. Transport Equipment-Group*

It is one of the smallest industrial groups of the public sector manufacturing enterprises. It subscribes to only 4.28% to the aggregate value added (for 8 industrial groups) and 1.37% to the GFC (**Table 4 (A)**). The two firms belonging to this group, i.e., Bharat Earth Movers Ltd (BEML) and Hindustan Aeronautics Limited (HAL) added 18.48% and 19.29%; 52.46% and 45.42% to value aded and GFC of the industry respectively in 1995-96. Thus, almost 70% is added by these two firms to value added and 65% to GFC (**Table 4 (B)**).

*(a) Estimates of factor productivities*

The detailed time trends of productivity estimates for both the industry and the firms are given in appendix **Tables 4.VII.I, 4.VII.2** and **4.VII.3**. However, their growth rates as depicted in **Tables 4 (C)** and **4 (D)** show that while the industry and the firm HAL behaved similarly, where TFPs grew moderately and capital productivity declined; in the case of BEML TFP indices also declined, especially sharply after 1986-87 and the annual growth rates are negative. Labour productivity on the contrary showed a positive growth rate of almost 5 percent in all the three cases. As capital intensity increased quite consistently, both within the industry and the firms (at the rate of 6.72 percent, 8.33 percent and 6.53 percent respectively), it might have led to the 'more machine per employee' effect thereby increasing labour productivity.

Table 4.VII. 4

**Production Function Estimates : Transport Equipment Group**

Coefficients of

| *Explanatory variable* / *Dependent Variable* | *Constant* | *Log (K/L)* | *Log L* | *T* | *Log (W)* | $\bar{R}^2$ | *DW* | *F/RHO* |
|---|---|---|---|---|---|---|---|---|
| **Transport Equipment Industry** | | | | | | | | |
| 1. **Cobb-Douglas** | -5.507 | -0.257 | 1.218*** | 0.068*** | | .925 | 1.417 | RHO=.609** |
| Log (V/L) | (-2.137) | (-0.478) | (2.000) | (1.883) | | | | (2.608) |
| 2. **CES** | -5.855 | | 1.154** | 0.034** | 0.765 | .936 | .512 | RHO=.656* |
| Log (V/L) | (-2.627) | | (2.418) | (2.351) | (1.730) | | | (3.286) |
| **BEML** | | | | | | | | |
| 1. **Cobb-Douglas** | -0.295 | 0.872 | 0.315 | -0.048 | | .621 | 1.869 | RHO=.710* |
| Log (V/L) | (-0.078) | (0.731) | (0.205) | (-0.366) | | | | (3.068) |
| 2. **CES** | -2.175 | | 0.673 | 0.023 | 1.548* | .674 | 1.544 | F=14.39 |
| Log (V/L) | (-0.821) | | (0.598) | (0.780) | (3.188) | | | (3,16) |

Contd. . . .

| | | | | | | | | |
|---|---|---|---|---|---|---|---|---|
| **HAL** | | | | | | | | |
| 1. **Cobb-Douglas** | -3.094 | 0.156 | 0.718 | 0.060** | | .910 | 1.865 | RHO=.510** |
| Log (V/L) | (-0.777) | (0.472) | (0.666) | (2.193) | | | | (2.322) |
| 2. **CES** | -3.899 | | 0.882 | 0.056* | 0.538 | .922 | 1.733 | RHO=.618* |
| Log (V/L) | (-1.026) | | (0.885) | (2.979) | (1.561) | | | (3.337) |

*Note* :
1. The significance of coefficient of W is tested for both zero and unity while that of the other coefficients are tested against zero.
2. Figures in brackets give the T-values.
3. * denotes significance at 1% level.
   ** denotes significance at 5% level.
   *** denotes significance at 10% level.
4. Figures in brackets in the last column i.e. F/RHO, give either the degree of freedom of F-values or t-values of RHO.

Table 4.VII. 5

**Regression Functions for Productivity Changes - Transport Equipment Group**

| *Explanatory variable*<br><br>*Dependent Variable Productivity* | *Constant* | *Log (V)* | *T* | *Log (WR)* | *Log (K/L)* | $\bar{R}^2$ | *DW* | *F/RHO* |
|---|---|---|---|---|---|---|---|---|
| **Transport Equipment Industry** | | | | | | | | |
| Labour Productivity | -8.730 | 0.824* | 0.127* | 0.070 | -0.179 | .995 | 1.876 | RHO=.970* |
| log (LP) | (-5.842) | (16.174) | (3.754) | (0.572) | (-1.522) | | | (6.395) |
| Kendrick (TFP) | -2.562 | 0.831* | 0.101** | 0.030 | -0.771* | .958 | 1.750 | RHO=.970* |
| log (TFPK) | (-1.573) | (14.987) | (2.731) | (0.227) | (-6.023) | | | (4.963) |
| Solow (TFP) | -4.146 | 0.750* | 0.119** | 0.113 | -0.707* | .910 | 1.876 | RHO=.975* |
| log (TFPS) | (-1.664) | (11.800) | (2.408) | (0.734) | (-4.823) | | | (5.390) |
| Translog (TFP) | -4.079 | 0.758* | 0.117** | 0.104 | -0.700* | .906 | 1.885 | RHO=.975* |
| log (TFPT) | (-1.580) | (11.531) | (2.282) | (0.657) | (-4.617) | | | (5.240) |
| **BEML** | | | | | | | | |
| Labour Productivity | -2.326 | 0.959* | -0.058* | 0.026 | 0.429** | .998 | 0.786 | RHO=.818* |
| log (LP) | (-10.605) | (20.949) | (-3.041) | (0.284) | (2.387) | | | (4.410) |

Contd. . . .

| | | | | | | | | |
|---|---|---|---|---|---|---|---|---|
| Kendrick (TFP) | 2.211 | 0.969* | -0.060* | 0.032 | -0.378*** | .983 | 0.783 | RHO=.818* |
| log (TFPK) | (10.175) | (21.150) | (-3.147) | (0.355) | (-2.115) | | | (5.057) |
| Solow (TFP) | 2.347 | 0.911* | -0.154* | 0.038 | 0.124 | .952 | 1.060 | RHO=.794* |
| log (TFPS) | (4.519) | (7.619) | (-3.196) | (0.158) | (0.263) | | | (4.106) |
| Translog (TFP) | 2.330 | 0.918 | -0.155 | 0.030 | 0.131 | .951 | 1.061 | RHO=.797* |
| log (TFPT) | (4.432) | (7.654) | (-3.186) | (0.124) | (0.277) | | | (4.122) |
| **HAL** | | | | | | | | |
| Labour Productivity | -4.051 | 0.938* | 0.038** | 0.031 | -0.075 | .996 | 0.878 | RHO=.896* |
| log (LP) | (-17.622) | (19.597) | (3.657) | (0.456) | (-1.276) | | | (6.129) |
| Kendrick (TFP) | 1.203 | 0.935* | 0.024** | 0.022 | -0.679* | .972 | 0.726 | RHO=.875* |
| log (TFPK) | (5.713) | (17.396) | (2.420) | (0.283) | (-10.173) | | | (4.799) |
| Solow (TFP) | -3.578 | 0.834* | 0.120* | 0.030 | -0.571* | .955 | 1.991 | RHO=.971* |
| log (TFPS) | (-2.108) | (15.503) | (3.133) | (0.385) | (-8.545) | | | (7.004) |
| Translog (TFP) | -3.077 | 0.843* | 0.113** | 0.025 | -0.595* | .953 | 2.016 | RHO=.970 |
| log (TFPT) | (-1.873) | (15.015) | (2.942) | (0.308) | (-8.246) | | | (6.492) |

*Note* :
1. Figures in brackets give T values.
2. * denotes significance at 1% level.
   ** denotes significance at 5% level.
   *** denotes significance at 10% level.
3. Figures in brackets in the last column; i.e. F/RHO, give either the degree of freedom of F-values or t-values of RHO.

*(b) Production Function Estimates*

The **Table 4.VII.4** incorporates the estimates obtained from production functions. It describes that the industry has increasing returns to scale, as the coefficient of log (L) in C-D function for the industry is significant. It exhibits a growth rate of 6.8 percent. Moreover, the coefficient of log (L) is also significant in CES function, thereby indicating that returns to scale is not constant. As log (W) is insignificant even for value zero this implies that elasticity of substitution is low but negative. It shows a TFP growth rate of 14.46 percent which is an overestimation. Bharat Earth Movers Limited exhibits a different trend for C-D function and concludes that returns to scale is constant (log (L) coefficient is not significant). The growth rate derived from the function is -4.8 percent, a slight underestimate. Since coefficient of log (L) is insignificant even in CES function, it supports the C-D function that returns to scale is constant. As log (w) is significant for value zero and insignificant for unity, it leads to the conclusion that elasticity of substitution is unity. The TFP growth rate given by CES is -4.19 percent. Hindustan Aeronautics Ltd confirms that returns to scale is constant since coefficient of log (L) is insignificant in both C-D and CES functions. It also infers that elasticity of substitution is very low, as log (W) coefficient is also insignificant. The TFP growth noticed from C-D function is 6.0 percent and 12.1 percent from CES function. Both show an overestimation but take the same direction as TFP estimates.

*(c) Estimates of functions explaining productivity changes : Transport Equipment Group*

**Table 4.VII.5** demonstrates that labour productivity and TFP for the industry and the two firms is significantly influenced by the change of scale, i.e., as scale increased over time, the labour productivity and TFP also increased. The time coefficient indicates that while improved labour-management relations and other institutional factors improved not only labour productivity but also TFP in the industry and Hindustan Aeronautics Ltd on the one hand, on the contrary in Bharat Earth Movers Ltd. the deteriorating relations has pushed down productivity. Capital intensity has played the expected role in this industry also, i.e., with capital deepening the TFP's have reduced both in the industry and the firm, Hindustan Aeronautics Ltd.

*VIII. Consumer Goods-Group*

**Table 4 (A)** shows that the share of consumer goods group, consisting of 19 units is 1.55% in the aggregate value added and 1.66% in GFC at current prices. Cement Corporation of India Ltd (CCIL) contributed 24.04% percent to the value added of the industry and 25.50% to GFC during 1995-96. On the other hand Hindustan Photo Films manufacturing Co.Ltd's (HPFMCL) comprised only 1.06% to value added and 22.08% to GFC in 1995-96 (**Table 4 (B)**). During the last few years, i.e., after 1991-92 the value added by HPFMCL has drastically reduced (**Table 5.VIII.3**).

*(a) Estimates of factor productivity*

**Tables 4.VIII.1**, **4.VIII.2** and **4.VIII.3** in the Appendix demonstrate the time trends of different productivity indices during the period. The trends suggest that there have been fluctuations in the indices but during the last four years, i.e., from 1992 to 1996, there has been a sharp decline in all productivity indices for the industry as well as the two firms, namely CCIL and HPFMCL. One significant reason for the change is noticed in the significant reduction in capacity utilization of the two firms during the four years.[7] **Table 4 (C)** depicts that while labour productivity in the industry grew at an annual rate of 2.31 percent the capital productivity and TFPK declined at the rate of -6.54 percent and -3.98 percent respectively. However, TFPS and TFPT remained almost static but the capital intensity increased at a high rate of 8.85 percent. Thus, the capital deepening did not increase labour productivity in a very significant way as it happened in the case of CCIL as presented by **Table 4 (D)**. In the case of CCIL the ratio of capital to labour increased at a pace of 10.63 percent and the labour productivity increased by 13.54 percent. The capital productivity and TFPK also showed an upward trend and increased at the rates of 2.91 percent and 4.70 percent respectively but TFPS and TFPT declined at the moderate rates of -0.90 percent and -0.70 percent. In the case of HPFMCL if the last four years are excluded, then the trend is almost similar to that of CCIL.

Table 4.VIII. 4

**Production Function Estimates : Consumer Goods Group**

| Explanatory variable / Dependent Variable | Constant | Log (K/L) | Log L | T | Log (W) | $\bar{R}^2$ | DW | F/RHO |
|---|---|---|---|---|---|---|---|---|
| | Coefficients of | | | | | | | |
| **Consumer Goods Industry** | | | | | | | | |
| 1. **Cobb-Douglas** | 0.469 | 1.250** | -0.597* | -0.030 | | .843 | 1.542 | RHO=.574 |
| Log (V/L) | (1.208) | (2.784) | (-5.160) | (-0.706) | | | | (1.685) |
| 2. **CES** | -0.008 | | -0.396** | 0.048 | 1.429 | .816 | 1.749 | RHO=.708* |
| Log (V/L) | (-0.010) | (-2.435) | | (1.642) | (1.513) | | | (3.320) |
| **CCI Ltd.** | | | | | | | | |
| 1. **Cobbs-Douglas** | -2.491 | 0.776 | 0.167 | 0.053 | | .881 | 1.431 | RHO=.539*** |
| Log (V/L) | (-0.846) | (1.041) | (0.200) | (0.747) | | | | (2.097) |
| 2. **CES** | .830 | | -0.508 | 0.056 | 0.586 | .885 | 1.698 | RHO=.756* |
| Log (V/L) | (.892) | | (-1.223) | (0.774) | (0.572) | | | (3.451) |

Contd. . . .

| | | | | | | | | |
|---|---|---|---|---|---|---|---|---|
| **HPFMCL** | | | | | | | | |
| 1. **Cobb-Douglas** | 3.814 | -0.282** | -3.531** | 0.151* | | .609 | 1.380 | 9.839 |
| Log (V/L) | (3.116) | (-2.403) | (-2.568) | (3.389) | | | | (3.14) |
| 2. **CES** | 1.034 | | -1.775*** | 0.042* | 2.085(5)* | .822 | 1.896 | 27.317 |
| Log (V/L) | (1.107) | | (-1.859) | (1.513) | (5.440) | | | (3.14) |

*Note* : 1. The significance of coefficient of W is tested for both zero and unity while that of the other coefficients are tested against zero.

2. Figures in brackets give the T-values.

3. * denotes significance at 1% level.

** denotes significance at 5% level.

*** denotes significance at 10% level.

4. Figures in brackets in the last column i.e. F/RHO, give either the degree of freedom of F-values or t-values of RHO.

5. The value of log (W) is significant for value unity also.

Table 4.VIII. 5

**Regression Functions for Productivity Changes - Consumer Goods Group**

| *Explanatory variable*<br>*Dependent Variable Productivity* | *Constant* | *Log (V)* | *T* | *Log (WR)* | *Log (K/L)* | $\bar{R}^2$ | *DW* | *F/RHO* |
|---|---|---|---|---|---|---|---|---|
| **Consumer Goods Industry** | | | | | | | | |
| Labour Productivity | -2.343 | 0.299 | 0.012* | 3.241* | -0.511 | .739 | 2.487 | RHO=.742* |
| log (LP) | (-2.759) | (1.053) | (0.210) | (3.176) | (-0.685) | | | (3.590) |
| Kendrick (TFP) | 3.207 | 0.296 | 0.001 | 3.264* | -1.184 | .763 | 2.442 | RHO=.700* |
| log (TFPK) | (4.135) | (1.075) | (0.025) | (3.245) | (-1.605) | | | (3.149) |
| Solow (TFP) | 2.542 | 0.599* | -0.003 | 2.422* | -0.940*** | .705 | 2.570 | RHO=.749* |
| log (TFPS) | (4.389) | (3.133) | (-0.088) | (3.532) | (-1.877) | | | (3.710) |
| Translog (TFP) | 2.519 | 0.602* | -0.006 | 2.447* | -0.920*** | .703 | 2.581 | RHO=.743* |
| log (TFPT) | (4.287) | (3.069) | (-0.144) | (3.471) | (-1.787) | | | (3.650) |
| **CCI Ltd.** | | | | | | | | |
| Labour Productivity | -4.917 | 1.047* | -0.024*** | 0.102 | 0.913* | .996 | 1.260 | RHO=.812* |
| log (LP) | (-14.506) | (22.952) | (-1.881) | (0.621) | (13.581) | | | (19.951) |

Contd. . . .

| | | | | | | | | |
|---|---|---|---|---|---|---|---|---|
| Kendrick (TFP) | 0.227 | 1.043* | 0.039*** | 0.108 | -0.004 | .989 | 1.866 | RHO=.901* |
| log (TFPK) | (0.374) | (24.893) | (1.796) | (0.759) | (-0.083) | | | (17.685) |
| Solow (TFP) | 0.664 | 1.101* | -0.064*** | -0.274 | 0.349** | .925 | 1.726 | RHO=.873* |
| log (TFPS) | (0.689) | (12.400) | (-1.788) | (-0.892) | (2.826) | | | (1.635) |
| Translog (TFP) | 0.610 | 1.113* | -0.066*** | -0.287 | 0.379* | .924 | 1.729 | RHO=.875* |
| log (TFPT) | (0.612) | (12.259) | (-1.768) | (-0.915) | (3.007) | | | (10.366) |
| **HPFMCL** | | | | | | | | |
| Labour Productivity | -0.950 | 0.966* | -0.031* | 0.230*** | 0.032 | .998 | 1.532 | 2480.21 |
| log (LP) | (-13.171) | (83.929) | (-7.878) | (1.905) | (1.330) | | | (4,14) |
| Kendrick (TFP) | 4.131 | 1.054* | -0.031* | 0.104 | -0.815* | .994 | 1.273 | 826.53 |
| log (TFPK) | (40.328) | (11.028) | (-5.317) | (0.412) | (-24.949) | | | (4,13) |
| Solow (TFP) | 3.979 | 1.103* | -0.047* | 0.098 | -0.761* | .994 | 1.781 | 746.00 |
| log (TFPS) | (35.033) | (10.408) | (-7.345) | (0.350) | (-20.992) | | | (4,13) |
| Translog (TFP) | 3.977 | 1.117* | -0.047* | 0.088 | 0.770* | .994 | 1.817 | 738.00 |
| log (TFPT) | (34.508) | (10.383) | (-7.263) | (0.310) | (-20.942) | | | (4,13) |

*Note* :
1. Figures in brackets give T values.
2. * denotes significance at 1% level.
   ** denotes significance at 5% level.
   *** denotes significance at 10% level.
3. Figures in brackets in the last column; i.e. F/RHO, give either the degree of freedom of F-values or t-values of RHO.

*(b) Production Function Estimates*

**Table 4.VIII.4** presents the summary of the production function estimates for both the industry and the two firms. The C-D function of the industry indicates that coefficients of log (L) and log (K/L) are statistically significant. It reveals that returns to scale is not constant but decreasing (as sign of log (L) is negative). The rate of TFP growth computed from it is -3.0 percent, an estimate close to that of TFPK. The CES function has log (L) as significant and log (w) as insignificant. Thus, it confirms the result derived from C-D function that returns to scale is not constant and elasticity of substitution is low. The growth rate on calculation is -11.18 percent, an overestimation. The CCIL's C-D function depicts that there are constant returns to scale in the firm as coefficient of log (L) is insignificant. The growth rate obtained from this function is 5.3 percent, close to TFPK, thus supporting the assumption of TFP estimation. The CES function also supports the result of C-D function, i.e., returns to scale is constant and elasticity of substitution is low. The growth rate, computed from it is 13.52 percent, an overestimation. The case of HPFMCL indicates that the coefficients of log (L) and log (w) are significant. Log (w) is significant for value unity also. Thus, there are no constant returns to scale and no unitary elasticity of substitution but elasticity is negative. The growth rates of TFP given by C-D function and CES function for the firm are 15.1 percent and -3.87 percent, both are overestimation but the latter takes the direction of TFPK and TFPS.

*(c) Estimates of functions explaining productivity changes : Consumer Goods*

The consumer goods industry shows a slightly different behaviour in **Table 4.VIII.5**. It shows that for the consumer goods industry the most important and significant coefficient is that of log (w) for all productivity regressions. Scale parameter, log (V) and capital intensity, log (K/L) are significant for only TFPS and TFPT. Thus, in the industry while labour, as well as, total factor productivity increased with increase in wage rate, the increase in scale and capital intensity significantly influenced only TFPS and TFPT. In the case of CCIL, the same trend is missing. For this firm labour productivity is significantly associated with coefficients of log (V), t and log (K/L). Thus, labour productivity increased as a result of an increase in the scale of production and capital intensity and declined because of adverse institutional factors. TFP for the firm also shows the same behaviour except for TFPK where capital intensity did not have any significant influence because of very low intensity of capital in the base year (**Table 4.VIII.2** (App.)). In case of HPFMCL, wage rate is also a significant coefficient, along with change in scale and labour-management relations, in explaining labour productivity variations. However, for TFPK, TFPS and TFPT the behaviour is same as is observed in CCIL, i.e., productivity increased with increase in scale of production but remained low because of high capital intensity and adverse labour-management relations and other institutional factors.

*Inter-Group Variations in Factor Productivities*

While analysing the productivity estimates of different industries and firms, in this study wide differences have been found in the growth rates of labour, capital and total factor productivities. The estimates of functions explaining productivity changes in these firms and industries make it clear that there exists a strong association between changes in productivity and value added. However, association with other factors like wage rate, capital intensity and institutional factors also does exist, though it may not be as consistent and strong as is the case with value added. It is argued that the positive association of value added to growth in productivity emanates from the fact that the faster an industry grows the more it has the opportunity to exploit the benefits of an expanding level of operations. The expansion allows the industry to exploit the economies of scale, both internal and external. Technological progress, either exogenous or endogenous, is another reason for the positive association. The empirical literature is full of studies establishing this relationship between growth in productivity and value added.[8] Apart from value added, other important variables like wage rate and capital deepening raises the issue of their impact on growth of productivities. The arguments advanced by 'efficiency wage hypothesis' make it imperative to find out, therefore, the impact of wage rates on productivity.

Capital deepening has been included so as to capture the direct impact of technological progress.

The section is further divided into two parts. Regression results for inter-industry variations in labour productivity and TFP are considered in section 4.4.3 (A) and those of the inter-firms are presented in section 4.4.3 (B).

*(A) Inter-Industry Variations in Productivity and their Determinants*

**Table 4 (C)** describes the variations in productivity growth rates between the eight broad industrial groups of the public enterprises manufacturing sector. While the labour productivity increased in all the industrial groups ranging from the lowest of 2.31 percent in consumer goods industries to 17.7 percent in the power industry, the capital productivity increased for first four groups and declined for the last four. The rates of growth in capital productivity are negligible in Steel and Petroleum industries and are significantly positive in Power (8.28 percent) and Fertilizer (2.95) but significantly negative in Consumer goods (-6.54 percent), Medium and Light engineering (-1.4 percent), Transport equipment (-1.55 percent), and Heavy engineering (-1.4 percent). TFPK fluctuated between the negative rate of -3.98 percent for consumer goods industries to a high growth rate of 8.7 percent for Power. TFPS and TFPT were significant only for Power (3.5 percent), Petroleum (-2 percent) and Fertilizers, Chemicals and Pharmaceuticals (3.2 percent), and were stagnant for other groups.

The regression function giving us the determinants of productivity change in different industries are limited by the small number (eight) of industrial groups and thus the degree of freedom is lost to only four. The results are summarized in **Table 4 (E)**. The results prove the Verdoon's law that growth in labour productivity has a positive relationship with growth in output (value added). However, because of limitation of data that explains low $\bar{R}^2$, the same result does not come out clearly for TFP though the coefficient of V is positive in all the three regressions. The coefficient of W is not significant in any of the regressions and is positive for TFPS and TFPT but negative for LP and TFPK. Thus there is no sufficient empirical evidence

Table 4 (E)

**Regression Functions for Productivity Changes - Inter Industry Variations**

| *Explanatory variable* <br> *Dependent Variable Productivity* | *Constant* | *Log (V)* | *Log (WR)* | *Log (K/L)* | $\bar{R}^2$ | *DW* | *F/RHO* |
|---|---|---|---|---|---|---|---|
| Labour Productivity | 8.783 | 0.789*** | -0.767 | -1.272 | .728 | 1.841 | 7.26 (3,4) |
| log (LP) | (0.820) | (2.070) | (-0.451) | (-0.825) | | | |
| Kendrick (TFP) | 5.598 | 0.540 | -0.156 | -1.372 | .494 | 1.797 | 3.28 (3,4) |
| log (TFPK) | (0.530) | (1.437) | (-0.093) | (-0.904) | | | |
| Solow (TFP) | -0.105 | 0.154 | 0.614 | -.397 | .545 | 2.404 | 3.80 (3,4) |
| log (TFPS) | (-0.019) | (.805) | (0.719) | (-0.513) | | | |
| Translog (TFP) | -0.112 | 0.154 | 0.609 | -0.392 | .528 | 2.372 | 3.61 (3,4) |
| log (TFPT) | (-0.020) | (0.787) | (0.699) | (-0.496) | | | |

Table 4 (F)

**Regression Functions for Productivity Changes - Inter-Firm Variations**

| *Explanatory variable* / *Dependent Variable Productivity* | *Constant* | *Log (V)* | *Log (WR)* | *Log (K/L)* | $\bar{R}^2$ | *DW* | *F/RHO* |
|---|---|---|---|---|---|---|---|
| Labour Productivity | -2.627 | 0.693* | 1.104** | -0.150 | .761 | 1.907 | 16.92 (3,12) |
| log (LP) | (-1.059) | (5.036) | (2.215) | (-0.651) | | | |
| Kendrick (TFP) | -2.287 | 0.475* | 1.368** | -0.816 | .721 | 1.623 | 13.97 (3,12) |
| log (TFPK) | (-0.881) | (3.302) | (2.621) | | | | |
| Solow (TFP) | -3.532 | 0.023 | 1.393** | -0.281 | .230 | 1.623 | 2.50 (3,12) |
| log (TFPS) | (-1.118) | (0.135) | (2.192) | (-0.958) | | | |
| Translog (TFP) | -3.862 | 0.011 | 1.420** | -0.239 | .260 | 1.582 | 2.75 (3,12) |
| log (TFPT) | (1.302) | (0.070) | (2.381) | (-0.869) | | | |

*Note :* 1. Figures in brackets give T values

2. * denotes significance at 1% level.

** denotes significance at 5% level.

*** denotes significance at 10% level.

about any kind of link between the growth in productivities and growth in wage rates at inter-industry level. The coefficient of K/L on the other hand is negative in all the regressions, though not statistically significant. For labour productivity this result is contrary to our earlier results for different industries but is in confirmity with TFP growth. It appears from the results that capital deepening did not necessarily help in improving either the labour productivity or the TFP across the industries.

*(B) Inter-Firm Variations in Productivity and their Determinants*

The variations in productivity growth rates between the sixteen firms are presented in **Table 4 (D)**. Except for National Hydro-Electric Power Corporation Ltd and Hindustan Photo Films Manufacturing Co. Ltd, labour productivity increased in all the firms, rates varying from 1.79 percent for HMT Ltd to a high of almost 23 percent for NTPC. Capital productivity, on the contrary declined for nine out of sixteen firms but was highest for Misra Dhatu Nigam Ltd (22.89 percent) and minimum for Hindustan Photo Films Manufacturing Co. Ltd, being -13.35 percent. The capital intensity rate is highest for NTPC and lowest for Bharat Heavy Plate and Vessels Ltd. It is to be noted that the firm with the highest capital intensity also has the highest labour productivity. TFPK growth rate is negative for five firms out of sixteen, indicating a fall in their TFP. Its value ranged from a low of -11.36 percent and -8.29 percent for Hindustan Photo Films Manufacturing Co. Ltd. and National-Hydro Electric Power Corp. Ltd. respectively to a high of 17.01 percent for Misra Dhatu Nigam Ltd. and 11.16 percent for NTPC. The growth rates for TFPS and TFPT show a very dismal picture. It indicates that for majority of firms, i.e., ten out of sixteen, the rates are negative. Thus, the TFP has been declining in these firms, the decline being highest in the National Hydro-Electric Power Corporation Ltd. Out of the six firms where TFP growth rate is positive, the highest rate is for Misra Dhatu Nigam Ltd.

The regression functions for productivity changes in different firms are given in **Table 4 (F)**. The result for labour productivity confirms the result of the industry about the validity of Verdoon's Law. It shows that labour productivity growth is significantly associated with value added growth rate. However, the regression function also indicates that wage rate growth is significantly and positively associated with labour productivity across the firms, thus supporting the efficiency wage hypothesis that higher wages may lead to higher labour productivity. Significantly, the same association is also clearly indicated by the regression functions of TFPK, TFPS and TFPT. Thus, wage rate has shown a significant and positive association not only with labour productivity but also with TFP when viewed across firms. The same cannot be held for the association of capital intensity with either LP or TFP as the coefficient though negative is not significant for any of the regressions. Value added does have a positive and significant relationship with TFPK but not with TFPS and TFPT. Thus, one may infer that variations in productivities across firms is mainly and conclusively associated with wage rate and partly with value added. There is, however, no sufficient statistical information to confirm such an association of capital intensity with variations in productivities across the firms.

**Summary**

In this chapter productivity trends at the firm level, the group level and the aggregate level have been presented and analysed for the period 1974-75 to 1995-96. Both the productivity approach and the production function approach have been adopted for various units over time. Attempt has been made to explain factor productivities of each unit. Inter-firm variations and inter-industry variations in productivities have also been analysed. The exercise is initially carried for the aggregate level.

The results show marked inter-firm and inter-industrial level differences in productivity growth. Estimates of TFP for Power, Fertilizers and Transport equipment show a rising trend in all the three direct measures of TFP. Labour productivity also increased in these groups but capital productivity increased in Power and Fertilizers and declined in Transport equipment. While for groups like Steel, Petroleum and Medium and Light engineering TFPK increased, there was a decline in TFPS and TFPT. In these groups we witness an increase in labour productivity while capital productivity gradually declined. In Consumer goods industry while labour productivity, TFPS and TFPT increased, the capital productivity and TFPK experienced a fall. However, it was only in Heavy Engineering industrial group that all the TFP indices showed a negative rate. At the firm level almost the same tendency is observed. Out of sixteen firms five firms have all the three TFP's growths to be positive. For these firms we also find both labour and capital productivities to be positive except Hindustan Aeronautics where capital productivity is negative. There are five firms where all the three TFP growth rates are negative and these firms also have negative capital productivity growth rates. However, out of these five firms labour productivity growth is positive in three and negative in two firms. The remaining six firms have positive TFPK growth but falling TFPS and TFPT growths. Thus, we witness a mixed trend in case of firms as we did in case of industries and aggregate of industries.

The Cobb-Dougles production function (C-D function) estimates reveal constant returns to scale in Steel, Power and Medium and Light engineering industrial groups. For other industrial groups it indicates the presence of increasing returns to scale except for Consumer goods industries where there are decreasing returns. The CES production function not only provides constant returns to scale (CRS) for Steel, Power and Medium and Light engineering, as was the case with C-D function, but also for Heavy engineering. For other groups, it supports the results obtained from C-D function estimates. For firms, the C-D function supports the assumption of constant returns to scale in eight out of sixteen firms and provides support for increasing returns to scale in five firms and decreasing returns to scale in the remaining three firms. The CES function on the other hand supports CRS in thirteen out of sixteen firms and decreasing returns to scale in the remaining three. The industry as a whole also experiences increasing returns to scale. The elasticity of substitution is unity only for the Consumer goods group, aggregate of industries and the two firms namely National Hydro-Electric Power Corporation Ltd and Bharat Earth Movers Ltd. For all other industrial groups and firms it is mainly very low. The elasticity of substitution is obtained to be negative for the firm NTPC and the Transport equipment industry. The estimates of growth rates of total factor productivity given by the two production function methods are different than those given by direct methods but are broadly consistent in terms of direction. It may be partly because of the presence of multicollinearity in few of the production function estimates and partly because of the differences in the underlying assumptions.

The variations in labour productivity and other three measures of TFP have been explained with the help of regression analysis which included value added, wage rate, capital intensity and a time variable embodying labour-management relations and other institutional factors. A significant positive relationship is observed with value added for almost all the firms and the industries under study. This is in agreement with other studies. On the other hand, 'time' has been observed to be a negative and significant coefficient in many units. Capital intensity generally is observed to have a positive relationship with labour productivity and negative association with TFP measures. Wage rate is found to be only occasionally associated, though positively, with increase in productivity. But it has been found to have a significant relationship in case of aggregate of industries and Steel, Petroleum and Consumer goods industries. The inter-industry variations and inter-firm variations in productivities are also analysed. Regression of inter-industry variation, which may suffer from multicollinearity, and inter-firm variations also support the broad results obtained for individual firms and industry except that in inter-firm variations, the significance of coefficient of log (W) is more strong and visible than in inter-industry variations. However, a detailed econometric analysis of the nexus between wages and productivity will be attempted in the sixth chapter.

## NOTES

1. Chandok, H.L. (1990).
2. Dutt (1969) p 168 - has shown that gross profit as percentage of capital employed ranged from 4.2 percent to 6.2 percent during the IV plan period but in V plan (1974-75 to 1977-78), the percentage showed distinct improvement and ranged between 7.5 percent to 9.4 percent.

3. Raj (1984), Hajela (1987), Krishna (1987), Patil (1987) have all discussed the turnabout in industrial growth.

4. Different committees were, (i) the Committee on Imports-Exports Policies and Procedures, headed by P.C. Alexander, Ministry of Commerce (1978), (ii) the Committee on Controls and Subsidies, headed by V. Dagli, Ministry of Finance (1979), (iii) the Committee on Export Strategy, headed by P. Tondon, Ministry of Commerce (1980), (iv) Arjun Sengupta's Committee on Public Enterprises (1985).

5. Source: Public Enterprises Survey (1993-94), Vol I.

6. Source: Survey op. cit.

7. Source: Survey op. cit.

8. Goldar (1986) has given a good coverage of the literature.

# 5

# WAGE TRENDS IN SELECTED PUBLIC SECTOR ENTERPRISES

## General

There is, generally, a growing gap between wage theory and actual practice. The unemployment of human resources existed in labour markets because the equilibrium therein could never be attained which could have cleared the labour market of excess labour supply. Thus, State intervention of wages, of one sort or the other, depending upon the socio-economic goals, took the place of laissez-faire in many sectors of an economy in many countries of the world in the past. As a result the wage structure in present day economies, too, abounds in disparities, distortions and anomalies between the government, public and private sectors and within each sector itself. Within the organised industrial sector, there are substantial inter-industry wage differentials for unskilled and semi-skilled labour, and within an industry there are marked occupational wage-differentials, for the same occupations also there are marked inter-firm (inter-industrial) wage differentials in the same industry.[1] However, wage structure in the public sector is expected to be relatively homogeneous owing to the different characteristics and objectives of the public sector.[2]

In the previous chapter we have estimated and analysed the productivity trends in selected public sector enterprises. There the productivity estimates and the regression analysis highlighted the differences which exist in the growth rates of productivities between firms and industries. The reasons for these differences were probed and the relationship between productivity differences with wages and other variables was analysed. In order to have a clear view of the nexus that exists between wages and productivity, it is necessary to have an insight into the behaviour of real wages in the selected public sector enterprises during the period of study, i.e., 1974-75 to 1995-96. Therefore, wage trends in selected public sector enterprises in India are being discussed in this chapter.

The present chapter is divided into four sections. Section 5.2 briefly outlines the concepts and the data used in this chapter. Wage trends in selected public sector enterprises will be discussed in section 5.3. Section 5.3 is further sub-divided into three parts. While 5.3.1 analyses the wage trends in aggregate of industries, section 5.3.2 deals with trends in eight industrial groups of public enterprises. Inter-group variations in growth rates are presented in section 5.3.3. Finally, section 5.4 gives a brief summary of the analysis.

**Concepts and Data**

The concept of employment represents the number of employees which includes both 'workers' and 'persons other than workers' as defined and adopted by different issues of Public Enterprises Survey. The number of manpower is expressed in thousands. Data on wages and salaries also includes benefits as received by the employees. The data is expressed at current year's values and are in terms of money wages and salaries. They are being deflated by the appropriate consumer price index for industrial workers with the base 1970-71=100 so as to obtain real wages by dividing the deflated values with employment. Friedman[3] assumed that neither employees nor employers suffer from any money illusion and argued that expected or anticipated changes in the price level of products will be fully incorporated into money wage settlements. Thus, we have also preferred to use real wages per worker instead of money wages. The real wages, thus reflect the real economic status of the human resources used in the public sector. However money wage rates can be and will be calculated by dividing the money wages and salaries by employment. Value added means the gross value added at current prices. Wage share in value added is obtained by dividing the wages and salaries including benefits by the gross value added at current prices. It gives the share of labour in the value added.

Wage shàre in an economy is generally affected by the type of technique which is being used in the economy. In a developing economy, like India, with emphasis on industrialization, capital-labour ratio is bound to change rapidly either through substitution of capital for labour or due to application of labour-saving techniques. This type of change will definitely affect the wage share over time.

Technical progress can be of three types- neutral, labour-saving and capital-saving. For given capital-labour ratio and neutral technical progress the ratio of marginal product of labour to marginal product of capital is unchanged and, hence, the income distribution between labour and capital will remain unaffected. On the other hand, if technical progress is labour saving the ratio of the two marginal products will fall, since the marginal product of capital is raised by more than that of labour and hence relative wage share will fall. At a given point in time this amounts to saying that between two industries the higher capital-labour ratio in one industry would mean a lower ratio of the marginal product of labour to that of capital as compared to other industry where capital-labour ratio is lower. Thus, the labour share can be expected to be negatively related to the capital-labour ratio in different industries. Hicks (1964) while discussing the impact of improvement in technique on the distribution of income assumed that an invention can only be profitably adopted if its ultimate affect is to increase the National Dividend. On this assumption it was concluded that increasing capital accompanied by stagnant invention may very well raise labour's relative share in the 'Dividend' (because elasticity of substitution will ultimately fall as more and more advantageous applications will be used up), but increasing capital with active invention is very likely to do the contrary. And since the activity of invention is definitely favourable to the growth of the Dividend, it is highly probable that periods of most rapidly rising real wages will also be periods of a falling relative share of labour.[4] In a developing country like India, thus, the trends in factor shares will be affected by the increase in the capital-labour ratio, caused by an improvement in technique, depending upon the elasticity of substitution between factors- labour and capital. The wage rate and the relative wage share are, therefore, to move in the opposite direction where the elasticity of substitution is greater than one. There is then an indication that wage share moves inversely with capital intensity and wage rate.

The data as mentioned earlier also, for all the variables has been collected and computed from various issues of Public Enterprises Survey. Data on consumer price index for industrial workers has been obtained from Chandok (1990), RBI Bulletins and Economic Survey (1996-97), and suitable conversion has been done to reduce data to the same base year. Though the indices have been computed and used for employment, real value added, real wages and salaries and the price deflators but they have not been reported because in the present analyses the absolute values give a comparatively better insight into the real trends. Few important limitations of using data from Public Enterprises Survey have been noted. Employment data does not include the casual workers in its scope but value added includes their contribution. Also if one finds the average emoluments from employment and wages, salaries and other benefits data, as given by the survey, then the average emoluments as measure of money wages comes out to be completely different from the values which have been provided by the Surveys for average emoluments. The present study has calculated real wages from the data of employment and of wages and salaries.

## Wage Trends in Selected Public Sector Enterprises - An Empirical Investigation

In this section an empirical analysis will be conducted of wage trends in selected public sector enterprises in India. The attempt here would be to examine the wage trends in the eight industrial groups of public enterprises along with the sixteen firms selected for the present study. The section will also cover the inter-firm and inter-industry variations in growth rates of wages and employment. The section will also find out the behaviour of the variables for the aggregate of industries.

*Wage Trends in Aggregate of Industries*

The term 'aggregate of industries' includes eight industrial groups of the public enterprises selected for the study. The groups are: Steel, Power, Petroleum, Fertilizers, Chemicals and Pharmaceuticals, Heavy engineering, Medium and Light engineering, Transport equipment and Consumer goods industries. The aggregate values have been obtained by adding the respective variable values for the eight industries and then the necessary computations have been done.

The wage trends for the aggregate of industries have been shown in **Table** 5(A). The employment trend highlights the pattern of employment in the aggregate of industries and indicates that employment, which was 534.2 thousand in 1974-75, increased upto 1990-91 when it reached 953.5 thousand, an increase of 178 percent. It started declining since then and reached a figure of 867.07 thousand in 1995-96. The decline in employment is a result of change in the Industrial policy of 1990, whereby (a) the number of reserved sectors for public enterprises have been reduced, (b) restructuring of public sector undertakings is being attempted, and (c) dis-investment of equity in public sector enterprises has been resorted to. Because of the change in the attitude of the Government towards public enterprises, the objectives of public enterprises, including the one of employment creation, have been redefined and more emphasis is now being laid on their commercial objectives. As a result of this new thinking, the employment has reduced over the last six years. The rate of annual growth in employment has been only 2.90 percent over the years, though the increase has been almost continuous over the period prior to 1990-91.

On the other hand, money wages and salaries paid by the aggregate of industries increased by 13.53 percent, i.e., during the same period from Rs. 52053 lakhs to Rs. 954199 lakhs. With an increase in consumer price index for industrial workers from 170 in 1974-75 (with base 1970-71=100) to 831 in 1995-96, an annual increase of 8 percent, the real increase in total wages and salaries is only 5.53 percent. As a result of this increase, the real wages per worker also increased at an annual rate of 2.08 percent. While money wages per worker were Rs. 9744 in 1974-

75, the real wages were Rs. 5731. The money wages, while increased almost continuously, the real wages experienced some fluctuations during the period. Money wages in 1995-96 reached a level of Rs. 110049, an increase of 1029% almost eleven times but real wages were only Rs. 13242, an increase of only 131%, more than double, in twenty two years. If the rate of increase in real wages is compared with the rise in national per capita income (at constant prices) which increased at the exponential rates of almost 2.06 percent[6] during the same period, then the rate of increase in wages does not appear very high. It, however, means that workers in these industries in public enterprises have been able to get their wages and salaries protected from price inflation, and the protection against erosion in the growth of their real income, commensurate with rise in national per capita income, is almost cent percent.

Though gross value added increased at an annual rate of 18.23 percent but the share of wages in value added declined over the period from 40.5 percent to 21.66 percent. The decline has taken place because of an increase in the capital-labour ratio at the rate of almost 9 percent[7]. Wage share has declined almost consistently, except in the last six years when it increased from 0.190 in 1990-91 to 0.216 in 1995-96, due to a fall in the employment level. The general increase in real wages per worker along with a general decline in wage share supports the hypothesis of capital-labour ratio to be negatively associated with wage share and the technical progress to be labour saving. On the other hand an 'active invention' increases both the national 'Dividend' and real wages per worker but reduces the relative share of labour.

Thus, there has been a general increase in employment, money wages and salaries, gross value added and real wages per worker, and a decline of the wage share in value added for the aggregate of selected eight industries in public enterprises. But contrary to popular perception, the increase in real wages of human resources is not more than the increase in national real per capia income. As a corollary to this, we may conclude that the popular belief about the strong trade union movement in public enterprises being able to get undue high wage rates is only a myth, as they have not been able to obtain more than the

Table 5 (A)

**Estimates of Wage Trends: Aggregate of Industries**

| *Variable* / *Year* | *Employment* *('000)* | *Wages and Salaries* *(Rs. Lakhs)* | *Value Added* *(Rs lakhs)* | *Consumer Price Index* | *Real Wages per worker* *('00,00)* | *Wages Share in Value added (Coeff.)* |
|---|---|---|---|---|---|---|
| 1974-75 | 534.204 | 52053 | 128348 | 170 | 0.5731 | 0.405 |
| 1975-76 | 571.618 | 60958 | 149782 | 170 | 0.6273 | 0.406 |
| 1976-77 | 634.398 | 66368 | 189833 | 162 | 0.6457 | 0.349 |
| 1977-78 | 661.017 | 79952 | 222675 | 174 | 0.6951 | 0.359 |
| 1978-79 | 663.526 | 87693 | 228781 | 178 | 0.7424 | 0.383 |
| 1979-80 | 690.596 | 97140 | 265718 | 194 | 0.7250 | 0.365 |
| 1980-81 | 708.777 | 109538 | 285751 | 216 | 0.7154 | 0.383 |
| 1981-82 | 787.373 | 132787 | 462512 | 242 | 0.6968 | 0.287 |
| 1982-83 | 831.175 | 154026 | 620438 | 261 | 0.7100 | 0.248 |
| 1983-84 | 853.210 | 183013 | 768885 | 294 | 0.7295 | 0.238 |
| 1984-85 | 882.687 | 206717 | 931438 | 313 | 0.7482 | 0.221 |
| 1985-86 | 901.302 | 233588 | 1089681 | 333 | 0.7782 | 0.214 |
| 1986-87 | 922.086 | 263748 | 1229879 | 362 | 0.7901 | 0.214 |
| 1987-88 | 935.058 | 296453 | 1551099 | 396 | 0.8006 | 0.191 |
| 1988-89 | 934.828 | 361532 | 1882028 | 423 | 0.9142 | 0.192 |

| | | | | | | |
|---|---|---|---|---|---|---|
| 1989-90 | 946.336 | 417621 | 2124765 | 458 | 0.9635 | 0.196 |
| 1990-91 | 953.554 | 469598 | 2468647 | 512 | 0.9618 | 0.190 |
| 1991-92 | 947.744 | 523649 | 2657325 | 580 | 0.9526 | 0.197 |
| 1992-93 | 929.493 | 577404 | 2900831 | 636 | 0.9767 | 0.199 |
| 1993-94 | 900.725 | 621623 | 3116723 | 684 | 1.0089 | 0.199 |
| 1994-95 | 878.178 | 733687 | 3631158 | 754 | 1.1080 | 0.202 |
| 1995-96 | 867.067 | 954199 | 4404860 | 831 | 1.3242 | 0.216 |
| Growth rate % | 2.90 | 13.53 | 18.23 (7.84) | 8.00 | 2.08 | |

*Notes* : 1. Data computed and compiled from various issues of Public Enterprises Survey, Chandok and RBI Bulletins.

2. Consumer Price Index refers to consumer price index for industrial workers with 1970-71=100.

3. Growth rates are annual exponential growth rates.

4. Figure in brackets in value added column indicates the growth rate of price of output.

minimum compensation they must receive to protect themselves against the erosion in their real per capita income. The results also get the support, indirectly, from the conclusions reached by Ramjash (1992) for the organised industry in India.

*Wage Trends in Eight Industrial Groups*

The section is further sub-divided into eight sections each describing the trends for an industrial group - an industry along with the two firms representing that industry.

*I. Steel-Group*

The trends of employment, wages and salaries, value added, consumer price index for industrial workers, real wages per employee and wages share in value added for the Steel group, comprising the Steel industry and the two firms, namely, SAIL and MDNL are presented in **Tables** 5.I.1, 5.I.2 and 5.I.3.

The Steel industry is one of the core industries in India. It was started during the Second Five Year Plan as part of the process of industrialization. Now it is not a reserve sector and faces some competition from the private sector. **Table** 5.I.1 provides information about few important variables concerning the steel industry in the public enterprises. It shows that employment in the industry grew from almost 161 thousand to 240 thousand during the period 1974-75 to 1995-96, at an annual exponential growth rate of 1.73 percent. The increase in employment has been continuous till 1984-85 but thereafter some fluctuations have been witnessed in the employment pattern. It remained almost stagnant till 1992-93, when it started declining. Thus during the last twelve years, i.e., from 1984-85 to 1995-96 there has been no increase in employment in the Steel industry. On the other hand, total wages and salaries, including benefits have been continuously increasing at an annual growth rate of 12.95 percent. But most of the increase in wages and salaries seems to have taken place because of the rise in consumer price index, which rose by 8.00 percent during the same period. Employees are generally expected to ask for the compensation for increase in prices so as to protect their real wages. Real wages per employee, which have been obtained from wages and salaries and employment data and not taken directly from the

Surveys, indicates that during the period it roughly doubled from Rs. 5639 to Rs. 13,416, and increased at a compound growth rate of 2.64 percent. The rise in real wages per worker is not very high if one compares them with the rise in national per capita income at constant prices over the same period which we find have increased at the rates of 2.6 percent, 3.2 percent,3.6 percent and 1.5 percent during 1974-79, 1980-85, 1985-90 and 1990-1994 respectively.[8] Thus, the employees in steel industry have kept pace with the improvement in national per capita income at constant prices, though their absolute wage levels are higher than the national per capita. Value added on the other hand increased at an impressive rate of almost 17 percent at current prices. If one were to exclude the effect of the price deflator, which rose by 9.12 percent, the real gross value added (at 1970-71 prices) increased by 7.03 percent which is higher than the increase in real wages. The same behaviour is also clearly visible from the trend of wage share in value added. It shows a decline in the share from 0.488 to 0.347, a decline of almost one-third of the original share. The share has, however, been increasing in the initial years till 1982-83 and only after employment's growth rate declined that the share also fell from a peak of 0.747 in 1982-83 to 0.347, i.e., less than half in 1995-96. The fell in wage share with an increase in wage rate is an indication of increase in capital intensity. So labour has been substituted by capital in the steel industry, and as Hicks puts it, the invention of capital has been 'active'. Thus, real wages per worker in steel industry have increased over the period while its share in value added has fallen because of increase in capital intensity.

**Table** 5.I.2 depicts the wage trends for Steel Authority of India Limited (SAIL) for the period 1978-79 to 1995-96. SAIL, though started earlier, it began contributing to value added only from 1978-79, when it employed almost 171 lakh employees, 81 percent of the total employment in the Steel Industry in public enterprises. The employment in SAIL increased upto 1985-86 when it reached a figure of 204.659 thousand, but then started decreasing continuously till 1993-94 when the employment figure declined to 182.896 thousand. The growth rate of employment has almost been negligible (0.13 percent only). The

Table 5.I. 1

**Estimates of Wage Trends: Steel Industry**

| *Variable* | *Employment* | *Wages and Salaries* | *Value Added* | *Consumer Price Index* | *Real Wages per worker* | *Wages Share in Value added (Coeff.)* |
|---|---|---|---|---|---|---|
| *Year* | *('000)* | *(Rs. Lakhs)* | *(Rs lakhs)* | | *('00,00)* | |
| 1974-75 | 160.777 | 15415 | 31552 | 170 | 0.5639 | 0.488 |
| 1975-76 | 162.139 | 17801 | 32338 | 170 | 0.6458 | 0.550 |
| 1976-77 | 203.648 | 20526 | 51025 | 162 | 0.6221 | 0.402 |
| 1977-78 | 214.736 | 26135 | 47309 | 174 | 0.6994 | 0.552 |
| 1978-79 | 211.018 | 27182 | 38987 | 178 | 0.7236 | 0.697 |
| 1979-80 | 222.634 | 30049 | 41559 | 194 | 0.6957 | 0.723 |
| 1980-81 | 228.333 | 33933 | 47487 | 216 | 0.6880 | 0.714 |
| 1981-82 | 235.228 | 39860 | 57394 | 242 | 0.7002 | 0.694 |
| 1982-83 | 247.474 | 47261 | 63187 | 261 | 0.7302 | 0.747 |
| 1983-84 | 248.443 | 54780 | 74075 | 294 | 0.7499 | 0.739 |
| 1984-85 | 250.312 | 59801 | 111933 | 313 | 0.7632 | 0.534 |
| 1985-86 | 250.179 | 66091 | 163827 | 333 | 0.7933 | 0.403 |
| 1986-87 | 246.676 | 73504 | 145701 | 362 | 0.8231 | 0.504 |

Contd. . .

| | | | | | | |
|---|---|---|---|---|---|---|
| 1987-88 | 240.525 | 85102 | 235842 | 396 | 0.8934 | 0.360 |
| 1988-89 | 236.381 | 100041 | 331388 | 423 | 1.00005 | 0.301 |
| 1989-90 | 241.754 | 114072 | 352188 | 458 | 1.0302 | 0.323 |
| 1990-91 | 250.617 | 125453 | 393639 | 512 | 0.9776 | 0.318 |
| 1991-92 | 251.170 | 149338 | 494675 | 580 | 1.0251 | 0.301 |
| 1992-93 | 250.197 | 163186 | 539353 | 636 | 1.0255 | 0.302 |
| 1993-94 | 243.233 | 187021 | 542388 | 684 | 1.1241 | 0.321 |
| 1994-95 | 243.649 | 214734 | 692581 | 754 | 1.1688 | 0.310 |
| 1995-96 | 240.530 | 268160 | 772422 | 831 | 1.3416 | 0.347 |
| Growth rate % | 1.73 | 12.95 | 17.05 (9.12) | 8.00 | 2.64 | |

*Notes* : 1. Data computed and compiled from various issues of Public Enterprises Survey, Chandok and RBI Bulletins.

2. Consumer Price Index refers to consumer price index for industrial workers with 1970-71=100.

3. Growth rates are annual exponential growth rates.

4. Figure in brackets in value added column indicates the growth rate of price of output.

Table 5.I. 2

**Estimates of Wage Trends: Steel Authority of India Ltd.**

| *Variable* / *Year* | *Employment* *('000)* | *Wages and Salaries* *(Rs. Lakhs)* | *Value Added* *(Rs lakhs)* | *Consumer Price Index* | *Real Wages per worker* *('00,00)* | *Wages Share in Value added (Coeff.)* |
|---|---|---|---|---|---|---|
| 1978-79 | 170.928 | 22378 | 38987 | 178 | 0.7355 | 0.573 |
| 1979-80 | 182.443 | 24783 | 38505 | 194 | 0.7002 | 0.643 |
| 1980-81 | 186.965 | 27798 | 40560 | 216 | 0.6883 | 0.685 |
| 1981-82 | 191.847 | 32459 | 45838 | 242 | 0.6991 | 0.708 |
| 1982-83 | 202.055 | 38741 | 50062 | 261 | 0.7346 | 0.773 |
| 1983-84 | 202.313 | 44686 | 58616 | 294 | 0.7512 | 0.762 |
| 1984-85 | 203.868 | 48375 | 99637 | 313 | 0.7581 | 0.485 |
| 1985-86 | 204.659 | 54427 | 142462 | 333 | 0.7986 | 0.382 |
| 1986-87 | 202.419 | 61165 | 125123 | 362 | 0.8347 | 0.488 |
| 1987-88 | 197.393 | 71488 | 215619 | 396 | 0.9145 | 0.331 |
| 1988-89 | 194.802 | 82595 | 308014 | 423 | 1.0023 | 0.268 |
| 1989-90 | 193.223 | 94643 | 324618 | 458 | 1.0694 | 0.291 |
| 1990-91 | 190.608 | 100747 | 357868 | 512 | 1.0323 | 0.281 |

Contd. . . .

| | | | | | | |
|---|---|---|---|---|---|---|
| 1991-92 | 189.193 | 120285 | 428772 | 580 | 1.0961 | 0.280 |
| 1992-93 | 188.352 | 128715 | 455788 | 636 | 1.0744 | 0.282 |
| 1993-94 | 182.896 | 147496 | 492886 | 684 | 1.1790 | 0.299 |
| 1994-95 | 184.185 | 168118 | 559146 | 754 | 1.2105 | 0.300 |
| 1995-96 | 182.787 | 210655 | 660620 | 831 | 1.3868 | 0.319 |
| Growth rate % | 0.13 | 12.73 | 20.11 (8.67) | 8.79 | 3.39 | |

*Notes* : 1. Data computed and compiled from various issues of Public Enterprises Survey, Chandok and RBI Bulletins.

2. Consumer Price Index refers to consumer price index for industrial workers with 1970-71=100.

3. Growth rates are annual exponential growth rates.

4. Figure in brackets in value added column indicates the growth rate of price of output.

Table 5.I. 3

Estimates of Wage Trends: Misra Dhatu Nigam Ltd.

| Variable<br>Year | Employment<br>('000) | Wages and Salaries<br>(Rs. Lakhs) | Value Added<br>(Rs lakhs) | Consumer Price Index | Real Wages per worker<br>('00,00) | Wages Share in Value added (Coeff.) |
|---|---|---|---|---|---|---|
| 1981-82 | 1.111 | 187 | 42 | 242 | 0.6955 | 4.452 |
| 1982-83 | 1.293 | 233 | 104 | 261 | 0.6904 | 2.240 |
| 1983-84 | 1.480 | 325 | 167 | 294 | 0.7469 | 1.946 |
| 1984-85 | 1.538 | 382 | 414 | 313 | 0.7935 | 0.922 |
| 1985-86 | 1.532 | 401 | 1007 | 333 | 0.7860 | 0.398 |
| 1986-87 | 1.509 | 457 | 1509 | 362 | 0.8366 | 0.302 |
| 1987-88 | 1.517 | 506 | 1355 | 396 | 0.8423 | 0.373 |
| 1988-89 | 1.409 | 578 | 1568 | 423 | 0.9697 | 0.368 |
| 1989-90 | 1.407 | 724 | 1680 | 458 | 1.1235 | 0.430 |
| 1990-91 | 1.522 | 938 | 1769 | 512 | 1.2036 | 0.530 |
| 1991-92 | 1.519 | 920 | 2198 | 580 | 1.0442 | 0.418 |
| 1992-93 | 1.503 | 1008 | 1855 | 636 | 1.0544 | 0.543 |

Contd. . . .

| | | | | | | |
|---|---|---|---|---|---|---|
| 1993-94 | 1.494 | 1111 | 2324 | 684 | 1.0871 | 0.478 |
| 1994-95 | 1.376 | 1852 | 3007 | 754 | 1.7850 | 0.616 |
| 1995-96 | 1.373 | 1523 | 3669 | 831 | 1.3348 | 0.415 |
| Growth rate % | 1.29 | 14.44 | 29.78 (7.22) | 8.61 | 4.06 | |

*Notes* :
1. Data computed and compiled from various issues of Public Enterprises Survey, Chandok and RBI Bulletins.
2. Consumer Price Index refers to consumer price index for industrial workers with 1970-71=100.
3. Growth rates are annual exponential growth rates.
4. Figure in brackets in value added column indicates the growth rate of price of output.

total wages and salaries at current prices, however, increased almost by nine and a half times from Rs. 22378 lakhs to Rs.210655 lakhs, thus the money wages per worker increased from Rs. 13092 to Rs. 115246, an increase of around nine times. But, the increase in real wages per worker is comparatively low, an increase from Rs. 7355 to Rs. 13868, which is less than double. The rate of annual increase is 12.73 percent and 3.39 percent in money wages per worker and real wages per worker respectively. But not only real wages per worker in SAIL have increased faster than the industry, the industry's rate being 2.64 percent, even the value added both in money value as well as real value, has increased faster than the industry. Annual growth rate in value added in SAIL is 20.31 percent and 11.64 percent in money value (i.e. at current prices) and real value (i.e. at constant prices) respectively. The rate of increase in the price of value added is 8.67 percent. Wage share in value added in SAIL followed the same trend as is followed by the industry. The wage-share increased continuously till 1982-83, when it was 0.773, it reduced almost gradually thereafter and reached in 1995-96 to roughly 0.32, i.e., 32 percent of the total value added. Thus, while wage share is slightly lower in SAIL as compared to the industry, the real wage rate per worker is higher. The phenomenon indicates that SAIL has either higher capital intensity or higher elasticity of substitution.

MDNL, which started operating in 1981-82, employed only 1.111 thousand employees, a meager .47 percent of total employment in the Steel industry in 1981-82. The employment reached the level of 1.373 thousand, in 1995-96, with an annual increase of 1.29 percent. The wages and salaries, etc. increased at an annual rate of 14.44 percent in money values and 5.83 percent at constant prices. This led to an increase in money wages per worker at a rate of 12.67 percent and real wages per worker at 4.06 percent, a rate higher than those of SAIL and the steel industry. The value added in MDNL also increased faster than both SAIL and the industry, it being about 30 percent at current prices and 22.56 percent at constant prices. But the higher growth rate in value added is partly due to a very small amount of value added in 1981-82, only Rs. 42 lakhs, even less than the wage bill, thus, showing us the wage share to be very high, i.e., 4.452. The price index of value added deflator for MDNL increased at an annual growth rate of 7.22 percent. The time trend of wage share in MDNL, however, shows a trend reverse to that of SAIL and the industry. While in the latter wage share reduced with increase in real wages per worker, in MDNL the wage share first reduced and then increased. The share was .302 in MDNL in 1986-87 but increased to 0.616 in 1994-95 and to 0.415 in 1995-96. Since the wage rate per worker and wage share are moving in the same direction, it implies that elasticity of substitution between factors, - capital and labour - is less than one.

Since the real wages per worker in the Steel industry, SAIL and MDNL grew by 2.64 percent, 3.39 percent and 4.06 percent respectively it can therefore, be argued that employees were not only able to protect themselves from general price rise but were also able to get their wages increased at a rate at least equal to or more than the rise in real per capita income, thus improving their relative economic position. It is also to be noted that in Steel industry, SAIL and MDNL real wages were higher than those of the aggregate of industries in 1995-96. But the Steel industry depicts the same trend for real wages as well as for employment as is being depicted by the aggregate of industries. However, within Steel industry real wages seems to have been influenced more by the Wage trends in SAIL, as while SAIL has improved its financial performance in recent years (it was fifth highest profit maker in 1992-93) and is making huge profits, the Steel industry as a whole which was incurring losses till 1993-94, is now making huge profits (Rs 1042 crores). With liberalisation and removal of price control since 1992, there is a hope of its becoming more efficient and competitive in near future.

*II. Power-Group*

Power industry is a very late entrant in public enterprises in India. It thus tried to learn from the experience of other public enterprises. It not only adopted the latest technique, though capital intensive, but also tried to control the alleged over-staffing. Despite all precautions, the employment in Power industry increased from 11.134 thousand in 1982-83 to 48.868

thousand in 1995-96, the indices being 100 and 439 respectively, showing an increase of almost four times at an annual growth rate of 13.43 percent. Money wages and salaries in the Power industry increased from Rs. 243 lakhs to Rs. 34407 lakhs, increasing at a phenomenal growth rate of almost 37 percent. The money wages per worker thus, were only Rs. 2182 and increased to Rs. 45703 in 1993-94 and Rs 70408 in 1995-96, increasing at a rate of 13.5 percent. However, since consumer price index increased at a rate of 8.66 percent during the same period, therefore, the two increases are only 28.78 percent and 4.86 percent. Though the increase in real wages per worker is higher (4.86 percent) in Power industry than in the Steel industry (2.64 percent) but the absolute real wages per worker are higher in Steel (Rs. 13,416) than in Power (Rs. 8472). The value added in Power industry grew faster, the rate being 38 percent. The index of value added in 1995-96, on computation, is 13018, i.e., an increase of 130 times in 14 years, an impressive performance in value added. The wage share in power industry has been not only low but fluctuating over the period. It reached a peak of .106 in 1984-85 and a low of 0.046 in 1985-86 because of a jump in value added from Rs.13585 lakhs to Rs. 36230 lakhs. But, the tendency has been to stagnate around 0.063. Such a low wage share is indicative of a very high capital intensity in the industry. Since the income distribution remained nearly unaffected, it therefore, means that technical progress in power industry has been neutral, with given capital-labour ratio.

National Hydro-Electric Power Corporation Ltd (NHPCL) employed 2.227 thousand employees in 1982-83, i.e., 20 percent of the total employment in power sector in public enterprises. The proportion increased to 24.5 percent as the employment in NHPCL reached a level of 11.992 thousand in 1995-96. The employment increased at the rate of 16.99 percent, which is faster than the increase in industry's. However, all other annual growth rates in NHPCL are lower than those of the industry (**Table** 5.II.2). The money wages and salaries increased at a rate of 27.56 percent on the one hand and value added at current prices at the rate of 23.40 percent on the other. Since the rate of increase in price deflators during the period 1982-83 to 1995-96 is 8.66 percent and 6.88 percent respectively, therefore, the

Table 5.II. 1

**Estimates of Wage Trends: Power Industry**

| *Variable* / Year | *Employment* ('000) | *Wages and Salaries* (Rs. Lakhs) | *Value Added* (Rs lakhs) | *Consumer Price Index* | *Real Wages per worker* ('00,00) | *Wages Share in Value added (Coeff.)* |
|---|---|---|---|---|---|---|
| 1982-83 | 11.134 | 243 | 4066 | 261 | 0.0836 | 0.059 |
| 1983-84 | 13.536 | 725 | 11053 | 294 | 0.1821 | 0.065 |
| 1984-85 | 17.739 | 1445 | 13585 | 313 | 0.2602 | 0.106 |
| 1985-86 | 20.142 | 1692 | 36230 | 333 | 0.2522 | 0.046 |
| 1986-87 | 22.673 | 2129 | 44366 | 362 | 0.2593 | 0.047 |
| 1987-88 | 33.321 | 3853 | 64510 | 396 | 0.2920 | 0.059 |
| 1988-89 | 36.066 | 6648 | 100337 | 423 | 0.4357 | 0.066 |
| 1989-90 | 40.331 | 8564 | 134552 | 458 | 0.4636 | 0.063 |
| 1990-91 | 39.330 | 11070 | 180719 | 512 | 0.5497 | 0.061 |
| 1991-92 | 45.658 | 14539 | 266033 | 580 | 0.5490 | 0.054 |
| 1992-93 | 47.533 | 16323 | 254041 | 636 | 0.5399 | 0.064 |
| 1993-94 | 44.975 | 20555 | 321344 | 684 | 0.6681 | 0.063 |
| 1994-95 | 45.706 | 29363 | 383486 | 754 | 0.8521 | 0.076 |
| 1995-96 | 48.868 | 34407 | 529312 | 831 | 0.8472 | 0.065 |
| Growth rate % | 13.43 | 37.44 | 38.07 (6.88) | 8.66 | 4.86 | |

*Notes* :
1. Data computed and compiled from various issues of Public Enterprises Survey, Chandok and RBI Bulletins.
2. Consumer Price Index refers to consumer price index for industrial workers with 1970-71=100.
3. Growth rates are annual exponential growth rates.
4. Figure in brackets in value added column indicates the growth rate of price of output.

Table 5.II. 2

**Estimates of Wage Trends: National Hydro-Electric Power Corp. Ltd.**

| *Variable* / *Year* | *Employment* *('000)* | *Wages and Salaries* *(Rs. Lakhs)* | *Value Added* *(Rs lakhs)* | *Consumer Price Index* | *Real Wages per worker* *('00,00)* | *Wages Share in Value added (Coeff.)* |
|---|---|---|---|---|---|---|
| 1982-83 | 2.227 | 73 | 2194 | 261 | 0.1255 | 0.033 |
| 1983-84 | 2.394 | 218 | 2667 | 294 | 0.3097 | 0.081 |
| 1984-85 | 3.115 | 295 | 3471 | 313 | 0.3025 | 0.084 |
| 1985-86 | 3.458 | 300 | 4621 | 333 | 0.2605 | 0.064 |
| 1986-87 | 4.643 | 367 | 5059 | 362 | 0.2183 | 0.072 |
| 1987-88 | 4.755 | 485 | 6600 | 396 | 0.2575 | 0.073 |
| 1988-89 | 5.125 | 1205 | 16248 | 423 | 0.5558 | 0.074 |
| 1989-90 | 8.428 | 1261 | 17089 | 458 | 0.3266 | 0.073 |
| 1990-91 | 5.841 | 1297 | 18505 | 512 | 0.4336 | 0.070 |
| 1991-92 | 13.003 | 2226 | 20275 | 580 | 0.2951 | 0.109 |
| 1992-93 | 12.938 | 1349 | 17717 | 636 | 0.1639 | 0.076 |
| 1993-94 | 12.437 | 1991 | 23469 | 684 | 0.2340 | 0.084 |
| 1994-95 | 12.138 | 3573 | 53566 | 754 | 0.3900 | 0.067 |
| 1995-96 | 11.992 | 3737 | 50781 | 831 | 0.3740 | 0.073 |
| Growth rate % | 16.99 | 27.56 | 23.40 (6.88) | 8.66 | 0.46 | |

*Notes* : 1. Data computed and compiled from various issues of Public Enterprises Survey, Chandok and RBI Bulletins.

2. Consumer Price Index refers to consumer price index for industrial workers with 1970-71=100.
3. Growth rates are annual exponential growth rates.
4. Figure in brackets in value added column indicates the growth rate of price of output.

Table 5.II. 3

**Estimates of Wage Trends: National Thermal Power Corp.**

| *Variable* | *Employment* | *Wages and Salaries* | *Value Added* | *Consumer Price Index* | *Real Wages per worker* | *Wages Share in Value added (Coeff.)* |
|---|---|---|---|---|---|---|
| *Year* | *('000)* | *(Rs. Lakhs)* | *(Rs lakhs)* | | *('00,00)* | |
| 1984-85 | 12.746 | 1125 | 9642 | 313 | 0.2819 | 0.116 |
| 1985-86 | 14.610 | 1351 | 31809 | 333 | 0.2776 | 0.042 |
| 1986-87 | 16.095 | 1749 | 39307 | 362 | 0.3001 | 0.044 |
| 1987-88 | 17.972 | 2605 | 51756 | 396 | 0.3660 | 0.050 |
| 1988-89 | 19.983 | 3842 | 70598 | 423 | 0.4545 | 0.054 |
| 1989-90 | 21.156 | 5314 | 109304 | 458 | 0.5484 | 0.048 |
| 1990-91 | 22.052 | 7345 | 137465 | 512 | 0.6505 | 0.053 |
| 1991-92 | 21.498 | 8976 | 214859 | 580 | 0.7198 | 0.041 |
| 1992-93 | 21.797 | 10982 | 219357 | 636 | 0.7921 | 0.050 |
| 1993-94 | 19.335 | 14529 | 289555 | 684 | 1.0985 | 0.050 |
| 1994-95 | 19.223 | 20755 | 310054 | 754 | 1.4319 | 0.067 |
| 1995-96 | 22.055 | 24512 | 418367 | 831 | 1.3374 | 0.058 |
| Growth rate % | 5.25 | 29.87 | 33.93 (5.69) | 8.95 | 8.48 | |

*Notes* : 1. Data computed and compiled from various issues of Public Enterprises Survey, Chandok and RBI Bulletins.
2. Consumer Price Index refers to consumer price index for industrial workers with 1970-71=100.
3. Growth rates are annual exponential growth rates.
4. Figure in brackets in value added column indicates the growth rate of price of output.

respective rates for real wages and salaries and value added are 18.90 percent and 16.52 percent. The real wages per worker in the firm rose at a very modest rate of only 0.46 percent, though the money wages per worker increased at a rate of 9.10 percent. The coefficient of wage share in value added has fluctuated over the years but there is an increase in its value. The coefficient increased from 0.033 in 1982-83 to 0.074 in 1995-96, an increase of about two and a half times. However, if the first year 1982-83 is excluded, then the coefficient is virtually stagnant. The low and stable value of the coefficient indicates not only the high capital intensity of the firm but also its elasticity of substitution to be close to unity.

**Table** 5.II.3 provides information about NTPC for only twelve years. During this period it employed 12.746 thousand employees in 1984-85 and 22.055 thousand employees in 1995-96. The share in the total employment of the industry being 71.85 percent and 45.02 percent. Thus, the share of NTPC in total employment of the industry has fallen. This, is also being reflected in the slow annual growth rate of employment in NTPC (5.25 percent) as compared to the industry (13.43 percent). Money wages and salaries in NTPC increased from Rs. 1125 lakhs to Rs. 24512 lakhs at an annual growth rate of almost 30 percent, with growth in money wage rate per worker being 17.43 percent. The money wages per worker in the two years are : Rs. 8826 in 1984-85 and Rs. 111,140 in 1995-96 with corresponding real wages per worker being only Rs. 2819 and Rs. 13,374. Real Wages increased at an annual growth rate of 8.48 percent. Gross value added at current prices by NTPC over the years 1984-85 to 1995-96, increased by nearly forty three times at a rate of 34 percent per annum with the growth rate in real gross value added to be 28.24 percent. The wage share in NTPC is comparatively lower, 0.050 in 1993-94 and 0.0585 in 1995-96, than in the industry (0.065). The wage share has been fluctuating around the value 0.050, the low value being indicative of comparative high capital-intensity.

Thus the analysis of the Power industry depicts that real wages per workers did not rise in any significant way in NHPCL and remained very low at close to 44 percent of the industry's real wages per worker. The real wages per worker in NTPC rose at quite a moderate rate of 8.48 percent which was not only higher than the industry's growth rate but also higher than the rise in national per capita income. The real wages per worker in NTPC are about 1.6 times higher than the industry and 4.7 times higher than the fellow firm NHPCL. Thus, this shows the wide disparity existing within the industry in real wages per worker. But a close look at the Power industry's real wages makes it obvious that the real wages in the industry and the two firms NHPCL and NTPC have remained very low throughout the period of study, as compared to the aggregate of industries. Though a detailed analysis of the relationship of real wages with some of the possible explanatory variables will be attempted in a subsequent chapter, but at the moment it is pertinent to point out that the real wages in the Power industry must have increased at a fast pace because, (a) Power industry in general and NTPC in particular have been making huge financial profits, (b) the industry must have strived hard to come at par with other industries in regard to the real wages per worker. **Table** 5.II.3 shows that whereas NTPC has succeeded in this goal, its real wages per worker were higher in 1995-96 than the aggregate of industries, NHPCL could not attain that objective.

### *III. Petroleum-Group*

It is one of the key groups amongst the public enterprises in India, as it is one of the highest contributers to the value added and has the most profitable firms in the public enterprises. The employment in petroleum industry was 44.687 thousand in 1974-75, nearly 8.34 percent of the total employment in the eight aggregate industries which increased to about 124 thousand in 1993-94, i.e., 13.76 percent of the aggregate employment but fell to 121.75 thousand in 1995-96; i.e. 14.4%. The growth in employment is, thus, only 5.91 percent. Money wages and salaries though, increased at a rate of 14 percent the annual growth rate of real wages and salaries is only 5.93 percent, thus, leaving the real wages per worker to grow at a negligible rate of 0.027 percent. Real wages per worker, fluctuated around the level of Rs 9800 till 1993-94 and increased to Rs 17415 in 1995-96. While money wages and salaries increased by 28.43 times, the money value added increased by 69.33 times over the same period. Gross value added at current prices was Rs 2915 lakhs in 1974-75 and it increased to Rs 2021307 lakhs in 1995-96, with an annual growth rate being 21.73 percent. Wage share in the Petroleum industry has been continuously falling from 1974-75 to 1990-91 when it increased slightly from 0.047 to .087. The falling wage share in Petroleum industry is a pointer towards increasing capital- labour ratio in the industry and the existence of labour saving technical progress.

Indian Oil Corporation Ltd (IOC LTD) employed about 14.5 thousand employees in 1974-75 and 33.28 thousand in 1995-96 (**Table** 5.III.2). The relative proportions in the total employment of the industry are 32.49 percent and 27.4 percent respectively. The employment has been almost continuously increasing at an annual growth rate of 4.77 percent, slightly lower than that of the industry as a whole. The money wages and salaries of the firm increased from Rs. 2226 lakhs to Rs. 72588 lakhs during the same period with an annual growth rate of 15.02 percent. But if we exclude the impact of increase in consumer price index, the growth rate of the deflated wages and salaries is 7.02 percent, more than the industry's rate. But not only the total wages and salaries rose faster in IOC Ltd even the real wages per worker increased at the rate of 2.66 percent which is faster than the industry's rate. The real wage rate per worker in IOC Ltd which was only Rs. 9016 in 1974-75, became Rs. 26,241 in 1995-96 as compared to Rs. 17,415 for the industry. On the other hand growth in value added has been slow, only 14.66 percent in IOC Ltd as compared to 21.73 percent in the industry. The rise in wages and salaries and value added is practically smooth. The Coefficient of wage share in value added for IOC Ltd has been fluctuating from a peak of .180 in 1981-82, when real wages per worker were low, to a bottom of .103 in 1987-88 but reached a proportion of 0.181 in 1995-96, almost double of 0.087 in the industry. Thus, while on the one hand the annual growth rates of employment and value added have been lower for IOC Ltd, on the other hand the rates of wages and salaries, real wages per worker and the coefficient of wage share have been higher for IOC Ltd as compared to the Petroleum industry, though the wage share within IOC Ltd has remained nearly constant.

**Table** 5.III.3 provides the time trend of employment, real wages per worker, etc. for ONGC for the years 1977-78 to 1995-96. The employment level in ONGC is higher than that of IOC Ltd. It employed 44548 employees in the firm during 1995-96 at an annual growth rate of 4.50 percent, a rate close to that of IOC Ltd. However, wages and salaries, and value added at current prices as well as at constant prices increased faster than IOC Ltd and the aggregate Petroleum industry, the rates being 13.91 percent for deflated wages and salaries and 18.49 percent for deflated value added in ONGC as compared to 7.02 percent and 9.54 percent respectively for IOC Ltd and 5.93 percent and 16.61 percent for the industry as a whole. Real wages per worker increased at a very modest rate of 1.31 percent in ONGC, which is higher than the industry's rate of 0.027 percent, and lower than the IOC's rate of 2.66 percent. However the absolute level of real wages as presented in the **Table** 5.III.3 for ONGC is very low as compared to the average emoluments data presented in the survey. Real wages per worker are defined in the study as deflated value of wages and salaries divided by employment. The difference in the two values is very large and irreconcilable. It, thus, puts a question mark regarding the reliability of results. However, if we assume that bias is uniform throughout the series then the dependability of the growth rates, at least, increases. The coefficient of wage share in value added remained the same for both initial as well as year 1993-94 of the study, i.e., being equal to 0.015. But it reached a low of 0.003 in 1982-83 and 1983-84 and attained the peak of 0.024 in 1995-96. Thus, the coefficient has been fluctuating between these two limits. The low value of the coefficient and the narrow range within which it has fluctuated depicts high capital intensity of the firm and low elasticity of substitution as real wages per worker and wage share in value added have generally moved in the same direction.

The trends of wages in Petroleum industry thus point to the fact that while the annual growth rate of real wages per worker in the industry remained almost constant, the growth rate is 2.66 percent and 1.31 percent in IOC Ltd and ONGC respectively. The growth of real wages per worker in IOCL and ONGC is not much higher than those of the national per capita income, rather

Table 5.III. 1

**Estimates of Wage Trends: Petroleum Industry**

| *Variable* / *Year* | *Employment* ('000) | *Wages and Salaries* (Rs. Lakhs) | *Value Added* (Rs lakhs) | *Consumer Price Index* | *Real Wages per worker* ('00,00) | *Wages Share in Value added (Coeff.)* |
|---|---|---|---|---|---|---|
| 1974-75 | 44.687 | 6202 | 29151 | 170 | 0.8163 | 0.212 |
| 1975-76 | 47.427 | 7114 | 33522 | 170 | 0.8823 | 0.212 |
| 1976-77 | 53.104 | 7926 | 42972 | 162 | 0.9213 | 0.184 |
| 1977-78 | 55.290 | 9493 | 74087 | 174 | 0.9867 | 0.128 |
| 1978-79 | 56.666 | 10090 | 77984 | 178 | 1.0003 | 0.129 |
| 1979-80 | 60.016 | 11256 | 87102 | 194 | 0.9667 | 0.129 |
| 1980-81 | 63.706 | 13454 | 100901 | 216 | 0.9777 | 0.133 |
| 1981-82 | 78.023 | 12578 | 206584 | 242 | 0.6661 | 0.060 |
| 1982-83 | 84.278 | 15085 | 312730 | 261 | 0.6857 | 0.048 |
| 1983-84 | 92.544 | 17400 | 394945 | 294 | 0.6395 | 0.044 |
| 1984-85 | 101.039 | 20893 | 460018 | 313 | 0.6606 | 0.045 |
| 1985-86 | 106.595 | 23877 | 508517 | 333 | 0.6726 | 0.046 |
| 1986-87 | 108.388 | 28562 | 606201 | 362 | 0.7279 | 0.047 |
| 1987-88 | 112.255 | 33026 | 774117 | 396 | 0.7429 | 0.042 |

| | | | | | | |
|---|---|---|---|---|---|---|
| 1988-89 | 114.690 | 40698 | 870608 | 423 | 0.8388 | 0.046 |
| 1989-90 | 117.935 | 47722 | 985123 | 458 | 0.8835 | 0.048 |
| 1990-91 | 121.057 | 57140 | 1192050 | 512 | 0.9218 | 0.047 |
| 1991-92 | 122.914 | 66254 | 1101592 | 580 | 0.9293 | 0.060 |
| 1992-93 | 123.280 | 75889 | 1260174 | 636 | 0.9678 | 0.060 |
| 1993-94 | 123.945 | 83308 | 1350773 | 684 | 0.9826 | 0.061 |
| 1994-95 | 122.595 | 112962 | 1590367 | 754 | 1.2220 | 0.071 |
| 1995-96 | 121.752 | 176205 | 2021307 | 831 | 1.7415 | 0.087 |
| Growth rate % | 5.91 | 13.93 | 21.73 (5.12) | 8.00 | 0.027 | |

*Notes* : 1. Data computed and compiled from various issues of Public Enterprises Survey, Chandok and RBI Bulletins.

2. Consumer Price Index refers to consumer price index for industrial workers with 1970-71=100.

3. Growth rates are annual exponential growth rates.

4. Figure in brackets in value added column indicates the growth rate of price of output.

Table 5.III. 2

**Estimates of Wage Trends: Indian Oil Corp. Ltd.**

| *Variable* | *Employment* | *Wages and Salaries* | *Value Added* | *Consumer Price Index* | *Real Wages per worker* | *Wages Share in Value* |
|---|---|---|---|---|---|---|
| *Year* | *('000)* | *(Rs. Lakhs)* | *(Rs lakhs)* | | *('00,00)* | *added (Coeff.)* |
| 1974-75 | 14.523 | 2226 | 22425 | 170 | 0.9016 | 0.099 |
| 1975-76 | 15.414 | 2554 | 22920 | 170 | 0.9746 | 0.111 |
| 1976-77 | 17.258 | 2845 | 29010 | 162 | 1.0175 | 0.098 |
| 1977-78 | 17.969 | 3407 | 29591 | 174 | 1.0896 | 0.115 |
| 1978-79 | 18.592 | 3547 | 28423 | 178 | 1.0718 | 0.124 |
| 1979-80 | 19.524 | 4177 | 32970 | 194 | 1.1027 | 0.126 |
| 1980-81 | 20.604 | 4804 | 38244 | 216 | 1.0794 | 0.125 |
| 1981-82 | 25.498 | 6180 | 34166 | 242 | 1.0015 | 0.180 |
| 1982-83 | 27.325 | 8296 | 47447 | 261 | 1.1632 | 0.174 |
| 1983-84 | 29.021 | 9778 | 58696 | 294 | 1.1460 | 0.166 |
| 1984-85 | 30.423 | 11010 | 61607 | 313 | 1.1562 | 0.178 |
| 1985-86 | 31.413 | 12580 | 73005 | 333 | 1.2026 | 0.172 |
| 1986-87 | 32.004 | 14113 | 116813 | 362 | 1.2181 | 0.120 |
| 1987-88 | 32.930 | 15118 | 146329 | 396 | 1.1593 | 0.103 |

| | | | | | | |
|---|---|---|---|---|---|---|
| 1988-89 | 33.100 | 18500 | 150782 | 423 | 1.3213 | 0.122 |
| 1989-90 | 33.365 | 21066 | 187001 | 458 | 1.3785 | 0.112 |
| 1990-91 | 33.303 | 24271 | 197884 | 512 | 1.4234 | 0.122 |
| 1991-92 | 33.480 | 27039 | 215658 | 580 | 1.3924 | 0.125 |
| 1992-93 | 33.829 | 31320 | 248952 | 636 | 1.4557 | 0.125 |
| 1993-94 | 34.035 | 33526 | 288898 | 684 | 1.4401 | 0.116 |
| 1994-95 | 33.589 | 41938 | 344795 | 754 | 1.6559 | 0.122 |
| 1995-96 | 33.287 | 72588 | 401371 | 831 | 2.6241 | 0.181 |
| Growth rate % | 4.77 | 15.02 | 14.66 (5.12) | 8.00 | 2.66 | |

*Notes* : 1. Data computed and compiled from various issues of Public Enterprises Survey, Chandok and RBI Bulletins.

2. Consumer Price Index refers to consumer price index for industrial workers with 1970-71=100.

3. Growth rates are annual exponential growth rates.

4. Figure in brackets in value added column indicates the growth rate of price of output.

Table 5.III. 3

**Estimates of Wage Trends: Oil and Natural Gas Commission**

| *Variable* / *Year* | *Employment* *('000)* | *Wages and Salaries* *(Rs. Lakhs)* | *Value Added* *(Rs lakhs)* | *Consumer Price Index* | *Real Wages per worker* *('00,00)* | *Wages Share in Value added (Coeff.)* |
|---|---|---|---|---|---|---|
| 1977-78 | 26.318 | 323 | 20394 | 174 | 0.0705 | 0.015 |
| 1978-79 | 25.326 | 342 | 27287 | 178 | 0.0758 | 0.012 |
| 1979-80 | 26.374 | 381 | 31752 | 194 | 0.0744 | 0.011 |
| 1980-81 | 28.138 | 473 | 33596 | 216 | 0.0778 | 0.014 |
| 1981-82 | 30.835 | 512 | 108029 | 242 | 0.0686 | 0.004 |
| 1982-83 | 33.020 | 588 | 194734 | 261 | 0.0682 | 0.003 |
| 1983-84 | 37.016 | 927 | 253743 | 294 | 0.0851 | 0.003 |
| 1984-85 | 41.591 | 1432 | 305799 | 313 | 0.1100 | 0.004 |
| 1985-86 | 43.940 | 1514 | 313963 | 333 | 0.1034 | 0.004 |
| 1986-87 | 43.349 | 1956 | 343920 | 362 | 0.1246 | 0.005 |
| 1987-88 | 44.000 | 2258 | 443545 | 396 | 0.1295 | 0.005 |
| 1988-89 | 45.420 | 2657 | 507964 | 423 | 0.1382 | 0.005 |
| 1989-90 | 46.956 | 3853 | 544175 | 458 | 0.1791 | 0.007 |
| 1990-91 | 48.198 | 4610 | 705676 | 512 | 0.1868 | 0.006 |

| | | | | | | |
|---|---|---|---|---|---|---|
| 1991-92 | 48.301 | 6699 | 559533 | 580 | 0.2391 | 0.011 |
| 1992-93 | 47.501 | 8124 | 597705 | 636 | 0.2689 | 0.013 |
| 1993-94 | 46.847 | 9229 | 599326 | 684 | 0.2880 | 0.015 |
| 1994-95 | 45.736 | 16234 | 705445 | 754 | 0.4707 | 0.023 |
| 1995-96 | 44.548 | 20553 | 850442 | 831 | 0.5551 | 0.024 |
| Growth rate % | 4.50 | 22.60 | 18.49 (3.96) | 8.69 | 1.31 | |

*Notes* : 1. Data computed and compiled from various issues of Public Enterprises Survey, Chandok and RBI Bulletins.

2. Consumer Price Index refers to consumer price index for industrial workers with 1970-71=100.

3. Growth rates are annual exponential growth rates.

4. Figure in brackets in value added column indicates the growth rate of price of output.

they are low in ONGC. Thus the workers have been able to get only the compensation against rise in consumer price index and full benefit of the rise in national per capita income has not been made available to them. However, the slow growth rate in real wages per worker in the industry and the firms, IOCL and ONGC, is surprising in view of the fact that Petroleum industry is the highest profit making industry in the public enterprises and IOCL and ONGC are respectively the number one and three among the most profitable firms under public enterprises. It implies that profit is not the sole criterion to determine the real wage rate per worker in the industry. Among the possible explanations for the slow rise in the real wage rate could be the high level of initial wage rate in the industry and IOCL; higher than the aggregate of industries. However, low real wages per worker in ONGC through out the period is irreconcilable.

*IV. Fertilizers, Chemicals and Pharmaceuticals - Group*

The group consists of the aggregate industry and its two firms National Fertilizers Ltd and Indian Petrochemicals Corporation Limited. **Tables** 5.IV.1, 5.IV.2 and 5.IV.3 provide information about the behaviour of the group in terms of employment, value added, wages and salaries and the real wage rate per worker.

**Table** 5.IV.1 indicates that the Fertilizers industry engaged 56.8 thousand employees in 1974-75, i.e., 10.6 percent of the aggregate employment in all the eight groups. However, this proportion changed to 9.10 percent in 1995-96 when the industry employed 78,701 employees. The employment increased continuously till 1986-87 when it fell for a year before increasing again till 1990-91. Since 1990-91 employment has been coming down from 87.88 thousand to nearly 78.7 thousand in 1995-96 because of the structural reforms programme and a change in policy towards public-sector enterprises. Wages and salaries at current prices increased rapidly from Rs. 4520 lakhs in 1974-75 to Rs. 99351 lakhs in the final year, an increase of over twenty two times, the rate of annual growth being 14.3 percent. But the real wages and salaries increased by 6.34 percent. On the other hand money wages per worker increased from Rs. 7956 to Rs. 126238, an increase of more than fifteen times but the deflated money wages, i.e., real wages increased from Rs. 4680 to Rs. 15191, i.e., about thrice the rate of growth of real wages per worker, it being 3.17 percent per annum. The rate is higher than the rate of growth of national per capita income over the period. Thus, the workers in the industry have been able to improve their relative economic status. Value added in the industry increased faster, at a rate of 16.80 percent, than the wages and salaries. As a result of this the wage share in value added declined over the period, the decline being faster in the beginning. The increasing real wages per worker along with falling wage share in value added demonstrates that capital intensity has increased in the industry and labour-saving technical progress has been made.

National Fertilizers Ltd's trends start from 1979-80 and are summarized in **Table** 5.IV.2. The basic trend is same as that of the industry. Employment in the firm increased marginally by 1.56 percent from 5725 in 1979-80 to 6805 in 1995-96 but decreased very insignificantly over the last five years. Money wages and salaries increased at a rate of 17 percent, slightly higher than that of the industry, as a result of which real wages per worker also increased faster at the rate of 6.22 percent as compared to 3.17 percent for the industry as a whole. The annual growth rate of real value added is virtually the same, 10.80 percent as that of the industry (10.60 percent). However, the wage share in value added for NFL, has been low, almost one-half, throughout the period. The wage share has been fluctuating between a low of 0.075 in 1984-85 to a high level of 0.187 in 1995-96. Therefore, while wages and salaries and real wages per worker increased faster in the firm, the employment growth rate and the wage share in value added are lower in the firm and higher in the industry. It tantamounts to the use of more labour saving technical progress and higher capital intensity in the firm as compared to the industry.

**Table** 5.IV.3 depicts the trends for Indian Petro-Chemicals Corporation Limited (IPCL). The employment in IPCL increased at a fast pace of 6.02 percent resulting in an increase in its share in the employment of the industry. The share increased from 7.42 percent to 15.4 percent. Thus, the relative size and importance of the firm grew within the industry. The number

Table 5.IV. 1

**Estimates of Wage Trends: Fertilizers, Chemicals and Pharmaceuticals Industry**

| *Variable* / *Year* | *Employment* *('000)* | *Wages and Salaries* *(Rs. Lakhs)* | *Value Added* *(Rs lakhs)* | *Consumer Price Index* | *Real Wages per worker ('00,00)* | *Wages Share in Value added (Coeff.)* |
|---|---|---|---|---|---|---|
| 1974-75 | 56.808 | 4520 | 13308 | 170 | 0.4680 | 0.339 |
| 1975-76 | 56.520 | 5189 | 13951 | 170 | 0.5400 | 0.371 |
| 1976-77 | 60.302 | 6157 | 17214 | 162 | 0.6302 | 0.357 |
| 1977-78 | 62.494 | 7165 | 19329 | 174 | 0.6589 | 0.370 |
| 1978-79 | 62.060 | 7354 | 25856 | 178 | 0.6657 | 0.284 |
| 1979-80 | 66.654 | 8590 | 36347 | 194 | 0.6643 | 0.236 |
| 1980-81 | 69.879 | 10446 | 42190 | 216 | 0.6920 | 0.247 |
| 1981-82 | 77.699 | 13485 | 59010 | 242 | 0.7171 | 0.228 |
| 1982-83 | 79.144 | 15278 | 73835 | 261 | 0.7396 | 0.206 |
| 1983-84 | 81.149 | 17720 | 85108 | 294 | 0.7427 | 0.208 |
| 1984-85 | 84.170 | 20516 | 99886 | 313 | 0.7787 | 0.205 |
| 1985-86 | 85.366 | 23673 | 109503 | 333 | 0.8327 | 0.216 |
| 1986-87 | 86.846 | 26606 | 127962 | 362 | 0.8462 | 0.207 |
| 1987-88 | 83.772 | 28023 | 138088 | 396 | 0.8447 | 0.202 |

| | | | | | | |
|---|---|---|---|---|---|---|
| 1988-89 | 83.596 | 32524 | 168563 | 423 | 0.9197 | 0.192 |
| 1989-90 | 85.004 | 38858 | 173464 | 458 | 0.9981 | 0.224 |
| 1990-91 | 87.889 | 48820 | 193002 | 512 | 1.0849 | 0.252 |
| 1991-92 | 86.683 | 56390 | 250009 | 580 | 1.1216 | 0.225 |
| 1992-93 | 83.671 | 58605 | 261132 | 636 | 1.1012 | 0.224 |
| 1993-94 | 82.008 | 61094 | 246043 | 684 | 1.0891 | 0.248 |
| 1994-95 | 78.411 | 73716 | 362472 | 754 | 1.2468 | 0.203 |
| 1995-96 | 78.701 | 99351 | 406330 | 831 | 1.5191 | 0.244 |
| Growth rate % | 2.33 | 14.34 | 16.80 (6.20) | 8.00 | 3.17 | |

*Notes* : 1. Data computed and compiled from various issues of Public Enterprises Survey, Chandok and RBI Bulletins.

2. Consumer Price Index refers to consumer price index for industrial workers with 1970-71=100.

3. Growth rates are annual exponential growth rates.

4. Figure in brackets in value added column indicates the growth rate of price of output.

Table 5.IV. 2

**Estimates of Wage Trends: National Fertilizers Ltd.**

| *Variable* / *Year* | *Employment* (*'000*) | *Wages and Salaries* (*Rs. Lakhs*) | *Value Added* (*Rs lakhs*) | *Consumer Price Index* | *Real Wages per worker* (*'00,00*) | *Wages Share in Value added (Coeff.)* |
|---|---|---|---|---|---|---|
| 1979-80 | 5.725 | 548 | 6316 | 194 | 0.4934 | 0.086 |
| 1980-81 | 5.653 | 784 | 6842 | 216 | 0.6420 | 0.114 |
| 1981-82 | 5.864 | 1019 | 7393 | 242 | 0.7180 | 0.137 |
| 1982-83 | 5.888 | 1171 | 8448 | 261 | 0.7619 | 0.138 |
| 1983-84 | 6.055 | 1368 | 16092 | 294 | 0.7684 | 0.085 |
| 1984-85 | 6.046 | 1392 | 18415 | 313 | 0.7355 | 0.075 |
| 1985-86 | 6.101 | 1578 | 18136 | 333 | 0.7767 | 0.087 |
| 1986-87 | 6.285 | 1913 | 19068 | 362 | 0.8408 | 0.100 |
| 1987-88 | 6.590 | 2260 | 20271 | 396 | 0.8660 | 0.111 |
| 1988-89 | 6.743 | 3100 | 28750 | 423 | 1.0868 | 0.107 |
| 1989-90 | 6.792 | 4359 | 30768 | 458 | 1.4012 | 0.141 |
| 1990-91 | 6.808 | 4747 | 37715 | 512 | 1.3618 | 0.125 |
| 1991-92 | 6.864 | 5440 | 42989 | 580 | 1.3664 | 0.126 |
| 1992-93 | 6.854 | 5315 | 46160 | 636 | 1.2192 | 0.115 |

| | | | | | | |
|---|---|---|---|---|---|---|
| 1993-94 | 6.820 | 6066 | 50209 | 684 | 1.3003 | 0.120 |
| 1994-95 | 6.803 | 8881 | 57076 | 754 | 1.7314 | 0.155 |
| 1995-96 | 6.805 | 9724 | 51909 | 831 | 1.7195 | 0.187 |
| Growth rate % | 1.56 | 17.03 | 15.60 (4.80) | 8.73 | 6.22 | |

*Notes* : 1. Data computed and compiled from various issues of Public Enterprises Survey, Chandok and RBI Bulletins.

2. Consumer Price Index refers to consumer price index for industrial workers with 1970-71=100.

3. Growth rates are annual exponential growth rates.

4. Figure in brackets in value added column indicates the growth rate of price of output.

Table 5.IV. 3.

**Estimates of Wage Trends: Indian Petro Chemical Corp. Ltd.**

| *Variable* / *Year* | *Employment* *('000)* | *Wages and Salaries* *(Rs. Lakhs)* | *Value Added* *(Rs lakhs)* | *Consumer Price Index* | *Real Wages per worker* *('00,00)* | *Wages Share in Value added (Coeff.)* |
|---|---|---|---|---|---|---|
| 1974-75 | 4.220 | 416 | 1526 | 170 | 0.5798 | 0.272 |
| 1975-76 | 4.199 | 477 | 2243 | 170 | 0.6682 | 0.212 |
| 1976-77 | 4.480 | 566 | 2368 | 162 | 0.7798 | 0.239 |
| 1977-78 | 4.643 | 659 | 1845 | 174 | 0.8157 | 0.357 |
| 1978-79 | 4.577 | 649 | 3503 | 178 | 0.7966 | 0.185 |
| 1979-80 | 4.986 | 855 | 6673 | 194 | 0.8839 | 0.128 |
| 1980-81 | 5.218 | 1054 | 10601 | 216 | 0.9351 | 0.099 |
| 1981-82 | 5.350 | 1291 | 13311 | 242 | 0.9971 | 0.096 |
| 1982-83 | 5.745 | 1562 | 14372 | 261 | 1.0417 | 0.108 |
| 1983-84 | 6.422 | 2016 | 13768 | 294 | 1.0677 | 0.146 |
| 1984-85 | 6.831 | 2692 | 18195 | 313 | 1.2590 | 0.147 |
| 1985-86 | 7.236 | 3176 | 21457 | 333 | 1.3180 | 0.148 |
| 1986-87 | 7.536 | 3387 | 21901 | 362 | 1.2415 | 0.154 |
| 1987-88 | 8.140 | 3753 | 24967 | 396 | 1.1642 | 0.150 |

| | | | | | | |
|---|---|---|---|---|---|---|
| 1988-89 | 8.430 | 4180 | 31634 | 423 | 1.1722 | 0.132 |
| 1989-90 | 10.322 | 5195 | 36986 | 458 | 1.0988 | 0.140 |
| 1990-91 | 10.037 | 6066 | 46827 | 512 | 1.1803 | 0.129 |
| 1991-92 | 11.189 | 7747 | 67317 | 580 | 1.1937 | 0.115 |
| 1992-93 | 11.742 | 10638 | 75563 | 636 | 1.4244 | 0.140 |
| 1993-94 | 11.858 | 10894 | 68734 | 684 | 1.3431 | 0.158 |
| 1994-95 | 11.249 | 13594 | 138040 | 754 | 1.6027 | 0.098 |
| 1995-96 | 12.101 | 29747 | 191713 | 831 | 2.9580 | 1.155 |
| Growth rate % | 6.02 | 17.75 | 20.62 (8.96) | 8.00 | 3.61 | |

*Notes* : 1. Data computed and compiled from various issues of Public Enterprises Survey, Chandok and RBI Bulletins.

2. Consumer Price Index refers to consumer price index for industrial workers with 1970-71=100.
3. Growth rates are annual exponential growth rates.
4. Figure in brackets in value added column indicates the growth rate of price of output.

of employees increased from 4220 in 1974-75 to 12101 in 1995-96. Both money as well as real wages and salaries and wages per worker increased at a faster rate because of the large size of the firm. While money wages and salaries increased at the rate of 9.75 percent, the increase in real wages per worker being only 3.61 percent, a rate closer to the industry's rate of growth (3.17 percent). Real wages in IPCL increased from Rs. 5798 to Rs. 29,580 and are also higher in absolute values as compared to both the industry and the firm NFL. But the coefficient of wage share in value added for IPCL has been lower throughout the period than that of the industry. The share has declined from 0.272 in the beginning of the period to 0.155 in 1995-96. Thus, the rising real wages per worker and falling wage share once again is an evidence of increasing capital intensity.

It follows from this that there has been an increase in real wages per worker and a decline in the wage share for both the industry and the two firms belonging to the group of Fertilizers, Chemicals and Pharmaceuticals. Nevertheless, the rates of growth in real wages per workers are different - it is highest for NFL (6.22 percent) and practically same for IPCL (3.61 percent) and the industry. The industry's real growth rate of real wages per worker (3.17 percent) is higher than the growth of national per capita income. The higher growth in the real wages for workers in both the industry and NFL appears to have taken place because of their urge to raise the initial low level of real wages per worker. Though the Fertilizer industry is not doing financially well in recent years, but the positive indices of all productivity measures suggest that productivity might have been a contributory factor to increase in the real wage rate per worker in the industry.

*V. Heavy Engineering-Group*

While **Table** 5.V.1 belongs to the industry, **Tables** 5.V.2 and 5.V.3 correspond to the two firms Bharat Heavy Electricals Ltd and Bharat Heavy Plate and Vessels Ltd respectively. Heavy engineering industry is one of the largest industries in public enterprises employing 12.75 percent of the total employment in the eight aggregate industries during 1995-96. However, the proportion was higher at 18.99 percent in 1974-75. The employment in Heavy Engineering industry increased continuously till 1983-84 and remained stable for three years before it started decreasing from 1985-86, the decrease being quite substantial during the last six years. The period of change coincides with the changes in the Industrial policy of India, first during 1985 and then in 1990, which basically emphasized upon liberal licensing and imports, dereservation of industries in the public sector, disinvestment of equity of public sector undertakings and other related reforms. As a result of the fall in employment in later years, the annual growth rate of employment is almost negligible (only 0.59 percent). Yet, on the other hand money wages and salaries have been continuously increasing at a rate of almost 12 percent with the deflated (i.e. real) wages increasing at the rate of 4 percent annually. Money wages and real wages per employee increased at the rates of 11 percent and 2.76 percent respectively during the same period. While the money wages per worker increased from Rs. 9615 in 1974-75 to Rs 123276, an increase of 12.8 times, real wages per worker increased from Rs. 5656 to Rs. 14835, an increase of 162 percent over the same period. The rate of increase of real income per worker (2.76 percent) is close to the average compound growth of national per capita income (2.6 percent). Thus, the relative position of labour is almost stagnant in this industry. Nevertheless in the behaviour of wage share, in Heavy engineering, we notice a departure from other industries. The wage share in value added in the Heavy engineering industry is on the rise instead of falling, as has happened in earlier industries. The wage share, though fluctuating, rose from 0.372 in 1974-75 to 0.549 in 1995-96. Thus, we notice an increase in both real wages per worker as well as wage share in value added. This trend along with the increase in capital-labour ratio implies, in Hicks' (1964) terminology that 'invention' has been 'stagnant' and technical progress is capital saving with low elasticity of substitution.

The general trend, as described by **Table** 5.V.2 for Bharat Heavy Electricals Ltd, is similar in nature as that of the industry. Employment in BHEL increased from 45 percent of the industry's total employment (i.e. 45,659) to 60 percent of the total (66,521). While the annual growth rate of employment for the

Table 5.V. 1

**Estimates of Wage Trends: Heavy Engineering Industry**

| *Variable* / *Year* | *Employment* ('000) | *Wages and Salaries* (Rs. Lakhs) | *Value Added* (Rs lakhs) | *Consumer Price Index* | *Real Wages per worker* ('00,00) | *Wages Share in Value added (Coeff.)* |
|---|---|---|---|---|---|---|
| 1974-75 | 101.464 | 9756 | 26184 | 170 | 0.5656 | 0.372 |
| 1975-76 | 123.302 | 12386 | 33725 | 170 | 0.5908 | 0.367 |
| 1976-77 | 125.011 | 12902 | 38327 | 162 | 0.6370 | 0.336 |
| 1977-78 | 127.009 | 14580 | 38446 | 174 | 0.6597 | 0.379 |
| 1978-79 | 130.809 | 17132 | 45188 | 178 | 0.7357 | 0.379 |
| 1979-80 | 133.752 | 19277 | 45436 | 194 | 0.7429 | 0.424 |
| 1980-81 | 138.951 | 22408 | 40010 | 216 | 0.7465 | 0.560 |
| 1981-82 | 144.047 | 26090 | 56208 | 242 | 0.7484 | 0.464 |
| 1982-83 | 145.636 | 29888 | 64818 | 261 | 0.7862 | 0.461 |
| 1983-84 | 146.893 | 35815 | 80163 | 294 | 0.8293 | 0.446 |
| 1984-85 | 146.115 | 37458 | 90697 | 313 | 0.8190 | 0.413 |
| 1985-86 | 146.172 | 42089 | 98341 | 333 | 0.8646 | 0.427 |

Contd. . .

| | | | | | | |
|---|---|---|---|---|---|---|
| 1986-87 | 145.995 | 47919 | 111691 | 362 | 0.9066 | 0.429 |
| 1987-88 | 145.210 | 48127 | 122930 | 396 | 0.8369 | 0.391 |
| 1988-89 | 143.637 | 61764 | 141833 | 423 | 1.0165 | 0.435 |
| 1989-90 | 142.192 | 69539 | 158802 | 458 | 1.0677 | 0.437 |
| 1990-91 | 139.589 | 79633 | 165210 | 512 | 1.1142 | 0.482 |
| 1991-92 | 133.929 | 79637 | 168955 | 580 | 1.0252 | 0.471 |
| 1992-93 | 127.951 | 86839 | 184102 | 636 | 1.0671 | 0.471 |
| 1993-94 | 119.333 | 85639 | 187248 | 684 | 1.0491 | 0.457 |
| 1994-95 | 115.475 | 97739 | 198107 | 754 | 1.1225 | 0.493 |
| 1995-96 | 110.556 | 136290 | 248028 | 831 | 1.4834 | 0.549 |
| Growth rate % | 0.59 | 11.95 | 10.83 (7.51) | 8.00 | 2.76 | |

*Notes* : 1. Data computed and compiled from various issues of Public Enterprises Survey, Chandok and RBI Bulletins.

2. Consumer Price Index refers to consumer price index for industrial workers with 1970-71=100.

3. Growth rates are annual exponential growth rates.

4. Figure in brackets in value added column indicates the growth rate of price of output.

Table 5.V. 2.

**Estimates of Wage Trends: Bharat Heavy Electrical Ltd.**

| *Variable* / *Year* | *Employment* ('000) | *Wages and Salaries* (Rs. Lakhs) | *Value Added* (Rs lakhs) | *Consumer Price Index* | *Real Wages per worker* ('00,00) | *Wages Share in Value added (Coeff.)* |
|---|---|---|---|---|---|---|
| 1974-75 | 45.659 | 4780 | 17629 | 170 | 0.6158 | 0.271 |
| 1975-76 | 55.486 | 6069 | 21539 | 170 | 0.6434 | 0.281 |
| 1976-77 | 56.255 | 6372 | 24972 | 162 | 0.6991 | 0.255 |
| 1977-78 | 57.154 | 7144 | 28547 | 174 | 0.7183 | 0.250 |
| 1978-79 | 59.720 | 8506 | 34674 | 178 | 0.8001 | 0.245 |
| 1979-80 | 62.571 | 9656 | 33940 | 194 | 0.7954 | 0.284 |
| 1980-81 | 66.760 | 11552 | 27693 | 216 | 0.8011 | 0.417 |
| 1981-82 | 69.508 | 13210 | 40382 | 242 | 0.7853 | 0.327 |
| 1982-83 | 71.750 | 15472 | 43545 | 261 | 0.8261 | 0.355 |
| 1983-84 | 73.180 | 18595 | 49900 | 294 | 0.8642 | 0.372 |
| 1984-85 | 72.503 | 21163 | 60188 | 313 | 0.9325 | 0.351 |
| 1985-86 | 73.719 | 24360 | 69983 | 333 | 0.9923 | 0.348 |

Contd. . .

| | | | | | | |
|---|---|---|---|---|---|---|
| 1986-87 | 73.762 | 28331 | 79216 | 362 | 1.0610 | 0.357 |
| 1987-88 | 73.976 | 28682 | 84044 | 396 | 0.9790 | 0.341 |
| 1988-89 | 74.329 | 37552 | 95892 | 423 | 1.1943 | 0.391 |
| 1989-90 | 73.735 | 41012 | 109229 | 458 | 1.2144 | 0.375 |
| 1990-91 | 72.785 | 49241 | 120367 | 512 | 1.3213 | 0.409 |
| 1991-92 | 72.030 | 48625 | 123202 | 580 | 1.1639 | 0.394 |
| 1992-93 | 71.307 | 53753 | 133631 | 636 | 1.1852 | 0.402 |
| 1993-94 | 69.765 | 56085 | 147244 | 684 | 1.1753 | 0.380 |
| 1994-95 | 68.479 | 68172 | 169861 | 754 | 1.3203 | 0.401 |
| 1995-96 | 66.521 | 103657 | 212463 | 831 | 1.8751 | 0.488 |
| Growth rate % | 1.81 | 13.57 | 11.17 (7.51) | 8.00 | 3.45 | |

Notes : 1. Data computed and compiled from various issues of Public Enterprises Survey, Chandok and RBI Bulletins.2. Consumer Price Index refers to consumer price index for industrial workers with 1970-71=100.

3. Growth rates are annual exponential growth rates.

4. Figure in brackets in value added column indicates the growth rate of price of output.

Table 5.V. 3.

**Estimates of Wage Trends: Bharat Heavy Plate and Vessels Ltd.**

| *Variable*<br>*Year* | *Employment*<br>*('000)* | *Wages and Salaries*<br>*(Rs. Lakhs)* | *Value Added*<br>*(Rs lakhs)* | *Consumer Price Index* | *Real Wages per worker*<br>*('00,00)* | *Wages Share in Value added (Coeff.)* |
|---|---|---|---|---|---|---|
| 1974-75 | 2.841 | 224 | 567 | 170 | 0.4637 | 0.3950 |
| 1975-76 | 3.452 | 285 | 779 | 170 | 0.4856 | 0.3658 |
| 1976-77 | 3.500 | 297 | 1077 | 162 | 0.5238 | 0.2757 |
| 1977-78 | 3.556 | 335 | 1125 | 174 | 0.5414 | 0.2977 |
| 1978-79 | 3.624 | 434 | 985 | 178 | 0.6727 | 0.4406 |
| 1979-80 | 3.825 | 463 | 1319 | 194 | 0.6239 | 0.3510 |
| 1980-81 | 3.943 | 500 | 1326 | 216 | 0.5870 | 0.3770 |
| 1981-82 | 4.009 | 572 | 1736 | 242 | 0.5895 | 0.3294 |
| 1982-83 | 4.041 | 706 | 3684 | 261 | 0.6693 | 0.1916 |
| 1983-84 | 4.188 | 926 | 3081 | 294 | 0.7520 | 0.3005 |
| 1984-85 | 4.255 | 981 | 3826 | 313 | 0.7365 | 0.2564 |
| 1985-86 | 4.266 | 1088 | 3990 | 333 | 0.7658 | 0.2726 |

Contd. . . .

| 1986-87 | 4.258 | 1171 | 4035 | 362 | 0.7597 | 0.2902 |
|---|---|---|---|---|---|---|
| 1987-88 | 4.226 | 1472 | 4791 | 396 | 0.8795 | 0.3072 |
| 1988-89 | 4.214 | 1777 | 5285 | 423 | 0.9969 | 0.3362 |
| 1989-90 | 4.159 | 2149 | 5979 | 458 | 1.1281 | 0.3590 |
| 1990-91 | 4.156 | 2378 | 6499 | 512 | 1.1175 | 0.3659 |
| 1991-92 | 4.161 | 2612 | 6813 | 580 | 1.0822 | 0.3833 |
| 1992-93 | 4.124 | 2839 | 8006 | 636 | 1.0824 | 0.3546 |
| 1993-94 | 4.090 | 3145 | 8544 | 684 | 1.1241 | 0.3680 |
| 1994-95 | 4.021 | 3565 | 10722 | 754 | 1.1758 | 0.332 |
| 1995-96 | 3.940 | 4258 | 11842 | 831 | 1.3004 | 0.359 |
| Growth rate % | 1.34 | 14.24 | 14.09 (7.51) | 8.00 | 3.76 | |

*Notes* : 1. Data computed and compiled from various issues of Public Enterprises Survey, Chandok and RBI Bulletins.

2. Consumer Price Index refers to consumer price index for industrial workers with 1970-71=100.

3. Growth rates are annual exponential growth rates.

4. Figure in brackets in value added column indicates the growth rate of price of output.

industry is only 0.59 percent, it is 1.81 percent for BHEL. The respective rates for increase in real wages and salaries and real wages per worker for BHEL are 5.57 percent and 3.45 percent. Both the rates are higher for BHEL than the industry. On the other hand wage share in value added in BHEL has been lower throughout the period. The share was 0.271 in 1974-75 and declined to a low of 0.245 in 1978-79 but increased soon after and kept fluctuating till it reached the level of 0.488 in 1995-96. So both the real wages per worker as well as the wage share in value added increased simultaneously indicating 'stagnant invention' and low elasticity of substitution.

**Table** 5.V.3 summarizes the trends for Bharat Heavy Plate and Vessels Ltd. The trends are not much different in nature from BHEL except for the wage share. The employment in Bharat Heavy Plate and Vessels Ltd. (BHPVL) increased from 2.8 thousand to 3.94 thousand at an annual growth rate of 1.34 percent. The real wages and salaries and real wages per worker increased at the respective rates of 6.24 percent and 3.76 percent, both slightly higher than those of BHEL. The money wages and salaries and money wage rates, on the other hand, grew by 14.25 percent and 11.75 percent respectively. The absolute levels of real wages in both BHEL and BHPVL are significantly different between themselves, being equal to Rs. 18,751 and Rs. 13,004 and are slightly away from the industry's level of Rs. 14834. The wage share in value added behaved slightly differently in BHPVL than in BHEL. While in BHEL it increased during the period, in BHPVL it has been fluctuating through out the period and remained almost at the same level in the final year of the study, i.e., 0.359in 1995-96, as it was in the second year of the study, i.e., 0.365 in 1975-76. The comparatively unchanged income distribution between factors in BHPVL speaks for the neutral technical progress and almost stable capital-labour ratio.

Thus, the experience of Heavy engineering group reveals that either the technical progress has been neutral, as in BHPVL, or it has been capital saving with 'stagnant invention'. This conclusion is supported by the comparatively slow growth of capital intensity in the industry and the firms (**Tables** 4 (C) and 4 (D)). However, we also observe that as a result of liberalisation and consequent competition the industry has now to face, there is a gradual decline in the employment as well as in the financial performance of the industry[9]. The industry which was a net profit earner till 1988-89 is now a loss making industry. However, the industry has always been a, comparatively a high wage industry except in the years 1974-75 to 1979-80 when the real wages per worker were lower than those of the aggregate of industries.

*VI Medium and Light Engineering Industry - Group*

Medium and Light Engineering industry employed 71685 employees in 1974-75, a proportion of 13.41 percent of total employment in the eight industrial groups. The number increased to 118.7 thousand in 1995-96 and the proportion increased to 13.69 percent. The employment reached its peak in 1990-91 when it employed 139.47 thousand employees and declined thereafter because of the change in the attitude of the government towards the public sector (**Table** 5.VI.1). The annual growth rate in employment has been 3.18 percent. On the other hand total money wages and salaries in the industry increased at the rate of 14.11 percent with total real wages increasing at a rate of 6.11 percent. Total money wages and salaries have been increasing continuously over the period. Gross value added at current prices, however, increased at the rate of 15.43 percent with deflated (or real) value added rising at the rate of 8.17 percent. Real wages per worker have been increasing continuously from an initial level of Rs. 6037 to Rs. 11,910 in the final year, i.e., 1995-96, with minor fluctuations in the last six years. The rate of increase is 2.37 percent during the period which is comparable to the increase in national per capita income. If the base year of the study is excluded then the wage share in value added is almost stagnant with a minor fall from 0.471 in 1975-76 to 0.434 in 1993-94 however, it increased to 0.689 in 1995-96. There have been only minor fluctuations in the wage share over the period.

Thus, an increase in real wages per worker along with a marginal change in wage share in the industry points out that either the technical progress has been neutral or labour saving.

**Table** 5.VI.2 highlights the required trends for Hindustan Machine Tools Ltd (HMT Ltd). The employment pattern of

Table 5.VI. 1

**Estimates of Wage Trends: Medium and Light Engineering Industry**

| *Variable* / *Year* | *Employment* *('000)* | *Wages and Salaries* *(Rs. Lakhs)* | *Value Added* *(Rs lakhs)* | *Consumer Price Index* | *Real Wages per worker* *('00,00)* | *Wages Share in Value added (Coeff.)* |
|---|---|---|---|---|---|---|
| 1974-75 | 71.685 | 7357 | 12094 | 170 | 0.6037 | 0.608 |
| 1975-76 | 78.880 | 8366 | 17732 | 170 | 0.6238 | 0.471 |
| 1976-77 | 85.800 | 9040 | 19759 | 162 | 0.6503 | 0.457 |
| 1977-78 | 92.718 | 11020 | 21936 | 174 | 0.6830 | 0.502 |
| 1978-79 | 96.898 | 12669 | 17630 | 178 | 0.7345 | 0.718 |
| 1979-80 | 102.168 | 13848 | 29129 | 194 | 0.6986 | 0.475 |
| 1980-81 | 103.720 | 13953 | 28342 | 216 | 0.6228 | 0.492 |
| 1981-82 | 105.628 | 18101 | 43119 | 242 | 0.7081 | 0.419 |
| 1982-83 | 108.886 | 21564 | 50888 | 261 | 0.7587 | 0.423 |
| 1983-84 | 112.764 | 26043 | 58259 | 294 | 0.7855 | 0.447 |
| 1984-85 | 115.573 | 30110 | 68264 | 313 | 0.8323 | 0.441 |
| 1985-86 | 119.264 | 34720 | 77684 | 333 | 0.8742 | 0.446 |

Contd. . . .

| | | | | | | |
|---|---|---|---|---|---|---|
| 1986-87 | 136.174 | 40016 | 93134 | 362 | 0.8117 | 0.429 |
| 1987-88 | 136.820 | 45561 | 101587 | 396 | 0.8409 | 0.448 |
| 1988-89 | 137.549 | 56136 | 124772 | 423 | 0.9648 | 0.449 |
| 1989-90 | 137.629 | 65516 | 148622 | 458 | 1.0393 | 0.440 |
| 1990-91 | 139.470 | 69693 | 160579 | 512 | 0.9759 | 0.434 |
| 1991-92 | 135.594 | 76233 | 181980 | 580 | 0.9693 | 0.418 |
| 1992-93 | 132.545 | 88219 | 204741 | 636 | 1.0465 | 0.430 |
| 1993-94 | 129.652 | 89046 | 204975 | 684 | 1.0041 | 0.434 |
| 1994-95 | 123.458 | 98654 | 175725 | 754 | 1.0598 | 0.561 |
| 1995-96 | 118.734 | 117522 | 170633 | 831 | 1.1910 | 0.689 |
| Growth rate % | 3.18 | 14.11 | 15.43 (7.26) | 8.00 | 2.37 | |

*Notes* : 1. Data computed and compiled from various issues of Public Enterprises Survey, Chandok and RBI Bulletins.

2. Consumer Price Index refers to consumer price index for industrial workers with 1970-71=100.

3. Growth rates are annual exponential growth rates.

4. Figure in brackets in value added column indicates the growth rate of price of output.

Table 5.VI. 2

**Estimates of Wage Trends: HMT Ltd.**

| *Variable* / *Year* | *Employment* ('000) | *Wages and Salaries* (Rs. Lakhs) | *Value Added* (Rs lakhs) | *Consumer Price Index* | *Real Wages per worker* ('00,00) | *Wages Share in Value added (Coeff.)* |
|---|---|---|---|---|---|---|
| 1974-75 | 17.419 | 1913 | 3251 | 170 | 0.6460 | 0.588 |
| 1975-76 | 19.168 | 2175 | 4560 | 170 | 0.6674 | 0.476 |
| 1976-77 | 20.849 | 2350 | 5058 | 162 | 0.6957 | 0.464 |
| 1977-78 | 22.530 | 2865 | 5550 | 174 | 0.7308 | 0.516 |
| 1978-79 | 23.237 | 3207 | 8303 | 178 | 0.7753 | 0.386 |
| 1979-80 | 24.722 | 3459 | 8936 | 194 | 0.7212 | 0.387 |
| 1980-81 | 25.596 | 3876 | 9625 | 216 | 0.7010 | 0.402 |
| 1981-82 | 26.637 | 4909 | 13084 | 242 | 0.7615 | 0.375 |
| 1982-83 | 27.238 | 5728 | 14434 | 261 | 0.8057 | 0.396 |
| 1983-84 | 27.906 | 6862 | 15758 | 294 | 0.8363 | 0.435 |
| 1984-85 | 28.716 | 7769 | 19495 | 313 | 0.8643 | 0.398 |
| 1985-86 | 29.417 | 9042 | 20471 | 333 | 0.9230 | 0.441 |

Contd. . . .

| | | | | | | |
|---|---|---|---|---|---|---|
| 1986-87 | 29.376 | 9677 | 21582 | 362 | 0.9099 | 0.448 |
| 1987-88 | 29.211 | 11074 | 19844 | 396 | 0.9573 | 0.558 |
| 1988-89 | 28.856 | 12929 | 23168 | 423 | 1.0592 | 0.558 |
| 1989-90 | 28.592 | 15274 | 25500 | 458 | 1.1663 | 0.598 |
| 1990-91 | 28.349 | 17066 | 29680 | 512 | 1.1757 | 0.575 |
| 1991-92 | 27.615 | 17753 | 36285 | 580 | 1.1084 | 0.489 |
| 1992-93 | 26.859 | 19280 | 32298 | 636 | 1.1286 | 0.596 |
| 1993-94 | 24.919 | 19746 | 23527 | 684 | 1.1584 | 0.839 |
| 1994-95 | 23.857 | 20488 | 27636 | 754 | 1.1390 | 0.741 |
| 1995-96 | 22.794 | 25041 | 32035 | 831 | 1.3220 | 0.782 |
| Growth rate % | 1.88 | 13.24 | 11.42 (7.74) | 8.00 | 2.99 | |

*Notes* : 1. Data computed and compiled from various issues of Public Enterprises Survey, Chandok and RBI Bulletins.

2. Consumer Price Index refers to consumer price index for industrial workers with 1970-71=100.

3. Growth rates are annual exponential growth rates.

4. Figure in brackets in value added column indicates the growth rate of price of output.

Table 5.VI. 3

**Estimates of Wage Trends: Indian Telephone Industries Ltd.**

| *Variable* / *Year* | *Employment* ('000) | *Wages and Salaries* (*Rs. Lakhs*) | *Value Added* (*Rs lakhs*) | *Consumer Price Index* | *Real Wages per worker* ('00,00) | *Wages Share in Value added* (*Coeff.*) |
|---|---|---|---|---|---|---|
| 1974-75 | 18.996 | 1766 | 4021 | 170 | 0.5468 | 0.439 |
| 1975-76 | 20.903 | 2008 | 4366 | 170 | 0.5650 | 0.459 |
| 1976-77 | 22.737 | 2170 | 5210 | 162 | 0.5891 | 0.416 |
| 1977-78 | 24.570 | 2645 | 5489 | 174 | 0.6186 | 0.481 |
| 1978-79 | 26.021 | 3425 | 5299 | 178 | 0.7394 | 0.646 |
| 1979-80 | 26.799 | 3460 | 6850 | 194 | 0.6655 | 0.505 |
| 1980-81 | 26.836 | 2972 | 5426 | 216 | 0.5127 | 0.547 |
| 1981-82 | 26.872 | 4113 | 9145 | 242 | 0.6324 | 0.449 |
| 1982-83 | 27.325 | 5242 | 10660 | 261 | 0.7350 | 0.491 |
| 1983-84 | 28.368 | 6576 | 12944 | 294 | 0.7884 | 0.508 |
| 1984-85 | 29.592 | 7445 | 14676 | 313 | 0.8037 | 0.507 |
| 1985-86 | 31.439 | 8365 | 17574 | 333 | 0.7990 | 0.475 |

Contd. . . .

| | | | | | | |
|---|---|---|---|---|---|---|
| 1986-87 | 32.023 | 9575 | 24821 | 362 | 0.8259 | 0.385 |
| 1987-88 | 32.447 | 10573 | 29026 | 396 | 0.8228 | 0.364 |
| 1988-89 | 32.369 | 13860 | 37751 | 423 | 1.0122 | 0.367 |
| 1989-90 | 32.298 | 16219 | 47638 | 458 | 1.0964 | 0.340 |
| 1990-91 | 32.215 | 16475 | 51936 | 512 | 0.9988 | 0.317 |
| 1991-92 | 30.280 | 18440 | 62480 | 580 | 1.0499 | 0.295 |
| 1992-93 | 29.730 | 24023 | 75406 | 636 | 1.2705 | 0.318 |
| 1993-94 | 28.633 | 22897 | 78328 | 684 | 1.1691 | 0.292 |
| 1994-95 | 27.477 | 22517 | 42335 | 754 | 1.0868 | 0.532 |
| 1995-96 | 26.272 | 26509 | 25955 | 831 | 1.2142 | 1.021 |
| Growth rate % | 2.13 | 14.35 | 17.22 (7.51) | 8.00 | 3.46 | |

*Notes* : 1. Data computed and compiled from various issues of Public Enterprises Survey, Chandok and RBI Bulletins.

2. Consumer Price Index refers to consumer price index for industrial workers with 1970-71=100.
3. Growth rates are annual exponential growth rates.
4. Figure in brackets in value added column indicates the growth rate of price of output.

HMT Ltd indicates that while employment has been increasing in the initial years, when it increased from 17.4 thousand to 29.4 thousand in 1985-86, it started decreasing since 1985-86 with a sharp decline in the last three years of the study. The trend reflects the same attitude of the government towards this industry and firm in particular which is evident in Medium and Light engineering industry, i.e., where the government wants to dilute its control and ownership in these non-crucial areas and is interested in reducing over-staffing in them, if it exists, through changes in its employment policy including the introduction of voluntary retirement schemes (VRS). The rate of growth of employment in HMT Ltd, thus, remained low at 1.88 percent. Total money wages and salaries, however, increased continuously despite a fall in employment at the rate of 13.24 percent, with the real wages rising at the rate of 5.24 percent. But the rise in real wages per worker was only 2.99 percent, with the wages increasing from Rs. 6460 in the base year to Rs 13220 in the final year. There is no marked fluctuation in the real wages per worker over the entire period. However, the wage share in value added has been fluctuating over the entire period with a value as high as 0.839 in 1993-94 and as low as 0.375 in 1981-82. The fluctuations in wage share have been caused more due to fluctuations in value added rather than in total wages and salaries. The high value of wage share as compared to other firms and industries hints at the use of labour-intensive technology by the firm.

Indian Telephone Industries Ltd (ITI Ltd), whose trends are presented in **Table** 5.VI.3, depicts a slightly different picture as compared to HMT Ltd, especially regarding wage share in value added especially during the last two years when value added declined from Rs 78328 lakhs in 1993-94 to Rs 25955 lakhs in 1995-96. The trend of employment in ITI Ltd is almost similar to that of HMT Ltd with employment increasing at the annual rate of 2.13 percent. Employment in ITI Ltd increased only upto 1987-88 and then gradually declined, as happened both in the industry and in HMT Ltd. Total money wages also increased almost continuously at the rate of 14.35 percent. The real wages per worker increased from Rs. 5468 in the base year to Rs. 12,142 in 1995-96 at the rate of 3.46 percent per year. But contrary to a clear trend in the industry and HMT Ltd the trend of wage share in ITI Ltd shows a decline over the period. Though some fluctuations in the values are visible but the value declined from 0.439 in 1974-75 to 0.292 in 1993-94 but increased to 1.021 in 1995-96. Thus, increasing real wages per worker along with falling wage share reveals the high capital intensity in the firm and the use of labour-saving technique by it. High growth rate of capital-intensity (11.46 percent) as revealed by **Table** 4 (D) supports the conclusion.

Thus, while the industry and ITI Ltd indicates generally a falling wage share, HMT Ltd has almost a constant share for most of the time period. The increase in real wage rate per worker is maximum in ITI Ltd and minimum in the industry, i.e., 3.46 percent, 2.99 percent and 2.37 percent for IIT Ltd., HMT Ltd and the industry respectively. Though HMT is now not performing financially well but the industry has been consistently contributing positive net profits till 1992-93 with a high ratio of gross profit to capital employed (17.36 percent in 1992-93), but is now incurring heavy losses with net profit being (-) 411.86 crores in 1995-96 and the ratio of gross profit to capital employed being only 2.63%. Thus, the real wage rates per worker in the industry has been almost at the level of that attained by the aggregate of industries.

*VII Transport Equipment - Group*

While 15.80 percent of the total employees were engaged in the Transport Equipment industry in 1974-75, the employment proportion is only 10.00 percent in 1995-96. The employment which was 84.4 thousand in 1974-75 increased to 86.6 thousand, at the annual growth rate of 1.10 percent (**Table** 5.VII.1). The employment increased continuously till 1987-88 when it started declining gradually as happened in the case of earlier two industries, i.e., Heavy Engineering and Medium and Light Engineering. Total money wages and salaries of the industry increased uninterrupted at the rate of 12.19 percent leading to a rise in real wages and salaries per worker from Rs. 5533 in 1974-75 to Rs. 12,570 in the final year, the annual growth rate being 2.42 percent. Gross value added at current prices increased faster than the increase in wages and salaries, the rate

Table 5.VII 1

**Estimates of Wage Trends: Transport Equipment - Industry**

| Variable / Year | Employment ('000) | Wages and Salaries (Rs. Lakhs) | Value Added (Rs lakhs) | Consumer Price Index | Real Wages per worker ('00,00) | Wages Share in Value added (Coeff.) |
|---|---|---|---|---|---|---|
| 1974-75 | 84.437 | 7943 | 14286 | 170 | 0.5533 | 0.555 |
| 1975-76 | 88.684 | 9140 | 16343 | 170 | 0.6062 | 0.559 |
| 1976-77 | 92.321 | 8799 | 18290 | 162 | 0.5883 | 0.481 |
| 1977-78 | 93.689 | 10323 | 19042 | 174 | 0.6332 | 0.542 |
| 1978-79 | 90.986 | 11851 | 20475 | 178 | 0.7317 | 0.578 |
| 1979-80 | 89.907 | 12620 | 23393 | 194 | 0.7235 | 0.539 |
| 1980-81 | 88.944 | 13611 | 23467 | 216 | 0.7084 | 0.580 |
| 1981-82 | 95.842 | 17663 | 34176 | 242 | 0.7615 | 0.516 |
| 1982-83 | 99.089 | 18795 | 43341 | 261 | 0.7267 | 0.433 |
| 1983-84 | 104.451 | 24010 | 56428 | 294 | 0.7818 | 0.425 |
| 1984-85 | 109.154 | 26810 | 73770 | 313 | 0.7847 | 0.363 |
| 1985-86 | 112.831 | 31061 | 81718 | 333 | 0.8266 | 0.380 |

Contd. . .

| | | | | | | |
|---|---|---|---|---|---|---|
| 1986-87 | 113.281 | 33113 | 84137 | 362 | 0.8074 | 0.393 |
| 1987-88 | 113.956 | 37743 | 88162 | 396 | 0.8363 | 0.428 |
| 1988-89 | 113.379 | 45072 | 114256 | 423 | 0.9397 | 0.394 |
| 1989-90 | 112.109 | 52930 | 130479 | 458 | 1.0308 | 0.405 |
| 0990-91 | 106.254 | 54175 | 133975 | 512 | 0.9958 | 0.404 |
| 1991-92 | 103.864 | 56172 | 135352 | 580 | 0.9324 | 0.415 |
| 1992-93 | 98.767 | 60858 | 148392 | 636 | 0.9688 | 0.410 |
| 1993-94 | 94.140 | 68215 | 176753 | 684 | 1.0593 | 0.385 |
| 1994-95 | 87.079 | 78213 | 183620 | 754 | 1.1912 | 0.426 |
| 1995-96 | 86.635 | 90502 | 188535 | 831 | 1.2570 | 0.480 |
| Growth rate % | 1.10 | 12.19 | 14.37 (8.10) | 8.00 | 2.42 | |

*Notes* : 1. Data computed and compiled from various issues of Public Enterprises Survey, Chandok and RBI Bulletins.

2. Consumer Price Index refers to consumer price index for industrial workers with 1970-71=100.

3. Growth rates are annual exponential growth rates.

4. Figure in brackets in value added column indicates the growth rate of price of output.

Table 5.VII. 2

**Estimates of Wage Trends: Bharat Earth Movers Ltd.**

| *Variable* / *Year* | *Employment* ('000) | *Wages and Salaries* (Rs. Lakhs) | *Value Added* (Rs lakhs) | *Consumer Price Index* | *Real Wages per worker* ('00,00) | *Wages Share in Value added (Coeff.)* |
|---|---|---|---|---|---|---|
| 1974-75 | 10.723 | 1080 | 2780 | 170 | 0.5924 | 0.388 |
| 1975-76 | 11.263 | 1243 | 2932 | 170 | 0.6491 | 0.423 |
| 1976-77 | 11.725 | 1197 | 3144 | 162 | 0.6301 | 0.380 |
| 1977-78 | 11.898 | 1404 | 3353 | 174 | 0.6781 | 0.418 |
| 1978-79 | 11.386 | 1631 | 3578 | 178 | 0.8047 | 0.455 |
| 1979-80 | 11.483 | 1722 | 4925 | 194 | 0.7729 | 0.349 |
| 1980-81 | 11.427 | 1433 | 3716 | 216 | 0.5805 | 0.384 |
| 1981-82 | 11.742 | 2038 | 7292 | 242 | 0.7172 | 0.279 |
| 1982-83 | 12.912 | 2568 | 13663 | 261 | 0.7620 | 0.187 |
| 1983-84 | 13.871 | 3215 | 16076 | 294 | 0.7883 | 0.199 |
| 1984-85 | 14.418 | 3803 | 14109 | 313 | 0.8427 | 0.269 |
| 1985-86 | 14.555 | 4201 | 19574 | 333 | 0.8667 | 0.214 |

Contd. . .

| | | | | | | |
|---|---|---|---|---|---|---|
| 1986-87 | 13.354 | 4558 | 22636 | 362 | 0.9428 | 0.201 |
| 1987-88 | 14.875 | 5421 | 17281 | 396 | 0.9202 | 0.313 |
| 1988-89 | 15.705 | 5369 | 21652 | 423 | 0.8081 | 0.247 |
| 1989-90 | 16.075 | 6121 | 25211 | 458 | 0.8313 | 0.242 |
| 1990-91 | 16.657 | 5225 | 27813 | 512 | 0.6126 | 0.187 |
| 1991-92 | 17.001 | 8301 | 28660 | 580 | 0.8418 | 0.289 |
| 1992-93 | 16.913 | 6414 | 33008 | 636 | 0.5962 | 0.194 |
| 1993-94 | 16.208 | 7593 | 32316 | 684 | 0.6849 | 0.234 |
| 1994-95 | 16.005 | 8360 | 29849 | 754 | 0.6927 | 0.280 |
| 1995-96 | 15.645 | 10527 | 34837 | 831 | 0.8097 | 0.302 |
| Growth rate % | 2.57 | 11.33 | 15.07 (7.51) | 8.00 | 0.57 | |

*Notes* :
1. Data computed and compiled from various issues of Public Enterprises Survey, Chandok and RBI Bulletins.
2. Consumer Price Index refers to consumer price index for industrial workers with 1970-71=100.
3. Growth rates are annual exponential growth rates.
4. Figure in brackets in value added column indicates the growth rate of price of output.

Table 5.VII. 3.

**Estimates of Wage Trends: Hindustan Aeronautics Ltd.**

| *Variable* / *Year* | *Employment ('000)* | *Wages and Salaries (Rs. Lakhs)* | *Value Added (Rs lakhs)* | *Consumer Price Index* | *Real Wages per worker ('00,00)* | *Wages Share in Value added (Coeff.)* |
|---|---|---|---|---|---|---|
| 1974-75 | 38.841 | 3495 | 7203 | 170 | 0.5293 | 0.485 |
| 1975-76 | 40.795 | 4021 | 8028 | 170 | 0.5798 | 0.500 |
| 1976-77 | 42.467 | 3872 | 8108 | 162 | 0.5628 | 0.477 |
| 1977-78 | 43.096 | 4542 | 8401 | 174 | 0.6057 | 0.540 |
| 1978-79 | 42.032 | 5558 | 9283 | 178 | 0.7428 | 0.598 |
| 1979-80 | 41.264 | 5704 | 9907 | 194 | 0.7125 | 0.575 |
| 1980-81 | 40.903 | 5733 | 9670 | 216 | 0.6488 | 0.592 |
| 1981-82 | 40.422 | 7453 | 14728 | 242 | 0.7618 | 0.506 |
| 1982-83 | 40.379 | 7555 | 16179 | 261 | 0.7168 | 0.466 |
| 1983-84 | 41.462 | 10007 | 22632 | 294 | 0.8209 | 0.442 |
| 1984-85 | 42.389 | 11148 | 27251 | 313 | 0.8402 | 0.409 |
| 1985-86 | 42.993 | 12269 | 33158 | 333 | 0.8569 | 0.370 |

Contd. . . .

| | | | | | | |
|---|---|---|---|---|---|---|
| 1986-87 | 44.123 | 14048 | 32664 | 362 | 0.8795 | 0.430 |
| 1987-88 | 44.043 | 16380 | 35003 | 396 | 0.9391 | 0.467 |
| 1988-89 | 43.663 | 20233 | 47490 | 423 | 1.0954 | 0.426 |
| 1989-90 | 42.678 | 23623 | 49679 | 458 | 1.2085 | 0.475 |
| 1990-91 | 41.530 | 26120 | 55390 | 512 | 1.2284 | 0.471 |
| 1991-92 | 40.336 | 23949 | 64330 | 580 | 1.0236 | 0.372 |
| 1992-93 | 38.700 | 27849 | 66499 | 636 | 1.1314 | 0.418 |
| 1993-94 | 36.946 | 30167 | 79095 | 684 | 1.1937 | 0.381 |
| 1994-95 | 35.545 | 38628 | 84797 | 754 | 1.4413 | 0.455 |
| 1995-96 | 35.245 | 47452 | 98911 | 831 | 1.6201 | 0.479 |
| Growth rate % | -0.09 | 12.27 | 13.90 (8.10) | 8.00 | 3.65 | |

*Notes* : 1. Data computed and compiled from various issues of Public Enterprises Survey, Chandok and RBI Bulletins.

2. Consumer Price Index refers to consumer price index for industrial workers with 1970-71=100.

3. Growth rates are annual exponential growth rates.

4. Figure in brackets in value added column indicates the growth rate of price of output.

of increase in gross value added being 14.37 percent. Wage share in value added has shown an uneven trend but it gradually declined to 0.480 in 1995-96 from 0.555 in 1974-75. So, whereas real wages per worker nearly doubled during the period, the wage share declined by about 15 percent. This reveals how the increase in capital intensity has led to labour saving technological progress.

**Table** 5.VII.2 depicts the trends in Bharat Earth Movers Ltd (BEML). The employment in BEML increased from 10.7 thousand to 15.645 thousand in 1995-96. Though there have been fluctuations in the employment level, and it declined during the last two years, the same trend as is witnessed in the industry is not clearly discernible in the case of BEML. The employment, thus, increased at a faster rate of 2.57 percent during the same period. Though gross value added at current prices increased at a slightly faster rate of 15.07 percent but total real wages and salaries increased at a lower rate (3.33 percent) than the industry (4.19 percent) leading to an almost negligible growth rate in real wages per worker, i.e., 0.57 percent in BEML. As a result of this the real wages per worker have been very low at Rs. 8097 in BEML as compared to Rs. 12,570 in the industry. Though the real wages per worker, which have been fluctuating, remained virtually stagnant, the money wages increased from Rs. 10071 in 1974-75 to Rs. 67286 in 1995-96. Wage share has the tendency to increase in the initial years but later on it declined from the original value of 0.388 to 0.302 in 1995-96. So the general tendency for wage share has been to decline over the years. Thus, the basic trend of real wages per worker and wage share in value added in BEML is same as that of the industry, i.e., while real wages per worker have slightly increased the wage share in value added has declined.

The trends for Hindustan Aeronautics Ltd are presented in **Table** 5.VII.3. It (HAL) is one of the major firms operating in Transport Equipment industry. It employed 46 percent of the total employees in the industry during 1974-75. But the share fell down to 40.68 percent in 1995-96 because the employment in HAL instead of increasing has decreased over the years at a rate of -0.09 percent. The employment, which was 38.8 thousand in the beginning is only 35.245 thousand in 1995-96. The employment in fact increased slowly till 1986-87 when it started falling gradually. Total wages and salaries at current prices, nonetheless, increased practically throughout the period at the rate of 12.27 percent as a result of which both money wages and real wages per worker increased continuously. The real wages nearly tripled from Rs. 5293 to Rs. 16,201 and increased at an annual growth rate of 3.65 percent. On the other hand wage share in value added, which was 0.485 in 1974-75 and reached a peak of 0.598 in 1978-79, came down to a level of 0.479 in 1995-96, a level close to the level of the industry. Thus, this shows that the firm supports the basic trends of the industry.

It follows from the discussion that there is a general tendency in the industry and the two firms for a decline in the level of employment along with an increase in real wages per worker. The falling share of wages in value added supports the general trend of other industrial groups in the public enterprises and highlights the increase in capital intensity in the industry. However, the examination of the trends of the real wages per worker in the industry exhibits that the two firms : BEML and HAL divulges different scenerio. In BEML not only real wages per worker are very low, as compared to HAL, but there are violant fluctuations also. Since 1986-87, the real wages per worker in BEML have declined sharply possibly, among other reasons, because of the decline in both capacity utilization (from 109.6 percent in 1986-87 to 57.2 percent in 1993-94) and gross profit to capital employed. However, the real wages per worker in the Transport equipment industry and HAL have been comparable with that of the aggregate of industries.

*VIII. Consumer Goods - Group*

The group was comparatively a small one in 1974-75 employing only 2.68 percent of the total employment but with the increase in employment to almost 7 percent in 1995-96 the significance of the group has increased. The increase in employment in consumer goods industry from 14.3 thousand to 61.3 thousand at an annual growth rate of 10.47 percent is one of the fastest in the public enterprises (**Table** 5.VIII.1). Moreover, money wages and salaries and gross value added at current prices also increased at very high rates of 21.21 percent and

Table 5.VIII. I

**Estimates of Wage Trends: Consumer Goods - Industry**

| *Variable* | *Employment* | *Wages and Salaries* | *Value Added* | *Consumer Price Index* | *Real Wages per worker* | *Wages Share in Value added (Coeff.)* |
|---|---|---|---|---|---|---|
| *Year* | ('000) | (Rs. Lakhs) | (Rs lakhs) | | ('00,00) | |
| 1974-75 | 14.346 | 860 | 1773 | 170 | 0.3526 | 0.485 |
| 1975-76 | 14.666 | 962 | 2171 | 170 | 0.3858 | 0.443 |
| 1976-77 | 14.212 | 1018 | 2246 | 162 | 0.4421 | 0.453 |
| 1977-78 | 15.081 | 1236 | 2526 | 174 | 0.4710 | 0.489 |
| 1978-79 | 15.089 | 1415 | 2661 | 178 | 0.5268 | 0.531 |
| 1979-80 | 15.465 | 1500 | 2752 | 194 | 0.4999 | 0.545 |
| 1980-81 | 15.244 | 1733 | 3354 | 216 | 0.5263 | 0.516 |
| 1981-82 | 50.906 | 5010 | 6021 | 242 | 0.4066 | 0.832 |
| 1982-83 | 55.034 | 5912 | 7573 | 261 | 0.4115 | 0.780 |
| 1983-84 | 53.430 | 6520 | 8854 | 294 | 0.4150 | 0.736 |
| 1984-85 | 58.585 | 9684 | 13285 | 313 | 0.5281 | 0.728 |
| 1985-86 | 60.753 | 10385 | 13861 | 333 | 0.5133 | 0.749 |

Contd. . .

| | | | | | | |
|---|---|---|---|---|---|---|
| 1986-87 | 62.053 | 11899 | 16687 | 362 | 0.5297 | 0.713 |
| 1987-88 | 69.199 | 15018 | 25863 | 396 | 0.5480 | 0.580 |
| 1988-89 | 69.530 | 18649 | 30271 | 423 | 0.6340 | 0.616 |
| 1989-90 | 69.382 | 20420 | 41535 | 458 | 0.6426 | 0.491 |
| 1990-91 | 69.348 | 23614 | 49473 | 512 | 0.6650 | 0.477 |
| 1991-92 | 67.932 | 25086 | 58729 | 580 | 0.6366 | 0.427 |
| 1992-93 | 65.549 | 27485 | 48896 | 636 | 0.6592 | 0.562 |
| 1993-94 | 63.439 | 26745 | 47199 | 684 | 0.6163 | 0.566 |
| 1994-95 | 61.805 | 28306 | 44800 | 754 | 0.6074 | 0.632 |
| 1995-96 | 61.291 | 31762 | 68293 | 831 | 0.6236 | 0.465 |
| Growth rate % | 10.47 | 21.21 | 20.77 (7.99) | 8.00 | 1.41 | |

*Notes* : 1. Data computed and compiled from various issues of Public Enterprises Survey, Chandok and RBI Bulletins.

2. Consumer Price Index refers to consumer price index for industrial workers with 1970-71=100.

3. Growth rates are annual exponential growth rates.

4. Figure in brackets in value added column indicates the growth rate of price of output.

Table 5.VIII. 2.

**Estimates of Wage Trends: Cement Corporation of India Ltd.**

| *Variable*<br>*Year* | *Employment*<br>*('000)* | *Wages and Salaries*<br>*(Rs. Lakhs)* | *Value Added*<br>*(Rs lakhs)* | *Consumer Price Index* | *Real Wages per worker ('00,00)* | *Wages Share in Value added (Coeff.)* |
|---|---|---|---|---|---|---|
| 1974-75 | 5.423 | 139 | 255 | 170 | 0.1507 | 0.545 |
| 1975-76 | 5.544 | 156 | 401 | 170 | 0.1655 | 0.389 |
| 1976-77 | 5.372 | 165 | 412 | 162 | 0.1895 | 0.400 |
| 1977-78 | 5.701 | 200 | 535 | 174 | 0.2016 | 0.373 |
| 1978-79 | 3.261 | 197 | 678 | 178 | 0.3393 | 0.290 |
| 1979-80 | 2.340 | 243 | 1115 | 194 | 0.5352 | 0.217 |
| 1980-81 | 4.579 | 342 | 1766 | 216 | 0.3457 | 0.193 |
| 1981-82 | 5.493 | 476 | 3145 | 242 | 0.3580 | 0.151 |
| 1982-83 | 6.094 | 872 | 7678 | 261 | 0.5482 | 0.113 |
| 1983-84 | 6.309 | 1041 | 6134 | 294 | 0.5612 | 0.169 |
| 1984-85 | 6.425 | 1253 | 7543 | 313 | 0.6230 | 0.166 |
| 1985-86 | 6.575 | 1366 | 7781 | 333 | 0.6238 | 0.175 |

Contd. . . .

| | | | | | | |
|---|---|---|---|---|---|---|
| 1986-87 | 6.579 | 1488 | 8583 | 362 | 0.6247 | 0.173 |
| 1987-88 | 6.699 | 2113 | 7187 | 396 | 0.7965 | 0.294 |
| 1988-89 | 6.663 | 2397 | 7998 | 423 | 0.8504 | 0.299 |
| 1989-90 | 6.703 | 2587 | 11356 | 458 | 0.8426 | 0.227 |
| 1990-91 | 6.677 | 3016 | 16311 | 512 | 0.8822 | 0.184 |
| 1991-92 | 6.713 | 3458 | 23698 | 580 | 0.8881 | 0.145 |
| 1992-93 | 6.530 | 4280 | 18610 | 636 | 1.0305 | 0.229 |
| 1993-94 | 6.371 | 4236 | 14383 | 684 | 0.9720 | 0.294 |
| 1994-95 | 6.218 | 4693 | 11051 | 754 | 1.0009 | 0.425 |
| 1995-96 | 6.048 | 5164 | 16417 | 831 | 1.0274 | 0.315 |
| Growth rate % | 2.43 | 20.37 | 23.36 (7.39) | 8.00 | 4.72 | |

*Notes* : 1. Data computed and compiled from various issues of Public Enterprises Survey, Chandok and RBI Bulletins.

2. Consumer Price Index refers to consumer price index for industrial workers with 1970-71=100.

3. Growth rates are annual exponential growth rates.

4. Figure in brackets in value added column indicates the growth rate of price of output.

Table 5.VIII. 3.

**Estimates of Wage Trends: Hindustan Photo Films Manufacturing Co.Ltd.**

| *Variable* / *Year* | *Employment* ('000) | *Wages and Salaries* (Rs. Lakhs) | *Value Added* (Rs lakhs) | *Consumer Price Index* | *Real Wages per worker* ('00,00) | *Wages Share in Value added (Coeff.)* |
|---|---|---|---|---|---|---|
| 1974-75 | 2.511 | 194 | 528 | 170 | 0.4544 | 0.367 |
| 1975-76 | 2.566 | 217 | 594 | 170 | 0.4974 | 0.365 |
| 1976-77 | 2.487 | 230 | 854 | 162 | 0.5708 | 0.269 |
| 1977-78 | 2.639 | 279 | 1026 | 174 | 0.6075 | 0.271 |
| 1978-79 | 2.535 | 302 | 1182 | 178 | 0.6692 | 0.255 |
| 1979-80 | 2.669 | 328 | 1255 | 194 | 0.6334 | 0.261 |
| 1980-81 | 2.827 | 426 | 1616 | 216 | 0.6976 | 0.263 |
| 1981-82 | 2.921 | 467 | 1614 | 242 | 0.6606 | 0.289 |
| 1982-83 | 3.036 | 525 | 1817 | 261 | 0.6625 | 0.288 |
| 1983-84 | 3.128 | 744 | 2458 | 294 | 0.8090 | 0.302 |
| 1984-85 | 3.226 | 657 | 2479 | 313 | 0.6506 | 0.265 |
| 1985-86 | 3.297 | 854 | 3095 | 333 | 0.7778 | 0.275 |

Contd. . . .

| | | | | | | |
|---|---|---|---|---|---|---|
| 1986-87 | 3.365 | 995 | 3590 | 362 | 0.8168 | 0.277 |
| 1987-88 | 3.440 | 989 | 3271 | 396 | 0.7260 | 0.302 |
| 1988-89 | 3.472 | 1010 | 3437 | 423 | 0.6877 | 0.293 |
| 1989-90 | 3.554 | 1185 | 4081 | 458 | 0.7280 | 0.290 |
| 1990-91 | 3.732 | 1553 | 4947 | 512 | 0.8127 | 0.313 |
| 1991-92 | 3.824 | 1688 | 5825 | 580 | 0.7610 | 0.289 |
| 1992-93 | 3.775 | 2036 | -141 | 636 | 0.8480 | -14.439 |
| 1993-94 | 3.633 | 1930 | 454 | 684 | 0.7766 | 4.251 |
| 1994-95 | 3.127 | 1913 | 228 | 754 | 0.8114 | 8.39 |
| 1995-96 | 3.046 | 1841 | 726 | 831 | 0.7273 | 2.54 |
| Growth rate % | 2.47 | 12.78 | 8.33 (7.66) | 8.00 | 1.49 | |
| | (2.67) | (13.13) | (13.05) | | (1.56) | |

*Notes* : 1. Data computed and compiled from various issues of Public Enterprises Survey, Chandok and RBI Bulletins.

2. Consumer Price Index refers to consumer price index for industrial workers with 1970-71=100.

3. Growth rates are annual exponential growth rates.

4. Figure in brackets in value added column indicates the growth rate of price of output.

20.77 percent respectively. But the increase in real wages per worker at 1.41 percent is not as impressive as the increase in total money wages and value added, rather it is one of the lowest among all the industries in public enterprises. Not only this, even the absolute level of real wages per worker at Rs. 6236 in 1995-96, is among the lowest. However, the coefficient of wage share in value added not only has the tendency to increase, it is also the highest among all the industrial groups in the public enterprises. The coefficient increased from 0.485 to 0.632 in 1994-95. The increase in both real wages per worker and wage share, along with a high value of wage share, indicates that capital-labour ratio is low in the industry and the technical progress is capital saving with low elasticity of substitution between factors.

The trend as shown in **Table** 5.VIII.2 for Cement Corporation of India Ltd (CCI Ltd) is at variance with the trend reported for the industry. CCI Ltd was a very important part of the consumer goods industry employing about 38 percent of the total employees in the industry. But its importance reduced over the period and now it employs less than 10 percent of the total employment. The rate of increase in employment in CCI Ltd is 2.43 percent per annum. Money wages and salaries in the firm increased at an impressive rate of 20.37 percent per annum but the real wages per worker grew from Rs. 1507 in 1974-75 to Rs. 10274 at the annual rate of only 4.72 percent. The rate is, however, higher than the increase in national per capita income (PCI) showing thereby that workers in the firm improved their economic position over the period. Wage share in value added has declined from 0.545 to 0.113 in 1982-83 but again increased to 0.315 in 1995-96. Thus, there is an increase in real wages per worker and a fall in the wage share during the period, a trend similar to that of the industry.

**Table** 5.VIII.3 highlights the trend of Hindustan Photo Films Manufacturing Co Ltd (HPFMC Ltd). The last four years, i.e., 1992-93 to 1995-96 have been comparatively abnormal years for the firm and are generally excluded from the discussion. **Table** 5.VIII.3 indicates that employment in the firm increased from 2.5 thousand to 3.05 thousand at an annual growth rate of 2.47 percent, nearly the same as in CCI Ltd. Both the total wages and salaries at current prices and real wages per worker increased over the period at the rates of 12.78 percent and 1.49 percent respectively, but the general level of real wages per worker remained low as compared to CCI Ltd. Excluding the last four years, the wage share shows a tendency to decline and reduced from 0.367 to 0.289 during 1974-75 to 1991-92. Hence, we observe a similar trend that has been observed for CCI.

Thus, we observe that in the Consumer goods industry not only the growth in the real wages per worker has been lower than the aggregate of industries but even the absolute level of wages has been low through out the period of study, despite a high employment growth rate. Thus the contention that the presence of strong trade-unions in the sector could pull the real wages up appears to be a myth, especially in Consumer goods industry.

While real wages per worker have increased for all the industries and firms, we do not find the same uniform behaviour for wage share. Wage share in value added has reduced for five out of eight industries and increased for Heavy Engineering and Consumer Goods industries but has remained practically constant for Power industry. Whereas in firms the wage share reduced for the eight firms, it remained virtually constant for six firms and increased for the remaining two firms, namely, Misra Dhatu Nigam Ltd and Bharat Heavy Electricals Ltd.

*Inter-Group Variations in Wage Rates*

The neo-classical explanation of inter-industry wage differentials is the variations in the skill-mix, or quality, of the labour force. High wage industries will be those which are relatively skill-intensive, and vice-versa. Changes in an industry's relative pay will reflect variation in occupational wage differentials in the entire economy, or alterations in its particular skill-mix. In the short run, demand factors may influence the industry wage levels but in the long run such demand factors will be generally irrelevent.

However, different empirical studies have found evidence in support of few other variables. Krueger and Summers (1986) found that high wage industries tend to pay all their workers well. Workers in the high wage industries are sharing in the monopoly rents. Dickens and Katz (1987) concluded that three factors stand out to explain the wage differentials : education, profitability and plant size (or the capital-labour ratio). So some comfort for human capital theory is afforded by the finding of Dickens and Katz. Strong correlation has also been found, by few studies, between the capacity to pay and plant size, union density, the capital-labour ratio and profits per worker. Neo-classical theory, generally, account for these differences in either unmeasured differences in the quality of labour, or compensation for non-pecuniary job attributes which serves to equalise net advantages between industries. Krueger and Summers (1986) have, however, raised objections to this neo-classical defence as they found no evidence to reconcile with orthodox theory: as workers move from industry to industry, their earnings change, while their individual endowments and personality traits do not.

However, wage differentials may also exist between different regions or in a particular locality. Some of the explanations advanced for regional wage differences are the differences in (a) the cost of living, (b) mobility of factors between regions, (c) regional economic development and (d) the institutional forces like wage policy, skill mix, racial factors, etc. On the other hand, there may be three possible explanations for wage differentials in a local market, all related to the conscious policy of the employer. First of these are : **Sorting by Worker Quality**. High-paying firms, it is suggested, select the most capable workers on the basis of their innate ability, educational qualifications or work experience etc. Second, **efficiency Wages**, concerns with relatively high rates of pay being used to motivate workers and encourage above-average efforts. Finally, there is the possibility of **rent-sharing**, which is confirmed by a number of pieces of evidence.

These factors indicate that earnings are significantly influenced by factors other than the occupation, industry and region of employment. In determining the level of pay, much depends on the policy of the individual employer. However, in segmented markets, characterized by internal labour markets of individual firms and isolated from one another, workers earnings depend upon the nature of the market, and on the characteristics of their employer, in addition to their own productive attributes.

*(a) Inter-Industry Variations in Wage Rates*

So far we have discussed the trends in wages individually for the eight industrial groups. Now we will analyse the inter-industry variations in growth rates of employment, wages and wage share in particular. The same analysis for firms will be undertaken in the next section.

In **Table** 5(B) we observe a different behaviour of each industry in the public enterprises. The annual rate of growth of employment varies from a very low rate of 0.59 percent in Heavy engineering industry to a high rate of 13.43 percent in the Power industry. While Transport equipment industry has a low growth rate of 1.10 percent, Steel industry, and Fertilizer and Chemical industry has a moderate rate of 1.73 percent and 2.33 percent respectively. On the other hand Petroleum industry, Consumer goods industry and Power industry have quite high growth rates of employment. These industries must have helped in achieving the national objective of employment generation by public enterprises. On the other hand wages, salaries and other benefits at current prices have increased at a minimum rate of almost 12 percent, for Steel, Heavy engineering and Transport equipment, to a high of 37 percent for Power industry. The rate is about 21 percent for Consumer goods industry. The different growth rates of total money wages and salaries have led to differences in growth rates of real wages per worker. While the growth rate is nearly zero in Petroleum industry and only 1.41 percent in Consumer goods industry, it is 2.37 percent in Medium and Light engineering, 2.42 percent in Transport equipment, 2.64 percent in Steel and 3.17 percent in Fertilizers, Chemicals and Pharmaceuticals. These rates are lower in the case of Petroleum and Consumer goods industries and slightly higher in others, than the exponential growth rate of national real per capita income. It is only in the Power sector, where real wages per worker increased at the rate of 4.86 percent, that one may definitely conclude that real wages have increased faster than the increase in national real PCI.

The trend of wage share in value added in different industries reveals that on the one hand there are industries like Power and Petroleum where wage share is very low, only about 6 percent in value added, indicating thereby very high capital intensity, on the other hand industries like Heavy engineering, Medium and Light engineering and Consumer goods have a share of more than 40 percent, it being 45.7 percent 43.4 percent and 56.6 percent respectively in 1993-94. The shares of Steel, Fertilizers and Chemicals and Transport equipment are 32.1 percent, 24.8 percent and 38.5 percent respectively. However, the wage share has not behaved uniformly in all the industries. While it reduced in Steel, Petroleum, Fertilizers, Chemicals and Pharmaceuticals, Medium and Light engineering and Transport equipment industries, it increased in Heavy engineering and Consumer goods industries and remained virtually constant in Power industry. We, thus, observe labour saving technical progress in those five industries where wage share has reduced, and capital saving technical progress in industries with increasing wage share and neutral technical progress in Power industry where it has remained unaffected.

*(b) Inter-Firm Variations in Wage Rates*

**Table** 5(C) has summarized the growth rates of employment, wages, salaries and other benefits, value added, consumer price index, real wages per worker and coefficients of wage share in 1993-94, for the sixteen firms selected for the study. We notice a lot of variation in the growth rates, as it is in the case of the industries.

Growth rate of employment is positive for all firms, except Hindustan Aeronautics Ltd. However, the growth rate is very low for few firms, only 0.13 percent for SAIL but comparatively high for others such as 16.99 percent for NHPC Ltd. There are seven firms with employment growth rates below 2 percent, six firms where growth rates very between 2 percent to 5 percent and the remaining three with rates above 5 percent. On the other hand, total wages and salaries including benefits at current prices have shown wider variations in growth rates, the lowest growth rate being 11.33 percent for Bharat Earth Movers Ltd, a firm with comparatively low growth rate of value added (15.07

percent). The higher growth in wages and salaries is observed for both the firms belonging to the power industry, i.e., NHPC Ltd and NTPC, firms also with high growth rates of value added. Though, there is a link between the growth rates of value added and of wages and salaries, a firm with higher growth rates of value added will have higher capacity to pay, but the link is not always proved as there are firms with higher growths in value added but lower, lower than value added, growth rates in wages and salaries and vice-versa.

The consumer price index for industrial workers increased at the rate of 8 percent during the period 1974-75 to 1993-94. Its effect is uniform on all the firms over the same time period. Deflation of money wages and salaries by consumer price index helped us to obtain the growth rates of real wages per worker. The variation in the growth rates of real wages reflects the disparities which exist between different firms. While the growth rate is highest for NTPC (8.48 percent), a firm belonging to Power industry, it is lowest (0.46 percent) for NHPCL, also a firm belonging to the same industry, i.e., Power. Thus, we find that within the same industry different firms have different growth rates of real wages per worker. Yet the variation between firrns seems to be minimum in the case of the firms BHEL and BHPVL belonging to Heavy engineering industry. Therefore, at this stage there seems to be a weak correlation between the growth of real wages per worker and the growth of gross value added. But this crucial question of link between real wages per worker and its determinants like value added and labour productivity will be analysed and discussed in detail in chapter VI.

The share of wages in value added also show a similar behaviour for the firms. While the share is very low for firms - ONGC (0.015), NTPC (0.050), and NHPCL (0.084), the share is quite high for some other firms such as HMT (.596), MDNL (0.478), HAL (o.381), BHEL (0.380) and BHPVL (0.368). The variations in wage share basically demonstrate the differences in capital intensities of the firm and the nature of their technological progress.

Table 5 (B)

**Estimates of Wage Trends: Inter-Industry Variations in Growth Rates(%)**

| *Variable*<br>*Year* | *Employment* | *Wages and Salaries* | *Value Added* | *Consumer Price Index* | *Real Wages per worker* | *Wages Share in Value added (Coeff.) (in 1995-96)* |
|---|---|---|---|---|---|---|
| **Industry** | | | | | | |
| Steel Industry | 1.73 | 12.95 | 17.05 | 8.00 | 2.64 | 0.347 |
| Power | 13.43 | 37.44 | 38.07 | 8.66 | 4.86 | 0.065 |
| Petroleum | 5.91 | 13.93 | 21.73 | 8.00 | 0.027 | 0.087 |
| Fertilizers | 2.33 | 14.34 | 16.80 | 8.00 | 3.17 | 0.244 |
| Chemicals and Pharmaceuticals | | | | | | |
| Heavy Engineering | 0.59 | 11.95 | 10.83 | 8.00 | 2.76 | 0.549 |
| Medium and Light Engineering | 3.18 | 14.11 | 15.43 | 8.00 | 2.37 | 0.689 |
| Transport Equipment | 1.10 | 12.19 | 14.37 | 8.00 | 2.42 | 0.480 |
| Consumer Goods | 10.47 | 21.21 | 10.77 | 8.00 | 1.41 | 0.465 |

Table 5 (C)

**Estimates of Wage Trends: Inter-Firm Variations in Growth Rates (%)**

| *Variable* / *Year* | *Employment* | *Wages and Salaries* | *Value Added* | *Consumer Price Index* | *Real Wages per worker* | *Wages Share in Value added (Coeff.) (in 1995-96)* |
|---|---|---|---|---|---|---|
| Firms | | | | | | |
| SAIL | 0.13 | 12.73 | 20.11 | 8.79 | 3.39 | 0.319 |
| MDNL | 1.29 | 14.44 | 29.78 | 8.61 | 4.06 | 0.415 |
| NHPCL | 16.99 | 27.56 | 23.40 | 8.66 | 0.46 | 0.073 |
| NTPC | 5.25 | 29.87 | 33.93 | 8.95 | 8.48 | 0.058 |
| IOC Ltd. | 4.77 | 15.02 | 14.66 | 8.00 | 2.66 | 0.181 |
| ONGC | 4.50 | 22.60 | 22.45 | 8.69 | 1.31 | 0.024 |
| NFL | 1.56 | 17.03 | 15.60 | 8.73 | 6.22 | 0.187 |
| IPCL | 6.02 | 17.75 | 20.62 | 8.00 | 3.61 | 0.155 |
| BHEL | 1.81 | 13.57 | 11.17 | 8.00 | 3.45 | 0.488 |
| BHPVL | 1.34 | 14.24 | 14.09 | 8.00 | 3.76 | 0.359 |
| HMT Ltd. | 1.88 | 13.24 | 11.42 | 8.00 | 2.99 | 0.782 |
| ITI Ltd. | 2.13 | 14.35 | 18.22 | 8.00 | 3.46 | 1.021 |
| BEML | 2.57 | 11.33 | 15.07 | 8.00 | 0.57 | 0.302 |
| HAL | -0.09 | 12.27 | 13.90 | 8.00 | 3.65 | 0.479 |
| CCI Ltd. | 2.43 | 20.37 | 23.36 | 8.00 | 4.72 | 0.315 |
| HPFMCL | 2.47 | 12.78 | 8.33 | 8.00 | 1.49 | 0.289* |

*The figure is for 1991-92.

**Summary**

In this chapter we have highlighted the wage trends for the aggregate of industries, for group level, including industries and firms and the variations in inter-group growth rates for the years 1974-75 to 1995-96. We have also presented the trends of employment, total wages and salâries including benefits at current prices, gross value added, consumer price index and wage share in value added.

The trends in aggregate of industries indicate that employment increased at an annual rate of 2.90 percent, with an absolute fall in employment during the last six years, i.e., since 1990-91, indicating a shift in the emphasis of the government about the objectives of the public enterprises. However, real wages per worker during the same period increased only at a rate of 2.08 percent, a rate almost equal to the increase in national real per capita, contrary to the popular perception about wages to be not only very high in the public sector enterprises but also increasing at a very fast rate in these enterprises.

On analyzing the inter group variations, it is noted that there exist vast differences in the rates of growth of real wages per worker. The differences are also noticeable in absolute values for the firms as well as the industries. The differences in growth rates of real wages range from 0.46 percent to 8.48 percent in the case of firms and 0.027 percent to 4.86 percent in the case of industries. However, we observe that industries/firms with initial low level of real wage rates have tried to have higher growth rates so as to come at par with other industries/firms. But while in some cases they have been successful in attaining these levels, in others the real wage rates remained depressed. On the other hand in industry like Petroleum with high initial level of real wages, the growth rate in real wage rates per worker remained low. Why do we observe such differences and what are their determinants? Such questions would be dealt with in the next chapter where we will find out these links.

Analysis of wage share in value added for different firms and industries also reveal wide differences reflecting upon the capital-intensity of the respective units. The coefficients range from 0.024 to 0.782 in the case of firms and vary between 0.065

to 0.689 in the case of industries. Thus, the range is narrow for the industries as compared to the firms. The range of wage share also reflects the diverse nature of industries and firms under public enterprises.

Thus, we observe wide differences between firms and industries in the growth rates of real wages and in coefficients of wage share in value added. Such inter-firm and inter-industry differences were also observed in their productivity growths in the last chapter. There is, thus, a need to find out the link between these differences in growth rates of real wages and productivity estimates.

## NOTES

1. Verma (1980), Ch. 1.
2. Courtheoux, Jean Paul (1974), p 142.
3. Friedman, M. (1968), pp 1-17.
4. Hicks (1964), pp 121-123.
5. Money wages are obtained by dividing the total money wages and salaries by the number of employees.
6. Computed from the data obtained from different issues of Economic Survey and Chandok (1990).
7. Source : **Table** 4(G).
8. Source: Economic Survey (1996-97).
9. For details about financial performance of different industries/ firms, see Public Enterprises Survey : 1995-96.

# 6

# WAGE-PRODUCTIVITY NEXUS: EXPERIENCE OF INDIAN PUBLIC SECTOR ENTERPRISES

### General

The wage - productivity relationship in public sector enterprises in India has come into sharp focus in recent years with the change in the Government's policy and attitude. The focus of the current economic reforms is to gradually 'privatize' the public sector in India either through outright closure or sale of some of these units or through dilution of government's ownership in them. The reason for the change in attitude is ascribed to the inefficiency and unprofitability of the public sector, the major blame for which is being shifted onto the workers. One of the main arguments advanced for the unprofitability of these enterprises is that wages of the workers in these enterprises have increased faster over the period and wages have no link with the worker's productivity.

The present chapter is devoted to the testing of the above mentioned contention that wages in the public sector have no link with labour productivity. The question of how the public sector productivity and wages have behaved during the last twenty two years has been dealt with in the discussions of the last two chapters, i.e., in chapter IV and V. While chapter IV had analysed the productivity trends in select public sector enterprises and had pointed out that labour productivity has almost consistently increased in all the groups, chapter V has led to the conclusion that real wage rates have also increased during the same period though wide inter-industry and inter-firm differences were noted.

Different studies and commissions have gone into the question of the link between wages and productivity and arguments for and against the link have been advanced. The importance of the link between wages and productivity for both the employer and employees was emphasized way back in 1932 by the Royal Commission on Labour in India when it had observed "...in certain occupations and industries the workers are getting a wage lower than the value of their marginal product..., the wages paid are themselves the cause of lower productivity".[1] In India the Committee on Fair Wages (1949) had suggested using labour productivity as one of the criteria to fix the `fair wage'; others being the prevailing rates of wages in the same or similar occupations in the same or neighbouring localities, the level of national income and its distribution and the place of the industry in the economy of the country.[2] The National Commission on Labour admitted that a rational wage policy should aim at a progressive increase in real wages. At the same time any sustained improvement in real wages cannot be brought about without increasing productivity.[3] Palekar (1962) also supported the link and has said, "It is true to say that in the long run a rise in productivity is the only sound basis for a rise in money wages".[4] Bowen (1969)[5] has linked the relationship through the profit position of firms, i.e., a higher productivity will lead to a higher capacity to pay through higher profits.

In practice, as distinct from theoretical positions no accepted approach to productivity-wage relationship has been found. As has been pointed out by Sinha and Sawhney in their study on productivity, what is at least as important as productivity for the creation of capacity to pay at the level of the industry or establishment is the rise in the money value of the product. Rising product prices and rising productivity together create the capacity of industry to pay. It is also generally accepted that the differential rates of productivity growth are largely due to technological and economic factors, and, therefore, they may not on the whole reflect differences in the contribution of employees to production.[6] Labour productivity is largely dependent on work conditions, work environment and plant conditions together with the technology adopted. Any increase in labour productivity does not necessarily mean that labour is working harder or is contributing more to production, irrespective of other factors.

The wage-productivity linkage is said to create a chaotic wage structure. The level of productivity may be very high in some industries and very low in some others depending on technological progress. If wages are strictly linked to productivity, the wage ratios would be disproportionately high in some industries and low in others for jobs requiring the same skill and responsibility. The level of productivity would change from time to time within the same industry, therefore, it is not practicable to raise or reduce wages in accordance with productivity trends. It is also being pointed out that if proportionate wage increases are given with large productivity increases then this will prevent industries from reducing their prices to consumers and from expanding output and employment.

However, while employer's representatives and government officials are of the opinion that any future upward revision of wages should be linked with productivity, trade unions are opposed to the idea. The unions generally argue that productivity by the management is being equated with labour productivity, and the unions do not like to accept responsibility for adverse performance attributable to other factors like inadequate power supply, raw-material shortages, cost overruns due to project delays and obsolete technology over which the workers have no control.

The rising cost of living as a result of rising prices also compels trade unions to demand higher wages. However, when the resulting wage increases are larger than the increases in productivity of labour, the labour cost per unit of output rises leading to a wage-price spiral. But in India, the workers would like to link the wage rates to the cost of living as prices are rising continuously and faster than productivity in industry.[7] However, linking wages to price levels is not generally favoured by employers who feel that such an arrangement is not only a major contributing factor to raising business costs, but it is detrimental to the economic system.[8] Gordon (1990)[9] has recently concluded, while analysing the US economy's Phillips Curve for 1954-87, that wage changes donot contribute statistically to the explanation of inflation. He also concludes that price changes are irrelevant for wage changes, i.e., that both prices and labour costs live a life of their own. He has thus, put a question mark on the wage-price linkage. However, wage-price linkage has one advantage. If our objective is to maintain a higher level of investment, the economy and the people will benefit more from the consumption angle, as emphasized by Keynesian approach than from the capital formation approach, because whatever is produced will be consumed through higher purchasing power. Gordon (1987) remarked, "Thus a stimulus to aggregate demand provides not only the direct benefit of raising output and employment, but also the indirect benefit of raising the real wage and creating substitution away from labour that boosts productivity and, if sustained, the nation's standard of living. With this dual benefit obtainable from demand expansion, the case against demand stimulation must rest with convincing evidence that such policies would create an unacceptable acceleration of inflation".[10] Khusro (1979), however, maintained that in the interests of the industry and the economy it is necessary that rise in industrial wage bill is less than the rise in industrial output. Thus, if a wage-price spiral kind of situation is to be avoided then it is necessary that prices increase at lower rates than productivity per man.

**The Indian Experience**

Some of the significant studies on wage-productivity link although were reviewed in an earlier chapter, i.e., Chapter II, where it was found that generally a link exists between wages and productivity still, in the Indian context, we find it necessary to mention some additional findings in this regard. However, though wage levels and productivity levels may be moving in the same direction in some of the industries, the employer's and worker's organization did not, in contrast, follow any consistent approach to productivity. Hence a rise in productivity does not automatically lead to a rise in wages. The golden rule of linking wages to productivity has generally been ignored. The National

Commission on Labour has pertinently pointed out[11] - "Increases in money wages of industrial workers since independence have not been associated with a rise in real wages nor have these been commensurate with improvements in productivity. Wage costs as a proportion of total costs of manufacture have registered a decline and same is true of worker's share in value added by manufacture".

One study[12] concluded that total emoluments per employee at constant prices increased by only 23 percent during 1960-71 as compared to a 53 percent increase in value added per employee at constant prices. Shivamaggi (1968) and Papola (1970) had also obtained the same conclusions for the earlier period. The study made by the Central Statistical Organisation entitled Wages and Productivity in Selected Industries in Organised Manufacturing Sector (1960-77) covers 20 major industries. The study revealed that indices of real wages during 1960-77 have generally lagged behind the indices of labour productivity in most industries.[13] The percentage shares of wages in value added during 1960-77 also showed a decline in most of the industries. Thus, workers in general did not receive their due share in gains from productivity - wages lagged behind productivity. There is no evidence that in industry generally real wages have outstripped productivity.

While linking wages to productivity is desirable, there is a feeling that labourer's wages are not moving alongwith productivity trends. Sundaram (1987)[14] shows that industrial wages in the organized sector of the manufacturing industries in the 1970's have lagged behind increased labour productivity. Tulpule and Datta (1988) and Jose (1994) have given us the same conclusions for organised industries in India for the periods 1960-84 and 1970-71 to 1987-88, respectively (as detailed earlier in chapter II).

Thus, the above-mentioned studies suggest that in actual practice there is no evidence of a direct relationship between wages and productivity in India's organised sector, though the two have generally moved in the same direction.

Gordon (1987) investigated the relationship between productivity, wages and prices inside and outside of manufacturing in the U.S., Japan and Europe during the period 1964-84. He divided the period into three stages, viz, 1964-72, 1972-79 and 1979-84 and found the relationships for aggregate level, manufacturing level and non-manufacturing level. He had concluded that U.S. productivity slow down after 1979 was mainly due to the slowdown in excess wage increase. He found broadly the same results for Japan and Europe. He also showed that output increases have a definite impact on wage changes except in U.S. manufacturing where wages were rigid as compared to Europe and Japan. He attributed the difference in U.S. productivity and Europe's productivity, after 1979 in manufacturing to the differences in excess wages besides the trend value. The paper confirms the real-wage elasticity of labour input and shows that the response of labour input and labour productivity to changes in real wage is roughly similar in three countries. The paper concludes, "The results have the interesting implication that a substantial component of the slowdown in productivity growth, especially after 1972 in US non-manufacturing and after 1979 in Japan and Europe, can be attributed to a shift from excessive to moderate real wage growth".

But apart from the practical difficulties of establishing an operational relationship between wages and productivity from year to year, there is the important consideration that in all countries, including India, productivity has in practice been considered to be only one of several criteria employed in wage determination. Other factors, as discussed here, which may influence the wage determination, especially in organised sector are the capacity to pay, the cost of living, the size of establishment, capacity utilization, capital intensity, unionization, and skill composition. Different Wage Board Awards in India; Committee on Fair Wages, 1949; The National Commission on Labour; and the Supreme Court - while adjudicating industrial disputes have made only casual references to the inclusion of productivity criterion for wage rate determination. Even in advanced countries limited use has been made of the productivity criterion in wage determination.

With such a limited applicability in general, the extension of the criterion to public sector enterprises, where there are non-commercial objectives along with the commercial ones, is doubtful. In public sector enterprises wages are generally determined through wage negotiations and agreements and are valid for a time duration. In such negotiations and agreements productivity may find a place but it certainly does not play a deciding or dominant role in wage fixation. However, this does not mean that productivity is altogether ignored. It only stresses the point that no exact quantitative relationship between productivity and wage rate has been put forward by Wage Boards and other wage determining institutions.

**An Econometric Analysis of the Relationship : The Models**

In order to clearly understand the link between wages and productivity in selected public sector enterprises this study has undertaken a simple econometric analysis. This section will concentrate on finding the link, through regression analysis, in aggregate of industries, individual industries and firms selected for the purpose.

In the first place different regression models, depending upon the number of variables included in the exercise, have been developed. The stepwise regresion will also identify and take care of the problem of multicollinearity, if it exists. The exercise includes real wage rate (Wr) as the dependent variable and trend variable (t), real value added (V), labour productivity (LP), capital-labour ratio (K/L) or capital intensity, and consumer price index for industrial workers (Pw) as the explanatory variables. Real value added has been replaced in some models by total factor productivity indices (TFP). Unionization has not been considered to be significant as (a) a number of empirical studies in India like Johri (1966), Suri (1976), Sen (1985) and Ramjash (1992) have found no positive influence of trade unions on the money earnings of workers in selected manufacturing industries in India; and (b) since Unions in the public sector enterprises are supported either by the State or by different political parties, it is, therefore, very difficult to separate the effect of unionization from State intervention. The complete set of the models used are :

Model I : $Wr = A\,(LP)^{\alpha}$

Model II : $Wr = A.\,e^{\lambda t}\,(LP)^{\alpha}$

Model III : $Wr = A. e^{\lambda t} (LP)^{\alpha}. (V)^{\beta}$

Model IV : $Wr = A. e^{\lambda t} (LP)^{\alpha}. (V)^{\beta} (K/L)^{\gamma}$

Model V : $Wr = A. e^{\lambda t} (LP)^{\alpha}. (V)^{\beta} (K/L)^{\gamma}. (Pw)^{\theta}$

Model VI : $Wr = A. e^{\lambda t} (LP)^{\alpha}. (TFPS)^{\beta 1} (K/L)^{\gamma}. (Pw)^{\theta}$

Model VII : $Wr = A. e^{\lambda t} (LP)^{\alpha}. (TFPT)^{\beta 2} (K/L)^{\gamma}. (Pw)^{\theta}$

Model VIII : $Wr = A. e^{\lambda t} (LP)^{\alpha}. (TFPK)^{\beta 3} (K/L)^{\gamma}. (Pw)^{\theta}$

Model IX : $Wr = A. (LP)^{\alpha}. (TFPS)^{\beta 1} (K/L)^{\gamma}$

Model X : $Wr = A. (LP)^{\alpha}. (TFPT)^{\beta 2} (K/L)^{\gamma}$

Model XI : $Wr = A. (LP)^{\alpha}. (TFPK)^{\beta 3} (K/L)^{\gamma}$

All the models are log-linear in coefficients.

The first model has only included labour productivity. It is generally expected, especially in neo-classical theory, that higher labour productivity leads to higher wages. The model has been extended to include the trend coefficient 't'. It captures the effect of size of the firm, change in managerial skills, and other labour embodiments. Value added has been considered in the third model because it is being argued that real value added reflects the firms `ability to pay' and is an important determinant of the wage rate. However, ability to pay may mean different things. Since it depends upon the level of productivity, of total factor productivity and not of labour alone, and also the product prices, therefore, value added has been substituted by total factor productivity indices in the subsequent models VI to XI. Further, Gahlen and Licht (1990) had not found any impact of `ability to pay' and of `establishment size' on wages. They had contended that all versions of the efficiency wage theory suggest that there is a positive relationship between firm size and remuneration but this relationship was not found in Germany because firm size effects were already captured in time series estimates. Such being the case one can expect that value added takes a negative sign in the regression analysis.[15] Thus, the negative sign of the coefficient of log (V) does not necessarily mean that value added has a negative relationship with wage rate, the negative sign may appear because the effect of value added is already captured by the trend coefficient and the two coefficients are not necessarily complementary to each other.

Capital intensity measured by capital-labour ratio is also expected to affect the wage rate of labour in a firm or in an industry. Rising capital-labour ratio, in neo-classical production function, increases labour productivity which leads to higher wages. Higher wages, in turn, induce a substitution of capital for labour. Thus, capital intensity via productivity is expected to have a positive relationship with wages. Sometimes the effect of capital intensity is captured either by the trend coefficient or by the value added coefficient through the route of capital intensity-productivity-value added. Therefore, capital intensity has been included in model IV to identify its relationship with wages.

Model V includes price of consumer goods for industrial workers (Pw) as an additional variable. Though, the dependent variable Wr has already tried to exclude the impact of price rise but employees in general, and especially in organised sector, expect their wages to be linked to the cost of living through change in dearness allowance. Since dearness allowance is granted only periodically and there is no automatic indexation, therefore, some degree of money illusion may creep in. Generally any increase in price of consumer goods has a tendency to depress real wages. Therefore,it is believed that the coefficient of Pw, broadly, takes a negative sign in its relationship with real wages.

We have extended this full model, i.e., model V, by replacing value added by its proxy variable total factor productivity. It is argued that value added depends upon total factor productivity and price of product. Though price of product and prices of inputs have been taken care of while calculating real value added but TFP is still a better alternative as it completely eliminates the impact of change in prices. However, TFP embodies labour productivity in a limiting sense, therefore, it can also be used as a substitute for labour productivity. Since the model includes both of them simultaneously, it is, therefore, expected that generally these will not be complementing each other and will be taking opposite signs in the regressions. The opposite signs will reveal that effect of rising productivity has been captured by one coefficient and the other coefficient is not complementing it; but if the two coefficients, i.e., of labour productivity and TFP take the same sign, it implies they are complementing each other.

In the last three models, i.e., IX, X and XI we have dropped the trend variable 't' and the money illusion variable Pw in order to find out their impact on the models.

As the variables introduced in different models, mostly, may have some direct or indirect relationship with each other, especially labour productivity, value added, and total factor productivity, therefore, problem of multicollinearity may arise. Different models have been tried so as to reduce multicollinearity to the maximum possible extent.

The models are estimated by Ordinary Least Square method (OLS) applied on log-linear forms. The coefficients of the variables, thus, give us the elasticity of response of the variable with wage rate. Preliminary results suggested that autocorrelation was a problem in the models. As a consequence, we corrected for a first order auto-regressive scheme in the error term and applied the Cochrane-Orcutt method of estimation. Out of the two, i.e., ordinary least square estimates and Cochrane-Orcutt estimates, we selected the latter wherever autocorrelation coefficient (RHO) was significant and incorporated the former (OLS estimates) in our results when auto-correlation was insignificant. The problem of autocorrelation was more severe when trend variable coefficient 't' was dropped from all the models, as it not only introduced autocorrelation but even the explaining power, i.e., $\bar{R}^2$ of the models declined. So 't' was retained in all the models except model I and the last three models. The results of the regression exercise, thus undertaken, have been presented in different tables, a separate one for each industry/firm.

While selecting the best model which explains the relationship of wage rate with its explanatory variables, the study has carefully kept certain factors into consideration. The factors which the model should have are : (a) the expected signs of the coefficients; (b) high $\bar{R}^2$, i.e., high explanatory power of the model; (c) absence of auto-correlation; and (d) absence of multicollinearity. A compromise, sometimes has been made between these considerations if there was a clash. However, the main emphasis has been on the correct signs of the variables and the value of $R^2$. The results have been presented and discussed in section 6.4.

**Empirical Results**

In this section we present and discuss the summarized results of the regression analysis undertaken to find out the link between real wage rate and labour productivity in public sector enterprises. The section is divided into three parts. In the first part we find out the link in the aggregate of industries. The second part will highlight the relationship, as found from the models, for the eight industrial groups along with the firms belonging to the industry. Inter-industry and inter-firm variations in wage rates will be examined in the third part.

*Aggregate of Industries*

The results of the different regression models for aggregate of industries (eight) in the public sector manufacturing enterprises are presented in **Table** 6(A).

In **Table** 6(A) model I gives us a positive relationship, though the value of LP coefficient is insignificant, between labour productivity and the real wage rate. The model had high degree of autocorrelation which was removed by the use of Cochrane-Orcutt adjustment method. But the model has been extended gradually by introducing more variables into it. The second model has not only increased $\bar{R}^2$ but has also shown the statistical significance of the time trend coefficient. Model III has further increased $\bar{R}^2$ and reduced the degree of autocorrelation present in the second model. Thus, the third model has lent significance to the coefficient of LP, and the newly introduced variable 'V' in addition to being negative is also significant. In model IV when we introduced (K/L) as another explanatory variable, it reduced $\bar{R}^2$ and took a negative sign, a sign opposite to what the theory suggests. Model V, which is a full model as it contains all the variables, is the best fit to describe the relationship between the dependent variable, the real wage rate and other explanatory variables. It gives the following relationship;

$$\log (Wr) = \underset{(3.071)}{6.875} + \underset{(1.326)}{0.056t} + \underset{(3.137)}{0.746 \log (LP)^*} - \underset{(-3.311)}{0.619 \log (V)^*}$$

$$+ \underset{(0.496)}{0.190 \log (K/L)} - \underset{(-4.411)}{0.555 \log (P_w)^*}$$

$$\bar{R}^2 = .970;\ D\text{–}W = 1.512;\ F_{5,14} = 127.60$$

The model provides not only the highest value for $\bar{R}^2$ but also indicates the expected signs of the coefficients. It reveals that while trend coefficient, LP coefficient and (K/L) coefficients are positive, with labour productivity to be statistically significant, the coefficients of 'V' and Pw are negative, where 'V' is statistically significant. Thus, the model depicts that real wage rates in the aggregate of industries in public sector enterprises are positively and significantly related to the labour productivity. Therefore, the model conclusively establishes the link between wages and productivity.

However, when we replace value added variable in Model V by its proxy variable TFP, we not only notice the fall in the value of $\bar{R}^2$ but also the presence of multicollinearity in models VI and VII. The coefficients of LP also get changed into negative values because of the introduction of TFPS and TFPT as they had acted as substitutes of LP and had captured its effect. But when the trend variable is dropped from these models resulting in new models IX and X, the effect which was earlier captured by the trend is now being shared by both LP and TFP(TFPS and TFPT) making both of them significant. TFPK and LP in models VIII and XI though, acted as substitutes, the major effect is captured by LP, thus, keeping its sign to be positive.

On screening of the different models, we thus found model V to be the best in explaining the required relationship. We also infer that time trend is positive along with a positive coefficient of LP. Thus, real wage rate is increasing and is positively associated with labour productivity in the aggregate of industries. The same relationship is being probed for the individual industries/firms in the next section.

Table 6 (A)

**Regression Function for Wages : Aggregate of Industries**

| *Dependent Variable* → *(Real Wage Rate)* | | | | | ——*MODEL NO.*—— | | | | | | |
|---|---|---|---|---|---|---|---|---|---|---|---|
| *Explanatory Variable* | 1 | 2 | 3 | 4 | 5 | 6 | 7 | 8 | 9 | 10 | 11 |
| Constant | 1.441 | 0.572 | 5.198 | 5.231 | 6.875 | -4.179 | -3.855 | 11.003 | -5.682 | -5.641 | 7.584 |
| | (4.318) | (7.962) | (3.872) | (2.311) | (3.071) | (-0.942) | (-0.842) | (2.838) | (-2.533) | (-2.472) | (1.774) |
| t | | ** 0.019 | * 0.023 | 0.023 | 0.056 | 0.062 | 0.059 | 0.011 | | | |
| | | (2.699) | (4.498) | (0.650) | (1.326) | (1.299) | (1.223) | (0.338) | | | |
| Log (LP) | 0.024 | 0.014 | * 0.873 | ** 0.878 | * 0.746 | -0.937 | -0.892 | ** 1.542 | ** -0.890 | ** -0.890 | 1.290 |
| | (.330) | (0.191) | (3.387) | (2.527) | (3.137) | (-1.532) | (-1.406) | (2.895) | (-2.620) | (-2.560) | (1.704) |
| Log (V) | | | * -0.715 | ** -0.719 | * 0.619 | | | | | | |
| | | | (-3.446) | (-2.587) | (-3.311) | | | | | | |
| Log (K/L) | | | | -0.005 | 0.190 | 0.665 | 0.658 | -0.564 | * 1.019 | * 1.015 | -0.774 |
| | | | | (-0.014) | (0.496) | (1.730) | (1.671) | (-0.864) | (3.367) | (3.293) | (-1.315) |

Contd. . . .

| | | | | | | | | | | | |
|---|---|---|---|---|---|---|---|---|---|---|---|
| Log ($P_w$) | | | | | -0.555* (-4.411) | -0.260 (-0.887) | -0.268 (-0.875) | -0.556* (-4.054) | | | |
| Log (TFPK) | | | | | | | | -1.523* (-2.960) | | | -1.273 (-1.735) |
| Log (TFPS) | | | | | | 1.074 (1.528) | | | 1.010** (2.608) | | |
| Log (TFPT) | | | | | | | 1.014 (1.402) | | | 1.003** (2.546) | |
| $\bar{R}^2$ | .927 | 0.932 | .959 | .956 | .970 | .949 | .948 | 0.968 | .953 | .952 | .943 |
| DW | 1.493 | 1.337 | 1.518 | 1.515 | 1.512 | 1.818 | 1.851 | 1.974 | 1.579 | 1.590 | 1.520 |
| F/RHO | 0.969* (13.726) | 0.721* (3.162) | 0.598* (3.314) | .599** (2.778) | 127.60* (5,14) | 0.711* (3.924) | 0.709* (3.828) | 116.08 (5,14) | .484*** (1.973) | .482*** (1.956) | 0.504*** (2.143) |

*Notes* : 1. Figures in the brackets give t-values or degree of freedom.
2. * indicates significance at 1% level.
** indicates significance at 5% level.
*** indicates significance at 10% level.

*VI. Group Level Regressions*

In this section we will describe the regression results obtained from different models for the eight industrial groups. The regressions will facilitate in finding out the relationship between wages and productivity in these industrial groups. The scheme of analysis being followed in this section is the same as was adopted in chapters IV and V.

*I. Steel-Group*

**Tables** 6.I.1, 6.I.2 and 6.I.3 provide the results of the regression analysis for the Steel industry group.

On analysing **Table** 6.I.1 for Steel industry, we find trend coefficient to be positive, indicating a rise in real wage rate in the Steel industry. The coefficient of labour productivity is also positive and significant, especially in many models. The coefficient of labour productivity creates problems only when we include both labour productivity and TFP into a model as they both try to capture the same effect. Thus, we find that if the coefficient of LP is positive then generally the TFP coefficients are negative and vice-versa. The coefficients of value added, as expected, are negative in all the three models and are significant. However, capital intensity coefficient is generally found to be negative because its effect is generally captured by any one of the other variables introduced into a model because of its close relationship with them. $P_w$ coefficient has also in general taken the expected sign, i.e. negative, depicting a negative relationship between the price of consumer goods and the real wage rate.

On close inspection of all the models for the steel industry, we observe model V to be the best in explaining the relationship of real wage rate with labour productivity and other variables. It portrays the following relationship:

$$\underset{}{\text{Log }(W_r)} = \underset{(3.88)}{6.08} + \underset{(4.72)}{0.07t^{*}} + \underset{(3.656)}{0.552\log(LP)^{*}} \underset{(-2.92)}{-0.49\log(V)^{**}} +$$

$$\underset{(0.26)}{0.025\log(K/L)} \underset{(-3.56)}{- 0.60\log(P_w)^{*}}$$

$\bar{R}^2 = 0.969$ D–W=1.822 $F_{5,14}$=123.69

The relationship conveys that wage rate is statistically related to the trend value, labour productivity, value added and price of consumer goods. Thus, labour productivity is a statistically significant variable related to the real wage rate in Steel industry and its elasticity with respect to wage rate is 0.552, implying that a 10 percent increase in labour productivity will lead to a 5.52 percent increase in real wage rate. The coefficient of LP is still higher in models III, IV, IX and X but they have been ignored in favour of model V because of the two following reasons; (i) $\bar{R}^2$ is high in model V implying thereby that it explains more variations in change in real wage rate; and (ii) in model V the sign of log (K/L) is positive, as is also supported by the theory.

**Table** 6.I.2 depicts the results of the regressions obtained for Steel Authority of India Limited (SAIL), a firm from Steel industry selected for analysis. On summarizing the results, it is clear that model III best explains the relationship between the real wage rate and the explanatory variables. Though the emphasis in our investigation is on the link between labour productivity and wages, yet we have not selected a model with the highest value of the coefficient of LP or highest $\bar{R}^2$; but as stated earlier, we have also considered the direction of the other coefficients included into the regression analysis. Any model with the same signs as expected by economic theory is generally preferred even though it might have lower coefficient values or lower $\bar{R}^2$. It is because of these reasons that model III is selected for SAIL. The values for both the coefficient of LP and $\bar{R}^2$ are higher in models IV and V, but since (K/L) take an opposite sign in these models, therefore, they have been ignored. The reason for ignoring model VIII is two fold: (i) it has lower $\bar{R}^2$ than model III, and (ii) (K/L) and TFPK in the model take opposite values and the net value of LP and TFPK, combined together, is less than the value of LP in model III. The relationship as expressed by model III is as follows:

$$\text{Log}(W_r) = 3.573 + 0.025t^{*} + 0.656 \log(LP)^{*} - 0.578 \log(V)^{**}$$

$$(3.230) \quad (5.024) \quad (3.463) \qquad\qquad (-2.670)$$

$\bar{R}^2 = .971$; DW = 1.939 ; $F_{3,12} = 173.58$

Table 6.I. 1

**Regression Function for Wages : Steel Industry**

| *Dependent Variable →* *(Real Wage Rate)* | ——*MODEL NO.*—— | | | | | | | | | | |
|---|---|---|---|---|---|---|---|---|---|---|---|
| *Explanatory Variable* | 1 | 2 | 3 | 4 | 5 | 6 | 7 | 8 | 9 | 10 | 11 |
| Constant | 1.613 | 0.573 | 3.222 | 4.276 | 6.08 | 2.434 | 2.383 | -0.338 | 3.24 | 3.081 | -11.467 |
| | (4.892) | (29.91) | (3.757) | (3.956) | (3.88) | (2.236) | (2.35) | (-0.04) | (3.29) | (3.34) | (-2.73) |
| t | | 0.020* | +0.026* | 0.040* | 0.07* | 0.025 | 0.024 | 0.034** | | | |
| | | (10.08) | (5.989) | (3.596) | (4.72) | (1.348) | (1.25) | (2.17) | | | |
| Log (LP) | 0.056* | 0.094* | 0.558* | 0.680* | 0.552* | 0.289 | 0.293 | -0.231* | .572* | .555** | -1.812** |
| | (1.002) | (3.94) | (3.592) | (3.985) | (3.656) | (1.226) | (1.271) | (-0.18) | (3.94) | (4.03) | (-2.58) |
| Log (V) | | | -0.495* | -0.628* | -0.49** | | | | | | |
| | | | (-3.074) | (-3.542) | (-2.92) | | | | | | |
| Log (K/L) | | | | -0.182 | 0.025 | -0.065 | -0.069 | 0.346 | -0.177 | -0.161 | 1.535* |

Contd. . . .

| | | | | | | | | | | | |
|---|---|---|---|---|---|---|---|---|---|---|---|
| | | | | (-1.362) | (0.26) | (-0.284) | (-0.304) | (0.35) | (-1.16) | (-1.117) | (3.429) |
| Log ($P_w$) | | | | | -0.60* | -0.174 | -0.161 | -0.289 | | | |
| | | | | | (-3.56) | (-0.772) | (-0.695) | (-1.742) | | | |
| Log (TFPK) | | | | | | | | 0.354 | | | 1.952** |
| | | | | | | | | (0.273) | | | (2.717) |
| Log (TFPS) | | | | | | 0.191 | | | | -0.505* | |
| | | | | | | (-0.741) | | | | (-3.378) | |
| Log (TFPT) | | | | | | | -0.192 | | | -0.477* | |
| | | | | | | | (-0.775) | | | (-3.44) | |
| $\bar{R}^2$ | .918 | .951 | 0.962 | 0.964 | .969 | .953 | .953 | .951 | .951 | .951 | .942 |
| DW | 2.06 | 1.559 | 1.843 | 1.705 | 1.822 | 2.164 | 2.169 | 1.955 | 2.150 | 2.156 | 1.387 |
| F/RHO | .967* | 187.3 | 0.497** | 0.546** | 123.67 | 78.88 | 79.16 | 76.21 | 123.95 | 125.95 | 104.93 |
| | (11.246) | (2,17) | (2.283) | (2.416) | (5,14) | (5,14) | (5,14) | (5,14) | (3,16) | (3,16) | (3,16) |

*Notes* : 1: Figures in the brackets give t-values or degree of freedom.

2. * indicates significance at 1% level.

** indicates significance at 5% level.

*** indicates significance at 10% level.

Table 6.I. 2

**Regression Function for Wages : SAIL**

| Dependent Variable → (Real Wage Rate) Explanatory Variable | MODEL NO. 1 | 2 | 3 | 4 | 5 | 6 | 7 | 8 | 9 | 10 | 11 |
|---|---|---|---|---|---|---|---|---|---|---|---|
| Constant | .791 | 0.621 | 3.573 | 4.263 | 6.374 | 1.219 | 1.297 | 18.677 | 0.353 | .0449 | 2.981 |
| | (4.73) | (14.020) | (3.230) | (3.701) | (2.027) | (0.435) | (0.461) | (1.870) | (0.165) | (0.211) | (0.393) |
| t | | 0.016* | 0.025* | +0.041* | 0.075 | 0.057 | 0.055 | 0.068 | | | |
| | | (3.669) | (5.024) | (3.529) | (1.566) | (1.005) | (0.927) | (1.193) | | | |
| Log (LP) | 0.267* | 0.156* | 0.656* | 0.675* | 0.724* | 0.038 | 0.059 | 2.996*** | 0.199 | 0.211 | 0.684 |
| | (10.096) | (4.565) | (3.463) | (3.729) | (3.677) | (0.134) | (0.208) | (2.081) | (0.745) | (0.789) | (0.500) |
| Log (V) | | | -0.578** | -0.599** | -0.682** | | | | | | |
| | | | (-2.67) | (-2.894) | (-2.833) | | | | | | |
| Log (K/L) | | | | -0.281 | -0.176 | -0.372 | -0.391 | -1.619** | 0.210 | 0.198 | 0.031 |
| | | | | (-1.487) | (-0.729) | (-0.966) | (-1.008) | (-2.294) | (0.741) | (0.697) | (0.056) |

| | | | | | | | | | | | |
|---|---|---|---|---|---|---|---|---|---|---|---|
| Log ($P_w$) | | | | | -0.406 | -0.043 | 0.025 | -0.262 | | | |
| | | | | | (-0.724) | (-0.065) | (-0.037) | (-0.407) | | | |
| | | | | | | | | *** | | | |
| Log (TFPK) | | | | | | | | -2.896 | | | -0.515 |
| | | | | | | | | (-1.958) | | | (-0.372) |
| Log (TFPS) | | | | | | 0.046 | | | -0.030 | | |
| | | | | | | (0.132) | | | (-0.091) | | |
| Log (TFPT) | | | | | | | 0.019 | | | -0.045 | |
| | | | | | | | (0.054) | | | (-0.136) | |
| $\bar{R}^2$ | .926 | .958 | .971 | .974 | .973 | .959 | .959 | .965 | .943 | .943 | .944 |
| | | | | | | *** | *** | | | | |
| DW | 1.657 | 1.527 | 1.939 | 1.719 | 1.835 | 2.127 | 2.139 | 1.575 | 1.756 | 1.757 | 1.843 |
| F/RHO | 0.261 | 174.53 | 173.58 | 143.89 | 110.24 | .575 | .567 | 84.13 | 84.73 | 84.51 | 85.39 |
| | (.819) | (2,13) | (3,12) | (4,11) | (5,10) | (2.152) | (2.129) | (5,10) | (3,12) | (3,12) | (3,12) |

*Notes* : 1. Figures in the brackets give t-values or degree of freedom.

2. * indicates significance at 1% level.

** indicates significance at 5% level.

*** indicates significance at 10% level.

Table 6.I. 3

**Regression Function for Wages : MDNL**

| *Dependent Variable →* *(Real Wage Rate)* | —MODEL NO.— | | | | | | | | | | |
|---|---|---|---|---|---|---|---|---|---|---|---|
| *Explanatory Variable* | 1 | 2 | 3 | 4 | 5 | 6 | 7 | 8 | 9 | 10 | 11 |
| Constant | 1.255 | 0.348 | 0.487 | -0.159 | 18.347 | 12.464 | 13.751 | 13.887 | 0.131 | 0.504 | 1.248 |
| | (15.65) | (2.232) | (2.086) | (-0.080) | (2.270) | (2.074) | (2.118) | (1.828) | (0.708) | (.355) | (0.989) |
| | | | * | ** | ** | ** | ** | *** | | | |
| t | | 0.040 | 0.038 | 0.036 | 0.411 | 0.356 | 0.344 | 0.301 | | | |
| | | (3.718) | (3.443) | (2.798) | (2.558) | (3.190) | (2.847) | (2.194) | | | |
| | | | | | | ** | *** | | | | |
| Log (LP) | -0.077 | 0.001 | 0.339 | 0.237 | -0.769 | -0.532 | -0.389 | -0.164 | -0.253 | -0.228 | -0.373 |
| | (-0.827) | (0.030) | (0.811) | (+0.441) | (-1.261) | (-2.355) | (-1.911) | (-0.350) | (-0.838) | (-0.863) | (-0.778) |
| Log (V) | | | -0.311 | -0.192 | 0.622 | | | | | | |
| | | | (-0.812) | (-0.356) | (1.119) | | | | | | |
| Log (K/L) | | | | 0.194 | 0.177 | -0.355 | -0.444 | -0.247 | -0.029 | -0.085 | -0.570 |
| | | | | (0.330) | (0.375) | (-0.959) | (-1.013) | (-0.222) | (-0.078) | (-0.207) | (-0.540) |

| | (1) | (2) | (3) | (4) | (5) | (6) | (7) | (8) | (9) | (10) | (11) |
|---|---|---|---|---|---|---|---|---|---|---|---|
| Log ($P_w$) | | | | | -4.005*** (-2.334) | -3.159** (-2.73) | -3.101** (-2.467) | -2.807*** (-1.938) | | | |
| Log (TFPK) | | | | | | | | 0.071 (0.153) | | | 0.302 (0.652) |
| Log (TFPS) | | | | | | 0.621*** (2.064) | | | 0.232 (0.655) | | |
| Log (TFPT) | | | | | | | 0.429 (1.592) | | | 0.201 (0.662) | |
| $\bar{R}^2$ | 0.773 | .788 | .780 | .756 | .843 | .885 | .864 | .816 | 0.726 | 0.727 | .725 |
| DW | 1.670 | 1.069 | 1.197 | 1.245 | 1.389 | 1.962 | 1.608 | 1.315 | 1.920 | 1.904 | 1.752 |
| F/RHO | .862 (7.69) | 23.30 (2,10) | 15.22** (3,9) | 10.31** (4,8) | 13.93 (5,7) | 19.52 (5,7) | 16.32 (5,7) | 11.65 (5,7) | .862* (8.084) | .856* (7.875) | .832* (6.359) |

*Notes* : 1. Figures in the brackets give t-values or degree of freedom.

2. * indicates significance at 1% level.

** indicates significance at 5% level.

*** indicates significance at 10% level.

The equation shows the elasticity of change in real wage rate with respect to labour productivity to be equal to 0.656, i.e., a 10 percent increase in labour productivity will induce a 6.56 percent change in real wage rate. Thus, we find that in SAIL labour productivity is a statistically significant variable in its relationship with wages.

The results of the regressions explaining the relationship in Misra Dhatu Nigam Limited (MDNL) are presented in **Table** 6.I.3. On scrutiny of the results we find it necessary to ignore the sign of labour productivity and select model VI to explain the relationship. The model provides the following estimates :

$$\log (W_r) = \underset{(2.074)}{12.464} + \underset{(3.190)}{0.356t^{**}} - \underset{(-2.355)}{0.532 \log(LP)^{**}} - \underset{(-0.959)}{0.355 \log (K/L)}$$

$$- \underset{(-2.730)}{3.159 \log P_w^{**}} + \underset{(2.064)}{0.621 \log (TFPS)^{***}}$$

$\bar{R}^2 = 0.885$ , DW = 1.962; $F_{5,7} = 19.52$

Though the signs of log (LP) and log (K/L) are negative and opposite to what the theory suggests but even then this model is selected because of the following four reasons : (i) it has the highest $\bar{R}^2$; (ii) it has the best DW, almost zero autocorrelation; (iii) the negative value of log (LP) is outweighted by the positive value of TFPS, thus the combined coefficient of two TFP measures is still positive, (0.089), and (iv) the negative value of log (K/L) is supported by raw data (**Table** 6 (E)). The coefficient of log (LP) in model VI also has the higher t value, thus it is statistically the most significant among all other models. We can, therefore, still conclude that in MDN Ltd the real wage rate is positively related to productivity, where productivity does not mean labour productivity alone but TFPS.

We may, thus, conclude that available statistical evidence points out that there is a positive link between real wage rate and productivity in the Steel industry and its associated two firms - SAIL and MDNL.

*II. Power-Group*

Power industry is a highly capital intensive industry and the proportion of wage share in value added is very low, almost lowest (**Tables** 4.II.1 (App.) and 5.II.1) with the highest growth rate in real wages. With such characteristic of an industry, it is a challenge to find out any long term relationship between real wage rate and labour productivity. The problem is compounded by the fact that power industry in public sector started adding to value added from 1982-1983, i.e., only eleven years ago. The results of the regression analysis point towards the absence of any significant relationship between the two in all the models except model I. We, therefore, choose the first model as it also has the highest statistical value of log (LP) coefficient. However, alternatively model II can be selected with highest value of $\bar{R}^2$ and 't' to be statistically significant. In fact, except for the first three models, all other models generally depict the presence of multicollinearity; but the first five models confirm the existence of a positive relationship between labour productivity and wages. It is to be noted that in almost all regressions all other variables K/L, $P_w$ and V take the expected signs, but K/L generally takes a negative sign with Kendrick index of TFP because TFPK ignores any change in capital-labour ratio during the period and considers only the base year prices of the factors. Models I and II give us the following regression equations:

**Model I**

$$\log (W_r) = 0.028 + 0.247 \log (LP)^*$$

$$(0.632) \quad (8.445)$$

$$\bar{R}^2 = .864 \text{ ; } DW = 1.800; F_{1,10} = 71.32$$

**Model II**

$$\log (W_r) = -0.278 + 0.041t^* + 0.041 \log (LP)$$

$$(-3.284) \quad (3.863) \quad (0.479)$$

$$\bar{R}^2 = .943; DW = 1.898; F_{2,9} = 92.79$$

The first model provides the elasticity of wages to productivity to be 0.247 while for the second it is only 0.041. But the second model captures most of the effects in trend

Table 6.II. 1

**Regression Function for Wages : Power Industry**

| *Dependent Variable →* *(Real Wage Rate)* *Explanatory Variable* | ——*MODEL NO.*—— | | | | | | | | | | |
|---|---|---|---|---|---|---|---|---|---|---|---|
| | 1 | 2 | 3 | 4 | 5 | 6 | 7 | 8 | 9 | 10 | 11 |
| Constant | 0.028 | -0.278 | -0.208 | -1.054 | 0.699 | -2.060 | -2.093 | 92.726 | -3.750 | -3.661 | 76.991 |
| | (0.632) | (-3.284) | (-1.177) | (-0.826) | (-0.124) | (-0.445) | (-0.450) | (1.087) | (-1.428) | (-1.375) | (1.397) |
| t | | 0.041* | +0.045** | 0.031 | 0.038 | 0.064 | 0.062 | 0.073 | | | |
| | | (3.863) | (3.115) | (1.245) | (0.344) | (0.589) | (0.565) | (0.695) | | | |
| Log (LP) | 0.247* | 0.041 | 0.093 | 0.070 | 0.077 | -0.216 | -0.24 | 11.063 | -0.169 | -0.162 | 9.552 |
| | (8.445) | (0.479) | (0.729) | (0.511) | (0.413) | (-0.845) | (-0.809) | (1.114) | (-0.738) | (-0.696) | (1.430) |
| Log (V) | | | -0.043 | -0.065 | -0.70 | | | | | | |
| | | | (-0.455) | (-0.632) | (-0.517) | | | | | | |

| | | | | | | | | | | | |
|---|---|---|---|---|---|---|---|---|---|---|---|
| Log (K/L) | | | | 0.263 | 0.247 | 0.318 | 0.316 | -10.420 | 0.747*** | 0.737*** | -8.603 |
| | | | | (0.670) | (0.507) | (0.676) | (0.668) | (-1.086) | (2.301) | (2.247) | (-1.345) |
| Log ($P_w$) | | | | | -0.061 | -0.243 | -0.225 | -0.482 | | | |
| | | | | | (-0.065) | (-0.269) | (-0.247) | (-0.501) | | | |
| Log (TFPK) | | | | | | | | -11.001 | | | -9.544 |
| | | | | | | | | (-1.115) | | | (-1.436) |
| Log (TFPS) | | | | | | 0.375 | | | 0.204 | | |
| | | | | | | (0.912) | | | (0.625) | | |
| Log (TFPT) | | | | | | | 0.365 | | | 0.193 | |
| | | | | | | | (0.871) | | | (0.582) | |
| $\bar{R}^2$ | .864 | .943 | .938 | .933 | .922 | .928 | .928 | .932 | .930 | .929 | .941 |
| DW | 1.800 | 1.898 | 1.910 | 1.681 | 1.686 | 1.866 | 1.862 | 1.881 | 1.428 | 1.424 | 1.664 |
| F/RHO | 71.32 | 92.79 | 56.48 | 39.55 | 27.14 | 29.70 | 29.37 | 31.55 | 49.80 | 49.47 | 60.25 |
| | (1,10) | (2,9) | (3,8) | (4,7) | (5,6) | (5,6) | (5,6) | (5,6) | (3,8) | (3,8) | (3,8) |

*Notes* : 1. Figures in the brackets give t-values or degree of freedom.

2. * indicates significance at 1% level.

** indicates significance at 5% level.

*** indicates significance at 10% level.

Table 6.II. 2

**Regression Function for Wages : National Hydro-Electric Power Corporation Ltd.**

| *Dependent Variable* → *(Real Wage Rate)* | ——*MODEL NO.*—— | | | | | | | | | | |
|---|---|---|---|---|---|---|---|---|---|---|---|
| *Explanatory Variable* | 1 | 2 | 3 | 4 | 5 | 6 | 7 | 8 | 9 | 10 | 11 |
| Constant | 0.024 | -0.073 | -0.102 | -0.369 | -1.066 | -3.589 | -3.460 | -246.96 | -1.645 | -1.680 | -115.969 |
| | (0.494) | (-0.657) | (-0.617) | (-0.657) | (-0.095) | (-0.325) | (-0.315) | (-0.930) | (-0.559) | (-0.551) | (-0.673) |
| t | | .505 | 0.015 | -0.001 | -0.016 | -0.222 | -0.021 | -0.164 | | | |
| | | (0.916) | (0.522) | (-0.025) | (-0.066) | (-0.126) | (-0.123) | (-0.732) | | | |
| Log (LP) | 0.266* | .265* | 0.309 | 0.196 | 0.180 | -0.054 | -0.047 | -33.502 | 0.013 | 0.010 | -16.100 |
| | (5.931) | (3.955) | (2.093) | (0.713) | (0.459) | (-0.085) | (-0.073) | (-0.921) | (0.032) | (.023) | (-0.662) |
| Log (V) | | | -0.058 | -0.022 | -0.013 | | | | | | |
| | | | (-0.336) | (-0.113) | (-0.054) | | | | | | |
| Log (K/L) | | | | 0.129 | 0.151 | 0.368 | 0.364 | 33.140 | .289 | .299 | 16.001 |
| | | | | (0.496) | (0.335) | (0.556) | (0:541) | (0.930) | (.639) | (.629) | (0.674) |

| | | | | | | | | | | | |
|---|---|---|---|---|---|---|---|---|---|---|---|
| Log ($P_w$) | | | | | 0.135 | 0.279 | 0.264 | 1.630 | | | |
| | | | | | (0.062) | (0.154) | (.146) | (0.710) | | | |
| Log (TFPK) | | | | | | | | 33.75 | | | 16.396 |
| | | | | | | | | (.926) | | | (.671) |
| Log (TFPS) | | | | | | 0.260 | | | 0.179 | | |
| | | | | | | (0.359) | | | (.475) | | |
| Log (TFPT) | | | | | | | 0.252 | | | 0.185 | |
| | | | | | | | (0.344) | | | (.469) | |
| $\bar{R}^2$ | .760 | .562 | .515 | .464 | .376 | .388 | .387 | .453 | .538 | .538 | .551 |
| DW | 2.300 | 1.756 | 1.787 | 2.012 | 1.99 | 2.094 | 2.086 | 2.050 | 2.128 | 2.122 | 2.097 |
| F/RHO | -0.093 | 8.08 | 4.89 | 3.38 | 2.32 | 2.40 | 2.394 | 2.82 | 5.28 | 5.27 | 5.50 |
| | (0.421) | (2,9) | (3,8) | (4,7) | (5,6) | (5,6) | (5,6) | (5,6) | (3,8) | (3,8) | (3,8) |

*Notes* : 1. Figures in the brackets give t-values or degree of freedom.

2. * indicates significance at 1% level.

** indicates significance at 5% level.

*** indicates significance at 10% level.

Table 6.II. 3

**Regression Function for Wages : National Thermal Power Corporation Ltd.**

| *Dependent Variable →* *(Real Wage Rate)* | | | | | —MODEL NO.— | | | | | | |
|---|---|---|---|---|---|---|---|---|---|---|---|
| *Explanatory Variable* | 1 | 2 | 3 | 4 | 5 | 6 | 7 | 8 | 9 | 10 | 11 |
| Constant | -0.090 | -1.011 | 0.573 | .594 | 8.40 | -7.443 | -7.605 | 150.68 | -15.021 | -15.317 | 110.01 |
| | (-0.693) | (-4.098) | (1.412) | (0.714) | (1.861) | (-0.951) | (-0.971) | (4.022) | (-2.299) | (-2.288) | (3.622) |
| | | ** | * | ** | ** | | | ** | | | |
| t | | 0.120 | 0.126 | 0.127 | 0.278 | 0.147 | 0.153 | 0.290 | | | |
| | | (3.932) | (7.496) | (3.733) | (3.069) | (0.780) | (0.805) | (3.017) | | | |
| | * | | ** | ** | ** | | | * | | | * |
| Log (LP) | 0.324 | -0.154 | 0.630 | .629 | 0.856 | -0.792 | -0.833 | 17.962 | -1.073 | -1.102 | 14.428 |
| | (5.184) | (-1.215) | (3.120) | (2.805) | (3.739) | (-1.062) | (-1.082) | (4.145) | (-1.904) | (-1.904) | (3.701) |
| | | | * | ** | * | | | | | | |
| Log (V) | | | -0.661 | -.659 | -0.890 | | | | | | |
| | | | (-4.143) | (-3.578) | (-4.371) | | | | | | |

| | | | | | | | | | | | |
|---|---|---|---|---|---|---|---|---|---|---|---|
| Log (K/L) | | | | -0.08 | 0.006 | 0.668 | 0.713 | -16.218* | 1.863 | 1.893** | -12.507** |
| | | | | (-0.030) | (0.026) | (0.610) | (0.640) | (-4.278) | (2.740) | (2.726) | (-3.511) |
| Log ($P_w$) | | | | | -1.557 | -0.286 | -0.347 | -2.432*** | | | |
| | | | | | (-1.750) | (-0.145) | (-0.174) | (-2.258) | | | |
| Log (TFPK) | | | | | | | | -17.990* | | | -14.401* |
| | | | | | | | | (-4.167) | | | (-3.714) |
| Log (TFPS) | | | | | | 1.182 | | | 1.773 | | |
| | | | | | | (0.955) | | | (1.906) | | |
| Log (TFPT) | | | | | | | 1.245 | | | 1.813 | |
| | | | | | | | (.978) | | | (1.904) | |
| $\bar{R}^2$ | .741 | .908 | .972 | .966 | .976 | .889 | .890 | .974 | .863 | .863 | .933 |
| DW | 1.244 | 1.408 | 1.776 | 1.790 | 1.517 | 1.747 | 1.746 | 2.007 | 1.508 | 1.527 | 2.003 |
| F/RHO | 28.43 | 45.47 | 106.06 | 66.30 | 75.56 | 15.42 | 15.57 | 69.79 | 19.91 | 19.89 | 43.04 |
| | (1,8) | (2,7) | (3,6) | (4,5) | (5,4) | (5,4) | (5,4) | (5,4) | (3,6) | (3,6) | (3,6) |

*Notes* : 1. Figures in the brackets give t-values or degree of freedom.

2. * indicates significance at 1% level.

** indicates significance at 5% level.

*** indicates significance at 10% level.

parameter. But whichever model one may choose the existence of a positive relationship between the real wage rate and labour productivity is never in doubt but it is significant in the first model.

When the same relationship is being tested for National Hydro-Electric Power Corporation Ltd (NHPCL) it is again found that model I is the most suitable to explain it. In fact, except models I and II, all other models seems to have suffered from multicollinearity and have very low $\bar{R}^2$'s (**Table** 6.II.2). But again the first five models have positive coefficients of log (LP) and all other variables take the expected signs indicating that real wage rate, is in fact affected by these variables included in the regression analysis, i.e., the theory is supported by empirical evidence. Model I selected to represent the relationship for the firm NHPCL is:

$$\log (W_r) = 0.024 + 0.266 \log (LP)^{*}$$
$$(0.494) \quad (5.931)$$
$$\bar{R}^2 = .760; \; DW = 2.300; \; RHO = -0.09$$
$$(0.421)$$

The regression gives us an elasticity of 0.266; and supports the result of the industry that wage rates are positively related to productivity.

The results of the regression models for NTPC are presented in **Table** 6.II.3. Model V represents the best relationship between wages and its explanatory variables. The full model has been preferred, as it not only provides the maximum explanation of the relationship and has the highest $\bar{R}^2 = .976$ but the model also supports the theoretical arguments advanced for the determination of wages. The model as obtained through regression analysis is:

$$\text{Log } (W_r) = 8.40 + 0.278t^{**} + 0.856 \log(LP)^{**} - 0.890 \log(V)^{*}$$
$$(1.861) \quad (3.069) \quad (3.739) \quad (-4.371)$$
$$+ 0.006 \log (K/L) - 1.557 \log P_w$$
$$(0.026) \quad (-1.750)$$
$$\bar{R}^2 = .976; \; DW = 1.517; \; F_{5,4} = 75.56.$$

The equation supports the positive link between real wage rate and labour productivity and capital intensity. As already argued earlier the negative sign of the coefficient of log (V) is not to be confused with a negative relationship between 'V' and 'Wr'. The model provides an elasticity of change in real wage rate to labour productivity as 0.856.

Thus, the analysis of **Tables** 6.II.1, 6.II.2 and 6.II.3, all belonging to Power sector, supports the conclusion reached for the Steel industry; i.e. there is evidence to show that wages and productivity are positively related in Power industry.

*III. Petroleum-Group*

Contrary to Power industry, Petroleum industry is the one which, though, has the lowest wage share in value added, has high capital intensity and the lowest rate of growth of real wages (**Tables** 4.III.1 (App.) and 5.III.1). This is despite the fact that financially it is one of the best performing industries. The difference in the structure is somewhat evident from the regression models. When the first two models are analysed, it is found that log (LP) has a negative coefficient. But on close examination of models we find a similar trend in other models as was found in the case of Power industry, with minor changes. The model that best explains the changes in real wage rate in Petroleum industry seems to be model V, as it has the highest $\bar{R}^2$ and includes the maximum explanatory variables with significant values. The coefficient of log (LP) also has the highest value of t-statistic. The model fully explains the significance of different variables. The model is

$$\text{Log}\,(W_r) = \underset{(5.637)}{11.312} + \underset{(3.525)}{0.180t^{*}} + \underset{(7.497)}{1.381\log(LP)^{*}} \underset{(-7.876)}{-1.264\log(V)^{*}}$$

$$\underset{(-1.298)}{-\,0.391\log(K/L)} \underset{(-2.819)}{-0.972\log(P_w)^{**}}$$

$\bar{R}^2 = 0.905$; D–W = 1.936; $F_{5,\,14} = 41.78$.

The regression model reveals that real wage rates in Petroleum industry, besides a trend, are significantly related to labour productivity, value added and consumer price index. The

Table 6.III.1

**Regression Function for Wages : Petroleum Industry**

| *Dependent Variable →* *(Real Wage Rate)* *Explanatory Variable* | ——*MODEL NO.*—— | | | | | | | | | | |
|---|---|---|---|---|---|---|---|---|---|---|---|
| | 1 | 2 | 3 | 4 | 5 | 6 | 7 | 8 | 9 | 10 | 11 |
| Constant | 1.024 | 0.826 | 6.245 | 5.957 | 11.312 | -12.166 | -12.33 | 59.331 | -10.398 | -14.240 | 36.045 |
| | (3.74) | (2.283) | (8.989) | (7.281) | (5.637) | (-1.988) | (-2.002) | (2.420) | (-3.627) | (-4.258) | (2.086) |
| t | | 0.016 | 0.069* | 0.056*** | 0.180* | -0.008 | -0.009 | -0.007 | | | |
| | | (0.712) | (6.474) | (2.127) | (3.525) | (-0.080) | (-0.099) | (-0.061) | | | |
| Log (LP) | -0.055 | -0.086 | 1.484* | 1.524* | 1.381* | -1.182** | -1.207** | 9.354*** | -1.574* | -1.263* | 5.873*** |
| | (-0.542) | (-0.758) | (6.973) | (6.725) | (7.497) | (-2.204) | (-2.228) | (2.108) | (-3.979) | (-3.748) | (2.022) |
| Log (V) | | | -1.409* | -1.448* | -1.264* | | | | | | |
| | | | (-7.732) | (-7.225) | (-7.876) | | | | | | |
| Log (K/L) | | | | 0.166 | -0.391 | 2.686* | 2.705* | -7.035** | 2.035 | 2.780* | -4.942 |
| | | | | (0.545) | (-1.298) | (3.209) | (3.231) | (-2.243) | (3.988) | (4.608) | (-2.007) |

| | | | | | | | | | | | |
|---|---|---|---|---|---|---|---|---|---|---|---|
| Log ($P_w$) | | | | | -0.972** | -0.136 | -0.120 | -0.928 | | | |
| | | | | | (-2.819) | (-0.206) | (-0.181) | (-1.131) | | | |
| Log (TFPK) | | | | | | | | -9.423*** | | | -5.881*** |
| | | | | | | | | (-2.124) | | | (-2.050) |
| Log (TFPS) | | | | | | 1.146*** | | | 1.582* | | |
| | | | | | | (2.019) | | | (3.839) | | |
| Log (TFPT) | | | | | | | 1.169*** | | | 1.229* | |
| | | | | | | | (2.045) | | | (3.429) | |
| $\bar{R}^2$ | .590 | .577 | .884 | .878 | .905 | .782 | .783 | .619 | .767 | .813 | .590 |
| DW | 1.700 | 1.689 | 1.868 | 1.751 | 1.936 | 2.123 | 2.128 | 1.725 | 2.443 | 2.117 | 1.734 |
| F/RHO | .844* | .825* | 0.470** | .435*** | 41.78 | .928* | .928* | .585** | .679* | .942* | .580* |
| | (5.346) | (4.931) | (2.296) | (1.800) | (5,14) | (9.139) | (9.147) | (2.725) | (2.984) | (47.43) | (3.265) |

*Notes* : 1. Figures in the brackets give t-values or degree of freedom.

2. * indicates significance at 1% level.

** indicates significance at 5% level.

*** indicates significance at 10% level.

Table 6.III.2

**Regression Function for Wages : Indian Oil Corporation Ltd**

| *Dependent Variable →* *(Real Wage Rate)* | MODEL NO. | | | | | | | | | | |
|---|---|---|---|---|---|---|---|---|---|---|---|
| *Explanatory Variable* | 1 | 2 | 3 | 4 | 5 | 6 | 7 | 8 | 9 | 10 | 11 |
| Constant | 1.006 | .828 | 1.2 | -0.318 | 5.098 | 0.474 | .494 | 19.974 | .791 | .805 | -12.086 |
| | (8.840) | (22.442) | (2.248) | (-0.261) | (1.173) | (0.293) | (.291) | (0.582) | (1.149) | (1.156) | (-.783) |
| t | | 0.023* | 0.030* | .001 | 0.097 | 0.057*** | 0.057*** | 0.057 | | | |
| | | (10.528) | (2.894) | (0.052) | (1.253) | (1.952) | (1.942) | (1.282) | | | |
| Log (LP) | 0.162* | 0.068** | 0.167 | -0.045 | 0.426 | -0.231 | -0.229 | 3.274 | 0.233** | 0.235* | -2.111 |
| | (2.753) | (2.559) | (1.160) | (-0.217) | (1.022) | (-0.722) | (-0.710) | (0.547) | (2.444) | (2.438) | (-0.733) |
| Log (V) | | | -0.125 | 0.148 | -0.413 | | | | | | |
| | | | (-0.698) | (0.561) | (-0.819) | | | | | | |
| Log (K/L) | | | | 0.259 | -0.209 | 0.205 | 0.207 | -2.819 | 0.180 | 0.177 | 2.387 |
| | | | | (1.377) | (-0.517) | (1.197) | (1.194) | (-0.514) | (1.185) | (1.157) | (0.925) |

| | | | | | | | | | | | |
|---|---|---|---|---|---|---|---|---|---|---|---|
| Log ($P_w$) | | | | | -0.514 | -0.234 | -0.234 | -0.458 | | | |
| | | | | | (-1.296) | (-1.165) | (-1.166) | (-0.983) | | | |
| Log (TFPK) | | | | | | | | -3.206 | | | 2.217 |
| | | | | | | | | (-0.533) | | | (0.763) |
| Log (TFPS) | | | | | | 0.306 | | | -0.154 | | |
| | | | | | | (0.994) | | | (-1.625) | | |
| Log (TFPT) | | | | | | | 0.304 | | | -0.156 | |
| | | | | | | | (0.980) | | | (-1.628) | |
| $\bar{R}^2$ | .860 | .920 | .917 | .922 | .925 | .927 | .926 | .923 | .918 | .918 | .908 |
| DW | 2.654 | 1.826 | 1.850 | 2.082 | 2.004 | 2.056 | 2.059 | 2.112 | 1.960 | 1.959 | 1.670 |
| | * | | | | | | | | | | |
| F/RHO | .748 | 110.659 | 71.71 | 57.27 | 48.23 | 49.33 | 49.24 | 46.89 | 72.66 | 72.70 | 64.04 |
| | (6.151) | (2,17) | (3,16) | (4,15) | (5,14) | (5,14) | (5,14) | (5,14) | (3,16) | (3,16) | (3,16) |

*Notes* : 1. Figures in the brackets give t-values or degree of freedom.

2. * indicates significance at 1% level.

** indicates significance at 5% level.

*** indicates significance at 10% level.

Table 6.III.3

**Regression Function for Wages : ONGC**

| Dependent Variable → (Real Wage Rate) | | | | | MODEL NO. | | | | | | |
|---|---|---|---|---|---|---|---|---|---|---|---|
| *Explanatory Variable* | 1 | 2 | 3 | 4 | 5 | 6 | 7 | 8 | 9 | 10 | 11 |
| Constant | 7.450 | -0.250 | 0.401 | 0.651 | -0.111 | -2.933 | -2.935 | 14.060 | -0.733 | -0.732 | 258.2 |
| | (3.573) | (-2.379) | (1.769) | (3.894) | (-0.166) | (-3.418) | (-3.418) | (0.632) | (-1.451) | (-1.450) | (2.738) |
| t | | 0.027 | 0.024* | 0.035* | 0.021 | -0.016 | -0.016 | 0.019 | | | |
| | | (5.24) | (7.985) | (11.469) | (1.648) | (-1.255) | (-1.256) | (1.270) | | | |
| Log (LP) | -0.020 | -0.015 | 0.129 | 0.062 | 0.069 | -0.086** | -0.086** | 2.149* | -0.019 | -0.019 | +38.820 |
| | (-1.486) | (-1.246) | (1.607) | (0.891) | (1.004) | (-3.150) | (3.150) | (0.637) | (-0.338) | (-0.338) | (2.739) |
| Log (V) | | | -0.146*** | -0.063 | -0.072 | | | | | | |
| | | | (-2.008) | (-1.006) | (-1.161) | | | | | | |
| Log (K/L) | | | | -0.175* | -0.159* | -0.032 | -0.032 | -2.289* | 0.235 | 0.235 | -38.307* |
| | | | | (-4.088) | (-3.601) | (-0.509) | (-0.508) | (-0.696) | (2.410) | (2.409) | (-2.727) |

| | | | | | | | | | | | |
|---|---|---|---|---|---|---|---|---|---|---|---|
| Log ($P_w$) | | | | | 0.157 | 0.556* | 0.556* | 0.151 | | | |
| | | | | | (1.175) | (4.312) | (4.312) | (1.085) | | | |
| Log (TFPK) | | | | | | | | -2.163 | | | -38.839** |
| | | | | | | | | (-0.640) | | | (-2.743) |
| Log (TFPS) | | | | | | 0.087* | | 0.135 | -0.023 | | |
| | | | | | | (3.246) | | (1.683) | (-0.373) | | |
| Log (TFPT) | | | | | | | 0.087* | | | -0.023 | |
| | | | | | | | (3.246) | | | (-0.373) | |
| $\bar{R}^2$ | .945 | .963 | .964 | .969 | .969 | .986 | .986 | .967 | .912 | .912 | .920 |
| DW | 1.866 | 2.598 | 2.152 | 2.089 | 2.242 | 2.900 | 2.900 | 2.314 | 1.461 | 1.460 | 1.404 |
| F/RHO | 0.997* | .856* | .547*** | 126.06 | 104.34 | -0.480*** | -0.480** | 96.235 | .752* | .752* | .472** |
| | (16.032) | (5.236) | (2.025) | (4,12) | (5,11) | (-2.241) | (-2.243) | (5,11) | (5.428) | (5.428) | (2.361) |

*Notes :* 1. Figures in the brackets give t-values or degree of freedom.

2. * indicates significance at 1% level.

** indicates significance at 5% level.

*** indicates significance at 10% level.

relationship is positive for labour productivity as the theory suggests, and is negative with value added and price index. The negative sign of the coefficient of log (V) has already been explained by its relationship with the trend variable. The statistical significance of log (Pw) implies that cost of living has been an important consideration in wage rate determination in the Petroleum industry. The negative sign of capital-intensity coefficient implies that its effect has been captured by either productivity coefficient or value added coefficient. Thus, we find that in Petroleum industry wages have been significantly related to labour productivity.

The evaluation of the regression models for Indian Oil Corporation Limited is being done on the basis of results contained in **Table** 6.III.2. On an examination of the results we come to the conclusion that model II is more suitable to explain wage changes in the firm because not only has the model high value of $\bar{R}^2$ but also has the coefficient of log (LP) to be significant. All other models either have multicollinearity or have lower value of $\bar{R}^2$. So the scale tilts in favour of this model. The model provides the following relationship:

$$\log(Wr) = .828 + 0.023\, t^{*} + 0.068 \log (LP)^{**}$$

$$(22.442)\ (10.528)\ \ (2.559)$$

$$\bar{R}^2 = .920;\quad D\text{-}W = 1.826;\quad F_{2,17} = 110.659$$

The model reports that labour productivity along with a time trend has a positive and significant relationship with real wage rate in Indian Oil Corporation Ltd. The elasticity of change in wage rate to change in labour productivity, however, is 0.068.

The regression model estimates for ONGC are summarized in **Table** 6.III.3. It reveals that the model III gives a better relationship between the dependent variable, real wage rate, and the explanatory variables. The relationship given is :

$$\log(Wr)=0.401 + 0.024t^{*} + 0.129\log (LP) - 0.146\log (V)^{***}$$

$$(1.769)\ \ (7.985)\ \ (1.607)\qquad\quad (2.008)$$

$$\bar{R}^2 =.964\ ;\ D\text{-}W = 2.152\ \ RHO = .547^{***}$$

$$(2.025)$$

The equation depicts that trend and value added coefficients are statistically significant, implying thereby that wage rate in ONGC has been following a trend and has been related to value added. It is also positively related, though not significantly, with labour productivity. The model has been preferred over other models as it gives the highest elasticity of wages to labour productivity and supports economic theory in its relationship with variables. The model also has quite high $\bar{R}^2$. Other models may have higher value of $\bar{R}^2$ but either they suffer from the presence of multicollinearity or the signs of the coefficients are not justified by any economic reasoning.

It is, therefore, found that in Petroleum industry group real wage rates though are positively related to labour productivity, they basically follow a trend pattern. That does not, however, undermine the link of change in real wage rates with labour productivity.

*IV. Fertilizers, Chemicals and Pharmaceuticals-Group*

The regression model outcomes are presented in **Tables** 6.IV.1, 6.IV.2 and 6.IV.3 for the Fertilizers, Chemicals and Pharmaceuticals group. On studying **Table** 6.IV.1 for the industry we observe that model VI is better than any other model to describe the desired relationship. Though, the model has a negative sign for labour productivity but even then the model is selected because it has more significant variables than any other model with positive coefficient of log (LP). In fact almost all the models with positive sign of log (LP) either seem to suffer from the problem of multicollinearity or have lower $\bar{R}^2$. Moreover, the negative sign of log (LP) is overshadowed by the greater positive value of TFPS. The model supplies us with the following equation:

$$\log(Wr) = -9.786 + 0.135t^{*} - 2.178\log(LP)^{*} + 1.237\ \log(K/L)^{*}$$
$$(-2.700)\quad (4.543)\quad (-4.016)\qquad (3.284)$$
$$-\ 0.680\ \log(p_w)^{***} + 2.392\ \log\ (TFPS)^{*}$$
$$(-2.888)\qquad\qquad (3.996)$$
$$\bar{R}^2 = .983;\ D\text{-}W = 1.415\ ;\ RHO = 0.853^{*}$$
$$(5.266)$$

Table 6.IV. 1

**Regression Function for Wages : Fertilizers,Chemicals and Pharmaceuticals Industry**

| *Dependent Variable →* *(Real Wage Rate)* | —MODEL NO.— | | | | | | | | | | |
|---|---|---|---|---|---|---|---|---|---|---|---|
| *Explanatory Variable* | 1 | 2 | 3 | 4 | 5 | 6 | 7 | 8 | 9 | 10 | 11 |
| Constant | 1.516 | 0.532 | 0.498 | 2.265 | 6.517 | -9.786 | -10.489 | 54.454 | -3.530 | -4.609 | 94.982 |
| | (5.218) | (7.077) | (0.525) | (0.872) | (1.576) | (-2.700) | (-2.740) | (1.328) | (-1.110) | (-1.374) | (3.242) |
| t | | 0.031* | 0.031* | 0.043** | 0.106* | 0.135* | 0.139* | 0.065 | | | |
| | | (4.753) | (4.474) | (2.623) | (2.033) | (4.543) | (4.576) | (1.389) | | | |
| Log (LP) | -0.017 | -0.038 | -0.047 | 0.283 | 0.482* | -2.178* | -2.338* | 8.128* | -1.892** | -2.021* | 15.108* |
| | (-0.206) | (-0.472) | (-0.169) | (0.548) | (.933) | (-4.016) | (-3.972) | (1.253) | (-2.977) | (-2.906) | (3.288) |
| Log (V) | | | .008 | -0.265 | -0.444 | | | | | | |
| | | | (.036) | (-0.667) | (-1.113) | | | | | | |
| Log (K/L) | | | | -0.234 | -0.548 | 1.237* | 1.302* | -6.744 | 1.278* | 1.341* | -11.996* |
| | | | | (-0.598) | (-1.229) | (3.284) | (3.288) | (-1.291) | (3.066) | (2.991) | (-3.125) |

| | | | | | | | | | | | |
|---|---|---|---|---|---|---|---|---|---|---|---|
| Log ($P_w$) | | | | | -0.549 | -0.680** | -0.690** | -0.411 | | | |
| | | | | | (-1.253) | (-2.888) | (-2.910) | (-0.953) | | | |
| Log (TFPK) | | | | | | | | -8.108 | | | -14.933* |
| | | | | | | | | (-1.269) | | | (-3.284) |
| Log (TFPS) | | | | | | 2.392* | | | 2.084* | | |
| | | | | | | (3.996) | | | (2.989) | | |
| Log (TFPT) | | | | | | | 2.537* | | | 2.200** | |
| | | | | | | | (3.952) | | | (2.914) | |
| $\bar{R}^2$ | 0.961 | .964 | .962 | .959 | .961 | .983 | .983 | .959 | .972 | .971 | .956 |
| DW | 1.009 | .995 | .991 | 1.050 | .967 | 1.415 | 1.393 | 0.992 | 1.923 | 1.863 | 1.305 |
| F/RHO | .951* | 0.649* | .654** | 0.527** | 0.509* | 0.853* | .855* | 0.401* | .992* | 0.911* | 0.417* |
| | (21.745) | (3.390) | (3.132) | (2.784) | (2.470) | (5.266) | (5.030) | (3.367) | (33.128) | (35.58) | (5.422) |

*Notes* : 1. Figures in the brackets give t-values or degree of freedom.

2. * indicates significance at 1% level.

** indicates significance at 5% level.

*** indicates significance at 10% level.

Table 6.IV. 2

**Regression Function for Wages : National Fertilizers Ltd.**

| Dependent Variable → (Real Wage Rate) | MODEL NO. | | | | | | | | | | |
|---|---|---|---|---|---|---|---|---|---|---|---|
| Explanatory Variable | 1 | 2 | 3 | 4 | 5 | 6 | 7 | 8 | 9 | 10 | 11 |
| Constant | 0.734 | 0.183 | -4.119 | -4.561 | 14.377 | 4.258 | 4.253 | 1122.481 | -4.510 | -4.52 | 1275.838 |
| | (8.667) | (.577) | (-1.358) | (-1.418) | (0.956) | (0.234) | (0.233) | (1.922) | (-0.729) | (-0.730) | (2.215) |
| t | | 0.052 | 0.024 | 0.024 | 0.369 | 0.212 | 0.212 | 0.332 | | | |
| | | (2.291) | (0.882) | (0.854) | (1.373) | (0.724) | (0.723) | (1.282) | | | |
| Log (LP) | 0.265 ** | 0.043 | -2.669 | -3.779 | -5.018 | -0.462 | -0.460 | 178.139 *** | -0.103 | -0.103 | 206.43 ** |
| | (2.727) | (0.278) | (-1.363) | (-1.368) | (-1.764) | (-0.839) | (-0.837) | (1.904) | (-0.145) | (-0.145) | (2.224) |
| Log (V) | | | 2.628 | 3.711 | 4.823 | | | | | | |
| | | | (1.391) | (1.385) | (1.763) | | | | | | |
| Log (K/L) | | | | -0.379 | -1.467 | 0.217 | 0.219 | -167.208 *** | 1.092 | 11.095 | -191.89 ** |
| | | | | (-0.588) | (-1.397) | (0.203) | (0.205) | (-1.907) | (1.101) | (1.100) | (-2.210) |

| | | | | | | | | | | | |
|---|---|---|---|---|---|---|---|---|---|---|---|
| Log ($P_w$) | | | | | -3.538 | -1.448 | -1.447 | -2.991 | | | |
| | | | | | (-1.288) | (-0.486) | (-0.486) | (-1.148) | | | |
| Log (TFPK) | | | | | | | | -178.126*** | | | -205.832** |
| | | | | | | | | (-1.904) | | | (-2.221) |
| Log (TFPS) | | | | | | 0.605 | | | 0.330 | | |
| | | | | | | (0.864) | | | (0.355) | | |
| Log (TFPT) | | | | | | | 0.603 | | | 0.331 | |
| | | | | | | | (0.862) | | | (0.356) | |
| $\bar{R}^2$ | .887 | .837 | .837 | .827 | .837 | .798 | .798 | .844 | .796 | .796 | .820 |
| DW | 1.732 | 1.372 | 1.133 | 1.252 | 1.215 | 1.086 | 1.086 | 1.369 | 1.351 | 1.351 | 1.519 |
| F/RHO | 0.793*** | 0.568 | 25.06 | 17.765 | 15.480 | 12.109 | 12.105 | 16.218 | .588** | .588** | 22.276 |
| | (5.030) | (2.123) | (3,11) | (4,10) | (5,9) | (5,9) | (5,9) | (5,9) | (2.348) | (2.348) | (3,11) |

*Notes* : 1. Figures in the brackets give t-values or degree of freedom.

2. * indicates significance at 1% level.

** indicates significance at 5% level.

*** indicates significance at 10% level.

Table 6.IV. 3

**Regression Function for Wages : Indian Petro-Chemicals Corporation Ltd.**

| *Dependent Variable →* *(Real Wage Rate)* | | | | | | —MODEL NO.— | | | | | |
|---|---|---|---|---|---|---|---|---|---|---|---|
| *Explanatory Variable* | 1 | 2 | 3 | 4 | 5 | 6 | 7 | 8 | 9 | 10 | 11 |
| Constant | 0.581 | 0.656 | 0.887 | 3.306 | 8.373 | 7.731 | 7.884 | -26.329 | -1.268 | -9.939 | -2.652 |
| | (17.561) | (3.787) | (1.224) | (3.102) | (2.336) | (2.075) | (2.363) | (-2.363) | (-0.594) | (-0.464) | (-0.243) |
| | | * | | ** | ** | ** | ** | * | | | |
| t | | 0.027 | 0.039 | 0.098 | 0.204 | 0.202 | 0.200 | 0.110 | | | |
| | | (3.382) | (1.093) | (2.638) | (2.871) | (2.373) | (2.348) | (2.090) | | | |
| | * | | | | | | | * | | | |
| Log (LP) | 0.156 | 0.072 | 0.230 | 0.616 | 0.869 | -0.274 | -0.243 | -5.031 | -0.582 | -0.532 | -0.686 |
| | (3.545) | (0.710) | (0.475) | (1.381) | (1.583) | (-0.736) | (-0.691) | (-3.127) | (-1.319) | (-1.236) | (-0.374) |
| Log (V) | | | -0.174 | -0.672 | -0.925 | | | | | | |
| | | | (-0.332) | (-1.349) | (-1.509) | | | | | | |
| | | | | ** | ** | | | ** | | | |
| Log (K/L) | | | | -0.504 | -0.385 | -0.157 | -0.181 | 3.835 | 0.263 | 0.220 | 0.482 |
| | | | | (-2.744) | (-2.278) | (-0.577) | (-0.701) | (2.885) | (0.926) | (0.811) | (0.329) |

| | | | | | | | | | | | |
|---|---|---|---|---|---|---|---|---|---|---|---|
| Log ($P_w$) | | | | | -1.081 | -1.666 | -1.653 | -0.560 | | | |
| | | | | | (-1.708) | (-2.050) | (-2.025) | (-1.007) | | | |
| | | | | | | | | * | | | |
| Log (TFPK) | | | | | | | | 0.403 | | | 0.725 |
| | | | | | | | | (3.164) | | | (0.400) |
| Log (TFPS) | | | | | | 0.403 | | | 0.666 | | |
| | | | | | | (0.911) | | | (1.465) | | |
| Log (TFPT) | | | | | | | 0.364 | | | 0.603 | |
| | | | | | | | (0.876) | | | (1.385) | |
| $\bar{R}^2$ | 0.836 | .860 | .852 | .892 | .875 | .863 | .862 | .915 | .851 | .849 | .831 |
| DW | 2.561 | 1.820 | 1.783 | 2.295 | 1.455 | 1.415 | 1.414 | 2.215 | 2.327 | 2.344 | 2.273 |
| | * | * | ** | ** | * | * | * | * | * | * | * |
| F/RHO | 0.739 | 0.565 | .556 | .330 | 27.69 | 24.978 | 24.86 | 42.176 | .880 | 0.877 | 0.873 |
| | (5.998) | (2.786) | (2.433) | (2.223) | (5,14) | (5,14) | (5,14) | (5,14) | (16.637) | (16.243) | (8.025) |

*Notes* : 1. Figures in the brackets give t-values or degree of freedom.

2. * indicates significance at 1% level.

** indicates significance at 5% level.

*** indicates significance at 10% level.

The model discloses that it has highest $\bar{R}^2$ and a significant trend coefficient. The joint elasticity of wages to productivity (both labour and total factor) is 0.214, i.e., lower than given by models IV and V; but models IV and V not only have lower $R^2$, but also have multicollinearity. Thus, the observed findings confirm that real wage rate in the industry is related to productivity, capital intensity and consumer price index.

**Table** 6.IV.2 exhibits the behaviour of regression functions in National Fertilizers Ltd. On scrutiny of the functions we discover that most of the models have the problem of multicollinearity. However, model I is free from the problem and explains the maximum. It also shows that labour productivity is not only positively but significantly related to the real wage rate in NFL. The coefficient gives the elasticity of response of wages to productivity to be equal to 0.265. The reported relationship is:

$$\log (Wr) = \underset{(8.667)}{0.734} + \underset{(2.727)}{0.265} \log (LP)^{**}$$

$$\bar{R}^2 = .887 \; ; \; D\text{-}W = 1.732 \; ; \; RHO = \underset{(5.030)}{0.793^{*}}$$

The high value of RHO shows that labour productivity has high degree of autocorrelation. There are other models with greater value of log (LP), i.e., models VIII and XI, but both these models also have very high negative values of TFP coefficients. Thus the joint effect is low. Besides these models also have comparatively low explanatory power as represented by $\bar{R}^2$.

The summary of regression functions for Indian Petrochemicals Corporation Ltd is reported in **Table** 6.IV.3. The evaluation of the models reveals that in all the models where only labour productivity is included as an explanatory variable either in isolation or with other variables, it takes a positive sign, disclosing a positive relationship between the real wage rate and labour productivity. However, if TFP indices are also included along with labour productivity then the sign changes to negative because then the effect of productivity change is captured by TFP indices. Thus, if we make a choice of a model with positive and high value of coefficient of log (LP) along with high $\bar{R}^2$, it is limited to model IV. The model is also free from multicollinearity and autocorrelation. Its equation is given below:

$$\log(Wr) = \underset{(3.102)}{3.306} + \underset{(2.638)}{0.098t^{*}} + \underset{(1.381)}{0.616}\log(LP) - \underset{(-1.349)}{0.672}\log(V) - \underset{(-2.744)}{0.504}\log(K/L)^{*}$$

$\bar{R}^2 = 0.892$, D-W = 2.295  RHO = 0.330** (2.223)

Two facts, however, may be noted about the regression. First, that though the value of coefficient of log (LP) is high, especially higher than model I but it is significant in case of model I and insignificant in model IV. Second, that in the selected model IV, capital intensity though takes a negative sign it is still significant. However, the first model is ignored because of low $\bar{R}^2$. Thus, we observe that in the case of Indian Petro-Chemicals Corporation Ltd it is labour productivity and capital intensity which seems to have influenced the level of real wage rate.

For the group as a whole we notice that productivity along with capital intensity has been related to the real wage rate.

*V. Heavy Engineering Group*

The Heavy Engineering group's regression functions are presented in **Tables** 6.V.1, 6.V.2 and 6.V.3. On study of **Table** 6.V.1, it is observed that labour productivity is positively related to real wage rate in Heavy engineering industry. A close scrutiny of different models, however, also reveal that capital intensity has acted, like TFP indices, as substitute of labour productivity and the sign of the two coefficients has moved into opposite direction, i.e., if capital intensity is introduced into the model, as in model IV, the sign of labour productivity is changed as its effect is captured by capital intensity. Similarly in model V the effect of capital intensity is merged into labour productivity and the sign of capital-intensity coefficient turns into negative. It is observed that model V gives the highest value

Table 6.V. 1

**Regression Function for Wages : Heavy Engineering - Industry**

| *Dependent Variable →* *(Real Wage Rate)* | *MODEL NO.* | | | | | | | | | | |
|---|---|---|---|---|---|---|---|---|---|---|---|
| *Explanatory Variable* | 1 | 2 | 3 | 4 | 5 | 6 | 7 | 8 | 9 | 10 | 11 |
| Constant | 0.950 | 0.525 | 0.214 | 0.066 | 7.634 | -0.752 | -0.670 | 5.420 | 1.573 | 1.630 | -17.487 |
| | (6.135) | (13.170) | (0.351) | (0.032) | (1.677) | (-0.369) | (-0.326) | (0.366) | (1.152) | (1.191) | (-1.752) |
| | | * | * | | *** | ** | ** | *** | | | |
| t | | 0.025 | 0.025 | 0.022 | 0.121 | 0.063 | 0.062 | 0.046 | | | |
| | | (8.711) | (7.737) | (0.771) | (2.002) | (2.777) | (2.718) | (1.998) | | | |
| | | | | | | | | * | | | |
| Log (LP) | 0.126 | 0.065 | 0.010 | -0.010 | 0.743 | -0.499 | -0.483 | 0.822 | 0.422 | 0.436 | -3.461 |
| | (1.019) | (0.742) | (0.072) | (-0.033) | (1.489) | (-1.051) | (-0.998) | (0.288) | (1.371) | (1.407) | (-1.707) |
| Log (V) | | | 0.063 | 0.083 | -0.650 | | | | | | |
| | | | (0.510) | (0.291) | (-0.351) | | | | | | |
| | | | | | | | | | | | ** |
| Log (K/L) | | | | 0.052 | -1.069 | -0.050 | -0.043 | -0.549 | 0.305 | 0.294 | 3.173 |
| | | | | (0.077) | (-1.215) | (-0.156) | (-0.132) | (-0.239) | (1.196) | (1.147) | (2.146) |

| | | | | | | | | | | | |
|---|---|---|---|---|---|---|---|---|---|---|---|
| Log ($P_w$) | | | | | -0.590*** | -0.187 | -0.191 | -0.254 | | | |
| | | | | | (-1.825) | (-1.031) | (-1.046) | (-1.160) | | | |
| Log (TFPK) | | | | | | | | -0.738 | | | 3.516*** |
| | | | | | | | | (-0.260) | | | (1.743) |
| Log (TFPS) | | | | | | 0.540 | | | -0.328 | | |
| | | | | | | (1.240) | | | (-1.214) | | |
| Log (TFPT) | | | | | | | 0.522 | | | -0.339 | |
| | | | | | | | (1.183) | | | (-1.252) | |
| $\bar{R}^2$ | 0.881 | 0.927 | 0.924 | 0.919 | 0.930 | 0.929 | 0.928 | 0.921 | 0.903 | 0.903 | 0.911 |
| DW | 2.557 | 1.538 | 1.542 | 1.543 | 1.800 | 1.799 | 1.790 | 1.611 | 1.427 | 1.428 | 1.619 |
| F/RHO | 0.888* | 123.13 | 78.60 | 55.29 | 51.77 | 50.77 | 50.30 | 45.70 | 60.08 | 60.441 | 65.951 |
| | (9.977) | (2,17) | (3,16) | (4,15) | (5,14) | (5,14) | (5,14) | (5,14) | (3,16) | (3,16) | (3,16) |

*Notes* : 1. Figures in the brackets give t-values or degree of freedom.

2. * indicates significance at 1% level.

** indicates significance at 5% level.

*** indicates significance at 10% level.

Table 6.V. 2

**Regression Function for Wages : Bharat Heavy Electricals Limited**

| Dependent Variable → (Real Wage Rate) | MODEL NO. | | | | | | | | | | |
|---|---|---|---|---|---|---|---|---|---|---|---|
| *Explanatory Variable* | 1 | 2 | 3 | 4 | 5 | 6 | 7 | 8 | 9 | 10 | 11 |
| Constant | 1.024 | 0.381 | 0.015 | 0.035 | 2.895 | 2.620 | 2.658 | -4.254 | -0.419 | -0.374 | 14.557 |
| | (4.660) | (4.377) | (0.021) | (0.044) | (0.973) | (1.200) | (1.215) | (-0.136) | (-0.264) | (-0.235) | (1.198) |
| | | * | * | ** | | *** | *** | *** | | | |
| t | | 0.030 | 0.028 | 0.036 | 0.080 | 0.075 | 0.075 | 0.076 | | | |
| | | (10.289) | (5.590) | (2.164) | (1.714) | (1.961) | (1.963) | (1.970) | | | |
| | | ** | | | | | | | | | |
| Log (LP) | 0.153 | 0.235 | 0.167 | 0.138 | 0.290 | 0.312 | 0.323 | -1.129 | 0.200 | 0.212 | 3.371 |
| | (1.165) | (2.345) | (0.946) | (0.732) | (1.196) | (0.732) | (0.756) | (-0.175) | (0.429) | (0.454) | (1.313) |
| Log (V) | | | 0.087 | 0.136 | -0.057 | | | | | | |
| | | | (0.475) | (0.650) | (-0.202) | | | | | | |
| Log (K/L) | | | | -0.204 | -0.399 | -0.460 | -0.471 | 0.621 | 0.639 | 0.628 | -1.975 |
| | | | | (-0.530) | (-0.924) | (-0.785) | (-0.803) | (0.129) | (1.587) | (1.555) | (-0.934) |

| | | | | | | | | | | | |
|---|---|---|---|---|---|---|---|---|---|---|---|
| Log ($P_w$) | | | | | -0.374 | -0.319 | -0.319 | -0.268 | | | |
| | | | | | (-0.997) | (-1.159) | (-1.159) | (-0.717) | | | |
| Log (TFPK) | | | | | | | | 1.392 | | | -3.175 |
| | | | | | | | | (0.213) | | | (-1.223) |
| Log (TFPS) | | | | | | -0.048 | | | 0.023 | | |
| | | | | | | (-0.159) | | | (0.071) | | |
| Log (TFPT) | | | | | | | -0.056 | | | 0.014 | |
| | | | | | | | (-0.185) | | | (0.043) | |
| $\bar{R}^2$ | 0.871 | 0.925 | 0.921 | 0.917 | 0.917 | 0.917 | 0.917 | 0.917 | 0.898 | 0.898 | 0.907 |
| DW | 2.789 | 1.680 | 1.700 | 1.710 | 1.696 | 1.725 | 1.726 | 1.729 | 1.650 | 1.651 | 1.654 |
| F/RHO | 0.892* | 118.32 | 75.36 | 54.05 | 43.43 | 43.380 | 43.410 | 43.44 | 57.18 | 57.16 | 63.010 |
| | (9,991) | (2,17) | (3,16) | (4,15) | (5,14) | (5,14) | (5,14) | (5,14) | (3,16) | (3,16) | (3,16) |

*Notes* :1. Figures in the brackets give t-values or degree of freedom.

2. * indicates significance at 1% level.

** indicates significance at 5% level.

*** indicates significance at 10% level.

Table 6.V. 3

**Regression Function for Wages : Bharat Heavy Plate and Vessels Ltd.**

| *Dependent Variable* → *(Real Wage Rate)* | *MODEL NO.* | | | | | | | | | | |
|---|---|---|---|---|---|---|---|---|---|---|---|
| *Explanatory Variable* | 1 | 2 | 3 | 4 | 5 | 6 | 7 | 8 | 9 | 10 | 11 |
| Constant | -1.536 | 0.354 | 1.462 | 0.386 | 3.938 | 1.284 | 1.309 | 64.855 | -0.211 | -0.195 | 41.162 |
| | (-3.314) | (3.864) | (2.146) | (0.277) | (1.863) | (0.659) | (0.673) | (1.359) | (-0.170) | (-0.157) | (0.950) |
| t | | 0.039 | 0.044* | 0.034 | 0.088** | 0.059** | 0.059** | 0.110 | | | |
| | | (5.479) | (7.003) | (1.522) | (2.686) | (2.836) | (2.835) | (1.204) | | | |
| Log (LP) | 0.029 | 0.004 | 0.833 | 0.261 | 0.677 | -0.081 | -0.080 | 11.450 | 0.069 | 0.070 | 7.998 |
| | (0.354) | (0.062) | (1.576) | (0.408) | (1.107) | (-0.513) | (-0.500) | (1.276) | (0.468) | (0.481) | (0.970) |
| Log (V) | | | -0.830 | -0.259 | -0.655 | | | | | | |
| | | | (-1.610) | (-0.434) | (-1.147) | | | | | | |
| Log (K/L) | | | | 0.268 | 0.384 | 0.926** | 0.924** | -7.222 | 1.074** | 1.069* | -4.059 |
| | | | | (0.447) | (0.706) | (2.805) | (2.801) | (-1.235) | (3.724) | (3.698) | (-0.748) |

| | | | | | | | | | | | |
|---|---|---|---|---|---|---|---|---|---|---|---|
| Log ($P_w$) | | | | | -0.658*** | -0.514 | -0.515 | -0.927 | | | |
| | | | | | (-2.092) | (-1.642) | (-1.647) | (-1.192) | | | |
| Log (TFPK) | | | | | | | | -11.452 | | | -7.979 |
| | | | | | | | | (-1.279) | | | (-0.971) |
| Log (TFPS) | | | | | | 0.112 | | | -0.127 | | |
| | | | | | | (0.460) | | | (-0.614) | | |
| Log (TFPT) | | | | | | | 0.109 | | | -0.129 | |
| | | | | | | | (0.445) | | | (-0.628) | |
| $\bar{R}^2$ | 0.920 | 0.934 | 0.937 | 0.921 | 0.935 | 0.930 | 0.930 | 0.940 | 0.941 | 0.941 | 0.943 |
| DW | 1.574 | 1.489 | 1.357 | 1.010 | 1.410 | 1.307 | 1.304 | 1.554 | 1.307 | 1.298 | 1.528 |
| F/RHO | 0.606** | 0.613** | 0.415*** | 56.638 | 56.389 | 52.120 | 52.071 | 0.517** | 0.346 | 0.346 | 0.399*** |
| | (2.706) | (2.871) | (1.899) | (4,15) | (5,14) | (5,14) | (5,14) | (2.261) | (1.961) | (1.964) | (1.939) |

*Notes* : 1. Figures in the brackets give t-values or degree of freedom.

2. * indicates significance at 1% level.

** indicates significance at 5% level.

*** indicates significance at 10% level.

for $\bar{R}^2$ and is comparatively free from problems of multicollinearity and autocorrelation, as they exist in many other models. In the selected model it is found that the variables, which are significantly related to the real wage rate, are time trend and consumer price index. Labour productivity, though not statistically significant at any of the standard levels, has quite a high t-statistic, therefore, must have influenced the real wage rate in the industry. In fact model V has the highest t-statistic for labour productivity coefficient, along with highest $\bar{R}^2$, justifying thereby its selection. The equation of the selected model is:

$$\log (Wr) = \underset{(1.677)}{7.634} + \underset{(2.002)}{0.121t^{***}} + \underset{(1.489)}{0.743 \log (LP)} - \underset{(-0.351)}{0.650 \log (V)}$$

$$- \underset{(-1.215)}{1.069 \log (K/L)} - \underset{(-1.825)}{0.590 \log (Pw)^{***}}$$

$\bar{R}^2 = .930$ D-W $= 1.800$ $F_{(5,14)} = 51.77$

The equation supplies with an elasticity of 0.743 of changes in wages to change in labour productivity. Thus the existence of a positive relationship between real wage rate and labour productivity in Heavy engineering industry is also beyond doubt.

The same conclusion, as we obtained for the industry is obtained for Bharat Heavy Electricalss Limited after carefully examining different regression models, as given in **Table** 6.V.2. The **Table** discloses that trend is the most important influence on the real wage rate in BHEL, but it also exhibits that the coefficient of log (LP) is positive in almost all models, disclosing again positive relationship between the real wage rate and labour productivity. The model best suited to explain the relationship is number II. It is:

$$\log (Wr) = \underset{(4.377)}{0.381} + \underset{(10.289)}{0.030\, t^{*}} + \underset{(2.345)}{0.235 \log (LP)^{**}}$$

$\bar{R}^2 = .925$ ; D-W $= 1.680$ $F_{(2,17)} = 118.32$

The model has been preferred over others as it gives the significant value of labour productivity coefficient and it not only provides highest $\bar{R}^2$ but is also free from both multicollinearity and autocorrelation. Comparing the results of BHEL with those of the industry, not much difference is noticed in the two except that at industry level consumer price index also appears to be an important significant variable influencing real wage rates.

An examination of **Table** 6.V.3 for Bharat Heavy Plate and Vessels Ltd shows that the real wage rates have been affected by the same set of variables as is the case for the industry. Model V again is preferred as it shows the significance of all the variables in the regressed relationship. Model III may be preferred on account of higher $\bar{R}^2$ and higher value of log (LP) coefficient but it ignores the effects of capital intensity and consumer price index. The selected model not only supports economic theory in explaining the relationship but also conforms to the model accepted by the industry. The preferred model is:

$$\log(Wr) = \underset{(1.863)}{3.938} + \underset{(2.686)}{0.088t^{**}} + \underset{(1.107)}{0.677 \log(LP)} - \underset{(-1.147)}{0.655 \log (V)}$$

$$+ \underset{(0.706)}{0.384 \log(K/L)} - \underset{(-2.092)}{0.658 \log (P_w)^{***}}$$

$\bar{R}^2 = 0.935$; D - W = 1.410; $F_{5,14} = 56.389$

The equation supports the relationship given by the industry, i.e., that besides labour productivity, trend and consumer price index are the other significant variables influencing real wage rates.

So the conclusions obtained for other industries are also valid for Heavy engineering industry, i.e., that there is statistical evidence to show a positive relationship between labour productivity and real wage rate in the Heavy engineering group.

*VI. Medium and Light Engineering-Group*

**Tables** 6.VI.1, 6.VI.2 and 6.VI.3 depict the conclusions of the different regression models for the Medium and Light engineering group. **Table** 6.VI.1 for the industry discloses that there are few significant variables in different models. They, thus, have the problem of multicollinearity. However, it is found that in all the models except the four - VI, VII, IX and X - where

TFPS and TFPT are also introduced as a proxy variable for value added, positive link is visible between labour productivity and the real wage rate in Medium and Light engineering industry. The coefficient of log (LP), i.e., labour productivity is statistically significant only in model I. Therefore, the choice of model falls on it. But if one looks into model II and III it is noted that $\overline{R}^2$ increases in both but it is more in II; however in model II the trend captures the entire effect of labour productivity. But the trend coefficient becomes insignificant in all other models except II and III as the effect is taken care of by the newly introduced variables, though multicollinearity also enters simultaneously. A close look of models VIII and IX, with higher $\overline{R}^2$, demonstrates that though capital intensity now is a significant variable, the joint elasticity of wages to labour and total productivity is low as compared to model I. Therefore, capital intensity seems to have captured the effect of productivity. For all these reasons model I is preferred. The model exhibits the following relationship:

$$\log(Wr) = \underset{(20.886)}{0.564} + \underset{(10.407)}{.436} \log(LP)^{*}$$

$$\overline{R}^2 = .849,\ D\text{-}W = 1.562,\ F_{1,18} = 108.30$$

Analysis of **Table** 6.VI.2 for Hindustan Machine Tools Limited is presented here. Model I discloses that if labour productivity is the only variable which is included in the regression analysis then it exhibits a positive relationship between the dependent variable Wr and labour productivity, howsoever small the coefficient may be. Inclusion of more variables into the model gives a clear picture about the relationship of real wage rate with these included variables. A better picture emerges from model number IV in which we observe that all the included variables except log (LP) are significant. The relationship that emerges is:

$$\log(Wr) = \underset{(4.475)}{1.889} + \underset{(4.104)}{0.071}t^{*} + \underset{(1.597)}{0.344}\log(LP) - \underset{(-2.022)}{0.263}\log(V)^{***} - \underset{(-2.209)}{0.731}\log(K/L)$$

$$\overline{R}^2 = 0.942,\ D\text{-}W = 1.229,\ F_{4,15} = 78.52 \qquad (4.15)$$

Though this model has comparatively lower $R^2$ but it has maximum t-statistics for log (LP) and does not contain multicollinearity. It gives elasticity of response of wage rate change to labour productivity as 0.344 and supports the positive relationship between the real wage rate and labour productivity.

**Table** 6.VI.3 divulges the regression trends for Indian Telephone Industries Ltd. It discloses that model II is more suitable to explain the changes in real wage rate in ITI Ltd. Other models with higher value of $\overline{R}^2$ are generally gripped with multicollinearity. Model I has higher value of the coefficient of log (LP) but its $\overline{R}^2$ is low as compared to model II. Same is true of model III. Model II shows that in ITI Ltd the real wage rate change is related positively and significantly to time trend and labour productivity. The model II gives the following relationship:

$$\log (Wr) = .489 + 0.014\, t^{**} + 0.263 \log (LP)^{*}$$

$$(14.814) \quad (2.294) \quad (3.433)$$

$$\overline{R}^2 = .909\ ,\ D - W = 1.778 \quad F_{2,17} = 96.65$$

The equation shows the elasticity of real wage rate to labour productivity to be equal to 0.263. The equation obtained for Model II is free from the problems of autocorrelation and multicollinearity.

Thus, we observe that in Medium and Light engineering industry all the variables included in full model V are not statistically significant, especially the consumer price index. The absence of consumer price index as a significant explanatory variable basically supports the contention that money illusion on the part of the workers is generally absent. Real wage rates generally follow a trend and they are linked with some degree to labour productivity.

*VII. Transport Equipment-Group*

The outcomes of the regression analysis for the Transport equipment group are reported in **Tables** 6.VII.1, 6.VII.2 and 6.VII.3. The Transport equipment industry is a comparatively less capital intensive industry with relatively high wage share in value added (**Table** 4.VII.1 (App.) and 5.VII. 1). Model I in

Table 6.VI. 1

**Regression Function for Wages : Medium and Light Engineering Industry**

| *Dependent Variable →* *(Real Wage Rate)* *Explanatory Variable* | 1 | 2 | 3 | 4 | 5 | 6 | 7 | 8 | 9 | 10 | 11 |
|---|---|---|---|---|---|---|---|---|---|---|---|
| | | | | | —MODEL NO.— | | | | | | |
| Constant | 0.564 | 0.556 | 0.981 | 0.534 | 3.044 | 0.156 | 0.193 | 9.436 | -0.448 | -0.406 | 2.959 |
| | (20.886) | (25.481) | (1.493) | (0.591) | (1.264) | (0.156) | (0.192) | (1.804) | (-0.616) | (-0.558) | (0.995) |
| t | | 0.017* | 0.020** | -0.006 | 0.019 | 0.017 | 0.016 | 0.015 | | | |
| | | (3.283) | (2.828) | (-0.166) | (0.441) | (0.540) | (0.495) | (0.491) | | | |
| Log (LP) | 0.436* | 0.126 | 0.221 | 0.112 | 0.366 | -0.186 | -0.177 | 1.625 | -0.097 | -0.090 | 0.621 |
| | (10.407) | (1.258) | (1.235) | (0.481) | (1.131) | (-0.909) | (-0.847) | (1.720) | (-0.531) | (-0.491) | (0.973) |
| Log (V) | | | -0.096 | -0.028 | -0.241 | | | | | | |
| | | | (-0.647) | (-0.162) | (-0.933) | | | | | | |
| Log (K/L) | | | | 0.374 | 0.457 | 0.508 | 0.512 | -0.426 | 0.418* | 0.413* | -0.052 |
| | | | | (0.735) | (0.896) | (1.074) | (1.074) | (-0.555) | (2.954) | (2.886) | (-0.133) |

| | | | | | | | | | | | |
|---|---|---|---|---|---|---|---|---|---|---|---|
| Log ($P_w$) | | | | | -0.330 | -0.238 | -0.232 | -0.405 | | | |
| | | | | | (-1.123) | (-1.171) | (-1.132) | (-1.600) | | | |
| Log (TFPK) | | | | | | | | -1.459 | | | -0.515 |
| | | | | | | | | (-1.642) | | | (-0.844) |
| Log (TFPS) | | | | | | 0.300 | | | 0.185 | | |
| | | | | | | (1.545) | | | (1.234) | | |
| Log (TFPT) | | | | | | | 0.285 | | | 0.176 | |
| | | | | | | | (1.461) | | | (1.175) | |
| $\bar{R}^2$ | 0.849 | 0.902 | 0.899 | 0.896 | 0.897 | 0.907 | 0.905 | 0.909 | 0.910 | 0.909 | 0.905 |
| DW | 1.562 | 1.452 | 1.446 | 1.440 | 1.387 | 1.783 | 1.771 | 1.627 | 1.648 | 1.644 | 1.512 |
| F/RHO | 108.30 | 88.98 | 57.43 | 41.97 | 34.41 | 38.21 | 37.57 | 38.98 | 65.21 | 64.63 | 61.94 |
| | (1,18) | (2,17) | (3,16) | (4,15) | (5,14) | (5,14) | (5,14) | (5,14) | (3,16) | (3,16) | (3,16) |

*Notes* : 1. Figures in the brackets give t-values or degree of freedom.

2. * indicates significance at 1% level.

** indicates significance at 5% level.

*** indicates significance at 10% level.

Table 6.VI. 2

**Regression Function for Wages : H.M.T. Ltd.**

| *Dependent Variable →* *(Real Wage Rate)* | MODEL NO. | | | | | | | | | | |
|---|---|---|---|---|---|---|---|---|---|---|---|
| *Explanatory Variable* | 1 | 2 | 3 | 4 | 5 | 6 | 7 | 8 | 9 | 10 | 11 |
| Constant | 3.109 | 0.524 | 1.132 | 1.889 | 4.036 | 3.207 | 3.347 | -23.840 | 7.570 | 7.014 | 9.146 |
| | (3.450) | (6.427)* | (1.162)* | (4.475)* | (2.027)** | (1.398)** | (1.525)** | (-1.498)* | (2.430) | (2.491) | (0.911) |
| t | | 0.031 | 0.031 | 0.071 | 0.102 | 0.110 | 0.110 | 0.159 | | | |
| | | (6.054) | (6.823) | (4.104) | (2.700) | (2.765) | (2.733) | (3.476) | | | |
| Log (LP) | 0.047 | 0.052 | 0.265 | 0.344 | 0.189 | -0.134 | -0.097 | -5.653 | 0.299 | 0.303 | -0.774 |
| | (0.571) | (0.612) | (0.729) | (1.597)*** | (0.422) | (-0.300) | (-0.230) | (-1.696) | (0.713) | (0.775) | (-0.338) |
| Log (V) | | | -0.189 | -0.263 | -0.132 | | | | | | |
| | | | (-0.616) | (-2.022)** | (-0.330) | | | | | | |
| Log (K/L) | | | | -0.731 | -0.281 | -0.097 | -0.131 | 2.909 | -0.481 | -0.475 | 0.133 |
| | | | | (-2.209) | (-0.848) | (-0.216) | (-0.304) | (1.543) | (-1.200) | (-1.255) | (0.104) |

| | | | | | | | | | | | |
|---|---|---|---|---|---|---|---|---|---|---|---|
| | | | | | | | | *** | | | |
| Log ($P_w$) | | | | | -0.610 | -0.719 | -0.710 | -0.695 | | | |
| | | | | | (-1.449) | (-1.717) | (-1.698) | (-2.182) | | | |
| Log (TFPK) | | | | | | | | 5.664 | | | 0.814 |
| | | | | | | | | (1.715) | | | (0.361) |
| Log (TFPS) | | | | | | 0.171 | | | -0.240 | | |
| | | | | | | (0.409) | | | (-0.608) | | |
| Log (TFPT) | | | | | | | 0.134 | | | -0.238 | |
| | | | | | | | (0.347) | | | (-0.665) | |
| $\bar{R}^2$ | 0.934 | 0.943 | 0.940 | 0.942 | 0.947 | 0.947 | 0.947 | 0.955 | 0.932 | 0.932 | 0.931 |
| DW | 1.541 | 1.415 | 1.393 | 1.229 | 1.751 | 1.884 | 1.866 | 1.783 | 1.458 | 1.458 | 1.549 |
| | * | * | ** | | * | * | * | * | * | * | * |
| F/RHO | 0.988 | 0.652 | 0.585 | 78.52 | 0.678 | 0.692 | 0.696 | 0.828 | 0.991 | 0.990 | 0.995 |
| | (15.251) | (3.441) | (2.279) | (4,15) | (3.368) | (3.693) | (3.790) | (7.207) | (21.453) | (21.107) | (11.483) |

*Notes* : 1. Figures in the brackets give t-values or degree of freedom.

2. * indicates significance at 1% level.

** indicates significance at 5% level.

*** indicates significance at 10% level.

Table 6.VI. 3

**Regression Function for Wages : ITI Ltd.**

| *Dependent Variable →* *(Real Wage Rate)* | —MODEL NO.— | | | | | | | | | | |
|---|---|---|---|---|---|---|---|---|---|---|---|
| *Explanatory Variable* | 1 | 2 | 3 | 4 | 5 | 6 | 7 | 8 | 9 | 10 | 11 |
| Constant | 0.558 | 0.489 | 0.790 | -2.628 | 2.327 | 1.233 | 1.616 | -0.930 | -1.030 | -0.882 | -1.472 |
| | (16.606) | (14.814) | (1.078) | (-1.220) | (0.448) | (0.415) | (0.538) | (-0.127) | (-0.886) | (-0.746) | (-0.283) |
| t | | 0.014* | 0.018 | 0.110*** | 0.117*** | 0.094*** | 0.098*** | 0.110** | | | |
| | | (2.294) | (1.578) | (1.977) | (2.094) | (1.813) | (1.871) | (2.293) | | | |
| Log (LP) | 0.409* | 0.263*** | 0.336 | -0.521 | 0.165 | 0.008 | 0.062 | -0.493 | -0.103 | -0.072 | -0.135 |
| | (10.215) | (3.433) | (1.739) | (-0.959) | (0.195) | (0.020) | (0.151) | (-0.355) | (-0.337) | (-0.228) | (-0.120) |
| Log (V) | | | -0.098 | 0.879 | 0.179 | | | | | | |
| | | | (-0.411) | (1.405) | (0.197) | | | | | | |
| Log (K/L) | | | | -1.062 | -0.609 | -0.213 | -0.259 | 0.146 | 0.402*** | 0.377 | 0.462 |
| | | | | (-1.677) | (-0.796) | (-0.532) | (-0.638) | (0.138) | (1.761) | (1.606) | (0.494) |

| | | | | | | | | | | | |
|---|---|---|---|---|---|---|---|---|---|---|---|
| Log ($P_w$) | | | | | -0.536 | -0.414 | -0.451 | -0.500 | | | |
| | | | | | (-1.049) | (-0.996) | (-1.078) | (-1.275) | | | |
| Log (TFPK) | | | | | | | | 0.898 | | | 0.492 |
| | | | | | | | | (0.596) | | | (0.386) |
| Log (TFPS) | | | | | | 0.275 | | | 0.386 | | |
| | | | | | | (0.829) | | | (1.349) | | |
| Log (TFPT) | | | | | | | 0.225 | | | 0.351 | |
| | | | | | | | (0.668) | | | (1.201) | |
| $\bar{R}^2$ | 0.897 | 0.909 | 0.905 | 0.914 | 0.915 | 0.919 | 0.917 | 0.917 | 0.908 | 0.906 | 0.898 |
| DW | 2.007 | 1.778 | 1.825 | 2.105 | 2.141 | 2.196 | 2.187 | 2.222 | 1.784 | 1.779 | 1.689 |
| F/RHO | 0.203 | 96.65 | 61.34 | 51.92 | 42.04 | 44.18 | 43.34 | 43.05 | 63.57 | 62.12 | 57.117 |
| | (0.910) | (2,17) | (3,16) | (4,15) | (5,14) | (5,14) | (5,14) | (5,14) | (3,16) | (3,16) | (3,16) |

*Notes* : 1. Figures in the brackets give t-values or degree of freedom.

2. * indicates significance at 1% level.

** indicates significance at 5% level.

*** indicates significance at 10% level.

**Table** 6.VII.1 reveals that if labour productivity is the sole variable included to explain the relationship then it is not only positive but is also significant. However, when trend variable is also included then the whole effect of labour productivity is taken by trend coefficient and labour productivity coefficient becomes insignificant, though it remains positive. But, when the models are extended and ultimately TFPK is introduced in model VIII as a proxy variable for value added, it provides us a better explanation of the relationship, not only with higher $\bar{R}^2$ but also with significant values of the coefficients. The equation of model VIII conveys that the real wage rate depends upon productivity, capital intensity, consumer price index and follows a time trend pattern. The negative value of the coefficient of log (K/L) can be due to comparatively high and positive value of the coefficient of 't', implying that trend value has taken the effect of capital intensity. The selected model can be represented as follows:

$$\log(Wr) = \underset{(2.902)}{15.160} + \underset{(4.392)}{0.072t^{*}} + \underset{(2.695)}{2.465}\log(LP)^{**} - \underset{(-2.849)}{1.666}\log(K/L)^{**}$$

$$- \underset{(-2.859)}{0.524}\log(Pw) - \underset{(-2.610)}{2.331}\log(TFPK)^{**}$$

$\bar{R}^2 = .942$; D-W = 1.562; $F_{(5,14)} = 63.30$

The joint elasticity of wages to productivity is 0.134. Thus, we observe a positive relationship between the real wage rate and productivity in Transport equipment industry too.

The same trend is visible when we examine **Table** 6.VII.2 for Bharat Earth Movers Ltd (BEML), i.e., that real wage rate depends upon labour productivity, (clearly noticeable from models I and II) capital intensity (noticeable in models V, VI and VII) and consumer price index (present in models V,VI and VII). Model VI is considered to be the best of these as it has the highest joint value of the coefficients of log (LP), which is also significant, and the value of coefficient of log (TFPS). It also has highest $\bar{R}^2$, except for model VIII which may suffer from multicollinearity. The model shows the following relationship:

$$\log (Wr) = 3.873 + 0.013t + 0.266 \log (LP)^{***} + 0.481 \log (K/L)^{***}$$
$$(2001) \quad (0.537) \quad (2.060) \qquad\qquad (1.968)$$
$$- 0.737 \log (Pw)^{***} + 0.032 \log (TFPS)$$
$$(- 2.539) \qquad\qquad (0.172)$$
$$\bar{R}^2 = 0.462;\ D\text{-}W = 2.122;\ RHO = - 0.487^{***}$$
$$(-1.896)$$

The equation also reveals that increasing capital intensity in BEML must have helped significantly to increase the real wage rate. But on the other hand increasing consumer price index has been a depressing factor to any such increase in real wage rate. Any significance of trend is, however, missing from the analysis.

On scrutiny of the regression results for Hindustan Aeronautics Ltd from **Table** 6.VII.3, it is observed that the firm follows the same relationship, i.e., the same variables have played the part in real wage rate determination for the firm as is the case with the industry. On close examination it is noted that model I has the highest coefficient of log(LP), and is also significant, as compared to models VIII and XI where joint values of log (LP) and log (TFPK) are lower. But model I is not preferred because it has lower value of $\bar{R}^2$ and does not show the possible effects of other variables. It is for these reasons that model VIII is selected to express the relationship, it is:

$$\log(Wr) = 18.243+0.055\, t^{**}+3.195 \log(LP)^{***}-1.879 \log (K/L)^{***}$$
$$(2.103)\ (2.64) \quad (2.025) \qquad\qquad (-1.890)$$
$$-0.480 \log (Pw)-3.007 \log (TFPK)^{***}$$
$$(-1.484) \qquad\qquad (-1.903)$$
$$\bar{R}^2 = 0.908\ ,\ D\text{ - }W = 1.552\ F_{5,14} = 38.87$$

The inter-relationship of capital intensity with labour productivity and trend variable has been emphasized many times earlier. The equation discloses a joint elasticity of wages to productivity to be of the order of 0.188.

Thus, we find that besides following a trend, real wage rates tend to be influenced by productivity, capital intensity and consumer price index. Moreover, the results of the Transport equipment group broadly support the economic theory.

Table 6.VII.1.

**Regression Function for Wages : Transport Equipment Industry**

| *Dependent Variable →* *(Real Wage Rate)* *Explanatory Variable* | ——*MODEL NO.*—— | | | | | | | | | | |
|---|---|---|---|---|---|---|---|---|---|---|---|
| | 1 | 2 | 3 | 4 | 5 | 6 | 7 | 8 | 9 | 10 | 11 |
| Constant | 0.734 | 0.545 | 1.102 | 0.925 | 3.540 | -5.622 | -4.757 | 15.160 | 1.844 | 3.430 | 27.159 |
| | (8.667) | (26.497) | (1.550) | (1.194) | (2.200) | (-1.026) | (-0.801) | (2.902) | (0.300) | (0.593) | (3.349) |
| t | | * 0.023 | * 0.022 | ** 0.0305 | * 0.048 | *** 0.036 | *** +0.036 | * 0.072 | | | |
| | | (5.052) | (4.752) | (2.383) | (3.130) | (2.038) | (1.884) | (4.392) | | | |
| Log (LP) | ** 0.265 | 0.013 | 0.177 | 0.129 | 0.451 | -1.054 | -0.910 | ** 2.465 | 0.473 | 0.760 | * 5.380 |
| | (2.727) | (0.156) | (0.784) | (0.533) | (1.575) | (-1.227) | (-0.985) | (2.695) | (0.433) | (0.733) | (3.428) |
| Log (V) | | | -0.123 | -0.060 | -0.289 | | | | | | |
| | | | (-0.783) | (-0.324) | (-1.345) | | | | | | |
| Log (K/L) | | | | -0.134 | -0.034 | 0.653 | 0.538 | ** -1.666 | -0.058 | -0.275 | * -3.280 |
| | | | | (-0.644) | (-0.169) | (1.004) | (0.780) | (-2.849) | (-0.072) | (-0.362) | (-3.21) |

Contd. . . .

| | | | | | | | | | | | |
|---|---|---|---|---|---|---|---|---|---|---|---|
| Log ($P_w$) | | | | | -0.340*** | -0.049 | -0.046 | -0.524** | | | |
| | | | | | (-1.818) | (-0.264) | (-0.224) | (-2.859) | | | |
| Log (TFPK) | | | | | | | | -2.331** | | | -5.161* |
| | | | | | | | | (-2.610) | | | (-3.267) |
| Log (TFPS) | | | | | | 1.277 | | | -0.253 | | |
| | | | | | | (1.338) | | | (-0.212) | | |
| Log (TFPT) | | | | | | | 1.105 | | | -0.557 | |
| | | | | | | | (1.086) | | | (-0.496) | |
| $\bar{R}^2$ | 0.887 | 0.917 | 0.915 | 0.912 | 0.924 | 0.924 | 0.921 | 0.942 | 0.824 | 0.876 | 0.927 |
| DW | 1.732 | 1.433 | 1.414 | 1.327 | 1.501 | 1.576 | 1.545 | 1.562 | 1.601 | 1.518 | 1.822 |
| F/RHO | 0.793* | 107.05 | 69.95 | 50 | 65 47.41 | 47.34 | 45.41 | 63.30 | 0.623* | 0.657* | 0.759* |
| | (5.030) | (2,17) | (3,16) | (4,15) | (5,14) | (5,14) | (5,14) | (5,14) | (2.943) | (3.263) | (7.254) |

*Notes* : 1. Figures in the brackets give t-values or degree of freedom.

2. * indicates significance at 1% level.

** indicates significance at 5% level.

*** indicates significance at 10% level.

Table 6.VII.2.

**Regression Function for Wages : Bharat Earth Movers Ltd.**

| Dependent Variable → (Real Wage Rate) | MODEL NO. | | | | | | | | | | |
|---|---|---|---|---|---|---|---|---|---|---|---|
| *Explanatory Variable* | 1 | 2 | 3 | 4 | 5 | 6 | 7 | 8 | 9 | 10 | 11 |
| Constant | 0.573 | 0.572 | 0.945 | 0.993 | 4.148 | 3.873 | 3.937 | -15.858 | -0.181 | -0.134 | -15.668 |
| | (10.394) | (10.548) | (0.890) | (0.915) | (3.107) | (2.001) | (2.036) | (-1.311) | (-0.176) | (-0.131) | (-1.817) |
| t | | -0.006 | -0.002 | -0.016 | 0.013 | 0.013 | 0.013 | -0.032 | | | |
| | | (-1.283) | (-0.212) | (-0.659) | (0.523) | (0.537) | (0.539) | (-0.920) | | | |
| | * | * | | | | *** | *** | | | | *** |
| Log (LP) | 0.175 | 0.247 | 0.411 | 0.465 | 0.324 | 0.266 | 0.271 | -3.788 | 0.130 | 0.136 | -3.530 |
| | (3.361) | (3.254) | (0.872) | (0.954) | (0.875) | (2.060) | (2.101) | (-1.543) | (0.837) | (0.878) | (-1.768) |
| Log (V) | | | -0.160 | -0.203 | -0.036 | | | | | | |
| | | | (-0.352) | (-0.433) | (-0.104) | | | | | | |
| | | | | | ** | *** | *** | *** | | | *** |
| Log (K/L) | | | | 0.178 | 0.458 | 0.481 | 0.474 | 3.716 | 0.138 | 0.125 | 2.852 |

Contd. . . .

| | | | | | | | | | | | |
|---|---|---|---|---|---|---|---|---|---|---|---|
| | | | | (0.639) | (2.327) | (1.968) | (1.938) | (1.887) | (0.500) | (0.455) | (1.843) |
| | | | | | ** | ** | ** | | | | |
| Log ($P_w$) | | | | | -0.744 | -0.737 | -0.742 | -0.285 | | | |
| | | | | | (-2.570) | (-2.539) | (-2.555) | (-0.770) | | | |
| Log (TFPK) | | | | | | | | 3.947 | | | 3.633 |
| | | | | | | | | (1.661) | | | (1.886) |
| Log (TFPS) | | | | | | 0.032 | | | 0.157 | | |
| | | | | | | (0.172) | | | (0.753) | | |
| Log (TFPT) | | | | | | | 0.023 | | | 0.148 | |
| | | | | | | | (0.127) | | | (0.708) | |
| $\bar{R}^2$ | 0.351 | 0.374 | 0.340 | 0.314 | 0.461 | 0.462 | 0.461 | 0.560 | 0.342 | 0.339 | 0.443 |
| DW | 1.724 | 1.981 | 1.992 | 2.098 | 2.104 | 2.122 | 2.115 | 1.971 | 2.090 | 2.079 | 2.146 |
| | | | | | *** | *** | *** | *** | | | |
| F/RHO | 11.29 | 6.67 | 4.26 | 3.18 | -0.478 | -0.487 | -0.484 | -0.512 | 4.30 | 4.26 | 6.03 |
| | (1,18) | (2,17) | (3,16) | (4,15) | (-1.849) | (-1.896) | (-1.881) | (-1.960) | (3,16) | (3,16) | (3,16) |

*Notes* : 1. Figures in the brackets give t-values or degree of freedom.

2. * indicates significance at 1% level.

** indicates significance at 5% level.

*** indicates significance at 10% level.

Table 6.VII. 3

**Regression Function for Wages : Hindustan Aeronautics Ltd.**

| *Dependent Variable* → *(Real Wage Rate)* | ——*MODEL NO.*—— | | | | | | | | | | |
|---|---|---|---|---|---|---|---|---|---|---|---|
| *Explanatory Variable* | 1 | 2 | 3 | 4 | 5 | 6 | 7 | 8 | 9 | 10 | 11 |
| Constant | 0.665 | 0.484 | -0.110 | -0.208 | 4.267 | -1.015 | -0.940 | 18.243 | 2.772 | 3.214 | 21.219 |
| | (8.675) | (13.414) | (-0.079) | (-0.143) | (0.764) | (-0.281) | (-0.237) | (2.103) | (0.558) | (0.625) | (1.875) |
| t | | 0.029* | 0.029* | 0.032 | 0.061 | 0.059** | 0.057** | 0.055** | | | |
| | | (3.982) | (3.907) | (3.266) | (1.678) | (2.387) | (2.327) | (2.640) | | | |
| Log (LP) | 0.439* | 0.121 | -0.039 | -0.043 | 0.553 | -0.380 | -0.356 | 3.195*** | 0.768 | 0.848 | 4.319 |
| | (4.438) | (1.050) | (-0.100) | (-0.108) | (0.668) | (-0.584) | (-0.499) | (2.025) | (0.906) | (0.957) | (2.009) |
| Log (V) | | | 0.159 | 0.204 | -0.322 | | | | | | |
| | | | (0.426) | (0.517) | (-0.429) | | | | | | |

Contd. . . .

| | (1) | (2) | (3) | (4) | (5) | (6) | (7) | (8) | (9) | (10) | (11) |
|---|---|---|---|---|---|---|---|---|---|---|---|
| Log (K/L) | | | | -0.078 | 0.058 | 0.358 | 0.343 | -1.879*** | -0.175 | -0.226 | -2.495 |
| | | | | (-0.443) | (0.240) | (0.823) | (0.724) | (-1.890) | (-0.290) | (-0.364) | (-1.744) |
| Log ($P_w$) | | | | | -0.537 | -0.363 | -0.347 | -0.480 | | | |
| | | | | | (-0.830) | (-1.058) | (-1.008) | (-1.484) | | | |
| Log (TFPK) | | | | | | | | -3.007*** | | | -4.030 |
| | | | | | | | | (-1.903) | | | (-1.831) |
| Log (TFPS) | | | | | | 0.649 | | | -0.441 | | |
| | | | | | | (0.928) | | | (-0.449) | | |
| Log (TFPT) | | | | | | | 0.618 | | | -0.528 | |
| | | | | | | | (0.808) | | | (-0.520) | |
| $\bar{R}^2$ | 0.884 | 0.899 | 0.894 | 0.889 | 0.886 | 0.891 | 0.890 | 0.908 | 0.872 | 0.872 | 0.893 |
| DW | 1.781 | 1.311 | 1.336 | 1.300 | 1.240 | 1.402 | 1.387 | 1.552 | 1.719 | 1.713 | 1.901 |
| F/RHO | 0.639* | 86.20 | 54.76 | 39.06 | 30.74 | 32.34 | 31.85 | 38.87 | 0.579** | 0.578** | 0.472** |
| | (3.502) | (2,17) | (3,16) | (4,15) | (5,14) | (5,14) | (5,14) | (5,14) | (2.723) | (2.729) | (2.187) |

*Notes* : 1. Figures in the brackets give t-values or degree of freedom.

2. * indicates significance at 1% level.

** indicates significance at 5% level.

*** indicates significance at 10% level.

*VIII. Consumer Goods Industry-Group*

**Tables** 6.VIII.1, 6.VIII.2, and 6.VIII.3 highlight the regression model outcomes for the group. The study of **Table** 6.VIII.1 reveals the positive relationship of labour productivity with the real wage rate in a more consistent manner, as in almost all the models the value of the coefficient is statistically significant. However, the trend coefficient also displays the presence of a trend in the real wage rate. The model which best exhibits the required relationship is the fifth which incorporates all the important variables. It shows that:

$$\log(Wr) = 2.339 + 0.037\, t^{*} + 0.129 \log (LP)^{*} - 0.044 \log (V)$$
$$(5.212) \quad (4.126) \quad (4.779) \qquad (-1.315)$$
$$+0.125 \log(K/L) - 0.400 \log (Pw)^{*}$$
$$(1.104) \qquad (-4.138)$$
$$\bar{R}^2 = 0.932;\ D\text{-}W = 2.082;\ F_{5,14} = 53.52$$

The model is considered to be the best because it has the highest $\bar{R}^2$, no autocorrelation or multicollinearity and conveys the effect of all variables. It displays that besides trend, while labour productivity has the effect of increasing the real wage rates, the consumer price index has a dampening effect.

In the case of Cement Corporation of India Ltd., the effect of consumer price index is missing, i.e., **Table** 6.VIII.2 does not provide any statistical evidence to the effect that consumer price index has any statistically significant relationship with the real wage rates in CCI Ltd, however, there is sufficient statistical evidence to support the positive link between labour productivity and real wage rate. Out of the models with no multicollinearity and high value of $\bar{R}^2$, the one with net coefficient of log (LP) to be the highest is model IV. It provides the following relationship:

$$\log(Wr) = 0.377 + 0.052t^{*} + 0.176 \log(LP)^{***} - 0.165 \log(V)^{***}$$
$$(1.740) \quad (7.217) \quad (1.742) \qquad (-1.948)$$
$$-0.024 \log (K/L)$$
$$(-0.455)$$
$$\bar{R}^2 = 0.957\ \ D\text{-}W = 1.944\ \ F_{4,15} = 107.64$$

The model shows the elasticity of real wages rate to labour productivity to be equal to 0.176.

Hindustan Photo Films Manufacturing Co. Ltd broadly supports the results, i.e., that trend coefficient and labour productivity coefficient are statistically significant in the relationship. Model II in **Table** 6.VIII.3 discloses this conclusion. The equation of the model is:

$$\log(Wr) = 0.344 + 0.007t^{*} + .300 \log (LP)^{*}$$

$$(9.083) \quad (3.387) \quad (5.549)$$

$$\bar{R}^2 = 0.875;\ D\text{-}W = 2.529;\ F_{2,15} = 60.60$$

The equation has been obtained after ignoring the last four abnormal years of the firm when it incurred losses in value added. The model has been selected because it not only has higher $\bar{R}^2$ but also the problems of autocorrelation and multicollinearity are absent from it.

Thus the Consumer goods industry group with one of the lowest rate of growth in real wage rates and almost highest wage share in value added also exhibits a positive link between the real wage rate and productivity.

### Inter-Group Wage Growth Differentials

This section is further sub-divided into two sections. While section 6.4.3 (a) will analyse the inter-industry wage growth differentials, the section 6.4.3 (b) will discuss the inter-firm wage growth differentials.

#### *(a) Inter-Industry Wage Growth Differentials*

Several studies[16] have been conducted by now to examine the various factors affecting the inter-industry wage differentials in the organised manufacturing sector in India. The basic theoretical frame for explaining the inter-industry wage structure adopted by most of these studies seems to be the one provided by David, G. Brown[17], who advanced the basic hypothesis that wage-level difference among manufacturing industries result primarily from industry -by-industry differences in the employer's estimates of their future abilities to pay wages.

Table 6.VIII. 1

**Regression Function for Wages : Consumer Goods Industry.**

| *Dependent Variable →* *(Real Wage Rate)* *Explanatory Variable* | 1 | 2 | 3 | 4 | 5 | 6 | 7 | 8 | 9 | 10 | 11 |
|---|---|---|---|---|---|---|---|---|---|---|---|
| | | | | | | ——*MODEL NO.*—— | | | | | |
| Constant | 0.581 | 0.423 | 0.515 | 0.511 | 2.399 | 2.719 | 2.725 | 1.845 | 1.070 | 1.079 | -7.943 |
| | (17.561) | (21.251) | (6.387) | (5.739) | (5.212) | (4.388) | (4.421) | (0.410) | (1.982) | (2.022) | (2.648) |
| t | | 0.011* | 0.016* | 0.015 | 0.037* | 0.036* | 0.036* | 0.039* | | | |
| | | (7.158) | (3.464) | (1.426) | (4.126) | (3.665) | (3.640) | (3.100) | | | |
| Log (LP) | 0.156* | 0.133* | 0.138* | 0.135* | 0.129* | 0.186* | 0.188* | 0.061 | 0.212** | 0.216** | -1.342** |
| | (3.545) | (4.697) | (4.880) | (3.461) | (4.779) | (3.251) | (3.245) | (0.090) | (2.627) | (2.646) | (-2.547) |
| Log (V) | | | -0.041 | -0.046 | -0.044 | | | | | | |
| | | | (-1.178) | (-0.942) | (-1.315) | | | | | | |
| Log (K/L) | | | | 0.020 | 0.125 | 0.057 | 0.059 | 0.086 | 0.102* | 0.102* | 1.193* |
| | | | | (0.127) | (1.104) | (0.607) | (0.624) | (0.175) | (3.947) | (3.986) | (3.087) |

| | | | | | | | | | | | |
|---|---|---|---|---|---|---|---|---|---|---|---|
| Log ($P_w$) | | | | | -0.400* | -0.402* | -0.401* | -0.387** | | | |
| | | | | | (-4.138) | (-4.023) | (-4.028) | (-2.427) | | | |
| Log (TFPK) | | | | | | | | 0.083 | | | 1.527** |
| | | | | | | | | (0.117) | | | (2.764) |
| Log (TFPS) | | | | | | -0.077 | | | -0.148 | | |
| | | | | | | (-0.878) | | | (-1.342) | | |
| Log (TFPT) | | | | | | | -0.078 | | | -0.150 | |
| | | | | | | | (-0.903) | | | (-1.374) | |
| $\bar{R}^2$ | 0.836 | 0.865 | 0.868 | 0.860 | 0.932 | 0.928 | 0.928 | 0.924 | 0.851 | 0.852 | 0.888 |
| DW | 2.561 | 1.301 | 1.299 | 1.265 | 2.082 | 2.106 | 2.096 | 2.178 | 1.106 | 1.098 | 1.438 |
| F/RHO | 0.739 | 62.18 | 42.86 | 30.17 | 53.52 | 50.09 | 50.25 | 47.37 | 37.31 | 37.52 | 51.30 |
| | (5.998) | (2,17) | (3,16) | (4,15) | (5,14) | (5,14) | (5,14) | (5,14) | (3,16) | (3,16) | (3,16) |

*Notes* : 1. Figures in the brackets give t-values or degree of freedom.

2. * indicates significance at 1% level.

** indicates significance at 5% level.

*** indicates significance at 10% level.

Table 6.VIII. 2

**Regression Function for Wages : Cement Corporation of India Ltd.**

| *Dependent Variable →* *(Real Wage Rate)* | MODEL NO. | | | | | | | | | | |
|---|---|---|---|---|---|---|---|---|---|---|---|
| *Explanatory Variable* | 1 | 2 | 3 | 4 | 5 | 6 | 7 | 8 | 9 | 10 | 11 |
| Constant | 0.936 | 0.106 | 0.287 | 0.377 | -3.235 | -2.105 | -1.898 | 5.460 | 2.700 | 2.635 | 37.911 |
| | (2.394) | (2.598) | (3.193) | (1.740) | (-0.918) | (-0.612) | (-0.559) | (0.821) | (9.158) | (9.359) | (1.953) |
| | | * | * | * | | | | | | | |
| t | | 0.042 | 0.050 | 0.052 | -0.013 | -0.043 | -0.043 | 0.027 | | | |
| | | (7.566) | (8.051) | (7.217) | (-0.206) | (-0.938) | (-0.951) | (0.428) | | | |
| | | | ** | *** | | | | | * | * | *** |
| Log (LP) | 0.115 | 0.034 | 0.139 | 0.176 | 0.085 | 0.214 | 0.234 | 0.921 | 0.438 | 0.434 | 5.622 |
| | (1.626) | (0.911) | (2.383) | (1.742) | (0.637) | (1.204) | (1.313) | (1.692) | (10.778) | (10.952) | (2.020) |
| | | | *** | *** | | | | | | | |
| Log (V) | | | -0.141 | -0.165 | -0.098 | | | | | | |
| | | | (-2.204) | (-1.948) | (-0.910) | | | | | | |
| | | | | | | | | | * | * | *** |
| Log (K/L) | | | | -0.024 | 0.101 | 0.038 | 0.033 | -0.656 | -0.152 | -0.138 | -4.784 |
| | | | | (-0.455) | (0.758) | (0.275) | (0.254) | (-1.331) | (-3.317) | (-3.117) | (-1.867) |

| | | | | | | | | | | | |
|---|---|---|---|---|---|---|---|---|---|---|---|
| Log ($P_w$) | | | | | 0.671 | 0.692 | 0.670 | 0.104 | | | |
| | | | | | (1.027) | (1.251) | (1.224) | (0.145) | | | |
| Log (TFPK) | | | | | | | | -0.923 | | | -5.568*** |
| | | | | | | | | (-1.750) | | | (-1.968) |
| Log (TFPS) | | | | | | -0.231 | | | -0.425* | | |
| | | | | | | (-1.414) | | | (-8.693) | | |
| Log (TFPT) | | | | | | | -0.245 | | | -0.414* | |
| | | | | | | | (-1.525) | | | (-8.892) | |
| $\bar{R}^2$ | 0.893 | 0.950 | 0.959 | 0.957 | 0.957 | 0.960 | 0.961 | 0.963 | 0.960 | 0.961 | 0.910 |
| DW | 2.268 | 2.091 | 1.981 | 1.944 | 2.058 | 2.173 | 2.170 | 2.182 | 1.859 | 1.895 | 1.483 |
| F/RHO | 0.938* | 182.52 | 150.93 | 107.64 | 86.64 | 93.70 | 95.68 | 100.11 | 154.14 | 160.14 | 0.572* |
| | (8.231) | (2,17) | (3,16) | (4,15) | (5,14) | (5,14) | (5,14) | (5,14) | (3,16) | (3,16) | (7.631) |

*Notes :* 1. Figures in the brackets give t-values or degree of freedom.

2. * indicates significance at 1% level.

** indicates significance at 5% level.

*** indicates significance at 10% level.

Table 6.VIII. 3

**Regression Function for Wages : Hindustan Photo Films Manufacturing Co. Ltd.**

| *Dependent Variable →* *(Real Wage Rate)* | | | | | ——*MODEL NO.*—— | | | | | | |
|---|---|---|---|---|---|---|---|---|---|---|---|
| *Explanatory Variable* | 1 | 2 | 3 | 4 | 5 | 6 | 7 | 8 | 9 | 10 | 11 |
| Constant | 0.318 | 0.344 | -0.061 | 0.271 | -0.762 | -0.159 | -0.155 | -0.503 | 0.757 | 0.770 | -3.936 |
| | (3.811) | (9.083) | (-0.221) | (0.886) | (-0.578) | (-0.206) | (-0.200) | (-0.196) | (0.637) | (0.649) | (-1.229) |
| | | * | | | | | | | | | |
| t | | 0.007 | -0.004 | 0.009 | 0.004 | 0.012 | 0.011 | 0.004 | | | |
| | | (3.387) | (-0.553) | (0.853) | (0.377) | (0.520) | (0.501) | (0.337) | | | |
| | * | * | | | | | | | *** | *** | |
| Log (LP) | 0.409 | 0.300 | -0.158 | 0.109 | 0.855 | 0.171 | 0.179 | 0.199 | 0.457 | 0.460 | -0.492 |
| | (4.656) | (5.549) | (-0.532) | (0.363) | (0.879) | (0.551) | (0.578) | (0.478) | (2.013) | (2.011) | (-0.751) |
| Log (V) | | | 0.466 | 0.145 | -0.574 | | | | | | |
| | | | (1.498) | (0.446) | (-0.604) | | | | | | |
| Log (K/L) | | | | -0.042 | -0.070 | 0.014 | 0.009 | 0.011 | -0.040 | -0.043 | 0.724 |
| | | | | (-0.789) | (-1.679) | (0.072) | (0.048) | (0.032) | (-0.200) | (-0.213) | (1.393) |

| | | | | | | | | | | | |
|---|---|---|---|---|---|---|---|---|---|---|---|
| Log ($P_w$) | | | | | 0.337 | 0.035 | 0.040 | 0.108 | | | |
| | | | | | (0.806) | (0.140) | (0.165) | (0.681) | | | |
| Log (TFPK) | | | | | | | | 0.070 | | | 0.827 |
| | | | | | | | | (0.166) | | | (1.320) |
| Log (TFPS) | | | | | | 0.077 | | | -0.090 | | |
| | | | | | | (0.316) | | | (-0.391) | | |
| Log (TFPT) | | | | | | | 0.070 | | | -0.093 | |
| | | | | | | | (0.291) | | | (-0.403) | |
| $\bar{R}^2$ | 0.865 | 0.875 | 0.847 | 0.869 | 0.864 | 0.861 | 0.861 | 0.860 | 0.819 | 0.819 | 0.537 |
| DW | 2.068 | 2.529 | 2.119 | 2.681 | 2.663 | 2.668 | 2.667 | 2.634 | 1.823 | 1.823 | 1.925 |
| | | | *** | | ** | ** | *** | ** | | | |
| F/RHO | 0.312 | 60.60 | -0.524 | -0.637 | -0.686 | -0.653 | -0.653 | -0.641 | 26.71 | 26.73 | 30.24 |
| | (1.226) | (2,15) | (-1.852) | (-2.539) | (-2.323) | (-2.332) | (-2.335) | (-2.315) | (3,14) | (3,14) | (3,14) |

*Notes* : 1. Figures in the brackets give t-values or degree of freedom.

2. * indicates significance at 1% level.

** indicates significance at 5% level.

*** indicates significance at 10% level.

A variety of factors such as productivity of labour, capital intensity, profitability, relative importance of wage costs, average size of the firms in an industry and degree of unionization have been considered in different studies, and with the help of the standard statistical techniques of multiple regression and correlation it has been shown that some of them are significantly related with wage variation while others are not. However, experience in public sector relating to wage fixation mechanisms such as adjudication, wage boards, or collective bargaining indicates that these mechanisms have operated more in favour of the welfare criterion rather than in inducing competitive behaviour in the labour market.

The basic hypothesis, which the present study attempts to postulate and test, is that the inter-industry wage differentials in India's public sector manufacturing enterprises result primarily from (a) the differences in the technological levels of different industries as reflected in the capital intensity, and (b) the differences in the industry's capacity to pay as reflected in the differences in average productivity of labour and average size of the industry as reflected by gross value added. Unionization has been excluded from the present analysis because, (a) there is no unanimous view in the available literature on the role of trade unions in wage rate determination[18], and (b) there is no substantial difference in the degree of unionization in India's public sector.

Thus, the following functional relationship is hypothesized:

W = f(LP, V, K/L)

In the explanation of inter-industry wage differentials, an important factor influencing the wage levels is expected to be the corresponding levels of labour productivity. Since income generated is the source out of which workers are paid, it is expected that the industries with higher productivity would have better capacity to pay higher wages compared to those which have low productivity.

It is natural to expect that a large industry, with an average size of plant to be large, would be in a better capacity to pay a high wage rate.

It is also expected that over the period of analysis, technological progress would result in higher output per unit of capital. This would increase money wages and, thus, real wages. However, in India's public sector since capital-output ratio has increased over the years as viewed in chapter IV, it is difficult to expect a positive link between capital intensity and wages.

The hypothesis is tested on the basis of the observations obtained from eight industrial groups of public enterprises. As explained in chapter IV, we did not pool the cross-section and time series data for fear of losing the differences which exist in different industries. Krueger and Summers (1986) has mentioned in this regard that aggregation may wipe out important differences that may exist in the structure of different units. Since the data is limited to only eight observations, therefore, the study at this point suffers from the limitation of having to accept regression with low $\bar{R}^2$. The regression obtained with the postulated relationship is:

$$W_r = 6.133 - 0.063\ LP + 0.241\ V^{***} - 0.850\ (K/L)^{**}$$
$$(4.815)\ (-0.451)\qquad (2.388)\qquad (-3.873)$$

$\bar{R}^2 = 0.705$, D-W $= 1.548$, $F_{3,4} = 6.58$

The regression reveals that growth in value added, representing size of the industry, is statistically significant and has the expected sign to be positive. However, labour productivity and capital intensity take the wrong sign but labour productivity is not significant, implying that wage rate growth differences between different industries cannot be explained with the help of labour productivity growth differences. But when growth in value added is replaced by its proxy variable TFP growth to represent capacity to pay as well as size of plant, then TFPS and TFPT give a better fit as compared to what we obtained earlier. The results are also summarized in **Table** 6(B). It is reproduced here for TFPS:

$$W_r = 3.758 + 0.099\ LP - 0.303\ (K/L) + 0.416\ TFPS$$
$$(3.052)\ (0.936)\qquad (-1.424)\qquad\qquad (1.795)$$

$\bar{R}^2 = 0.604$, D-W $= 1.738$, $F_{3,4} = 4.560$

This regression equation is a better explanation of the relationship as the signs are correct for LP and TFPS, but both these are insignificant. Hence the regression may have multicollinearity. Thus, the regression analysis does not provide any statistical evidence to support the hypothesis that inter-industry wage differences can be explained with the help of differences in labour productivity. Moreover, the raw data in **Table** 6.(D) show that growth in real wage rate in different industries is accompanied by growths in labour productivity, value added and capital intensity, but no clear trend is visible.

*(b) Inter-Firm Wage Growth Differentials*

The same regression models which we tested for inter-industry wage growth differentials are also tested for explaining the inter-firm wage differentials and the results are presented in **Table** 6 (C). These regressions also suffer from the limitation of few observations and a low $R^2$. The first model with almost the highest value of $R^2$ displays that labour productivity is not only positive but significant, i.e., it explains the differences in growth in wage rates in different firms.

The equation is :

$$W_r = 1.947 + 0.180\ LP^*$$

$$(3.147)\quad(3.084)$$

$$\bar{R}^2 = 0.362,\ DW = 2.28,\ F_{1,14} = 9.512$$

A close look at other models shows that while models IV, V and VI suffer from multicollinearity, models II and III provide the same conclusions as are obtained from model I. They also demonstrate that coefficients of growth rates of 'V' and K/L are not significantly related to growth rates of real wages.

Thus, differences in growth rates of real wages are linked to differences in labour productivity alone. Raw data in **Table** 6 (E) corroborates how growth in real wage rates are broadly associated with growths in labour productivity.

**Summary**

In this chapter we have examined the relationship between the real wage rate and labour productivity in the selected public

Table 6 (B)

**Regression Function for Wages : Inter-Industry Differences (In growth rates)**

| *Dependent Variable →* *(Real Wage Rate)* *Explanatory Variable* | MODEL NO. 1 | 2 | 3 | 4 | 5 | 6 |
|---|---|---|---|---|---|---|
| Constant | 1.560 | 1.583 | 6.133 | 3.758 | 3.781 | 4.207 |
| | (1.789) | (1.648) | (4.815) | (3.052) | (3.051) | (2.070) |
| (LP) | 0.121 | 0.161 | -0.063 | 0.099 | 0.103 | 0.152 |
| | (1.204) | (0.652) | (-0.451) | (0.936) | (0.971) | (0.189) |
| (V) | | -0.026 | 0.241*** | | | |
| | | (-0.181) | (2.388) | | | |
| (K/L) | | | -0.850** | -0.303 | -0.310 | -0.419 |
| | | | (-3.873) | (-1.424) | (-1.455) | (-0.542) |
| TFPK | | | | | | 0.094 |
| | | | | | | (0.098) |
| TFPS | | | | 0.416 | | |
| | | | | (1.795) | | |
| TFPT | | | | | 0.408 | |
| | | | | | (1.761) | |
| $\bar{R}^2$ | 0.060 | -0.119 | 0.705 | 0.604 | .597 | 0.286 |
| DW | 2.726 | 2.773 | 1.548 | 1.738 | 1.728 | 2.240 |
| F | 1.451 | 0.625 | 6.58 | 4.560 | 4.463 | 1.938 |
| | (1,6) | (2,5) | (3,4) | (3,4) | (3,4) | (3,4) |

*Notes :* 1. Figures in the brackets give t-values or degree of freedom.

2. * indicates significance at 1% level.

** indicates significance at 5% level.

*** indicates significance at 10% level.

Table 6 (C)

**Regression Function for Wages : Inter-Firm Differences (In growth rates)**

| *Dependent Variable →* *(Real Wage Rate)* | ——MODEL NO.—— | | | | | |
|---|---|---|---|---|---|---|
| *Explanatory Variable* | 1 | 2 | 3 | 4 | 5 | 6 |
| Constant | 1.947 | 2.355 | 2.314 | 2.292 | 2.372 | 1.922 |
| | (3.147) | (2.994) | (2.155) | (2.265) | (2.362) | (1.984) |
| (LP) | 0.180* | 0.261** | 0.262* | 0.125 | 0.117 | -0.146 |
| | (3.084) | (2.343) | (2.215) | (1.669) | (1.585) | (-0.651) |
| (V) | | -0.091 | -0.093 | | | |
| | | (-0.853) | (-0.810) | | | |
| (K/L) | | | 0.006 | 0.023 | 0.024 | 0.262 |
| | | | (0.059) | (0.211) | (0.221) | (1.240) |
| TFPK | | | | | | 0.384 |
| | | | | | | (1.508) |
| TFPS | | | | 0.132 | | |
| | | | | (1.219) | | |
| TFPT | | | | | 0.154 | |
| | | | | | (1.383) | |
| $\bar{R}^2$ | 0.362 | 0.349 | 0.295 | 0.338 | 0.358 | 0.375 |
| DW | 2.28 | 2.137 | 2.137 | 1.961 | 1.907 | 2.107 |
| F | 9.512 | 5.028 | 3.096 | 3.561 | 3.800 | 4.001 |
| | (1,14) | (2,13) | (3,12) | (3,12) | (3,12) | (3,12) |

*Notes :* 1. Figures in the brackets give t-values or degree of freedom.

2. * indicates significance at 1% level.

** indicates significance at 5% level.

*** indicates significance at 10% level.

sector enterprises. The link between wages and productivity has been established by several studies in manufacturing industries both in India and abroad. These studies have focussed on the desirability of linking wages to productivity but generally have concluded that productivity can be only one of the several other criteria while determining wages. Others being capacity to pay, capital intensity, cost of living and unionization.

The present study basically focussed on the relationship of the real wage rate with (i) labour productivity, (ii) value added by the unit, (iii) capital intensity, (iv) price of consumer goods for industrial workers and (v) a time trend. The study, however, started with a two variable relationship, i.e., between the real wage rate and labour productivity but extended it to include other variables gradually. Value added has also been replaced by a proxy variable, total factor productivity. So in all, eleven different models were formulated to find out the link.

The link was first examined for the aggregate of eight industrial groups of public sector enterprises. It was disclosed by the regression analysis that the real wage rate is positively and significantly related to the labour productivity with elasticity of response of wage change to labour productivity being 0.746. However, changes in real wage rates in the industry are also being explained by other factors such as value added and consumer price index. The link between wages and productivity is conclusively established by different models for the aggregate of industries.

Through group level regressions, the same relationship was investigated for the individual industries and firms selected for the study. Generally, it has been found that the link is present in almost all the units though with different elasticities of response. However, as in the case of aggregate of industries, other factors like trend, value added, capital intensity, $P_w$ and TFP indices are also related to the real wage rate. In some of the units they are significant while in others they are insignificant depending upon the structure and size of the unit. But the positive relationship between the real wage rate and labour productivity in these units is supported by the available statistical evidence beyond doubt.

While trying to study the variations in inter-industry and inter-firm growth rates in real wage rates and productivity and establish a link between them, the exercise is limited by the few number of observations. Even then, new regressions were applied with labour productivity, value added and capital intensity. The available statistical information did not provide any significant relationship between the two, i.e., the real wage rate and labour productivity in the case of inter-industry differences. Value added, which represents capacity to pay and size of the unit, is the central determinant of inter-industry wage variation. But the relationship is again established in the case of inter-firm differences.

Thus, the available statistical information points towards the existence of a positive relationship between the real wage rate and labour productivity in the selected public sector enterprises in India.

## NOTES

1. Report of the Royal Commission on Labour (1932), p 11.
2. Committee on Fair Wages (1949).
3. The National Commission on Labour (1969).
4. Palekar, S.A. (1962), p 166.
5. Bowen (1969), p 227.
6. I.L.O. (1966), pp. 126-127.
7. Khusro (1979), p 68.
8. Kehar Sangha (1964), p 54.
9. Gordon (1990), pp 1-25.
10. Gordon (1987), p 686.
11. Report of the National Commission on Labour, opcit, p 15.
12. Basu, Sreelekha (1974).
13. Commerce (1982), Nov, 20. p 761.
14. Sundaram I. Satya (1987), pp 107-108.
15. Gahlen and Licht (1990), pp 129-149.

16. Studies by Verma (1971), Papola (1972), Dholakia (1976), Suri (1976), etc.

17. Brown, David G (1962), p 45.

18. Ramjash (1992) for details about the effect of trade unions on wages.

Table 6(D)

**Inter-Industry Growth Rates (%)**

| *Industry* | | *(Value-Added)* | *(Real Wage Rate)* | *(Labour Productivity)* | *(K/L)* |
|---|---|---|---|---|---|
| I | Steel | 17.05 | 2.64 | 6.20 | 6.10 |
| II | Power | 38.07 | 4.86 | 17.70 | 9.40 |
| III | Petroleum | 21.73 | 0.027 | 10.69 | 10.23 |
| IV | Fertilizers, Chemicals & Pharmaceuticals | 16.80 | 3.17 | 8.26 | 5.31 |
| V | Heavy Engineering | 10.83 | 2.76 | 2.70 | 4.19 |
| VI | Medium & Light Engineering | 15.43 | 2.37 | 4.99 | 7.11 |
| VII | Transport Equipment | 14.37 | 2.42 | 5.17 | 6.72 |
| VIII | Consumer goods | 20.77 | 1.41 | 2.31 | 8.85 |

Table 6(E)

**Inter-Firm Growth Rates (%)**

| *Industry* | | *(Value-Added)* | *(Real Wage Rate)* | *(Labour Productivity)* | *(K/L)* |
|---|---|---|---|---|---|
| I | SAIL | 20.11 | 3.39 | 11.51 | 5.63 |
| II | MDNL | 29.78 | 4.06 | 21.26 | -1.63 |
| III | NHPCL | 23.40 | 0.46 | -0.46 | 8.06 |
| IV | NTPCL | 33.93 | 8.48 | 22.99 | 12.99 |
| V | IOCL | 14.66 | 2.66 | 4.76 | 5.18 |
| VI | ONGC | 22.45 | 1.31 | 13.99 | 11.28 |
| VII | NFL | 15.60 | 6.22 | 9.23 | 3.80 |
| VIII | IPCL | 20.62 | 3.61 | 5.63 | 6.02 |
| IX | BHEL | 11.17 | 3.45 | 1.85 | 4.83 |
| X | BHPVL | 14.09 | 3.76 | 5.20 | 2.60 |
| XI | HMT | 11.42 | 2.99 | 1.79 | 5.21 |
| XII | ITI | 17.22 | 3.46 | 7.58 | 11.46 |
| XIII | BEML | 15.07 | 0.57 | 4.99 | 8.33 |
| XIV | HAL | 13.90 | 3.65 | 5.89 | 6.53 |
| XV | CCIL | 23.36 | 4.72 | 13.54 | 10.63 |
| XIV | HPFMCL | 13.06 | 1.56 | 2.72 | 10.61 |

# 7

# SUMMARY AND CONCLUSION

In this study we have analysed the Wage-productivity relationship in selected public sector enterprises in India for the period 1974-75 to 1995-96. This period is commensurate with the turnaround in India's industrial development which put an end to the deceleration and relative stagnation of mid-sixties to mid-seventies. The public sector in India has been an important instrument of Indian development strategy. It was visualized by the founding 'Fathers' of the Indian plans that public sector will occupy commanding heights in the shaping of Indian economy. With this objective in mind the public sector in India has grown manifolds from 5 enterprises in 1950-51 with an investment of Rs 29 crores to 243 in 1995-96 with the total investment of Rs 178628 crores. However, its performance in terms of physical and financial targets has not been satisfactory giving rise to a debate about its role and relevance. It is now being argued that such an inefficient large public sector is a drain on precious national resources. It is also being blamed for overmanning, labour inefficiency and excessive unionization. The present public enterprise reforms bring into focus the questions about the productivity and efficiency of all the factors especially human resources, which have been used in the public enterprises.

The productivity and efficiency of labour has been examined through the Wage-productivity nexus. The Wage-productivity nexus has earlier been examined at the theoretical as well as empirical level by several studies both within India and abroad. The link has been found directly through the marginal productivity theory and efficiency wage theories, and indirectly through the effect of productivity on 'capacity to pay' of an industry. Most of the studies, especially in India, focussed on either the manufacturing sector as a whole or to a particular industry. The present study, therefore, has been extended to the public sector enterprises. Separate analysis of productivity trends, by both the parametric (Cobb-Dougles and CES production functions) and non-parametric methods (partial and total factor productivity indices) (Chapter IV) and wage trends (Chapter V), have been carried out before using a multiple regression framework for analysing the productivity growths (with productivities as dependent variable and host of explanatory variables) (Chapter IV) and wage-productivity relationship (with the real wage rate as dependent variable and labour productivity along with few more, as the explanatory variables) (Chapter VI).

Our empirical analysis at the aggregate level and at a detailed level of disaggregation (for eight industrial groups of public enterprises at one level and for the sixteen firms at another) has clearly brought out the poor performance of public enterprises with respect to the total factor productivity growth for the entire period. The decline in all the three TFP indices is noteworthy after 1988-89. At the aggregate level, total factor productivity by Solow and Translog measures declined at the rate of 0.44 percent and 0.40 percent respectively while the Kendrick index increased marginally at the rate of 0.68 percent. At the disaggregate level of industries we observe that the three total factor productivity indices namely TFPK, TFPS and TFPT increased only in three industries - Power, Fertilizers and Transport Equipment. While in Power and Fertilizers the increase has been substantial, 3.5 percent in TFPT for Power and 3.24 percent in TFPT for Fertilizers, it is marginal in Transport Equipment (only 0.24 percent). On the other hand, whereas in Heavy Engineering industry all the three indices are negative, the remaining industries exhibit a mixed trend. Our estimates of productivity (TFP) for the aggregate of eight industries and for the individual industries do not show any significant improvement since 1990-91, when the roots of reforms were laid down. At the disaggregate level of firms also we observe the same behaviour as has been observed for the industries. Out of the sixteen firms, five have shown positive values for the three TFP indices, and, there are five firms with the negative signs for all the three TFP indices, and the remaining show a mixed trend. Our findings of TFPT growth for the aggregate of manufacturing and individual industries are broadly in agreement with the findings of earlier studies for the organised manufacturing industries in India (e.g. Ahluwalia, 1991).

Our estimates of partial productivities - labour and capital and capital intensity show a significant rising trend in labour productivity and capital intensity and a significantly falling trend in capital productivity for the aggregate of industries. While labour productivity increased at the rate of 7.49 percent and capital intensity by 9.06 percent during 1974-75 to 1995-96 the capital productivity declined by 1.56 percent. At the disaggregate level the estimates reveal that labour productivity increased in all the industries and firms except one (NHPC) and the rate of growth ranged from 2.31 percent to 17.7 percent in case of industries and -0.46 percent to almost 23 percent in the case of firms. On the other hand the average annual growth rate of capital intensity in industries ranged from a low of 4.19 percent in the case of Heavy engineering to a high of 10.23 percent for Petroleum, and in the case of firms from a low of (-)1.63 percent in MDNL to 13 percent in NTPC. The growth in labour productivity and capital intensity has been almost continuous throughout the period in all the industries and firms. The estimates of capital productivity at the disaggregate level exhibit wide fluctuations in growth rates. Capital productivity has increased in two (Power and Fertilizers) out of the eight and remained stagnant in another two (Steel and Petroleum) while it declined in the remaining four industries (Heavy Engineering, Medium and Light Engineering, Transport Equipment and Consumer goods). Capital productivity for the industries varied between (-)6.54 percent for Consumer goods to 8.28 percent for Power. In the case of firms capital productivity declined for nine firms out of sixteen and ranged from (-)7.89 percent for HPFMC Ltd to 22.89 percent for MDN Ltd. It is observed that capital productivity is negative in those industries where wage share in value added is comparatively higher. Though no such trend is clearly visible in the case of firms.

Estimates of the Cobb-Douglas production function and the CES function discloses a mixed trend. The aggregate of industries shows increasing returns to scale, contrary to the assumption of constant returns to scale implicit in the TFP indices. The CES function also reveals the presence of unitary elasticity of substitution for the aggregate of industries. Estimates of the rate of technological progress obtained from production functions are broadly consistent in terms of direction with the results based on TFP indices especially TFPS and TFPT. At the disaggregate level the Cobb-Douglas production function (C-D function) estimates reveal constant returns to scale (CRS) in Steel, Power and Medium and Light engineering industrial groups. For other industrial groups it indicates the presence of increasing returns to scale except for Consumer goods industry where there are decreasing returns. The CES production function not only provides constant returns to scale (CRS) for Steel, Power and Medium and Light Engineering, as has been revealed by the C-D functions, but also for Heavy Engineering. For the remaining groups, it supports the results obtained from C-D function. For firms, the C-D function supports the assumption of constant returns to scale in eight out of sixteen firms and provides support for increasing returns to scale in five firms and decreasing returns to scale in the remaining three firms. The CES production function on the other hand supports constant returns to scale in thirteen out of sixteen firms and decreasing returns to scale in the remaining three. The elasticity of substitution comes out to be unity only for the Consumer goods industry and the two firms - namely, NHPC Ltd and BEML. For all other industrial groups and firms it is mainly very low, and it is negative for the Transport Equipment industry and the firm NTPC.

The regression analysis for variations in labour productivity and total factor productivity measures (TFPK, TFPS and TFPT) suggests a significant positive relationship with value added for both the aggregate level of industries and the disaggregate level of industries and firms. This is in agreement with the finding of many earlier studies for India and other countries for the manufacturing industries (e.g., Goldar, 1986 and Gordon, 1987). This association takes place because rapid growth in value added generally induces technological progress and generates scale economies. The analysis also discloses a negative relationship of the variable 'time' with productivity. It implies that deterioration in labour-management relations has been responsible for low productivity growth in public enterprises. Capital intensity has been, generally, positively related with labour productivity but negatively with total factor productivity. High capital intensity is expected to lead to 'more machine per worker' effect, thereby increasing labour productivity. However, total factor productivity may not increase with increase in capital intensity because of overcapitalization[1] and prevalence of excess capacity. All the productivity indices have also been found to be positively related with real wage rate per worker at the aggregate level and for the three industries - Steel, Petroleum and Consumer goods. At the disaggregate level of firms the relationship has been found to be generally missing.

The analysis of inter-industry and inter-firm differentials in labour and total factor productivity growth highlights the importance of the growth in value added for labour productivity growth, as it has been found to be significantly related to labour productivity. The available evidence is not sufficient to obtain a similar relationship for total factor productivity. However, real wages per worker have been found to be a significant variable in explaining inter-firm differences in productivity estimates.

If the poor productivity growth is a serious concern for policy makers then an increase in employment in the public enterprises in the early phase and the decline since 1990-91 should be a hopeful event, as it is in tune with the objectives of the policy makers at different points of time. Employment in the aggregate of the eight industrial groups increased at the rate of 2.90 percent per annum during the period 1974-75 to 1995-96. However, the employment has been increasing only till 1990-91 when a turnaround started, possibly due to a change in the Government's objectives and perceptions about the role of public enterprises in India. There has been a continuous fall in the employment level during the last six years. The fall in employment is distinctly visible in all the industries except Power and Petroleum which already have very high capital intensity and low wage share in value added. It is observed that while employment generation objective has been fulfilled by a few industries whose growth rates of employment have been from moderate to impressive, others did not generate sufficiently large employment and the growth rate remained comparatively low. The analysis also reveals differences in the growth rates of employment generation by the firms where the range of growth rate has been from (-)0.09 percent to 16.99 percent.

The real wages per worker during the period under study, i.e., 1974-75 to 1995-96, increased at an exponential rate of 2.08 percent for the aggregate of industries. The rate of increase is almost equal to the exponential increase in real per capita income of 2.06 percent during the same period. However, the growth in real wages per worker has been almost continuous and there is no fall in real wages during the last six years, unlike as in employment. But the growth in real wages per worker has not been uniform at the disaggregate level of industries and firms. The uniformity is missing even at the absolute level of real wages. The inter-industry variations in annual growth rates of real wages per worker ranged from almost zero percent in Petroleum industry to 4.86 percent in Power industry. Though the real wages in Power industry grew at the highest rate of 4.86 percent per year but the absolute level of real wages in it, along with Consumer goods industry, have remained very low throughout the entire period of study. Our estimates also disclose that those industries and firms which had initially low absolute real wage rates attempted to reach the level of real wages enjoyed by workers elsewhere. In all such cases (as in the case of NTPC), generally, the real wages per worker grew faster than the others, but wherever high growth rates could not be obtained (as in the case of NHPC and ONGC) the real wages per worker remained depressed. On the other hand industries and firms which already had high real wages per worker in the beginning, i.e., 1974-75, could increase the real wages only at a low rate (as in the case of Petroleum). Moreover, the estimates of growth rates of real wages per worker for different firms divulge more differences in the inter-firm growth rates than the industry and they vary from 0.46 percent in case of NHPC to 8.48 percent for NTPC, both firms belonging to the same industry-Power. This reflects the existence of inter-firm differences, even, within the same industry.

The estimates of Wage share in value added also highlights wide differences between industries and firms. At the aggregate level the wage share has declined from more than 40 percent in 1974-75 to around 20 percent in 1995-96. This has happened mainly because of the increase in capital intensity. It has been found that industries and firms with high capital intensity generally have low wage share in value added. Thus, the differences in wage share also, to some extent, reflect the differences in capital intensity of the units. The coefficients of wage share in value added during the year 1995-96 varied from 0.065 to 0.689 in the case of industries and from 0.024 to 0.782 in the case of firms.

In an attempt to find the wage-productivity relationship, real wage rates have been regressed on a number of possible determinants of the real wage rates. The regression analysis discloses that in the aggregate of the eight industrial groups of public enterprises the real wage rates are positively and significantly related to the labour productivity, with elasticity of response of wage changes to labour productivity changes being 0.748. Value added and consumer price index are the other significant variables explaining changes in real wage rates. The group level regressions for different industries also exhibits the same relationship, i.e., there is statistical evidence to support the positive relationship of real wage rates with labour productivity in these industries though the elasticity varies between them from 0.129 in Consumer goods industry to 1.381 in Petroleum industry. Other factors like trend, value added, capital intensity and price of Consumer goods are significant in some industries and insignificant in others. The firm level investigation under the study also conclusively supports the broad results of the industry level analysis, i.e., the firms also generally display a positive relationship between the real wage rates and labour productivity - the elasticity ranging from 0.068 in IOC Ltd. to 0.856 in NTPC. Inter-industry variations in real wage rate growths do not show any significant statistical evidence of a link between the two, i.e., the real wage rates and labour productivity. It is value added, which represents capacity to pay, that explains these variations. But, if value added is replaced by its proxy variable, total factor productivity, then both labour productivity and TFP show a positive relationship between wage rate variations and productivity variations. Inter-firm variations in the growth of real wage rates, however, are positively and significantly related to labour productivity.

**Conclusion**

The estimates of TFP for the period 1974-75 to 1995-96 bring out the fact that the TFP growth in India's public enterprises during 1974-75 to 1995-96 have been sluggish. It can, therefore, be seen that public sector enterprises have not performed efficiently during the period. It is interesting to note that during the same period the index of industrial production for Indian manufacturing industry increased faster (5.9 percent) but TFPT had declined by 0.4 percent during the same period. Even the high growth of gross value added at constant prices, 10.49 percent per annum, did not induce TFP to increase in the select public enterprises. Factor productivities of labour and capital indicate the efficiency of operations with respect to the production function. Our finding of a declining capital productivity (and rising labour productivity) with a rising capital intensity in most of the industries and firms implies that, (i) there is an under utilization of capacities, and (ii) growth in employment has seriously lagged behind the growth in investment and output. These two facts along with a slow growth in employment (only 2.90 percent) raise doubts about the presence of over-staffing in public enterprises.

The problem of over-staffing and labour inefficiency, especially in the light of poor performance by public enterprises, is related to the link between wages and productivity. Several empirical studies have found that the relationship between wages and productivity does exist in the manufacturing sector, both in India and abroad. The findings of our study reveal that there is statistical evidence of the existence of the Wage-productivity relationship in India's public sector enterprises. The existence of the relationship both in the public sector enterprises and in the private organised sector in India and abroad basically imply that ownership *per se* is not important and does not affect the relationship, and the productivity, as there are examples of very efficeintly run public enterprises and of loss making private enterprises.

In India's public sector enterprises productivity may not have played a direct role in wage rate determination but the findings show that the real wage rates have increased faster in those industries (three out of eight, namely - Power; Fertilizers, Chemicals and Pharmaceuticals and Transport Equipment) and firms (five out of the sixteen, namely - SAIL, MDNL, NTPC, NFL and HAL) where total factor productivity growth rates have been positive. Our findings, thus, confirm the indirect role of productivity in wage rate determination in India's public sector enterprises. The role of productivity has now been recognized openly by the Government by providing weightage to the performance of the public enterprises while signing MOUs with them.

An interesting finding of the study is that contrary to popular belief, the real wage rate increase in public enterprises in India has been generally slower than the increase in their labour productivity. The rate of increase of real wage rates is even slower than the increase in national real per capita income in many industries and firms. Thus, the employees in the public sector enterprises, who may be over-paid as compared to the national real per capita income or to the income of the employees in other sectors, are generally not overpaid if viewed from the angle of their productivity. From this, one may conclude that the general perception of strong trade unions in public enterprises being able to extract unduly high wages from the government is a myth, as workers have not been able to corner more than their proportionate contribution. Therefore, the blame on them for every malaise in public enterprises seems to be misplaced.

Nevertheless, the general inefficiency in the public enterprises cannot be denied. Therefore, the question that arises is *who is to be blamed if not the public sector workers?* The blame appears to lie somewhere else. There could be some possible explanations as to why public sector enterprises show lower efficiency as measured by total factor productivity indices. The poor performance of public enterprises can be due to inappropriate location and technology choice decisions, irrational product mixes, forced marketing decisions, irrational pricing policies, inadequate attention to R&D and human resources development, and the policies of the government. Many times political considerations rather than economic criteria have been the basis of these decisions. However, in instances wherever the public sector has been freed from the above mentioned shackles, its efficiency has shown improvement. The public sector enterprises reforms, which were started in 1990, focussed at improving their performance. But the reforms seems to have started more on pragmatic rather than ideological grounds. The inability of the State to continue to subsidize the public sector through budgetary support compelled the Government to initiate the reforms. Some steps have been taken towards the 'marketization' of public enterprises with a view to making those enterprises behave like competitive units. A large number of Memoranda of Understanding (MOUs), 114 in 1996-97, were being entered into with public enterprises. Nevertheless, the present study clearly points out that during the last six years, i.e., since 1990-91, though the number of employees in the aggregate of select industries have declined, and labour productivity has increased there is no visible improvement in their total factor productivity. The finding implies that the response of the reforms so far has been slow, mainly because of the resistance against these reforms from different sections which have long enjoyed the profits and perks of the public sector. But if the economic profitability for the public enterprises is to be ensured then the steps toward marketization and privatization of these enterprises have to be taken on ideological grounds. These steps may strike at the very *raison d'etre* of public enterprises but just a few cosmetic changes will not be sufficient to help the public enterprises generate desired amount of internal resources. A detailed analysis of the same needs to be undertaken for further research.

## NOTES

1. Ahluwalia (1991) has also shown that the higher the capital-labour ratio in an industry the lower is its growth in total factor productivity (p. 196).

# APPENDICES

Table 4.I.1

**Estimates of Productivity and Capital Intensity: Steel Industry**

| *Variable* | *Indices of Single Factor Productivity* | | *Indices of Total Factor Productivity* | | | *Capital Intensity* |
|---|---|---|---|---|---|---|
| *Year* | *Labour* | *Capital* | *Kendrick* | *Solow* | *Translog* | *(Rs' 000)* |
| 1974-75 | 100.00 | 100.00 | 100.00 | 100.00 | 100.00 | 8.78 |
| 1975-76 | 94.87 | 86.95 | 90.68 | 90.92 | 90.66 | 9.58 |
| 1976-77 | 117.01 | 115.87 | 116.43 | 108.09 | 107.36 | 8.86 |
| 1977-78 | 102.18 | 94.18 | 97.95 | 90.04 | 88.90 | 9.52 |
| 1978-79 | 75.89 | 62.32 | 68.33 | 55.27 | 53.86 | 10.69 |
| 1979-80 | 63.03 | 49.50 | 55.35 | 43.95 | 42.80 | 11.18 |
| 1980-81 | 66.64 | 49.05 | 56.38 | 45.50 | 44.32 | 11.92 |
| 1981-82 | 64.22 | 44.00 | 52.07 | 42.91 | 41.82 | 12.81 |
| 1982-83 | 57.53 | 39.09 | 46.41 | 38.09 | 37.11 | 12.92 |
| 1983-84 | 62.60 | 40.43 | 48.97 | 40.68 | 39.65 | 13.59 |
| 1984-85 | 84.23 | 52.23 | 64.24 | 50.29 | 49.18 | 14.16 |
| 1985-86 | 105.98 | 63.01 | 78.73 | 59.39 | 58.21 | 14.76 |
| 1986-87 | 94.93 | 53.72 | 68.32 | 50.93 | 49.78 | 15.51 |
| 1987-88 | 150.92 | 80.69 | 104.67 | 68.47 | 67.12 | 16.42 |
| 1988-89 | 187.74 | 94.28 | 124.89 | 79.18 | 77.74 | 17.48 |
| 1989-90 | 203.13 | 98.35 | 131.83 | 83.17 | 81.62 | 18.13 |
| 1990-91 | 200.14 | 73.62 | 106.88 | 68.84 | 67.61 | 23.87 |
| 1991-92 | 243.84 | 82.57 | 122.44 | 77.34 | 76.00 | 25.93 |
| 1992-93 | 234.91 | 75.32 | 113.17 | 71.51 | 70.28 | 27.38 |
| 1993-94 | 241.89 | 73.21 | 111.49 | 70.84 | 69.57 | 29.01 |
| 1994-95 | 268.76 | 77.55 | 119.69 | 75.63 | 74.35 | 30.43 |
| 1995-96 | 280.02 | 75.43 | 118.21 | 75.42 | 73.92 | 32.57 |
| Growth rate% | 6.19 | 0.02 | 2.24 | -0.30 | -0.35 | 6.17 |

*Notes:* 1. Data computed and compiled from various issues of Public Enterprises Survey, Deptt. of Public Enterprises, GOI, New Delhi.

2. Growth rates are annual exponential growth rates over time.

Table 4.I.2

**Estimates of Productivity and Capital Intensity : Steel Authority of India Ltd. (SAIL)**

| *Variable* | *Indices of Single Factor Productivity* | | *Indices of Total Factor Productivity* | | | *Capital Intensity* |
|---|---|---|---|---|---|---|
| *Year* | *Labour* | *Capital* | *Kendrick* | *Solow* | *Translog* | *(Rs' 000)* |
| 1978-79 | 100.00 | 100.00 | 100.00 | 100.00 | 100.00 | 10.47 |
| 1979-80 | 76.06 | 72.06 | 74.75 | 68.76 | 68.59 | 11.05 |
| 1980-81 | 74.19 | 64.64 | 70.90 | 65.37 | 65.10 | 12.02 |
| 1981-82 | 67.12 | 54.18 | 62.43 | 57.30 | 57.00 | 12.98 |
| 1982-83 | 59.70 | 47.34 | 55.17 | 50.32 | 50.03 | 13.21 |
| 1983-84 | 64.93 | 48.54 | 58.69 | 53.68 | 53.39 | 14.01 |
| 1984-85 | 98.25 | 69.87 | 87.12 | 70.41 | 70.38 | 14.73 |
| 1985-86 | 120.25 | 82.03 | 104.87 | 81.47 | 81.59 | 15.35 |
| 1986-87 | 106.03 | 68.89 | 90.65 | 68.43 | 68.32 | 16.12 |
| 1987-88 | 179.45 | 110.27 | 149.86 | 94.59 | 94.74 | 17.05 |
| 1988-89 | 226.00 | 130.98 | 183.99 | 110.35 | 110.69 | 18.07 |
| 1989-90 | 250.02 | 135.45 | 197.45 | 115.89 | 116.17 | 19.34 |
| 1990-91 | 255.35 | 126.49 | 193.35 | 111.12 | 111.43 | 21.15 |
| 1991-92 | 299.49 | 134.39 | 215.98 | 120.04 | 120.38 | 23.35 |
| 1992-93 | 281.45 | 117.76 | 195.78 | 106.46 | 106.76 | 25.04 |
| 1993-94 | 290.59 | 113.9 | 195.46 | 117.87 | 118.29 | 26.73 |
| 1994-95 | 306.44 | 113.08 | 199.41 | 119.12 | 119.76 | 28.39 |
| 1995-96 | 336.39 | 116.11 | 210.43 | 124.49 | 125.10 | 30.34 |
| Growth rate% | 11.51 | 5.88 | 9.17 | 4.55 | 4.60 | 5.63 |

*Notes:* 1. Data computed and compiled from various issues of Public Enterprises Survey, Deptt. of Public Enterprises, GOI, New Delhi.

2. Growth rates are annual exponential growth rates over time.

Table 4.I.3

**Estimates of Productivity and Capital Intensity: Misra Dhatu Nigam Ltd.**

| *Variable* | *Indices of Single Factor Productivity* | | *Indices of Total Factor Productivity* | | | *Capital Intensity* |
|---|---|---|---|---|---|---|
| *Year* | *Labour* | *Capital* | *Kendrick* | *Solow* | *Translog* | *(Rs' 000)* |
| 1981-82 | 100.00 | 100.00 | 100.00 | 100.00 | 100.00 | 33.56 |
| 1982-83 | 182.49 | 211.58 | 107.27 | 121.85 | 106.70 | 28.95 |
| 1983-84 | 238.09 | 266.43 | 154.35 | 150.22 | 132.02 | 29.99 |
| 1984-85 | 509.52 | 743.51 | 195.57 | 230.63 | 182.92 | 23.00 |
| 1985-86 | 1069.10 | 1539.48 | 417.85 | 349.96 | 278.22 | 23.31 |
| 1986-87 | 1615.10 | 2286.72 | 646.51 | 465.93 | 370.63 | 23.70 |
| 1987-88 | 1381.57 | 1956.23 | 552.97 | 387.61 | 308.33 | 23.70 |
| 1988-89 | 1497.61 | 1961.06 | 679.04 | 400.13 | 318.35 | 25.63 |
| 1989-90 | 1673.09 | 2170.64 | 771.28 | 440.05 | 350.02 | 25.87 |
| 1990-91 | 1488.33 | 2081.04 | 606.79 | 404.41 | 322.92 | 24.00 |
| 1991-92 | 1800.36 | 2505.64 | 739.13 | 473.54 | 378.21 | 24.11 |
| 1992-93 | 1351.54 | 1831.60 | 578.34 | 308.88 | 246.07 | 24.76 |
| 1993-94 | 1579.25 | 2110.33 | 691.53 | 351.42 | 280.07 | 25.11 |
| 1994-95 | 2076.31 | 2621.21 | -- | 430.71 | 341.57 | 27.36 |
| 1995-96 | 2341.22 | 2909.09 | -- | 476.37 | 377.85 | 27.70 |
| Growth rate % | 21.26 | 22.89 | 17.01 | 10.31 | 9.10 | -1.63 |

*Notes:* 1. Data computed and compiled from various issues of Public Enterprises Survey, Deptt. of Public Enterprises, GOI, New Delhi.

2. Growth rates are annual exponential growth rates over time.

Table 4.II.1

**Estimates of Productivity and Capital Intensity : Power Industry**

| *Variable* | *Indices of Single Factor Productivity* | | *Indices of Total Factor Productivity* | | | *Capital Intensity* |
|---|---|---|---|---|---|---|
| *Year* | *Labour* | *Capital* | *Kendrick* | *Solow* | *Translog* | *(Rs' 000)* |
| 1982-83 | 100.00 | 100.00 | 100.00 | 100.00 | 100.00 | 51.61 |
| 1983-84 | 189.02 | 167.68 | 169.11 | 130.06 | 130.03 | 58.18 |
| 1984-85 | 166.14 | 141.96 | 143.53 | 113.13 | 113.03 | 60.41 |
| 1985-86 | 332.42 | 230.58 | 236.01 | 145.09 | 145.52 | 74.41 |
| 1986-87 | 311.06 | 200.52 | 206.02 | 127.57 | 127.95 | 80.07 |
| 1987-88 | 280.01 | 169.62 | 174.79 | 113.02 | 113.32 | 85.21 |
| 1988-89 | 380.32 | 197.74 | 205.14 | 126.75 | 127.04 | 99.27 |
| 1989-90 | 569.66 | 280.05 | 291.17 | 158.64 | 159.01 | 104.99 |
| 1990-91 | 733.04 | 300.79 | 314.72 | 169.65 | 170.08 | 125.79 |
| 1991-92 | 838.67 | 329.78 | 345.53 | 182.29 | 182.77 | 131.27 |
| 1992-93 | 688.70 | 284.84 | 297.97 | 152.65 | 153.10 | 124.80 |
| 1993-94 | 721.05 | 260.55 | 273.68 | 140.82 | 141.23 | 142.84 |
| 1994-95 | 764.51 | 253.10 | 267.00 | 137.80 | 138.19 | 155.92 |
| 1995-96 | 941.15 | 320.03 | 332.00 | 158.29 | 163.89 | 154.08 |
| Growth rate % | 17.75 | 8.28 | 8.72 | 3.53 | 3.55 | 9.47 |

*Notes:* 1. Data computed and compiled from various issues of Public Enterprises Survey, Deptt. of Public Enterprises, GOI, New Delhi.

2. Growth rates are annual exponential growth rates over time.

Table 4.II.2

**Estimates of Productivity and Capital Intensity: National Hydro-Electric Power Corp Ltd.**

| *Variable* | *Indices of Single Factor Productivity* | | *Indices of Total Factor Productivity* | | | *Capital Intensity* |
|---|---|---|---|---|---|---|
| *Year* | *Labour* | *Capital* | *Kendrick* | *Solow* | *Translog* | *(Rs' 000)* |
| 1982-83 | 100.00 | 100.00 | 100.00 | 100.00 | 100.00 | 38.50 |
| 1983-84 | 95.72 | 95.90 | 95.89 | 96.00 | 96.00 | 38.43 |
| 1984-85 | 89.64 | 87.68 | 87.76 | 89.39 | 89.39 | 39.36 |
| 1985-86 | 91.58 | 75.50 | 76.06 | 79.27 | 79.40 | 46.70 |
| 1986-87 | 64.29 | 50.64 | 51.10 | 51.77 | 51.84 | 48.88 |
| 1987-88 | 74.48 | 46.40 | 47.15 | 48.89 | 48.96 | 61.80 |
| 1988-89 | 160.85 | 63.92 | 65.57 | 58.04 | 58.11 | 96.90 |
| 1989-90 | 128.41 | 59.86 | 61.23 | 54.79 | 54.85 | 82.60 |
| 1990-91 | 187.46 | 57.75 | 59.48 | 54.76 | 54.87 | 124.98 |
| 1991-92 | 83.24 | 48.21 | 49.07 | 43.23 | 43.75 | 66.48 |
| 1992-93 | 65.45 | 37.47 | 38.15 | 30.96 | 31.34 | 67.25 |
| 1993-94 | 70.63 | 36.00 | 36.75 | 30.08 | 30.44 | 75.55 |
| 1994-95 | 149.11 | 57.63 | 4.68 | 39.37 | 39.92 | 99.47 |
| 1995-96 | 136.42 | 47.11 | 3.82 | 31.66 | 32.09 | 111.67 |
| Growth rate% | -0.46 | -8.53 | -8.29 | -10.48 | -10.37 | 8.06 |

*Notes:* 1. Data computed and compiled from various issues of Public Enterprises Survey, Deptt. of Public Enterprises, GOI, New Delhi.

2. Growth rates are annual exponential growth rates over time.

Table 4.II.3

**Estimates of Productivity and Capital Intensity : NTPC**

| *Variable* | *Indices of Single Factor Productivity* | | *Indices of Total Factor Productivity* | | | *Capital Intensity* |
|---|---|---|---|---|---|---|
| *Year* | *Labour* | *Capital* | *Kendrick* | *Solow* | *Translog* | *(Rs' 000)* |
| 1984-85 | 100.00 | 100.00 | 100.00 | 100.00 | 100.00 | 64.44 |
| 1985-86 | 245.18 | 192.69 | 199.27 | 133.77 | 134.46 | 81.99 |
| 1986-87 | 236.78 | 170.51 | 178.21 | 119.75 | 120.36 | 89.48 |
| 1987-88 | 253.93 | 141.66 | 152.04 | 104.05 | 104.51 | 115.51 |
| 1988-89 | 294.53 | 152.94 | 165.20 | 110.82 | 111.30 | 124.10 |
| 1989-90 | 537.68 | 261.28 | 283.80 | 151.77 | 152.44 | 132.61 |
| 1990-91 | 606.10 | 257.91 | 283.01 | 151.07 | 151.70 | 151.44 |
| 1991-92 | 876.76 | 293.73 | 327.33 | 167.33 | 168.21 | 192.35 |
| 1992-93 | 790.37 | 279.46 | 310.44 | 157.98 | 158.85 | 182.25 |
| 1993-94 | 921.10 | 266.91 | 299.77 | 152.72 | 153.57 | 222.39 |
| 1994-95 | 895.49 | 245.23 | 276.00 | 140.52 | 141.25 | 235.13 |
| 1995-96 | 1004.27 | 307.69 | 344.00 | 167.37 | 168.16 | 210.41 |
| Growth rate% | 22.99 | 9.99 | 11.16 | 4.89 | 4.92 | 12.99 |

*Notes:* 1. Data computed and compiled from various issues of Public Enterprises Survey, Deptt. of Public Enterprises, GOI, New Delhi.

2. Growth rates are annual exponential growth rates over time.

Table 4.III.1

**Estimates of Productivity and Capital Intensity : Petroleum Industry**

| *Variable* | *Indices of Single Factor Productivity* | | *Indices of Total Factor Productivity* | | | *Capital Intensity* |
|---|---|---|---|---|---|---|
| *Year* | *Labour* | *Capital* | *Kendrick* | *Solow* | *Translog* | *(Rs' 000)* |
| 1974-75 | 100.00 | 100.00 | 100.00 | 100.00 | 100.00 | 11.96 |
| 1975-76 | 102.66 | 90.21 | 94.35 | 93.44 | 93.44 | 13.61 |
| 1976-77 | 112.38 | 86.59 | 94.42 | 92.27 | 92.42 | 15.52 |
| 1977-78 | 182.65 | 116.99 | 134.47 | 113.33 | 113.94 | 18.67 |
| 1978-79 | 185.88 | 103.19 | 122.98 | 102.43 | 102.96 | 21.54 |
| 1979-80 | 150.93 | 73.92 | 90.65 | 70.11 | 70.48 | 24.42 |
| 1980-81 | 118.52 | 52.03 | 65.27 | 46.12 | 46.34 | 27.24 |
| 1981-82 | 173.00 | 71.75 | 91.01 | 56.02 | 56.37 | 28.84 |
| 1982-83 | 242.46 | 86.31 | 112.52 | 63.89 | 64.33 | 33.60 |
| 1983-84 | 282.61 | 89.60 | 119.00 | 66.07 | 66.55 | 37.60 |
| 1984-85 | 299.70 | 87.73 | 117.89 | 65.09 | 65.56 | 40.86 |
| 1985-86 | 287.93 | 77.69 | 105.58 | 57.97 | 58.38 | 44.33 |
| 1986-87 | 340.82 | 82.49 | 113.65 | 61.22 | 61.66 | 49.41 |
| 1987-88 | 451.27 | 97.03 | 135.50 | 69.37 | 69.88 | 55.63 |
| 1988-89 | 485.97 | 96.17 | 135.47 | 69.07 | 69.56 | 60.44 |
| 1989-90 | 594.95 | 109.68 | 155.58 | 77.00 | 77.54 | 64.88 |
| 1990-91 | 646.28 | 113.82 | 162.13 | 79.76 | 80.33 | 67.92 |
| 1991-92 | 579.63 | 96.81 | 138.56 | 66.92 | 67.37 | 71.61 |
| 1992-93 | 650.66 | 99.35 | 143.25 | 68.82 | 69.28 | 78.34 |
| 1993-94 | 574.09 | 78.58 | 114.25 | 53.04 | 53.39 | 87.38 |
| 1994-95 | 654.63 | 78.90 | 116.12 | 53.68 | 54.01 | 99.23 |
| 1995-96 | 832.96 | 91.84 | 135.91 | 64.02 | 64.37 | 108.48 |
| Growth rate% | 10.69 | 0.46 | 2.25 | -2.02 | -1.99 | 10.23 |

*Notes:* 1. Data computed and compiled from various issues of Public Enterprises Survey, Deptt. of Public Enterprises, GOI, New Delhi.

2. Growth rates are annual exponential growth rates over time.

Table 4.III.2

**Estimates of Productivity and Capital Intensity : Indian Oil Corporation Ltd.**

| *Variable* | *Indices of Single Factor Productivity* | | *Indices of Total Factor Productivity* | | | *Capital Intensity* |
|---|---|---|---|---|---|---|
| *Year* | *Labour* | *Capital* | *Kendrick* | *Solow* | *Translog* | *(Rs' 000)* |
| 1974-75 | 100.00 | 100.00 | 100.00 | 100.00 | 100.00 | 14.21 |
| 1975-76 | 91.24 | 85.23 | 86.19 | 85.44 | 85.40 | 15.22 |
| 1976-77 | 98.62 | 84.27 | 86.39 | 85.28 | 85.29 | 16.64 |
| 1977-78 | 94.83 | 69.78 | 73.03 | 71.94 | 71.85 | 19.32 |
| 1978-79 | 87.23 | 56.66 | 60.22 | 58.75 | 58.63 | 21.89 |
| 1979-80 | 74.19 | 43.70 | 46.96 | 44.37 | 44.27 | 24.13 |
| 1980-81 | 58.68 | 32.09 | 34.75 | 30.63 | 30.57 | 25.99 |
| 1981-82 | 36.98 | 22.32 | 23.92 | 18.20 | 18.24 | 23.56 |
| 1982-83 | 47.93 | 28.82 | 30.90 | 22.03 | 22.07 | 23.64 |
| 1983-84 | 56.58 | 33.37 | 35.85 | 24.87 | 24.92 | 24.10 |
| 1984-85 | 56.31 | 31.98 | 34.49 | 24.04 | 24.08 | 25.03 |
| 1985-86 | 59.26 | 32.25 | 34.95 | 24.39 | 24.44 | 26.12 |
| 1986-87 | 93.96 | 48.26 | 52.57 | 32.05 | 32.14 | 27.68 |
| 1987-88 | 122.84 | 60.99 | 66.65 | 38.44 | 38.56 | 28.63 |
| 1988-89 | 123.20 | 57.87 | 63.56 | 36.75 | 36.84 | 30.26 |
| 1989-90 | 168.64 | 73.21 | 80.94 | 44.12 | 44.25 | 32.75 |
| 1990-91 | 164.75 | 65.04 | 72.44 | 39.56 | 39.66 | 36.01 |
| 1991-92 | 175.99 | 63.75 | 71.44 | 39.24 | 39.33 | 39.24 |
| 1992-93 | 197.89 | 66.78 | 75.19 | 41.21 | 41.31 | 42.13 |
| 1993-94 | 188.90 | 58.06 | 65.74 | 36.03 | 36.13 | 46.25 |
| 1994-95 | 218.91 | 57.57 | 65.74 | 36.40 | 36.91 | 54.04 |
| 1995-96 | 255.61 | 56.79 | 63.36 | 37.00 | 37.35 | 64.00 |
| Growth rate % | 4.76 | -0.42 | 0.11 | -3.86 | -1.83 | 5.18 |

*Notes:* 1. Data computed and compiled from various issues of Public Enterprises Survey, Deptt. of Public Enterprises, GOI, New Delhi.

2. Growth rates are annual exponential growth rates over time.

Table 4.III.3

**Estimates of Productivity and Capital Intensity : ONGC**

| *Variable* | *Indices of Single Factor Productivity* | | *Indices of Total Factor Productivity* | | | *Capital Intensity* |
|---|---|---|---|---|---|---|
| *Year* | *Labour* | *Capital* | *Kendrick* | *Solow* | *Translog* | *(Rs' 000)* |
| 1977-78 | 100.00 | 100.00 | 100.00 | 100.00 | 100.00 | 18.98 |
| 1978-79 | 137.76 | 108.29 | 108.98 | 106.53 | 106.57 | 24.15 |
| 1979-80 | 118.52 | 80.01 | 80.79 | 75.66 | 75.68 | 28.12 |
| 1980-81 | 84.58 | 49.89 | 50.51 | 38.38 | 38.38 | 32.18 |
| 1981-82 | 216.72 | 108.11 | 109.74 | 54.35 | 54.39 | 38.06 |
| 1982-83 | 364.81 | 143.67 | 146.30 | 64.30 | 64.35 | 48.21 |
| 1983-84 | 429.74 | 149.36 | 152.30 | 66.25 | 66.30 | 54.63 |
| 1984-85 | 458.20 | 148.31 | 151.34 | 65.88 | 65.93 | 58.66 |
| 1985-86 | 408.27 | 119.20 | 121.75 | 52.18 | 52.21 | 65.03 |
| 1986-87 | 457.69 | 114.40 | 116.99 | 50.32 | 50.35 | 75.96 |
| 1987-88 | 624.49 | 141.45 | 144.77 | 58.94 | 58.97 | 83.82 |
| 1988-89 | 677.81 | 141.43 | 144.82 | 58.95 | 58.99 | 90.99 |
| 1989-90 | 781.43 | 151.50 | 155.20 | 62.50 | 62.54 | 97.93 |
| 1990-91 | 909.71 | 170.15 | 174.34 | 68.96 | 69.00 | 101.51 |
| 1991-92 | 709.27 | 125.41 | 128.54 | 45.79 | 45.81 | 107.38 |
| 1992-93 | 758.24 | 118.99 | 122.04 | 43.63 | 43.65 | 120.99 |
| 1993-94 | 637.99 | 108.47 | 111.20 | 38.93 | 38.94 | 111.68 |
| 1994-95 | 736.87 | 88.60 | 90.95 | 32.89 | 32.82 | 157.89 |
| 1995-96 | 906.87 | 100.55 | 103.95 | 36.65 | 36.58 | 171.31 |
| Growth rate % | 13.99 | 2.71 | 2.84 | -3.45 | -3.45 | 11.28 |

*Notes:* 1. Data computed and compiled from various issues of Public Enterprises Survey, Deptt. of Public Enterprises, GOI, New Delhi.

2. Growth rates are annual exponential growth rates over time.

Table 4.IV.1

**Estimates of Productivity and Capital Intensity : Fertilizers, Chemicals and Pharmaceuticals Industry.**

| *Variable* | *Indices of Single Factor Productivity* | | *Indices of Total Factor Productivity* | | | *Capital Intensity* |
|---|---|---|---|---|---|---|
| *Year* | *Labour* | *Capital* | *Kendrick* | *Solow* | *Translog* | *(Rs' 000)* |
| 1974-75 | 100.00 | 100.00 | 100.00 | 100.00 | 100.00 | 12.23 |
| 1975-76 | 100.54 | 79.45 | 85.43 | 87.30 | 86.96 | 15.48 |
| 1976-77 | 120.41 | 81.85 | 91.64 | 93.46 | 93.17 | 18.00 |
| 1977-78 | 130.46 | 79.89 | 91.76 | 94.78 | 94.43 | 19.98 |
| 1978-79 | 172.67 | 86.35 | 103.63 | 105.58 | 105.95 | 24.47 |
| 1979-80 | 208.99 | 104.64 | 125.56 | 122.76 | 123.29 | 24.44 |
| 1980-81 | 188.77 | 93.78 | 112.70 | 109.53 | 109.90 | 24.63 |
| 1981-82 | 208.23 | 107.77 | 128.45 | 121.91 | 122.29 | 23.64 |
| 1982-83 | 257.77 | 127.27 | 153.13 | 140.54 | 141.04 | 24.78 |
| 1983-84 | 278.97 | 130.46 | 158.64 | 145.23 | 145.74 | 26.17 |
| 1984-85 | 307.62 | 137.96 | 169.07 | 153.71 | 154.25 | 27.28 |
| 1985-86 | 316.41 | 135.50 | 167.44 | 152.56 | 153.06 | 28.57 |
| 1986-87 | 342.14 | 135.97 | 170.19 | 155.29 | 155.54 | 30.79 |
| 1987-88 | 360.45 | 132.39 | 167.82 | 153.74 | 154.32 | 33.32 |
| 1988-89 | 414.24 | 143.05 | 183.03 | 166.31 | 166.99 | 35.44 |
| 1989-90 | 399.65 | 134.33 | 172.55 | 156.95 | 157.52 | 36.41 |
| 1990-91 | 406.61 | 136.01 | 174.83 | 159.00 | 159.57 | 36.58 |
| 1991-92 | 470.49 | 150.29 | 194.45 | 175.27 | 175.99 | 38.31 |
| 1992-93 | 443.19 | 133.65 | 174.26 | 156.21 | 156.86 | 40.58 |
| 1993-94 | 401.27 | 116.40 | 152.53 | 134.99 | 135.84 | 42.19 |
| 1994-95 | 552.93 | 148.25 | 196.16 | 165.20 | 166.03 | 45.64 |
| 1995-96 | 573.32 | 144.67 | 193.69 | 166.63 | 166.13 | 48.47 |
| Growth rate % | 8.26 | 2.95 | 4.00 | 3.21 | 3.24 | 5.31 |

*Notes:* 1. Data computed and compiled from various issues of Public Enterprises Survey, Deptt. of Public Enterprises, GOI, New Delhi.

2. Growth rates are annual exponential growth rates over time.

Table 4.IV.2

**Estimates of Productivity and Capital Intensity : National Fertilizers Ltd.**

| *Variable* | *Indices of Single Factor Productivity* | | *Indices of Total Factor Productivity* | | | *Capital Intensity* |
|---|---|---|---|---|---|---|
| *Year* | *Labour* | *Capital* | *Kendrick* | *Solow* | *Translog* | *(Rs' 000)* |
| 1979-80 | 100.00 | 100.00 | 100.00 | 100.00 | 100.00 | 41.73 |
| 1980-81 | 75.57 | 74.14 | 74.26 | 65.59 | 65.56 | 42.53 |
| 1981-82 | 69.83 | 70.34 | 70.30 | 61.83 | 61.83 | 41.43 |
| 1982-83 | 78.30 | 78.68 | 78.65 | 68.37 | 68.36 | 41.53 |
| 1983-84 | 150.57 | 154.18 | 153.90 | 101.44 | 101.39 | 40.75 |
| 1984-85 | 175.85 | 173.72 | 173.87 | 112.73 | 112.70 | 42.24 |
| 1985-86 | 168.79 | 147.48 | 148.88 | 96.27 | 96.17 | 47.76 |
| 1986-87 | 159.21 | 123.66 | 125.76 | 81.32 | 81.16 | 53.73 |
| 1987-88 | 161.58 | 113.06 | 115.66 | 75.62 | 75.44 | 59.64 |
| 1988-89 | 224.05 | 153.90 | 157.59 | 95.02 | 94.79 | 60.75 |
| 1989-90 | 240.89 | 165.07 | 169.04 | 101.42 | 101.17 | 60.90 |
| 1990-91 | 291.52 | 199.03 | 203.86 | 118.67 | 118.38 | 61.13 |
| 1991-92 | 262.93 | 179.85 | 184.21 | 106.07 | 105.81 | 61.01 |
| 1992-93 | 226.81 | 153.76 | 157.56 | 88.31 | 88.10 | 61.56 |
| 1993-94 | 220.06 | 147.31 | 151.05 | 84.61 | 84.41 | 62.34 |
| 1994-95 | 222.29 | 140.44 | 144.35 | 81.42 | 81.17 | 66.07 |
| 1995-96 | 192.04 | 108.45 | 112.02 | 61.57 | 61.22 | 73.94 |
| Growth rate % | 9.23 | 5.42 | 5.66 | 1.76 | 1.74 | 3.80 |

*Notes:* 1. Data computed and compiled from various issues of Public Enterprises Survey, Deptt. of Public Enterprises, GOI, New Delhi.

2. Growth rates are annual exponential growth rates over time.

Table 4.IV.3

**Estimates of Productivity and Capital Intensity : Indian Petrochemical Corporation Ltd.**

| *Variable* | *Indices of Single Factor Productivity* | | *Indices of Total Factor Productivity* | | | *Capital Intensity* |
|---|---|---|---|---|---|---|
| *Year* | *Labour* | *Capital* | *Kendrick* | *Solow* | *Translog* | *(Rs' 000)* |
| 1974-75 | 100.00 | 100.00 | 100.00 | 100.00 | 100.00 | 12.78 |
| 1975-76 | 143.14 | 79.97 | 92.69 | 95.37 | 96.70 | 22.87 |
| 1976-77 | 149.17 | 58.37 | 72.00 | 78.60 | 79.34 | 32.66 |
| 1977-78 | 111.03 | 36.54 | 46.18 | 44.80 | 44.51 | 38.83 |
| 1978-79 | 194.12 | 61.33 | 77.90 | 62.78 | 62.51 | 40.45 |
| 1979-80 | 266.58 | 90.16 | 113.52 | 81.98 | 81.52 | 37.78 |
| 1980-81 | 318.15 | 107.89 | 135.80 | 94.87 | 94.34 | 37.68 |
| 1981-82 | 367.32 | 122.77 | 154.82 | 106.05 | 105.46 | 38.23 |
| 1982-83 | 355.81 | 119.75 | 150.88 | 103.47 | 102.89 | 37.97 |
| 1983-84 | 285.32 | 100.70 | 126.07 | 84.45 | 84.06 | 36.21 |
| 1984-85 | 388.52 | 121.26 | 151.49 | 97.93 | 97.49 | 35.68 |
| 1985-86 | 330.91 | 112.99 | 142.09 | 92.12 | 91.70 | 37.43 |
| 1986-87 | 322.43 | 86.04 | 111.44 | 73.45 | 73.06 | 47.89 |
| 1987-88 | 336.26 | 74.84 | 98.69 | 66.66 | 66.33 | 57.42 |
| 1988-89 | 381.37 | 75.85 | 101.02 | 68.34 | 68.05 | 64.26 |
| 1989-90 | 299.74 | 64.81 | 85.70 | 57.32 | 57.10 | 59.10 |
| 1990-91 | 358.91 | 68.57 | 91.62 | 61.06 | 60.87 | 66.89 |
| 1991-92 | 396.31 | 77.46 | 103.30 | 67.35 | 67.13 | 65.39 |
| 1992-93 | 367.87 | 71.63 | 95.55 | 62.18 | 61.97 | 65.64 |
| 1993-94 | 307.73 | 57.69 | 77.19 | 48.21 | 48.03 | 68.17 |
| 1994-95 | 582.28 | 97.18 | 131.15 | 66.65 | 66.65 | 76.57 |
| 1995-96 | 699.77 | 112.75 | 152.59 | 75.24 | 74.92 | 79.33 |
| Growth rate % | 5.63 | -0.38 | 0.45 | -1.99 | -2.03 | 6.02 |

*Notes:* 1. Data computed and compiled from various issues of Public Enterprises Survey, Deptt. of Public Enterprises, GOI, New Delhi.

2. Growth rates are annual exponential growth rates over time.

Table 4. V.1

**Estimates of Productivity and Capital Intensity : Heavy Engineering Industry.**

| *Variable* | *Indices of Single Factor Productivity* | | *Indices of Total Factor Productivity* | | | *Capital Intensity* |
|---|---|---|---|---|---|---|
| *Year* | *Labour* | *Capital* | *Kendrick* | *Solow* | *Translog* | *(Rs' 000)* |
| 1974-75 | 100.00 | 100.00 | 100.00 | 100.00 | 100.00 | 3.15 |
| 1975-76 | 95.58 | 102.72 | 100.16 | 100.08 | 100.07 | 2.93 |
| 1976-77 | 108.64 | 109.09 | 108.93 | 107.65 | 107.73 | 3.14 |
| 1977-78 | 106.03 | 98.26 | 100.79 | 99.97 | 99.87 | 3.40 |
| 1978-79 | 114.32 | 102.10 | 105.98 | 104.82 | 104.72 | 3.53 |
| 1979-80 | 97.26 | 84.40 | 88.40 | 85.17 | 85.02 | 3.63 |
| 1980-81 | 75.25 | 65.28 | 68.38 | 61.18 | 61.07 | 3.64 |
| 1981-82 | 92.91 | 78.39 | 82.82 | 71.52 | 71.47 | 3.74 |
| 1982-83 | 100.66 | 81.74 | 87.37 | 75.55 | 75.50 | 3.88 |
| 1983-84 | 116.39 | 90.39 | 97.87 | 83.86 | 83.83 | 4.06 |
| 1984-85 | 126.54 | 93.02 | 102.30 | 87.98 | 88.02 | 4.29 |
| 1985-86 | 124.68 | 87.25 | 97.25 | 84.25 | 84.26 | 4.51 |
| 1986-87 | 134.41 | 90.14 | 101.60 | 88.35 | 88.36 | 4.71 |
| 1987-88 | 142.97 | 92.15 | 104.91 | 91.56 | 91.63 | .90 |
| 988-89 | 151.61 | 93.52 | 107.64 | 94.59 | 94.58 | 5.12 |
| 1989-90 | 152.24 | 89.93 | 104.58 | 92.71 | 92.70 | 5.34 |
| 1990-91 | 148.62 | 83.42 | 98.16 | 87.97 | 87.85 | 5.62 |
| 1991-92 | 137.08 | 72.27 | 86.23 | 77.31 | 77.24 | 5.99 |
| 1992-93 | 140.92 | 69.58 | 84.17 | 76.81 | 76.73 | 6.39 |
| 1993-94 | 149.09 | 67.78 | 83.34 | 77.78 | 77.75 | 6.94 |
| 1994-95 | 147.70 | 63.90 | 79.26 | 73.78 | 73.82 | 7.30 |
| 1995-96 | 179.62 | 73.04 | 91.74 | 83.15 | 83.27 | 7.76 |
| Growth rate % | 2.7 | -1.4 | -0.3 | -0.9 | -0.9 | 4.19 |

*Notes:* 1. Data computed and compiled from various issues of Public Enterprises Survey, Deptt. of Public Enterprises, GOI, New Delhi.

2. Growth rates are annual exponential growth rates over time.

Table 4. V.2

**Estimates of Productivity and Capital Intensity : BHEL.**

| *Variable* | *Indices of Single Factor Productivity* | | *Indices of Total Factor Productivity* | | | *Capital Intensity* |
|---|---|---|---|---|---|---|
| *Year* | *Labour* | *Capital* | *Kendrick* | *Solow* | *Translog* | *(Rs' 000)* |
| 1974-75 | 100.00 | 100.00 | 100.00 | 100.00 | 100.00 | 3.26 |
| 1975-76 | 90.67 | 98.16 | 96.18 | 96.41 | 96.45 | 3.01 |
| 1976-77 | 105.14 | 99.76 | 101.05 | 100.75 | 100.94 | 3.44 |
| 1977-78 | 116.93 | 96.60 | 100.97 | 101.13 | 101.36 | 3.95 |
| 1978-79 | 128.42 | 99.08 | 105.06 | 104.96 | 105.22 | 4.23 |
| 1979-80 | 103.80 | 77.47 | 82.70 | 78.86 | 78.99 | 4.37 |
| 1980-81 | 72.45 | 52.23 | 57.00 | 46.21 | 46.21 | 4.44 |
| 1981-82 | 92.46 | 64.53 | 69.78 | 54.32 | 54.42 | 4.67 |
| 1982-83 | 91.75 | 61.12 | 66.67 | 52.37 | 54.43 | 4.89 |
| 1983-84 | 97.20 | 62.01 | 68.16 | 53.89 | 53.93 | 5.11 |
| 1984-85 | 113.11 | 67.18 | 74.75 | 59.11 | 59.19 | 5.49 |
| 1985-86 | 117.59 | 67.35 | 75.37 | 59.96 | 60.05 | 5.69 |
| 1986-87 | 126.11 | 68.76 | 77.55 | 62.17 | 62.24 | 5.98 |
| 1987-88 | 128.24 | 67.27 | 76.31 | 61.65 | 61.75 | 6.22 |
| 1988-89 | 132.39 | 67.70 | 77.08 | 62.63 | 62.69 | 6.38 |
| 1989-90 | 134.97 | 65.78 | 75.41 | 61.99 | 62.07 | 6.69 |
| 1990-91 | 138.80 | 64.16 | 74.09 | 61.81 | 61.84 | 7.06 |
| 1991-92 | 124.23 | 54.93 | 63.79 | 52.84 | 52.88 | 7.38 |
| 1992-93 | 122.67 | 52.29 | 61.01 | 51.01 | 51.05 | 7.65 |
| 1993-94 | 134.04 | 55.00 | 64.47 | 54.23 | 54.29 | 7.95 |
| 1994-95 | 142.72 | 56.26 | 66.26 | 56.28 | 56.33 | 8.28 |
| 1995-96 | 170.88 | 63.81 | 75.59 | 64.28 | 64.18 | 8.74 |
| Growth rate % | 1.85 | -2.9 | -2.1 | -3.2 | -3.2 | 4.83 |

*Notes:* 1. Data computed and compiled from various issues of Public Enterprises Survey, Deptt. of Public Enterprises, GOI, New Delhi.

2. Growth rates are annual exponential growth rates over time.

Table 4. V.3

**Estimates of Productivity and Capital Intensity : Bharat Heavy Plate & Vessels Ltd.**

| *Variable* | *Indices of Single Factor Productivity* | | *Indices of Total Factor Productivity* | | | *Capital Intensity* |
|---|---|---|---|---|---|---|
| *Year* | *Labour* | *Capital* | *Kendrick* | *Solow* | *Translog* | *(Rs' 000)* |
| 1974-75 | 100.00 | 100.00 | 100.00 | 100.00 | 100.00 | 4.03 |
| 1975-76 | 101.97 | 118.84 | 112.11 | 110.22 | 110.02 | 3.46 |
| 1976-77 | 141.00 | 161.32 | 153.30 | 138.88 | 138.72 | 3.53 |
| 1977-78 | 143.29 | 161.65 | 154.46 | 139.72 | 139.53 | 3.58 |
| 1978-79 | 116.30 | 128.91 | 124.03 | 106.56 | 106.25 | 3.64 |
| 1979-80 | 127.66 | 144.17 | 137.70 | 116.78 | 116.36 | 3.57 |
| 1980-81 | 113.64 | 126.17 | 121.31 | 101.61 | 101.22 | 3.63 |
| 1981-82 | 133.32 | 142.66 | 139.12 | 113.94 | 173.58 | 3.77 |
| 1982-83 | 266.63 | 280.58 | 275.35 | 168.95 | 168.54 | 3.83 |
| 1983-84 | 202.88 | 211.21 | 208.11 | 116.50 | 116.13 | 3.87 |
| 1984-85 | 237.03 | 236.78 | 236.93 | 129.61 | 129.29 | 4.04 |
| 1985-86 | 224.13 | 211.90 | 216.18 | 117.09 | 116.75 | 4.27 |
| 1986-87 | 215.28 | 191.59 | 199.56 | 107.39 | 107.02 | 4.53 |
| 1987-88 | 247.56 | 210.06 | 222.28 | 118.00 | 117.55 | 4.76 |
| 1988-89 | 249.00 | 203.42 | 217.90 | 115.76 | 115.26 | 4.94 |
| 1989-90 | 253.41 | 198.98 | 215.81 | 114.89 | 114.33 | 5.14 |
| 1990-91 | 253.91 | 196.10 | 213.77 | 113.92 | 113.36 | 5.22 |
| 1991-92 | 230.06 | 175.35 | 191.92 | 101.20 | 100.70 | 5.29 |
| 1992-93 | 245.85 | 183.53 | 202.13 | 106.40 | 105.90 | 5.41 |
| 1993-94 | 256.66 | 182.81 | 204.13 | 107.81 | 107.27 | 5.67 |
| 1994-95 | 297.03 | 203.28 | 229.50 | 119.82 | 119.29 | 5.90 |
| 1995-96 | 311.10 | 207.47 | 236.08 | 123.39 | 122.80 | 6.06 |
| Growth rate % | 5.2 | 2.6 | 3.5 | -0.47 | -0.47 | 2.6 |

*Notes:* 1. Data computed and compiled from various issues of Public Enterprises Survey, Deptt. of Public Enterprises, GOI, New Delhi.

2. Growth rates are annual exponential growth rates over time.

Table 4. VI. 1

**Estimates of Productivity and Capital Intensity: Medium and Light Engineering Industry**

| *Variable* | *Indices of Single Factor Productivity* | | *Indices of Total Factor Productivity* | | | *Capital Intensity* |
|---|---|---|---|---|---|---|
| *Year* | *Labour* | *Capital* | *Kendrick* | *Solow* | *Translog* | *(Rs' 000)* |
| 1974-75 | 100.00 | 100.00 | 100.00 | 100.00 | 100.00 | 1.63 |
| 1975-76 | 120.16 | 108.40 | 114.67 | 110.55 | 111.15 | 1.81 |
| 1976-77 | 124.83 | 107.91 | 116.76 | 112.05 | 112.69 | 1.89 |
| 1977-78 | 126.76 | 105.14 | 116.22 | 111.53 | 112.08 | 1.97 |
| 1978-79 | 92.10 | 72.31 | 82.18 | 69.77 | 69.49 | 2.08 |
| 1979-80 | 124.86 | 91.31 | 107.45 | 84.75 | 84.96 | 2.24 |
| 1980-81 | 109.23 | 75.35 | 91.16 | 70.40 | 70.54 | 2.37 |
| 1981-82 | 148.68 | 96.48 | 120.04 | 86.36 | 86.68 | 2.52 |
| 1982-83 | 161.69 | 95.77 | 124.03 | 88.89 | 89.21 | 2.76 |
| 1983-84 | 168.54 | 91.24 | 122.70 | 88.30 | 88.53 | 3.03 |
| 1984-85 | 184.18 | 89.32 | 125.43 | 90.60 | 90.86 | 3.37 |
| 1985-86 | 184.64 | 81.50 | 118.50 | 86.45 | 86.68 | 3.71 |
| 1986-87 | 183.80 | 81.42 | 118.23 | 86.27 | 86.49 | 3.70 |
| 1987-88 | 191.80 | 76.93 | 115.64 | 85.37 | 85.51 | 4.08 |
| 1988-89 | 213.05 | 81.24 | 124.19 | 91.54 | 91.69 | 4.29 |
| 1989-90 | 236.91 | 83.77 | 131.16 | 97.03 | 97.22 | 4.63 |
| 1990-91 | 223.47 | 74.01 | 118.19 | 87.83 | 88.02 | 4.94 |
| 1991-92 | 235.33 | 70.70 | 116.10 | 87.51 | 87.77 | 5.45 |
| 1992-93 | 243.63 | 67.27 | 112.99 | 86.44 | 86.65 | 5.93 |
| 1993-94 | 241.93 | 63.44 | 107.96 | 83.30 | 83.49 | 6.25 |
| 1994-95 | 197.22 | 47.44 | 82.44 | 58.56 | 59.16 | 6.81 |
| 1995-96 | 185.00 | 41.05 | 72.66 | 53.00 | 53.56 | 7.38 |
| Growth rate % | 4.99 | -2.12 | 0.69 | -0.66 | -0.66 | 7.11 |

*Notes:* 1. Data computed and compiled from various issues of Public Enterprises Survey, Deptt. of Public Enterprises, GOI, New Delhi.

2. Growth rates are annual exponential growth rates over time.

Table 4. VI. 2

**Estimates of Productivity and Capital Intensity : HMT Ltd.**

| *Variable* | *Indices of Single Factor Productivity* | | *Indices of Total Factor Productivity* | | | *Capital Intensity* |
|---|---|---|---|---|---|---|
| *Year* | *Labour* | *Capital* | *Kendrick* | *Solow* | *Translog* | *(Rs' 000)* |
| 1974-75 | 100.00 | 100.00 | 100.00 | 100.00 | 100.00 | 2.07 |
| 1975-76 | 98.91 | 83.64 | 90.88 | 91.66 | 92.45 | 2.45 |
| 1976-77 | 98.81 | 83.23 | 90.60 | 91.40 | 92.18 | 2.46 |
| 1977-78 | 97.84 | 83.09 | 90.09 | 90.90 | 91.69 | 2.44 |
| 1978-79 | 134.55 | 104.80 | 118.29 | 110.46 | 111.91 | 2.66 |
| 1979-80 | 118.26 | 84.97 | 99.40 | 91.23 | 92.42 | 2.88 |
| 1980-81 | 120.56 | 83.82 | 99.45 | 91.21 | 92.37 | 2.98 |
| 1981-82 | 132.93 | 88.63 | 107.02 | 97.11 | 98.40 | 3.11 |
| 1982-83 | 133.03 | 82.69 | 102.74 | 93.31 | 94.48 | 3.33 |
| 1983-84 | 130.29 | 76.44 | 97.15 | 88.50 | 89.51 | 3.53 |
| 1984-85 | 153.10 | 81.99 | 107.82 | 96.81 | 98.05 | 3.87 |
| 1985-86 | 140.64 | 73.88 | 97.84 | 87.43 | 88.52 | 3.94 |
| 1986-87 | 139.98 | 70.28 | 94.57 | 84.88 | 85.92 | 4.13 |
| 1987-88 | 122.98 | 59.28 | 80.89 | 71.57 | 72.26 | 4.30 |
| 1988-89 | 136.08 | 64.00 | 88.05 | 77.77 | 78.52 | 4.41 |
| 1989-90 | 143.55 | 65.19 | 90.73 | 80.77 | 81.49 | 4.56 |
| 1990-91 | 153.92 | 65.53 | 93.11 | 84.10 | 84.91 | 4.87 |
| 1991-92 | 168.64 | 66.69 | 96.90 | 88.49 | 89.61 | 5.24 |
| 1992-93 | 139.74 | 51.61 | 76.49 | 67.25 | 67.78 | 5.61 |
| 1993-94 | 107.83 | 36.48 | 55.38 | 44.82 | 44.43 | 6.12 |
| 1994-95 | 123.00 | 39.59 | 60.81 | 50.01 | 49.68 | 6.44 |
| 1995-96 | 139.96 | 42.98 | 66.90 | 55.82 | 55.40 | 6.75 |
| Growth rate % | 1.79 | -3.41 | -1.41 | -2.20 | -2.22 | 5.21 |

*Notes:* 1. Data computed and compiled from various issues of Public Enterprises Survey, Deptt. of Public Enterprises, GOI, New Delhi.

2. Growth rates are annual exponential growth rates over time.

Table 4. VI. 3

**Estimates of Productivity and Capital Intensity: Indian Telephone Industries Ltd.**

| *Variable* | *Indices of Single Factor Productivity* | | *Indices of Total Factor Productivity* | | | *Capital Intensity* |
|---|---|---|---|---|---|---|
| *Year* | *Labour* | *Capital* | *Kendrick* | *Solow* | *Translog* | *(Rs' 000)* |
| 1974-75 | 100.00 | 100.00 | 100.00 | 100.00 | 100.00 | 0.68 |
| 1975-76 | 88.97 | 74.94 | 80.03 | 81.00 | 80.85 | 0.81 |
| 1976-77 | 98.75 | 71.53 | 80.47 | 82.29 | 82.36 | 0.95 |
| 1977-78 | 95.27 | 60.86 | 71.23 | 74.85 | 74.62 | 1.07 |
| 1978-79 | 82.05 | 46.14 | 56.02 | 60.47 | 59.59 | 1.22 |
| 1979-80 | 89.10 | 44.72 | 55.95 | 61.99 | 61.53 | 1.37 |
| 1980-81 | 64.33 | 29.87 | 38.09 | 36.06 | 35.69 | 1.48 |
| 1981-82 | 98.66 | 40.00 | 52.60 | 46.08 | 45.83 | 1.69 |
| 1982-83 | 107.43 | 37.83 | 51.20 | 46.75 | 46.38 | 1.95 |
| 1983-84 | 118.48 | 37.17 | 51.38 | 48.53 | 48.11 | 2.19 |
| 1984-85 | 123.10 | 33.72 | 47.67 | 47.37 | 46.96 | 2.51 |
| 1985-86 | 126.13 | 29.66 | 42.88 | 45.14 | 44.84 | 2.92 |
| 1986-87 | 165.81 | 33.54 | 49.43 | 51.93 | 51.87 | 3.40 |
| 1987-88 | 183.94 | 33.26 | 49.65 | 53.53 | 53.52 | 3.80 |
| 1988-89 | 218.03 | 36.62 | 55.10 | 59.51 | 59.49 | 4.09 |
| 1989-90 | 244.82 | 38.24 | 57.95 | 63.27 | 63.32 | 4.40 |
| 1990-91 | 246.49 | 36.58 | 55.70 | 61.54 | 61.62 | 4.63 |
| 1991-92 | 273.01 | 36.82 | 56.54 | 63.70 | 63.84 | 5.10 |
| 1992-93 | 302.46 | 38.32 | 59.14 | 67.33 | 67.44 | 5.43 |
| 1993-94 | 316.49 | 37.09 | 57.58 | 66.72 | 66.90 | 5.87 |
| 1994-95 | 161.53 | 17.69 | 27.88 | - | - | 6.28 |
| 1995-96 | 96.37 | 9.72 | 15.23 | - | - | 6.82 |
| Growth rate % | 7.58 | -3.88 | -1.72 | -1.04 | -1.00 | 11.76 |

*Notes:* 1. Data computed and compiled from various issues of Public Enterprises Survey, Deptt. of Public Enterprises, GOI, New Delhi.

2. Growth rates are annual exponential growth rates over time.

Table 4. VII. 1

**Estimates of Productivity and Capital Intensity: Transport Equipment Industry**

| Variable | Indices of Single Factor Productivity | | Indices of Total Factor Productivity | | | Capital Intensity |
|---|---|---|---|---|---|---|
| Year | Labour | Capital | Kendrick | Solow | Translog | (Rs' 000) |
| 1974-75 | 100.00 | 100.00 | 100.00 | 100.00 | 100.00 | 2.40 |
| 1975-76 | 99.99 | 99.98 | 99.98 | 99.98 | 99.98 | 2.40 |
| 1976-77 | 109.22 | 93.87 | 101.16 | 101.10 | 101.63 | 2.79 |
| 1977-78 | 109.63 | 88.86 | 98.42 | 98.88 | 99.22 | 2.96 |
| 1978-79 | 111.64 | 95.89 | 103.37 | 103.27 | 103.74 | 2.79 |
| 1979-80 | 104.88 | 83.21 | 93.07 | 92.87 | 93.45 | 3.02 |
| 1980-81 | 92.97 | 68.09 | 78.92 | 77.81 | 78.15 | 3.28 |
| 1981-82 | 110.89 | 77.21 | 91.46 | 87.76 | 88.25 | 3.45 |
| 1982-83 | 131.31 | 87.58 | 105.62 | 98.93 | 99.64 | 3.60 |
| 1983-84 | 162.87 | 100.76 | 125.25 | 113.21 | 114.05 | 3.88 |
| 1984-85 | 193.55 | 101.45 | 134.20 | 119.85 | 121.25 | 4.58 |
| 1985-86 | 180.33 | 83.26 | 115.00 | 102.78 | 103.87 | 5.20 |
| 1986-87 | 176.63 | 74.76 | 106.16 | 95.47 | 96.42 | 5.67 |
| 1987-88 | 173.31 | 69.10 | 99.90 | 90.50 | 91.31 | 6.02 |
| 1988-89 | 198.75 | 75.51 | 110.72 | 99.56 | 100.52 | 6.32 |
| 1989-90 | 217.90 | 79.05 | 117.42 | 105.70 | 106.69 | 6.62 |
| 1990-91 | 216.79 | 78.33 | 116.48 | 104.86 | 105.85 | 6.64 |
| 1991-92 | 200.28 | 69.75 | 104.77 | 93.75 | 94.61 | 6.89 |
| 1992-93 | 214.21 | 70.03 | 106.95 | 96.60 | 97.51 | 7.34 |
| 1993-94 | 244.38 | 75.72 | 117.21 | 105.86 | 106.92 | 7.54 |
| 1994-95 | 274.46 | 78.79 | 124.21 | 106.07 | 107.19 | 8.36 |
| 1995-96 | 266.07 | 74.47 | 117.85 | 103.01 | 103.49 | 8.58 |
| Growth rate % | 5.17 | -1.55 | 0.94 | 0.20 | 0.24 | 6.72 |

*Notes:* 1. Data computed and compiled from various issues of Public Enterprises Survey, Deptt. of Public Enterprises, GOI, New Delhi.

2. Growth rates are annual exponential growth rates over time.

Table 4. VII. 2

**Estimates of Productivity and Capital Intensity: Bharat Earth Movers Ltd.**

| *Variable* | *Indices of Single Factor Productivity* | | *Indices of Total Factor Productivity* | | | *Capital Intensity* |
|---|---|---|---|---|---|---|
| *Year* | *Labour* | *Capital* | *Kendrick* | *Solow* | *Translog* | *(Rs' 000)* |
| 1974-75 | 100.00 | 100.00 | 100.00 | 100.00 | 100.00 | 1.59 |
| 1975-76 | 90.54 | 86.52 | 87.91 | 87.62 | 87.54 | 1.66 |
| 1976-77 | 94.35 | 85.45 | 88.42 | 88.29 | 88.31 | 1.75 |
| 1977-78 | 98.01 | 84.74 | 89.04 | 89.25 | 89.20 | 1.84 |
| 1978-79 | 103.34 | 82.76 | 89.09 | 90.33 | 90.15 | 1.98 |
| 1979-80 | 122.07 | 92.91 | 101.56 | 101.18 | 101.21 | 2.09 |
| 1980-81 | 84.48 | 61.32 | 67.97 | 53.05 | 52.98 | 2.19 |
| 1981-82 | 147.00 | 99.57 | 112.51 | 72.52 | 72.61 | 2.35 |
| 1982-83 | 237.93 | 156.65 | 178.37 | 96.22 | 96.42 | 2.41 |
| 1983-84 | 245.72 | 146.48 | 171.11 | 92.29 | 92.43 | 2.67 |
| 1984-85 | 198.32 | 106.88 | 127.90 | 64.84 | 64.64 | 2.94 |
| 1985-86 | 247.76 | 119.68 | 146.72 | 72.43 | 72.39 | 3.29 |
| 1986-87 | 296.07 | 106.03 | 137.50 | 69.01 | 69.11 | 4.44 |
| 1987-88 | 195.04 | 69.67 | 90.38 | 36.81 | 36.85 | 4.45 |
| 1988-89 | 210.44 | 70.30 | 92.18 | 37.66 | 37.78 | 4.76 |
| 1989-90 | 212.54 | 63.38 | 84.53 | 35.03 | 35.15 | 5.33 |
| 1990-91 | 208.44 | 56.98 | 76.91 | 32.08 | 32.27 | 5.82 |
| 1991-92 | 182.11 | 47.98 | 65.07 | 26.73 | 26.83 | 6.04 |
| 1992-93 | 190.02 | 47.72 | 65.11 | 26.83 | 26.99 | 6.33 |
| 1993-94 | 188.34 | 45.06 | 61.82 | 25.57 | 25.69 | 6.65 |
| 1994-95 | 159.71 | 37.41 | 51.42 | 20.66 | 20.77 | 6.79 |
| 1995-96 | 177.24 | 40.22 | 55.50 | 22.27 | 22.39 | 7.02 |
| Growth rate % | 4.99 | -03.34 | -1.50 | -7.56 | -7.52 | 8.33 |

*Notes:* 1. Data computed and compiled from various issues of Public Enterprises Survey, Deptt. of Public Enterprises, GOI, New Delhi.

2. Growth rates are annual exponential growth rates over time.

Table 4.VII. 3

**Estimates of Productivity and Capital Intensity: Hindustan Aeronautics Ltd.**

| *Variable* | *Indices of Single Factor Productivity* | | *Indices of Total Factor Productivity* | | | *Capital Intensity* |
|---|---|---|---|---|---|---|
| *Year* | *Labour* | *Capital* | *Kendrick* | *Solow* | *Translog* | *(Rs' 000)* |
| 1974-75 | 100.00 | 100.00 | 100.00 | 100.00 | 100.00 | 2.89 |
| 1975-76 | 97.42 | 80.13 | 87.06 | 89.05 | 88.92 | 3.52 |
| 1976-77 | 96.21 | 82.40 | 88.06 | 89.81 | 89.64 | 3.38 |
| 1977-78 | 96.06 | 96.79 | 96.46 | 96.85 | 97.15 | 2.87 |
| 1978-79 | 100.09 | 108.73 | 104.68 | 103.96 | 104.51 | 2.66 |
| 1979-80 | 88.41 | 87.34 | 87.81 | 85.90 | 86.46 | 2.93 |
| 1980-81 | 76.10 | 67.91 | 71.35 | 68.47 | 68.85 | 3.24 |
| 1981-82 | 103.51 | 80.80 | 89.61 | 82.53 | 83.36 | 3.71 |
| 1982-83 | 109.88 | 81.68 | 92.29 | 85.22 | 86.16 | 3.90 |
| 1983-84 | 150.32 | 109.90 | 124.96 | 106.78 | 107.98 | 3.96 |
| 1984-85 | 168.18 | 94.71 | 117.76 | 103.70 | 105.26 | 5.14 |
| 1985-86 | 175.42 | 88.41 | 113.67 | 101.15 | 102.89 | 5.75 |
| 1986-87 | 160.82 | 75.45 | 99.00 | 88.32 | 89.63 | 6.18 |
| 1987-88 | 162.63 | 70.10 | 94.09 | 85.48 | 86.61 | 6.72 |
| 1988-89 | 195.95 | 80.29 | 109.17 | 97.70 | 99.08 | 7.07 |
| 1989-90 | 199.08 | 79.07 | 108.33 | 97.66 | 98.96 | 7.30 |
| 1990-91 | 209.48 | 82.02 | 112.77 | 101.89 | 103.26 | 7.40 |
| 1991-92 | 223.91 | 84.57 | 117.28 | 106.33 | 107.93 | 7.67 |
| 1992-93 | 223.80 | 80.86 | 113.29 | 103.47 | 104.93 | 8.02 |
| 1993-94 | 254.55 | 87.32 | 123.75 | 113.18 | 114.87 | 8.45 |
| 1994-95 | 267.02 | 87.48 | 125.16 | 105.11 | 106.87 | 8.86 |
| 1995-96 | 313.49 | 97.95 | 142.42 | 118.25 | 120.18 | 9.29 |
| Growth rate % | 5.89 | -0.63 | 1.51 | 0.82 | 0.91 | 6.53 |

*Notes:* 1. Data computed and compiled from various issues of Public Enterprises Survey, Deptt. of Public Enterprises, GOI, New Delhi.

2. Growth rates are annual exponential growth rates over time.

Table 4. VIII. 1

**Estimates of Productivity and Capital Intensity: Consumer Goods Industry**

| *Variable* | *Indices of Single Factor Productivity* | | *Indices of Total Factor Productivity* | | | *Capital Intensity* |
|---|---|---|---|---|---|---|
| *Year* | *Labour* | *Capital* | *Kendrick* | *Solow* | *Translog* | *(Rs' 000)* |
| 1974-75 | 100.00 | 100.00 | 100.00 | 100.00 | 100.00 | 2.16 |
| 1975-76 | 120.52 | 113.07 | 116.38 | 113.29 | 113.41 | 2.30 |
| 1976-77 | 125.53 | 108.54 | 115.73 | 112.94 | 113.02 | 2.49 |
| 1977-78 | 132.24 | 110.35 | 119.43 | 116.44 | 116.46 | 2.58 |
| 1978-79 | 124.18 | 96.73 | 107.66 | 105.26 | 105.11 | 2.77 |
| 1979-80 | 98.64 | 76.35 | 85.19 | 78.38 | 78.26 | 2.79 |
| 1980-81 | 116.98 | 87.10 | 98.68 | 89.38 | 89.29 | 2.90 |
| 1981-82 | 60.90 | 40.22 | 47.65 | 64.22 | 63.68 | 3.27 |
| 1982-83 | 66.39 | 39.82 | 48.79 | 67.94 | 67.51 | 3.60 |
| 1983-84 | 71.95 | 44.37 | 53.85 | 73.87 | 73.36 | 3.50 |
| 1984-85 | 80.27 | 37.33 | 49.49 | 76.36 | 75.89 | 4.64 |
| 1985-86 | 83.72 | 36.16 | 48.93 | 78.08 | 77.55 | 5.00 |
| 1986-87 | 100.66 | 40.38 | 55.70 | 89.39 | 88.87 | 5.38 |
| 1987-88 | 131.94 | 39.75 | 58.54 | 100.02 | 100.76 | 7.17 |
| 1988-89 | 139.00 | 40.16 | 59.64 | 103.51 | 104.20 | 7.47 |
| 1989-90 | 158.83 | 44.10 | 66.00 | 114.40 | 115.42 | 7.78 |
| 1990-91 | 172.42 | 45.18 | 68.35 | 120.05 | 121.17 | 8.24 |
| 1991-92 | 192.84 | 47.32 | 72.43 | 128.58 | 129.97 | 8.80 |
| 1992-93 | 154.24 | 34.85 | 54.08 | 90.61 | 90.87 | 9.56 |
| 1993-94 | 142.53 | 30.43 | 47.64 | 80.68 | 80.90 | 10.12 |
| 1994-95 | 126.06 | 25.81 | 40.66 | 66.85 | 67.64 | 10.54 |
| 1995-96 | 175.93 | 35.05 | 55.42 | 85.83 | 86.81 | 10.84 |
| Growth rate % | 2.31 | -6.54 | -3.98 | 0.05 | 0.10 | 8.85 |

*Notes:* 1. Data computed and compiled from various issues of Public Enterprises Survey, Deptt. of Public Enterprises, GOI, New Delhi.

2. Growth rates are annual exponential growth rates over time.

Table 4. VIII. 2
**Estimates of Productivity and Capital Intensity: Cement Corporation of India Ltd.**

| *Variable* | *Indices of Single Factor Productivity* | | *Indices of Total Factor Productivity* | | | *Capital Intensity* |
|---|---|---|---|---|---|---|
| *Year* | *Labour* | *Capital* | *Kendrick* | *Solow* | *Translog* | *(Rs' 000)* |
| 1974-75 | 100.00 | 100.00 | 100.00 | 100.00 | 100.00 | 2.29 |
| 1975-76 | 133.13 | 80.79 | 99.32 | 100.84 | 103.84 | 3.77 |
| 1976-77 | 138.73 | 51.40 | 73.29 | 80.74 | 82.91 | 6.18 |
| 1977-78 | 166.87 | 45.11 | 69.00 | 80.69 | 83.14 | 8.47 |
| 1978-79 | 332.85 | 39.47 | 67.86 | 94.87 | 101.14 | 19.32 |
| 1979-80 | 653.77 | 45.86 | 82.08 | 117.53 | 127.39 | 32.67 |
| 1980-81 | 520.98 | 63.71 | 109.18 | 138.21 | 149.22 | 18.74 |
| 1981-82 | 667.68 | 90.27 | 153.10 | 173.85 | 187.42 | 16.95 |
| 1982-83 | 1087.65 | 149.53 | 253.15 | 236.70 | 255.12 | 16.67 |
| 1983-84 | 725.32 | 91.59 | 156.47 | 107.02 | 114.78 | 18.15 |
| 1984-85 | 796.88 | 82.37 | 143.38 | 100.56 | 107.89 | 22.17 |
| 1985-86 | 754.92 | 70.37 | 123.53 | 87.14 | 93.45 | 24.59 |
| 1986-87 | 872.54 | 74.90 | 132.30 | 93.19 | 99.94 | 26.70 |
| 1987-88 | 707.73 | 56.92 | 100.99 | 67.80 | 72.33 | 28.50 |
| 1988-89 | 782.53 | 59.40 | 105.79 | 71.63 | 76.41 | 30.20 |
| 1989-90 | 1336.42 | 98.01 | 174.94 | 99.28 | 106.00 | 31.25 |
| 1990-91 | 1646.43 | 118.62 | 211.96 | 116.62 | 124.55 | 31.81 |
| 1991-92 | 2088.54 | 149.11 | 266.60 | 140.28 | 149.84 | 32.10 |
| 1992-93 | 1584.81 | 109.28 | 195.79 | 90.64 | 96.60 | 33.24 |
| 1993-94 | 1264.34 | 84.62 | 151.87 | 65.17 | 69.36 | 34.25 |
| 1994-95 | 879.58 | 57.55 | 92.23 | 33.79 | 36.08 | 35.19 |
| 1995-96 | 1157.73 | 73.13 | 118.26 | 40.98 | 43.69 | 36.31 |
| Growth rate % | 13.54 | 2.91 | 4.70 | -0.90 | -0.70 | 10.63 |

*Notes:* 1. Data computed and compiled from various issues of Public Enterprises Survey, Deptt. of Public Enterprises, GOI, New Delhi.

2. Growth rates are annual exponential growth rates over time.

Table 4. VIII. 3

**Estimates of Productivity and Capital Intensity: Hindustan Photo Films Manufacturing Co. Ltd.**

| *Variable* | *Indices of Single Factor Productivity* | | *Indices of Total Factor Productivity* | | | *Capital Intensity* |
|---|---|---|---|---|---|---|
| *Year* | *Labour* | *Capital* | *Kendrick* | *Solow* | *Translog* | *(Rs' 000)* |
| 1974-75 | 100.00 | 100.00 | 100.00 | 100.00 | 100.00 | 2.77 |
| 1975-76 | 105.88 | 104.37 | 104.85 | 104.54 | 104.55 | 2.81 |
| 1976-77 | 157.06 | 139.21 | 144.57 | 131.75 | 132.28 | 3.13 |
| 1977-78 | 176.70 | 159.62 | 164.82 | 147.29 | 147.87 | 3.07 |
| 1978-79 | 188.63 | 152.24 | 162.47 | 144.82 | 145.53 | 3.43 |
| 1979-80 | 171.40 | 139.81 | 148.76 | 132.08 | 132.73 | 3.40 |
| 1980-81 | 182.11 | 153.41 | 161.73 | 142.41 | 143.13 | 3.29 |
| 1981-82 | 171.99 | 145.89 | 153.49 | 134.98 | 135.67 | 3.27 |
| 1982-83 | 162.67 | 138.01 | 145.19 | 127.56 | 128.21 | 3.27 |
| 1983-84 | 192.32 | 159.02 | 168.55 | 144.45 | 145.17 | 3.35 |
| 1984-85 | 180.45 | 145.20 | 155.09 | 132.48 | 133.20 | 3.44 |
| 1985-86 | 212.92 | 113.40 | 133.82 | 120.51 | 120.93 | 5.21 |
| 1986-87 | 232.58 | 115.49 | 138.20 | 124.72 | 125.15 | 5.58 |
| 1987-88 | 179.78 | 57.42 | 73.82 | 58.52 | 58.17 | 8.68 |
| 1988-89 | 154.40 | 42.75 | 55.96 | 43.54 | 43.32 | 10.02 |
| 1989-90 | 181.62 | 41.36 | 55.30 | 44.56 | 44.34 | 12.18 |
| 1990-91 | 204.70 | 35.84 | 49.04 | 42.61 | 42.29 | 15.85 |
| 1991-92 | 218.77 | 33.30 | 46.04 | 41.43 | 41.18 | 18.23 |
| 1992-93 | -4.93 | -0.58 | -0.82 | 1802.19 | 1857.77 | 23.26 |
| 1993-94 | 15.52 | 1.66 | 2.35 | 4882.75 | 3219.50 | 25.86 |
| 1994-95 | 7.85 | 6.88 | 0.93 | - | - | 31.83 |
| 1995-96 | 22.91 | 17.94 | 2.57 | - | - | 35.44 |
| Growth rate % | -1.82 | -13.35 | -11.36 | 4.43 | 3.83 | 12.07 |
| | (2.72)* | (-7.891)* | (-5.9)* | (-6.73)* | (-6.79)* | (10.61)* |

*Notes:* 1. Data computed and compiled from various issues of Public Enterprises Survey, Deptt. of Public Enterprises, GOI, New Delhi.

2. Growth rates are annual exponential growth rates over time.

* The growth rates in the brackets are obtained after excluding the last four years.

# BIBLIOGRAPHY

Ahluwalia, I.J. (1985) *Industrial Growth in India: Stagnation Since the Mid-Sixties*. Delhi: Oxford University Press.

Ahluwalia, I.J. (1991) *Productivity and Growth in Indian Manufacturing*. New Delhi: Oxford University Press.

Ahluwalia, I.J. (1995) Policies, Enterprises, and Privatization, in Cassen, Robert and Joshi, Vijay. (Eds.) *India: The Future of Economic Reforms*. Delhi: Oxford University Press.

Akerlof, G. and Yeller, J. (1986) *Efficiency Wage Models of Labour Market*. Cambridge: Cambridge University Press.

Arrow, K.J. (1962) The Economic Implications of Learning by Doing. *Review of Economic Studies*. Vol. 29, June, pp 155-73.

Arrow, K.J., Chenery, H.B., Minhas, B.S. and Solow, R.M. (1961) Capital-Labour Substitution and Economic Efficiency. *Review of Economics and Statistics*. Vol. 43, August, pp 225-50.

Asian Development Bank (1991) Human Resource Policy and Economic Development. ADB, Philippines.

Balakrishnan, P. and Pushpangadan, K. (1994) Total Factor-Productivity Growth in Manufacturing Industry: A Fresh Look. *Economic and Political Weekly*. July 30, pp 2028-35.

Banerji, A. (1975) *Capital Intensity and Productivity in Indian Industry*. New Delhi: Macmillan Co. of India Ltd.

Bardhan, P. (1984) *The Political Economy of Development in India*. Oxford: Basil Blackwell.

Barna, T. (1959) Alternative Methods of Measuring Capital, in Goldsmith, R. and Saunder, C. (Eds.) *Income and Wealth Series*. VIII. London: Bower and Bower.

Basu, S. (1974) Share of Labour in Manufacturing Industries. *Economic and Political Weakly*. July 13, p 1110.

Berglas, E. (1965) Investment and Technological Change. *Journal of Political Economy*. Vol. 73(2), April, pp 173-80.

Berndt, E.R. and Khaled, M.S. (1978) Parametric Productivity Measurement and Choice Among Flexible Functional Forms. *Journal of Political Economy*. December, pp 1220-45.

Bhagwati, J. and Desai, P. (1970) *India: Planning for Industrialization*. London: Oxford University Press.

Bhalla, G.S. and Mehta, S.S. (1970) Rates of Return in Public and Private Sector Industries in India. *Lok Udyog*. May, pp 147-56.

Bhaya, H. (1990) Management Efficiency in the Private and Public Sectors in India, in Heath, J. (Ed.) *Public Enterprises at the Crossroads*. London: Routledge.

Boardman, A.E. and Vining, A.R. (1989) Ownership and Performance in Competitive Environments: A Comparison of the Performance of Private, Mixed, and State-Owned Enterprises. *Journal of Law and Economics*. Vol. 32, pp 1-33.

Bodkin, R.G. (1966) The Wage-Price-Productivity Nexus. Philadelphia: University of Pennsylvania Press.

Bodkin, R. and Klein, L. (1967) Non-linear Estimation of Aggregate Production Functions. *Review of Economics and Stastics*. Vol. 49(1), Feburary, pp. 28-44.

Bos, D. (1991) *Privatization: A Theoretical Treatment*. Oxford: Clarendon Press.

Bowen, W.G. (1969) *The Wage-Price Issue: A Theoretical Analysis*. Princeton: Princeton University Press.

Brahmananda, P.R. (1982) *Productivity in the Indian Economy: Rising Inputs for Falling Outputs*. Delhi: Himalaya Publishing House.

Brown, D.G. (1962) Expected Ability to Pay and Inter-Industry Wage Structure in Manufacturing. *Industrial and Labour Relations Review*. Vol. XII, No. 1, October.

Bruno, M. (1978) Duality, Intermediate Inputs and Value Added, in Fuss, M and McFadden, D. (Eds.) *Production Economics: A Dual Approach to Theory and Applications*. Amsterdam: North Holland Publishing Co.

Bruno, M. (1984) Raw Materials, Profits and the Productivity Slowdown. *Quarterly Journal of Economics*. Vol. 1, pp 1-29.

Caves, D.W. and Christiansen, L.R. (1980) The Relative Efficiency of Public and Private Firms in a Competitive Environment: The Case of Canadian Railroads. *Journal of Political Economy*. Vol. (88), pp 958-76.

Chandok, H.L. and the Policy Group. (1990) *India Data Base*. Vol. 1 and 2. New Delhi: Living Media India Ltd.

Chattopadhyay, P. (1975) Public Enterprises - A Trend Report, in *A Survey of Research in Economics*. Vol. V, Industry. Delhi: ICSSR.

Chen, E.K.V. (1976) The Empirical Relevence of the Endogenous Technological Progress Function. Kyklos, Vol. 29(2), pp 256-71.Chinchankar, P.Y. (1969) *Wages and Productivity in Indian Industries*. Bombay: Vora and Co.

Chitale, V.P. (1986) *Capital-Output Ratio in the Indian Economy*. Delhi: ESRF, Radiant Publishers.

Christensen, L.R. and Jorgenson, D.W. (1969) The Measurement of U.S. Real Capital Input, 1929-1967. *Review of Income and Wealth*. Vol. 15(4) December, pp 293-320.

Christensen, L.R. and Jorgenson, D.W. (1970) U.S. Real Product and Real Factor Input, 1929-1967. *Review of Income and Wealth*. Vol. 16(1), March, pp 19-50.

Christensen, L.R. and Jorgenson, D.W. (1973) Measuring Economic Performance in the Private Sector, in Moss, Milton. (Ed.)The Measurement of Economic and Social performance. *Studies in Income and Wealth*. Vol. 38. New York: NBER.

Christensen, L.R., Cummings, D. and Jorgenson, D.W. (1980) Economic Growth, 1947-73: An International Comparison, in Kendrick, J.W. and Vaccara, B.N. (Eds.) *New Development in Productivity Measurement and Analysis*. New York: NBER.

Christensen, L.R., Jorgenson, D.W. and Lau, L.J. (1971) Conjugate Duality and the Transcendental Logarithmic Production Function. *Econometrica*. 39, No. 4 (July), pp 225-256.

Christensen, L.R., Jorgenson, D.W. and Lau, L.J. (1973) Transcendental Logarithmic Production Frontiers. *Review of Economis and Statistics*. February, pp 28-45.

Clark, J.B. (1899) *The Distribution of Wealth*. New York.

Cook, P. and Kirkpatrick, C. (Eds.) (1988) *Privatization in Less Developed Countries*. Brighton: Wheatsheaf Press.

Courtheoux, J.P. (1974) The Public Sector, in *Wage Determination*, p. 142. Paris: OECD (papers Presented at an International Conference).

Cowning, T.G. and Stevenson, R.F. (Eds.) (1981) *Productivity Measurement in Regulated Industries*. New York: Academic Press.

Dadi, M.M. (1973) *Income Share of Factory Labour in India*. New Delhi: Shri Ram Centre.

David, P.A. (1975) *Technological Choice, Innovation and Economic Growth*. Cambridge: Cambridge University Press.

Denison, E.F. (1957) Theoretical Aspects of Quality Change, Capital Consumption and Net Capital Formation. *Studies in Income and Wealth*. Vol. 19. Princeton: NBER.

Denison, E.F. (1961) Measurement of Labour Input: Some Questions of Definition and Adequacy of Data, in *Output, Input and Productivity Measurement*. New York: NBER.

Denison, E.F. (1962). The Sources of Economic Growth in the U.S. and the Alternatives Before Us. *Committee for Economic Development*. New York: Library of Congress.

Denison, E.F. (1964) The Unimportance of the Embodied Question. *American Economic Review*. Vol. (54(2) March, pp 90-94.

Denison, E.F. (1967) *Whay Growth Rates Differs: Post War Experience in Nine Western Countries*. Washington DC: The Brookings Institution.

Dension, E.F. (1972) Some Major Issues in Productivity Analysis. *Survey of Current Business*. Vol. 49(5), May, pp 1-28.

Denison, E.F. (1974) *Accounting for United States Economic Growth, 1929 to 1969*. Washington DC: The Brookings Institution.

Dhankar, R.S. (1975) Managing Public Sector Undertakings Finance. New Delhi: Westvill Publishing House.

Dhesi, Autar S. (1979) Human Capital formation and its utilization. Sterling Publishers Pvt. Ltd., New Delhi.

Dholakia, B.H. (1976) Determinants of Inter-Industry Wage Structure in India. *Indian Journal of Industrial Relations*. April, pp 445-58.

Dholakia, B.H. (1978) Relative Performance of Public and Private Manufacturing Enterprises in India: TFP Approach. *Economic and Political Economy*. Vol XIII, No. 8, Feburary 25, pp M4-M11.

Dholakia, B.H. (1980) *The Changing Efficiency of Public Enterprises in India*. Delhi: Somaiya Publications.

Dickens, W.T. and Katz, L.F. (1987) Inter-Industry Wage Differences and Industry Characteristics, in Lang, K. and Leonard, J.S. (Eds.) *Unemployment and the Structure of Labour Markets*. London: Basil Blackwell.

Diewert, W.E. (1971) An Application of the Shepherd Duality Theorem: A Generalised Leontief Production Function. *Journal of Political Economy*. May-June, pp 481-501.

Diewert, W.E. (1973) Functional Forms for Profit and Transformation Functions. *Journal of Economic Theory*. Vol. 6, June, pp 284-316.

Diewert, W.E. (1978) Hicks Aggregation Theorem and the Existence of a Real Value Added Function, in Fuss, M. and McFadden, D. (Eds.) Production Economics: A Dual Approach to Theory and Applications. Amsterdam: North Holland Pub. Co.

Dogramaci, A. (Ed.) (1981) Productivity Analysis: A Range of Perspectives. (Studies in Productivity Analysis). Boston: Martinus Nijhoff.

Dogramaci, A. (Ed.) (1983) Developments in Econometric Analysis of Productivity - Measurement and Modelling Issues. (Studies in Productivity Analysis) Boston: Kluwer-Nijhoff.

Dutt, R. and Sundaram, K.P.M. (1989) *Indian Economy*. New Delhi: S. Chand & Company (Pvt) Ltd.

Fabricant, S. (1959) *Basic Facts on Productivity Change*. New York: Columbia University Press, NBER.

Fazal, M. (1969) Criteria for Measuring Performance of Managements in Public Undertaking. *Lok Udyog*. November, pp 903-05.

Ferguson, C. (1965) Time Series Production Functions and Technological Progress in American Manufacturing Industry. *Journal of Political Economy*. Vol. 73(2), April, pp 135-147.

Fisher, F. (1969) The Existence of Aggregate Production Functions. *Econometrica*. Vol. 37, October, pp 553-557.

Fishlaw, A. (1990) The Latin American State. *Journal of Economic Perspectives*. Vol. 4, no. 3, pp 61-74.

Flynn, N. (1993) *Public Sector Management*. London: Harvester-Wheatsheaf.

Fonseca, A.J. (1975) Wage Issues in a Developing Economy. Bombay: Oxford University Press.

Frank, R. (1984) Are Workers Paid Their Marginal Product? *American Economic Review*. Vol. LXXIV, September, pp 971-91.

Frank, R.H. and Cook, P.J. (1995) *The Winner-Take - All Society*. New York: The Free Press. Martin Kessler Books.

Freeman, R.B. (1986) Unionism Comes to the Public Sector. *Journal of Economic Literature*. Vol. XXIV, March, pp 41-86.

Freeman, R.B. and Medoff, J.L. (1984) *What Do Unions Do*? New York: Basic Books.

Friedman, M. (1968) The Role of Monetary Policy. *American Economic Review*. Vol. 58, No. 1, pp 1-17.

Gahlon, B. and Licht, G. (1990) The Efficiency Wage Theories and Inter-Industry Wage Differentials, in Konig, Heinz. (Ed.) *Economics of Wage Determination*. New York: Springer-Verlag.

Gelb, A., Knight, J.B. and Sabot, R.H. (1991) Public Sector Employment, Rent Seeking and Economic Growth. *The Economic Journal*. Vol. 101. September, pp 1186-99.

Ghosh, A. (1984) Efficiency and Productivity of Indian Manufacturing Industry: A Few Case Studies. *Economic and Political Weekly*. Annual Number.

Ghosh, A. (1988) Industrial Productivity: Some Issues Relevant for Policy Making. *Productivity*. Vol. 29, No. 3, October-December, pp 303-310.

Goldar, B.N. (1986) *Productivity Growth in Indian Industry*. New Delhi: Allied Publishers Private Ltd.

Goldsmith, R.W. (1951) A Perpetual Inventory of National Wealth. *Studies in Income and Wealth*. Vol. 14, NBER.

Gordon, R.J. (1982) Why U.S. Wage and Employment Behaviour Differs from that in Britain and Japan. *Economic Journal*. Vol. 92, pp 13-44.

Gordon, R.J. (1987) Productivity, Wages and Prices Inside and Outside of Manufacturing in the U.S., Japan and Europe. *European Economic Review*. Vol. 31, pp 685-739.

Gordon, R.J. (1990) U.S. Inflation, Labour's Share, and the Natural Rate of Unemployment, in Konig, Heinz. (Ed.) *Economic of Wage Determination*. New York: Springer-Verlag.

Government of India (1949) *Report of the Committee on Fair Wages. Ministry of Labour.*

Government of India (1956) *Industrial Policy Resolution*. April 30.

Government of India (1969) *Report of the National Commission on Labour*. Ministry of Labour.

Government of India (1988) *Estimates of Capital Stock of Indian Economy*. C.S.O. Department of Statistics. New Delhi: Ministry of Planning.

Government of India. *Economic Survey 1994-95*. New Delhi: Ministry of Finance.

Government of India. *Eighth Five Year Plan 1992-97*. New Delhi: Planning Commission.

Government of India. *Index Numbers of Wholesale Prices in India*. New Delhi: Ministry of Industry.

Government of India. *Public Enterprises Survey*. New Delhi: Department of Public Enterprises.

Griliches, Z. (1967) Production Functions in Manufacturing: Some Preliminary Results, in Brown, M. (Ed.) *The Theory and Empirical Analysis of Production*. New York: NBER.

Griliches, Z. and Jorgenson, D.W. (1966) Sources of Measured Productivity Change: Capital Input. *American Economic Association Papers*. May.

Griliches, Z. and Jorgenson, D.W. (1967) The Explanation of Productivity Change. *Review of Economic Studies*. Vol (34), July, pp 249-83.

Griliches, Z. and Ringstad, V. (1971) *Economies of Scale and the Form of the Production Function*. Amsterdan: North Holland Publishing Co.

Gupta, M. (1982) Measurement of Productivity - Comparison Between Public Sector and Private Sector Industry. *Indian Economic Review*. Vol. 17, No. 2-4, pp 165-86.

Hajela, P.D. (1987) India's Industrial Development, in Brahmananda, P.R. and Panchamukhi, V.R. (Eds.) *The Development Process of the Indian Economy*. Delhi: Himalaya Publishing House.

Hajra, S. (1993) *Productivity Growth in Industry*. Delhi: Allied Publishers Co.

Harbison Frederick H. and Myers, Charles A. (1964) Education, Manpower and Economic Growth. New York: McGraw Hill Book Co.

Harbison Frederick H. and Myers, Charles A. (1965) Manpower and Education. New York: McGraw Hill Book Company.

Harbison, Frederick H. (1973) Human Resource as the Wealth of Nations. London: Oxford University Press.

Hart, R.A. (1984) *Economics of Non-Wage Labour Cost*. London: George Allen and Unwin.

Hasim, B.R. and Dadi, M.M. (1973) Capital Output Relationship in Indian Manufacturing (1946-64). Baroda: M.S. University of Baroda.

Herrick, B. and Kindleberger, C.P. (1983) *Economic Development*. London: McGraw Hill.

Hicks, J.R. (1964) *The Theory of Wages*. London: Macmillan and Company Ltd.

Hirschman, A.O. (1980) The Welfare State in Trouble: Systemic Crises or Growing Pains. *American Economic Review*. Vol. 70, No. 2, pp 113-16.

Hirschman, A.O. (1982) *Shifting Involvements: Private Interest and Public Action*. Oxford: Martin Robertson.

Hodges, D. (1969) A Note on Estmation of Cobb-Douglas and CES Production Function Models. *Econometrica*. Vol. 37 (4), October, pp 721-25.

Holzer, H.J. (1990) The Determinants of Employee Productivity and Earnings. *Industrial Relations*. Vol. 29, No. 3, pp 403-22.

International Labour Organisation (1966) *Prices, Wages and Income Policies in Industrialized Market Economies*. Geneva: ILO.

Iyer, R.R. (1991) *A Grammer of Public Enterprises: Exercises in Clarification*. New Delhi: CPR.

Jalan, B. (1991) *India's Economic Crisis: The Way Ahead*. Delhi: Oxford University Press.

Jha, R. and Sahni, B.S. (1992) Measures of Efficiency in Private and Public Sector Industries: The Case of India. *Annals of Public and Cooperative Economics*. Vol. 63, pp 489-95.

Johri, C.K. and Agarwal, N.C. (1966) Inter-Industry Wage Structure in India, 1950-61: An Analysis. *Indian Journal of Industrial Relations*. April, pp 379-413.

Jorgenson, D.W. (1966) The Embodiment Hypothesis. *Journal of Political Economy*. Vol. 74(1), February, pp 1-17.

Jorgenson, D.W. and Griliches, Z. (1967) The Explanation of Productivity Changes. *Review of Economic Studies*. Vol. 34(3), July, pp 249-84.

Jorgenson, D.W. and Griliches, Z. (1970) The Sources of Economic Growth: A Reply to Edward F. Denison. mimeo. *Harvard Institute of Economic Research*

Jorgenson, D.W. and Griliches, Z. (1972) Issues in Growth Accounting: A Reply to Edward F. Denison. *Survey of Current Business*. May.

Jose, A.V. (1994) Earnings, Employment and Productivity Trends in the Organised Industries of India, in Deshpande, L.K. and Rodgers, Gerry. (Eds.) *The Indian Labour Market and Economic Structural Change*. Delhi: B.R. Publishing Corporation.

Joshi, Vijay and Little I.M.D. (1994) *India: Macro Economics and Political Economy 1964-1991*. Delhi: Oxford University Press.

Kay, J.A. and Thomson, D.J. (1986) Privatization: A Policy in Search of a Rationale. *The Economic Journal*. Vol. 96, March, pp 18-32.

Kehar, S. (1964) *Productivity and Economic Growth*. Bombay: Asia Publishing House.

Kendrick, J.W. (1956) Productivity Trends: Capital and Labour. *Review of Economics and Statistics*. Vol. (38), August, pp 248-57.

Kendrick, J.W. (1961) *Productivity Trends in the United States*. Princeton: Princeton University Press, NBER.

Kendrick, J.W. (1964) Measuring the Nation's Wealth. *Studies in Income and Wealth*. Vol. 29. New York: NBER.

Kendrick, J.W. (1973) Post War Productivity Trends in U.S. 1948-69. New York: NBER.

Khusro, A.M. (1979) *The Indian Economy: Stability and Growth*. New Delhi: Prachi Prakashan.

Khusro, A.M. (1985) Shaping India through Planning. *Yojana*. Vol. 28(11), pp 4-7.

King, J.E. (1990) *Labour Economics*. London: Macmillan.

Kmenta, J. (1967) On Estimation of the CES Production Function. *International Economic Review*. Vol. 8(2), June, pp 180-89.

Krishna, K.L. (1987) Industrial Growth and Productivity in India, in Brahmananda, P.R. and Panchmukhi, V.R. (Eds.) *The Development Process of the Indian Economy*. Delhi: Himalaya Publishing House.

Krueger, A.O. (1974) The Political Economy of the Rent Seeking Society. *American Economic Review*. Vol. 64, No. 3 (June), pp 291-303.

Krueger, A. and Summers, L.H. (1986) Reflections on the Inter-Industry Wage Structure, in Lang, K. and Leonard, J.S. (Eds.) *Unemployment and the Structure of Labour Markets*. London: Basil Blackwell.

Krueger, A.B. and Summers, L.H. (1988) Efficiency Wages and Inter-Industry Wage Structure. *Econometrica*. Vol. 56, pp 259-93.

Kumari, A. (1993) Productivity in Public Sector. *Economic and Political Weekly*. Vol. XXVIII, No. 48, November 27, pp M145-M162.

Levhari, E., Kleiman, E. and Halevi, N. (1966) The Relationship Between Two Measures of Total Productivity. *Review of Economics and Statistics*. Vol. 48(3), August, pp 345-47.

Levy, V. (1981) On Estimating Efficiency Differentials Between Public and Private Sectors in a Developing Economy-Iraq. *Journal of Comparative Economics*. Vol. 5, pp 235-50.

Lindback, A. and Snower, D.J. (Eds.) (1988) *Insider-Outsider Theory of Employment and Unemployment*. Cambridge-Mass: MIT Press.

Lucas, R.E.B. (1988) India's Industrial Policy, in Lucas, R.E.B. and Papanek, G.F. (Eds.) *The Indian Economy: Recent Development and Future Prospects*. New Delhi: Oxford University Press.

Lydall, H.F. (1968) Technological Progress in Australian Manufacturing. *Economic Journal*. Vol. 78, December, pp 807-26.

Macus, R. (1994) Thematic Section on Strategic Concerns of the Public Sector in India. *Public Enterprises*. Vol. 14, nos. 3-4, pp 183-96.

Madan, B.K. (1977) *The Real Wages of Industrial Labour in India*. New Delhi: Management Development Institute.

Majumdar, S.K. (1995) Public, Joint and Private Sectors in Indian Industry. *Economic and Political Weekly*. February, pp M25-M33.

Marshall, A. (1957) *Principles of Economics* (Eighth Edition). New York: Macmillan.

Massell, B.F. (1962) Is Investment Really Important. *Metroeconomica*. April/August/December.

McFadden, D.L. (1978) Cost, Revenue and Profit Functions, in Fuss, M. and McFadden, D. (Eds.) *Production Economics: A Dual Approach and Application*. Vol. I. Amsterdam: North Holland.

Mehdi, H. (1989) *State Owned Enterprises in a Mixed Economy*. London: West View Press.

Mehta, S.S. (1974) Growth and Productivity in Indian Industries. *Anvesak*. Vol. 4(1), June, pp 1-11.

Mendelowitz, A.I. (1971) The Measurement of Economic Depreciation. Proceedings of the Business and Economic Section of the American Statistical Association.

Mohanty, N. (1994) Public Sector Enterprises in India—Need for Basic Reforms. *Public Enterprises*. Vol. 14, No. 3-4, pp 197-213.

Nadiri, M.I. (1970) Some Approaches to the Theory and Measurement of Total Factor Productivity: A Survey. *Journal of Economic Literature*. Vol. VIII, pp 1137-1177.

Nadiri, M.I. (1972) International Studies of Factor Inputs and Total Factor Productivity: A Brief Survey. *Review of Income and Wealth*. June, pp 129-54.

Nagaraj, R. (1989) Growth in Manufacturing Output since 1980. *Economic and Political Weekly*. Vol. XXIV, No. 26, July, pp 1481-84.

Nagraj, R. (1991) Public Sector Performance in the Eighties - Some Tentative Findings. *Economic and Political Weekly*. December 14, pp 2877-83.

Nayar, B.R. (1990) *The Political Economy of India's Public Sector: Policy and Performance*. Bombay: Popular Prakashan.

Nelson, R.R. (1965) The CES Production Function and Economic Growth Projections. *Reveiw of Economics and Statistics*. Vol. 47(3), August, pp 326-28.

Nelson, R.R. (1973) Recent Exercises in Growth Accounting: New Understanding or Dead End? *American Economic Review*. Vol. 63, June, pp 462-68.

Nelson, R.R. (1981) Research on Productivity Growth and Productivity Differences: Dead Ends and New Departures. *Journal of Economic Literature*. Vol. 19(3), September, pp 1029-64.

Palekar, S.A. (1962) *Problems of Wage Policy for Economic Development: With Special Reference to India*. Bombay: Asia Publishing House.

Papola, T.S. (1970) Productivity and Wage Structure in Indian Industries, in Sandesara, J.C. and Deshpande, L.K. (Eds.) *Wage Policy and Wage Determination in India*. Bombay: University of Bombay.

Papola, T.S. (1972) Inter-Industry Wage Structure: Technology Hypothesis. *Anvesak*. June, pp 50-74.

Patil, R.H. (1987) Industrial Growth in India during the Post-Independence Period: Facts and Issues, in Brahmananda, P.R. and Panchmukhi, V.R. (Eds.) *The Development Process of the Indian Economy*. Delhi: Himalaya Publishing House.

Perlman, R. (1969) *Labour Theory*. London: Wiley.

Picard, P. (1993) *Wages and Unemployment*. New York: Cambridge University Press.

Picchio, A. (1992) *Social Reproduction - The Political Economy of Labour Market*. New York: Cambridge University Press.

Powell, V. (1987) *Improving Public Enterprises Performance*. Management Development Series. Geneva: ILO Office.

Prasad, L. (1966) Remuneration Policy of Public Undertakings. *Indian Journal of Commerce*. April-June, pp 149-55.

Raj, K.N. (1984) Some Observation on Economic Growth in India over the Period 1952-53 to 1982-83. *Economic and Political Weekly*. Vol. XIX, No. 41, October 13, pp 1801-04.

Ramanadham, V.V. (1989) *Privatization in Developing Countries*. London: Routledge.

Ramanadham, V.V. (1991) *The Economics of Public Enterprises*. London: Routledge.

Ramanadham, V.V. (Ed.) (1993) *Privatization: A Global Perspective*. London: Routledge.

Ramaswamy, K. and Renforth, W. (1994) Evaluating the Performance of State Owned Enterprises and Privately Owned Firms: The Indian Experiences. *Academy of Management Proceedings*. pp 297-301.

Ramjash (1992) *Trade Unions and Productivity in Indian Industries*. New Delhi: Radha Publications.

Rao, K.C.S. and Latha, K.M. (1990) Productivity and operating Efficiency in Public Enterprises: A Study. *Prajnan*, Vol. (XIX), No. 1.

Rapping, L. (1965) Learning and World War II Production Functions. *Review of Economics and Statistics*. Vol. 47(1), February, pp 81-86.

Report of the Royal Commission on Labour (1932).

Reports/Recommendations of Various Committees on Public Enterprises (1990). New Delhi: A SCOPE Publication.

Report of C.S.O. (1982) Wages and Productivity in Organised Industry. *Commerce*. November 20, p 761.

Reserve Bank of India Bulletin. Bombay: Reserve Bank of India.

Robertson, D.J. (1961) *The Economics of Wages*. London: Macmillan and Co. Ltd.

Robinson, J. (Mrs.) (1960) The Production Function and the Theory of Capital. *Collected Economic Papers*. Vol. II. Oxford: Basil Blackwell.

Ruggles, R. and Ruggles, N. (1961) Concepts of Real Capital Stocks and Services, in Output, Input and Productivity Measurement. *Studies in Income and Wealth*. Vol. 25, New York: NBER.

Sandesara, J.C. and Deshpande, L.K. (Eds.) (1970) *Wage Policy and Wage Determination in India*. Bombay: Bombay University Press.

Sapsford, D. and Tzannatos, Z. (1993) *The Economics of the Labour Market*. London: Macmillan Press Ltd.

Sarna, J.V.M. and Rao, M.G. (1988) *Financing Public Sector Development Expenditure in Selected Countries - India*. Manila: Asian Development Bank.

Sawhney, P.K. (1969) Inter-Industry Wage Differentials in India. *Indian Economic Journal*. pp. 28-47.

Schultz, T.W. (1971) *Investing in Human Capital*. New York: The Free Press.

Schultz, T.W. (1981) *Investing in People*.California: University of California Press.

Seetharam, G.N. (1984) Increased Socialisation of Economy Brightens Future of Public Sector. *Yojana*. Vol. 28(4), pp 14-17.

Seetharam, G.N. (1984) Public Sector in West Germany. *Yojana*. Vol. 28(6), p 13.

Seetharam, G.N. (1984) Contribution of Public Enterprises in Economy. Trends in Public Sector in U.K. *Yojana*, Vol. 28(5), p 21.

Sen, S.K. (1985) Inter-Industry Differentials in Growth of Real Earnings: Some Implications for Wage Policy. *Economic and Political Weekly*. Vol. 20, No. 13, 30th March, pp 556-64.

Sen. G. and Palas, R. (1988) Social Commitment and Efficiency Measurement in Indian Public Enterprises. *Public Enterprises*. Vol. 8, No. 4, pp 299-304.

Seth, V.K. (1994) Labour Market Restructuring and Structural Adjustment. *Indian Journal of Labour Economics*. Vol. 37, No. 4, pp 523-34.

Shephard, R.W. (1970) *Theory of Cost and Production Functions*. Princeton: Princeton University Press.

Sheshinsky, E. (1967) Tests of the Learning by Doing Hypothesis. *Review of Economics and Statistics*. November.

Shivamaggi, H.B., Rajagopalan, N. and Venketachalam, T.R. (1968) Wages, Labour Productivity and Costs of Production. *Economic and Political Weekly*. Vol. 3, No. 18, May, 710-16.

Sikorski, D. (1989) Competitive Advantage of State Owned Enterprises - Comparative Case Studies of National and Private Companies in Singapore. *Public Enterpries*. Vol. 9, No. 1, pp 65-88.

Sinha, J.N. and Sawhney, P.K. (1970) *Wages and Productivity in Selected Indian Industries*. New Delhi: Vikas Publishing House.

Sinha, P.R.N. (1971) *Wage Determination*. New Delhi: Asia Publishing House.

Sinha, R.K. (1995) The Times of India. October 16, p. 17.

Solow, R. (1957) Technical Change and the Aggregate Production Function. *Review of Economic Statistic*. Vol. 39(3), August, pp 312-20.

Solow, R. (1959) Investment and Technical Progress, in Arrow, K; Karlin, S. and Suppes, P. (Eds.) *Mathematical Methods in the Social Sciences*. Stanford: Stanford University Press.

Song, D.H. (1988) A New Performance Evaluation System of Korean Enterprises: Policies and Experiences. *Public Enterprises*. Vol. 8, No. 1, pp 84-91.

Srivastava, S.C. (1984) *Wages, Profits and Productivity in Selected Industries of India Since 1950: An Econometric Study*. Delhi: Himalaya Pub. House.

Stoneman, P. and Francis, N. (1992) The Measurment of Output and Productivity in U.K. Manufacturing 1979-89. Mimeo. Coventry: Warwick Business School.

Subramanian, K.N. (1977) Wages in India. New Delhi: Tata McGraw-Hill Publishing Co. Ltd.

Sundaram, S.I. (1987) *National Wage Policy*. Delhi: B.R. Publishing Corporation.

Suri, G.K. (1976) Productivity, Wages and Industrial Relations. New Delhi: Affiliated East-West Press Pvt. Ltd.

Swamy, T.L.N. (1993) Verdoorn's Law of Productivity Growth. *Productivity*. Vol. 34, No. 1, April-June, pp 109-11.

Swamy, T.L.N. (1994) Public and Private Sector Industries in India: A Comparative Analysis. *Productivity*. Vol. 35, No. 1, April-June, pp 128-31.

Tinbergen, J. (1942) Zur Theorie der Langfristigen Wirtschaft Sentwicklung. *Weltwirschaftliches Archiv*. May.

Todaro, M.P. (1989) *Economic Development in the Third World*. London: Longman.

Trivedi, P. (1986) Public Sector Performance: Perception Versus Reality. *Indian Journal of Public Administration*. Vol. 32, pp 1007-35.

Trivedi, P. (1987) Sen Gupta Committee Report on Public Enterprises: Eloquent Fuzziness at its Best. *Economic and Political Weekly*. Vol. XXII, No. 22, May, pp M55-M66.

Tulpule, B. and Datta, R.C. (1988) Real Wages in Indian Industry. *Economic and Political Weekly*. October 29, pp 2275-78.

Usher, D. (Ed.) (1981) *Measurement of Capital*. Chicago: The University of Chicago Press.

Uzawa, H. (1964) Duality Principles in the Theory of Cost and Production. *International Economic Review*. Vol. 5(2), pp 216-20.

Vashist, D.C. and Kundu, T.R. (1990) Productivity of Public and Private Enterprises. *Productivity*. Vol. 31, No. 2, July-September, pp 197-204.

Verma, P. (1971) Inter-Industry Wage Structure in India: Further Evidence. *Indian Journal of Industrial Relations*. pp 289-95.

Verma, P. (1980) *Wage Determination: Concepts and Cases*. New Delhi: Wiley Eastern Ltd.

Verma, P. (1985) Operational Efficiency of Public Enterprises in India. *Lok Udyog*. August, pp 35-39.

Verma, P. and Subbayamma, G. (1985) The Inter-Industry Wage Structure in India: Recent Experience. *Indian Journal of Labour Economics*. Vol. XXVII, October, p 171.

Vickers, J. and Yarrow, G. (1988) *Privatization: An Economic Analysis*. Cambridge: MIT Press.

Walters, A.A. (1968) *Introduction to Econometrics*. London: Macmillan.

Wicksen, M.R. (1970) Estimation of the Vintage Cobb-Douglas Production Function for the United States 1900-1960. *Review of Economics and Statistics*. Vol. 52(2), May, pp 187-93.

World Bank (1983) *World Development Report 1983*. Washington DC: The World Bank.

Wright, T.P. (1936) Factors Affecting the Cost of Airplanes. *Journal of Aeronautical Sciences*. February.

Yellen, J.L. (1984) Efficiency Wage Models of Unemployment. *American Economic Review*. Vol. 74, pp 200-205.

You, J.K. (1976) Embodied and Disembodied Technical Progress in the United States, 1929-1968. *Review of Economics and Statistics*. Vol. 58, February, pp 123-27.

Zellnor, A., Kmenta, J. and Dreze, J. (1966) Specifications and Estimations of Cobb-Douglas Production Function Models. *Econometrica*, Vol. 34(4), October, pp 784-95.

